ARCHITECTURE IN TRANSLATION

ARCHITECTURE

IN TRANSLATION

*Germany, Turkey, &
the Modern House*

ESRA AKCAN

DUKE UNIVERSITY PRESS
DURHAM & LONDON 2012

© 2012 Duke University Press
All rights reserved.
Designed by Jennifer Hill
Typeset in Garamond Premier Pro by Tseng Information Systems, Inc.

Library of Congress Cataloging-in-Publication Data appear on the last printed page of this book.

Duke University Press gratefully acknowledges the support of the Graham Foundation for Advanced Studies in the Fine Arts, which provided funds toward the publication of this book.

MM Publication of this book has been aided by a grant from the Millard Meiss Publication Fund of the College Art Association.

to my parents, Selma Akcan and Tuncer Akcan

Translation is the most intimate act of reading.

> GAYATRI CHAKRAVORTY SPIVAK,
> "The Politics of Translation"

CONTENTS

Acknowledgments ix

Introduction MODERNITY IN TRANSLATION 1

Translation beyond Language 6
The Theoretical Possibility or Impossibility of
   Translation 9
Appropriating and Foreignizing Translations 15
The Historical Unevenness of Translation 17
The Ubiquity of Hybrids and the Scarcity of
   Cosmopolitan Ethics 21

1 MODERNISM FROM ABOVE
A Conviction about Its Own Translatability 27

New City: Traveling Garden City 30
New House: Representative Affinities 52
New Housing: The Ideal Life 76
From Ankara to the Whole Nation: Translatability
   from Above and Below 93

2 **MELANCHOLY IN TRANSLATION**   101

    The Melancholy of İstanbul   107
    A Journey to the West   119
    The Birth of the "Modern Turkish House"   133

3 *SIEDLUNG* **IN SUBALTERN EXILE**   145

    Siedlung and the Metropolis   148
    Siedlung and the Generic Rational Dwelling   175
    Siedlung and the Subaltern   195

4 **CONVICTIONS ABOUT UNTRANSLATABILITY**   215

    Untranslatable Culture and Translatable Civilization   215
    "The Original"   218
    Against Translation? The National House and *Siedlung*   233

5 **TOWARD A COSMOPOLITAN ARCHITECTURE**   247

    Ex Oriente Lux   249
    Melancholy of the East   252
    Weltarchitektur—Translation of a Treatise   263
    Toward another Cosmopolitan Ethics in Architecture   277

Epilogue   283

Notes   291

Bibliography   337

Sources of Illustrations   375

Index   383

ACKNOWLEDGMENTS

For books that take as long to prepare as this one, writing the acknowledgments means going through a labyrinthine memory lane with circuitous routes of research, doubt, writing, erasing, rewriting, editing, and reediting. During the very early stages of conceiving this book I had the opportunity to discuss my ideas with incredibly gifted and helpful people. Among these I would like to start by mentioning my deep gratitude to my doctoral advisors at Columbia University, Kenneth Frampton, Andreas Huyssen, and Mary McLeod. If it were not for Ken's curiosity and love for architecture, Andreas's commitment to theory, and Mary's scholarly rigor, this book would not have taken its current form. Before arriving in the United States, my professors at Middle East Technical University, Emel Aközer, Kemal Aran, Ali Cengizkan, Ünal Nalbantoğlu, and Haluk Pamir, were inspiring in shaping my initial interest in Turkish modernization. During my studies at Columbia I was exceptionally fortunate to discuss parts of this work with Joan Ockman, Edward Said, and Gwendolyn Wright, as well as Jonathan Crary, David Eng, Reinhold Martin, Grahame Shane, and

Mark Wigley. Careful reading and suggestions from the members of my dissertation committee, Barry Bergdoll, Sibel Bozdoğan, and Gayatri Chakravorty Spivak, guided the rewriting of the book version. Sibel later became a co-author, close colleague, and friend, and I am delighted to have met her. I also thank Dean Bernard Tschumi and David Hinkle for their persistent commitment to launching and maintaining the Ph.D. program in architecture at Columbia, in addition to its other graduate programs. As an architect pursuing scholarly research, I benefited tremendously from what I considered one of the liveliest architectural centers of the world, and I thank the whole faculty of the Graduate School of Architecture, Planning and Preservation for contributing to the making of this environment. Needless to say, my fellow doctoral students were constant inspiration: Dear Cesare Birignani, Shantel Blakely, Lucy Creagh, Kimberly Elman, Jennifer Louise Gray, Hyun Tae Jung, Eeva Pelkonen, David Rifkind, Ioanna Theocharopoulou, Sjoukje van der Meulen, Nader Voussoughian—I know I will be following your work for many years to come. The architecture studio faculty and the graduate students who took my architecture classes at Columbia, Parsons the New School for Design, and Pratt Institute were perpetual mirrors for self-checking. Additionally, Philip Kitcher trusted me in teaching political philosophy and ethics at the Core Program of Columbia, which undoubtedly broadened my knowledge and perspective. Looking back, I see once again how much all of the scholars, architects, and students at Columbia, as well as the intellectual life in New York, influenced my work in more ways than any of us might have anticipated.

The archival research for this book took place in thirteen cities in Turkey, Germany, Austria, Switzerland, Canada, and the United States. I owe tremendous debts to the staff members of archives and libraries, including Avery Library (New York), the Akademie der Künste (Berlin), the Kunstbibliothek (Berlin), the Turkish Chamber of Architects Archive (Ankara), Ankara Belediyesi Arşivi (Ankara), Milli Saraylar Arşivi (Istanbul), Stuttgart University Archives (Stuttgart), Special Collections at ETH Library (Zurich), Architekturmuseum der Technischen Universität (Munich), the Bauhausarchiv (Berlin), Universität für Angewandte Kunst Bibliothek (Vienna), Graphische Sammlung Albertina (Vienna), Plansammlung der technischen Universität (Berlin), Germanisches Nationalmuseum (Nürnberg), Stadtarchiv (Frankfurt), Landesarchiv (Berlin), Universität für angewandte Kunst Sammlung (Vienna), T. C. Başbakanlık Cumhuriyet Arşivleri (Ankara), the Getty Research Institute (Los Angeles), and the Canadian Center for Architecture (Montreal). In addition to the staff members in these institutions, I thank those who generously opened their personal collections for my research, including Kemal Ahmet Aru, Edhem Eldem, Neşe Ergin, and Melih Şallı in Istanbul; Peter Dübers in Stuttgart; Thomas Elsaesser in Munich; Manfred Speidel in Aachen; and Bernd Nicolai (then) in Trier. I owe special thanks to Speidel and Nicolai for their incredibly helpful guidance during my research in Germany.

While the early version of this book was written in New York, Berlin, and Istanbul, my carreer took me to new cities during the rewriting process. As an assistant professor at the University of Illinois, Chicago, I had the endless support of my dear colleagues, Ellen Baird, Catherine Becker, Bob Bruegmann, Nina Dubin, Heather Grossman, Peter Hales, Hannah Higgins, Dean Judith Kirshner, Victor Margolin, Jonathan Mekinda, Virginia Miller, Bob Munman, Annie Pedret, Martha Pollak, and David Sokol. As an architect and scholar, I appreciated being able to participate in discussions at the architecture studios and receiving suggestions from both architecture and art history students. Most importantly, this book would not have been possible if the Art History Department at UIC had not been so strongly committed to the advancement of architectural scholarship, and had not allowed me to take educational leaves to accept fellowships at the Getty Research Institute in Los Angeles, the Canadian Center for Architecture in Montreal, and Clark Art Institute in Williamstown, where parts of this book were written and edited.

I think I speak on behalf of all scholars that our debt to research institutes such as Clark, CCA, and Getty is immeasurable. There are so few institutions that support scholarly research and writing in the humanities in general and architecture in particular that I cannot express enough my gratitude for their financial and intellectual support. Thank you to Thomas Geahtgens and Wim de Wit at the Getty Research Institute, Phyllis Lambert and Alexis Sornin at the Canadian Center for Architecture, and Michael Ann Holly and Aruna D'Souza at the Clark Institute, to mention just a few directors at these institutions. Above all, I was extremely fortunate during my years as a visiting scholar at these institutions to work with other fellows. Scholarly deliberations with Thierry de Duve, Rob Linrothe, Mary Roberts, and Avinoam Shalem, as well as Drew Armstrong, Susan Babaie, Ali Behdad, Carolin Behrmann, Jean-Louis Cohen, Tony Cokes, Jorge Coronado, Hartmut Dorgerloh, Hannah Feldman, Claire Fox, Alessia Frassani, Talinn Grigor, Courtney Martin, Sina Najafi, John Onians, Jennifer Purtle, Andrew Schulz, Peter-Klaus Schuster, Volker Welter, and Lisa Young, helped me both for this book and for future projects. Something very special happened at the Getty Research Institute, where those of us working on different periods and places shared an interest in the remaking of art and architecture history as a discipline better equipped for a global future. I met not only colleagues whom I deeply respect but also lifetime friends at these research institutes.

This book was financially supported by many institutions. During the research and early writing stages, I received grants from Columbia University, the Graham Foundation, the Mellon Foundation, German Academic Exchange Service (DAAD), Kinne, and KRESS/ARIT. For rewriting and publication, I received support from Columbia University, the Getty Research Institute, the Canadian Center for Architecture, the College Art Association, and the Graham Foundation. Needless to say, the book would not have existed without their generous financial support. Journal and book editors including Ali Cengizkan, Andreas Huyssen, Ruth Oldenziel and Karin Zachman, Jilly Traganou and Miodrag Mitrasinovic, Efe Çakmak and Şeyda Öztürk, Dora Wiebenson, and Jean François Lejeune and Michelangelo Sabatino took interest in my research and inspired me to rework or translate some ideas by integrating them into articles.

In the very last stages, the review and editing processes at Duke University Press were extremely rigorous and friendly. I would like to thank Ken Wissoker, the editorial board, and the reviewers for enabling solid and creative scholarship that challenge disciplinary assumptions. Jade Brooks, Jeanne Ferris, Fred Kameny, Bonnie Perkel, Jennifer Hill, Christine Dahlin, and Amanda Sharp worked with diligence and attention. It was reassuring to be in such good hands, and an honor to be part of the Duke University Press list. Let me also thank Eileen Quam for her careful work on the index.

I was also privileged to share my ideas, hopes, and doubts with friends around the world. The fellow students, visiting scholars, and faculty mentioned above were much more than colleagues to me, but dear friends. I discussed my ideas at length with Peter Lang and Orhan Pamuk, and their ideas undoubtedly found their way into this work. My warmest thanks to Zafer Akay, İpek Akpınar, Anthony Alofsin, Cihan Arın, Aybars Aşçı, İhsan Bilgin, Can Çinici, Penelope Dean, Sevil Erginsoy, Elvan Altan Ergut, Namık Erkal, Mualla Erkılıç, Ebru Gencer, Jette Gindner, Berin Gür, Sharon Haar, David Haney, Esen Karol, Carsten Krohn, Burcu Kütükçüoğlu, Mehmet Kütükçüoğlu, Alex Lehnerer, Brian McGrath, Aslı Özbay, Füsun Sevgen, Bülent Tanju, Pamela Theocharapoulou, Belgin Turan, İpek Türeli, Aydan Volkan, and Şebnem Yalınay for their friendship, generous help, and encouragement during this long process. Onur Yüce Gün witnessed the preparation of the book's final stages, and I feel very lucky for having not only his personal support but also his help in the selection of this book's illustrations. Finally, two people watched the growth of this book as well as its author very closely: my exceptionally supportive and caring parents, Selma Akcan and Tuncer Akcan.

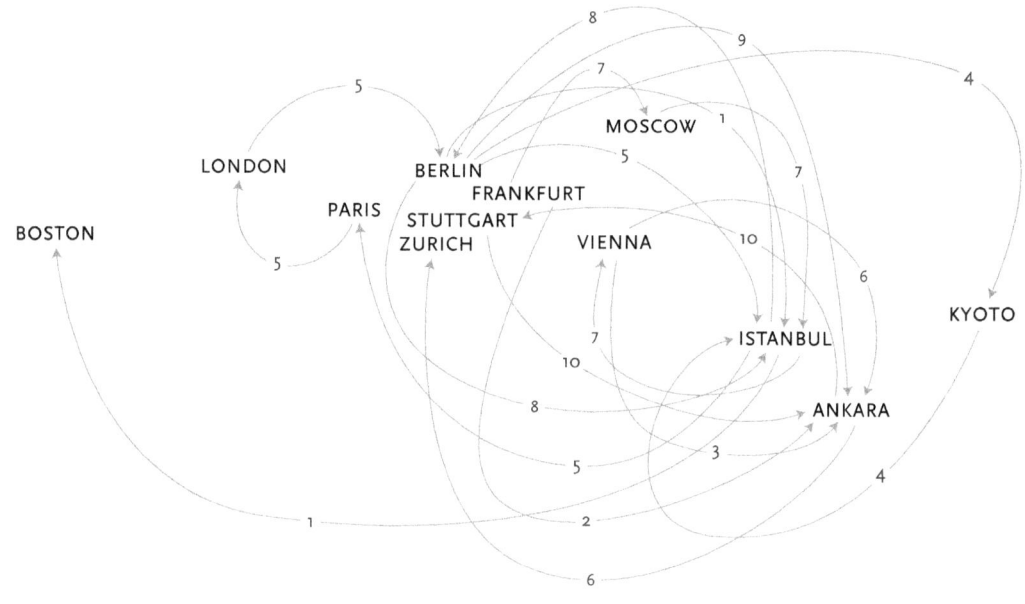

1 – Martin Wagner
2 – Martin Elsaesser
3 – Clemens Holzmeister
4 – Bruno Taut
5 – Sedad Eldem
6 – Ernst Egli
7 – Margarete Schütte-Lihotzky
8 – Seyfi Arkan
9 – Hermann Jansen
10 – Paul Bonatz

This diagram traces the stylized paths of some of the immigrating and traveling architects as they are discussed in the book.

INTRODUCTION | Modernity in Translation

In a newspaper article that was by no means particularly unusual, a Turkish reporter informed his readers in 1935 about a housing project in Germany, which the German architect and urban planner Hermann Jansen suggested be used in Turkey for modernizing the country's residential architecture. The Turkish reporter praised the project for the same reasons that were cited as prewar garden city ideals in Germany: detached low-rise houses in private gardens; ample green space between buildings; hygienic urban space; rational, functional houses; orderly streets; a unified neighborhood; functioning infrastructure; affordable construction; and so on.[1] This article expresses a view common among professional European and Turkish architects at the time: the design of a group of houses in Germany could be repeated in Turkey, according to Jansen, who sent the project to the officials in the Turkish government for their consideration. Additionally, the Turkish journalist considered it appropriate, even ideal, to apply a housing project designed for Germany to a site in Turkey. Both the reporter and Jansen seem convinced that modernism was smoothly translatable.

Jansen was only one of the few hundred professionals connecting Germany and Turkey during the first half of the twentieth century. When one maps the influential German- and Turkish-speaking architects and urban planners who migrated or traveled back and forth between Europe and Turkey in the early twentieth century, at times moving even farther east and west, the scope of interactions between the two regions will be evident. After founding the Turkish Republic in 1923 by overthrowing the Ottoman Empire, the Kemalist state invited numerous experts from the German-speaking ally countries to assist in the construction of the country's modern cities, buildings, and architectural schools, a process very similar to the one in today's China, Gulf States, and ex-Soviet nations. In the first decade of the republic, most of the architects designed their projects for Turkey while remaining based in their home country, communicating through countless translated letters. Their visions were meant to infiltrate the lives of the Turkish nation from the largest to the smallest scale. The prewar garden city model, for example — which developed in Germany partly as a result of a dialogue with British architects and authors — was applied not only in the capital of Ankara, but in master plans all over Turkey, such as in collective housing neighborhoods for the new government officials and in residential villages for immigrants arriving after the exchange of populations with the Balkan countries. Individual houses for the new leader, Mustafa Kemal Atatürk, and other elite officials increased the popularity of flat roofs rather than pitched ones, plain stucco façades rather than ornamental patterns, transparent surfaces rather than wooden shutters, winter gardens rather than courtyards, and fashionable modern furniture rather than built-in *divans*. However, even in the most obvious examples of the official westernization program, the results were never a direct copy of what happened in German modernism, but significantly modified visions. They were transformed during translation, to use the term to be elaborated on in this book. But this term involves much nuance, since these translations varied from excessive domestication to abrupt intervention, and since they were set in motion by multiple agents, including invited foreign professionals, their clients, state officials, and Turkish architects — all of whom had varying opinions about the translatability and untranslatability of architecture. Meanwhile, a group of authors and architects in İstanbul initiated an alternative path to modern architecture in Turkey through both a welcoming of translation and a productively melancholic appreciation of the existing wooden houses in the city. The German-Turkish connection was intensified after the National Socialist (Nazi) regime came to power in Germany in 1933, which forced many German architects and city planners into exile in Turkey, where they occupied a variety of intellectual and political positions. Although some stayed in Turkey as promoters of National Socialism and its classical, monumental architecture, others who had fled from the Nazis fought against this propaganda in Turkey. Most of these architects took part in educating the new generation of Turkish architects and collaborated with local professionals—a dialogue that had an impact that lasted beyond the period of their sojourns in Turkey. Translations in the opposite directions from Turkey to Germany also existed, although exposing and criticizing asymmetry and inequality in modern cross-cultural encounters is part of my intention. While in Turkey, many German architects and planners outlined the future of postwar Germany and came to influential posts afterward; some returned to Europe and advocated new positions in urban design based on their migrant experience. After the 1960s, generations of Turkish immigrants moved to Germany and left their traces in the migrant neighborhoods. To summarize, such cross-cultural exchanges in the twentieth century mobilized by immigrants, exiles, travelers, international students, officials, and collaborating local architects significantly transformed the urban and residential culture in Germany and Turkey.

The acknowledgment of earlier cross-cultural relations in a globalizing world has motivated this book. The routes of Turkish- and German-speaking architects are analyzed here, but maps of such cultural circulation for other countries would be similar. Moving from one place to another during this process are not only people (exiled, immigrating, or traveling architects and international students), but also capital, ideas (architectural movements and theories), technologies (reinforced concrete and equipment for kitchens and baths), information (including graphic standards), and images (drawings and photographs). These circulations and their transformative effects have been so ubiquitous during modern times that one can hardly think of any pure "local" architecture that is produced at a place completely closed to other locations, or any pure "global" building produced in some abstract space outside the influence of local conditions. Rather, the diverse types of continuous translations have shaped and are still shaping history, perpetually mutating definitions of the local and the foreign.

This book explores the concept of translation to explain interactions between places. Bi- and multilateral international transportation of people, ideas, technology, information, and images generates processes of change that I am defining as *translations*—a term I particularly find accessible since it is a common experience, whether one has translated between two languages, mediums, or places. Translation, as it is conceptualized in this book, takes place under any condition where there is a cultural flow from one place to another.[2] It is the process of transformation during the act of transportation.

Conducting research for this book, I arrived at the concept of translation for an architectural culture better equipped for a global future. As common as the words *globalization*, *multinational*, and *cross-cultural* might be, the future remains unclear, since the forces of history are acting in contrary directions. We live in a world where institutions in power seem to perceive a benefit in perpetual conflict—today between "the West" and "Islam"—a world where continuing geopolitical hierarchies foreclose the promise of intertwined futures. Global historiographical and design practices remain equally underdeveloped and undertheorized. This book offers translation as a way of transforming architecture into a discipline that advocates more exchange between geographic locations and more sophisticated knowledge about the entire world, while simultaneously eschewing both the hidden orientalist and isolationist studies that also claim to have this intention. It offers translation as an alternative in order not just to explore the potentials and missed opportunities of intertwined histories, but also to expose the tensions that block what is defined here as a rewarding cosmopolitan ethic.

I participate in lingual translation theories that challenge its preconception as a second-hand and inferior copy where the "origin" gets lost. On the contrary, it is through translations that a place opens itself to what was hitherto foreign, modifying and enriching its political institutions and cultural forms while simultaneously negotiating local norms with the other. This view of the foreign as a rejuvenating force, rather than a threat, sharply differentiates this book from nationalist positions at the time that it covers, as well as from mainstream geopolitical ones today. Additionally, translation reveals the voice of both sides of a cross-cultural exchange, which differentiates it from narratives that emphasize Western agency alone. The book also demystifies the idea of translation as a neutral bridge between cultures, since no translation has been devoid of the geographical distribution of power or capital. As the reader will realize, in the following pages I record many historical conditions that can hardly be considered a neutral exchange between equals, and thus I analyze both the liberating and the colonizing forces of translation. Translations establish a contact zone that not only makes cultural exchanges possible, but also reveals the tensions and conflicts created by the perceived inequalities between places. This is a contested zone where geopolitical tensions and psychological anxieties are exposed, and one where the possibility of a cosmopolitan ethic emerges or is foreclosed.

As a historical account of one such interaction, this book treats reciprocal translations as a field of study that identifies the qualifying terms to help us understand and evaluate such exchanges. Looking at specific examples and episodes in detail, it develops a terminology based on translation, such as convictions about smooth translatability and untranslatability, appropriating and foreignizing translations, melancholy as a tension produced by translations, and translations for the sake of hybridity and for the sake of a cosmopolitan ethic. It offers the trope of translation for globalization studies not only to reject the thesis of a clash of civilizations between the West and its other, but also to offer an alternative to indistinct concepts such as hybrid and transculturation, and to passive metaphors such as import, influence, and transfer—all of which deny agency to the receiving location. As it will become clearer to the reader, this book writes the history of a continuing translation process, while avoiding three common narratives: It does not perpetuate the colonial terms of cultural criticism, such as *civilized* and *backward*, *progressive international style* and *regressive regionalism*. It does not uphold the myth of problem-free modernization and the westernization of the world, which is predicated on the premise of smooth translatability. Nor does it support the convictions of untranslatability that glorify traditional origins and closed borders.

The following chapters focus on the history of German-Turkish exchanges in residential architecture in the twentieth century, analyzing the geographical circulation of major modern housing models and ideas such as the garden city, mass housing, the formal potentials of new technological inventions, and the typological study of so-called national houses. On the one hand, the book traces the translation of the garden city ideal in Germany at the beginning of the twentieth century up to World War I, and then its transformation into the Weimar *Siedlungen* during the interwar period in Germany. On the other hand, it also traces the translation of the garden city and then of the Weimar *Siedlung* theories in Turkey, as well as their different hybridizations with the "Turkish house" discourse during the early republican period in Turkey. Because the world's urban population has outnumbered the rural, housing remains one of the major quandaries of world cities today, as informal settlements perpetuate environments with no convenient city services and hence bring into being an urban poor living outside the social contract. This book integrates architecture and urbanism through the study of housing, which has so far lacked sufficient dialogue between the two disciplines. While discussing visions of innovative, alternative, or paradigmatic housing, it simultaneously demonstrates how these visions shaped and were shaped by the urban culture beyond residential architecture. The book is therefore an attempt to write an intertwined history of the modern city and architecture, told through its visions of house and housing.

How is translation possible in the first place? What makes different languages interchangeable, and different places compatible with each other? How do products and ideas pertaining to visual culture, art, and architecture get translated, and what are the ethical and political consequences of these translations? Should a cultural circulation conceal the differences between two places by domesticating the imported artifact in its new location, or should it reveal some differences by letting a deliberate awkwardness and an estranging effect persist in the translated artifact? To use the well-known words of Friedrich Schleiermacher, should a "translator leave the writer alone as much as possible and move the reader toward the writer," or "leave the reader alone as much as possible and move the writer toward the reader"?[3] Is the test of a good translation whether or not it looks like a translation? Is the ethical translation the one that resists the implementation of a new set of standards in the local context and appropriates the imported artifact into the local conditions, or the one that refuses to assimilate the foreign into the local and intentionally manifests the foreignness of the translated artifact? Who speaks and who cannot speak during the process of translation? Translation as a field of study explores every example in the light of such questions.

TRANSLATION BEYOND LANGUAGE

> It is the translator's infidelity, his happy and creative infidelity that must matter to us. — JORGE LUIS BORGES, "The Translators of the Thousand and One Nights" (trans. Esther Allan)

Baudolino, the main character of Umberto Eco's novel with the same title, was born with a peculiar gift. He could learn to speak any language after practicing a few sentences with a newfound companion who spoke it. Not burdened by the multiplicity of languages as ordinary humans are, Baudolino could have been the perfect peacemaker: he could have easily bridged the gaps between any two groups of dissimilar tongues, resolved any misunderstandings, and enjoyed communicating with people in whichever language they spoke.[4] Can Baudolino's talent for languages serve as a metaphor for translation in nonlinguistic mediums, such as the visual arts and architecture? Does something similar operate in the visual medium, which also seems, at first sight, to be emancipated from the burden of multiple languages? Although a linguistic text needs to be converted for reception in another language, no such conversion is required for visual culture. The visual original does not need to be transformed in order to circulate across geographical space. Can those who operate in a visual medium adjust themselves easily to the norms of any locale, just like Baudolino, and are they able to represent themselves equally well in any place in the world? Is there something liberating, limiting, or deceiving in the easy transferability of the visual image — in its relative universality, in the facile communicability of its denoted meanings — that bypasses the multiplicity of languages and hence the difficulty of lingual translation? If we disregarded, for one moment, the connoted or culturally coded nature of images,[5] we would have to conclude that the smooth transportability of visual culture from one place to another, in comparison to the linguistic, has facilitated its flow on a global scale and has thus accelerated the hybridization of different populations around the world. Although I understand the point of view that such connections are only shallow interactions between countries, this book nevertheless points out their potential in constructing dialogues. However, the visual medium is not devoid of connoted meanings, and, as I hope the following chapters illustrate, cross-cultural conversations have hardly been untouched by the politically charged hierarchies that have shaped the world. They have, thus, been neither smooth nor egalitarian. It takes a Baudolino, the historian who lies, to claim that one could speak in all languages. Yet it also takes a Baudolino, the historian who is deeply concerned about the future of the world, to set this as a human aspiration.

The definition of *translation* includes any act of changing from one place, position, condition, medium, or language. As etymologists point out, using the word commonly to mean a conversion between languages is only a modern phenomenon. Despite the paucity of working theories, translation has been an integral part of architectural design. Translations in architecture can be discussed in relation to converting from drawing to building, from diagram to project, from one place to another, from a different discipline to architecture, and from text to visual image.[6] I explore here translations involving the movement of entities from one location to another, and their impact on the built environment. Naturally, translations in architecture engage both the linguistic and the visual, since the reception of one or more architects' texts, concepts, and theories in another language is possible through linguistic translation, while the movement of images, space-making principles, and representational styles involves visual translation.

Theories of literary translation have formed a rich body of literature, even though their explanatory power for visual culture is not without limits. Linguistic and visual, or literary and architectural, translations differ in respect to the status of the original, the expectation of fidelity, levels of transformation, and amounts of hybridization. The original is given priority in many Western theories of linguistic translation, but as scholars have argued, the seemingly de facto superiority of the original and the notion of intellectual ownership are only recent phenomena connected to the spread of printing and literacy.[7] Nevertheless, the history of modern literary translation can hardly be written without taking into account the hierarchical status of the source text. The success of a particular literary translation is measured by its ability to transport (or rewrite) the original in the receiving language, even though the appropriate definition of *fidelity* and ways to achieve it have long been under discussion.[8] In the case of the notion of translation that I would like to explore here however, there is no one determinable original created by a single author to be converted by a single translator for its reception in another context. Every translation, linguistic or visual, is a transformation, but modern literary translation aims at the maximum possible closeness to the original, whereas architectural translation more often than not aims at a distance, distortion, or transmutation. There can be missed opportunities of translation, but mistranslation is an oxymoron in architecture. Unlike literary translation, in which translators aim to sustain a decent level of fidelity to the original text — trying to capture its meaning or feeling in their own language through word-to-word translation, interpretation, or other means — architectural translation is not burdened by fidelity. If there could ever be anything like an ultimate transformation during the act of translation in architecture, which there could not, it would be when absolutely no source could be detected in the work. If there could ever be anything like no transformation during the act of translation, which there could not, it would be the case when the identical conditions are attained in the places of departure and arrival. In this book, the category of translation includes a broad range of conversions approaching both ends in infinite opposition (the ultimate transformation and no transformation). I look at multiple degrees and types of translations that affected the history of the built environment in order to define the qualifying concepts and come to terms with them.

The medium-specific differences of translations notwithstanding, linguistic translation as a conceptual metaphor tells us more about the world than about human languages alone. The relatively facile transportability of the image assists in its geographical circulation. Yet artifacts of visual culture — including spaces, objects, and images — also have connoted social meanings, which complicate the translation process. As the following sections aim to demonstrate, there are as important similarities between linguistic and other mediums of translation as there are differences. For this reason, I suggest linguistic translation as a trope to understand the transformations in form, meaning, or function of a transported architectural artifact in its new destination, whether this is an image, an idea of space, technology, or information. In what follows, I am not using language as a system whose modes of operation are equivalent to those of architecture. I do not treat buildings as artifacts that can be read using the same methods we would apply to a linguistic text. Rather, I explore architectural translation in relation to broader theories of translation, but always by registering the limits of the metaphor so that linguistic discourse inspires but does not limit the visual discourse. In other words, I do not intend to use language as an analogue for architecture, but rather to use linguistic translation as a conceptual metaphor, and to think through linguistic theories in order to construct a terminology for architectural translation. Due to the easy transportability of the visual image, we are often oblivious to the complex translation processes that happen during this transportation process — something that has been explored attentively in linguistic translation.

THE THEORETICAL POSSIBILITY OR IMPOSSIBILITY OF TRANSLATION

> Nothing which is harmonized by the bond of the Muses can be changed from its own to another language without destroying all its sweetness. — DANTE, quoted in Reuben Brower, "Bibliography by Bayard Quincy Morgan"

> Deny translation . . . then you must be consistent and deny all speech. Translation is, and always will be, the mode of thought and understanding.
> — G. GENTILE, "Il dritto e il torto delle traduzioni," quoted in George Steiner, *After Babel*

If the limit of one's language is the limit of one's world, as Wittgenstein once said, are there as many worlds as there are languages?[9] Is there a truth before language that can be repeated in any tongue? If not, can it be that translation is actually impossible? If translation is not possible, how does it nevertheless come to exist? As elementary as these questions may seem, thinking about the theoretical possibility of translation will bring us face to face with the perplexities of what are now popularly called cross-cultural exchanges.[10] Translation as a concept and practice has no bounded place; it has commonly been seen as a channel for communication for as long as our historiographical tools allow us to detect.[11] Moreover, linguistic translation discloses the laborious work that a true exchange requires.

Theories of linguistic translation over the course of the twentieth century were preoccupied with multiple questions about fidelity and freedom, meaning and function, language as communication and as constitution, but the most important for our purposes is the question about the abstruse notion of translatability.[12] Theories and practices of translation have shown plenty of times that texts cannot be fully transmitted in all aspects, and that translators need to decide whether to give priority to each separate word's meaning, the overall feeling of the text, or something else. Translation was hardly ever viewed as a smooth and untroubled activity, yet authors diverge in their responses to the question of translation's theoretical possibility, to such an extent that one's opinion on the translatability or untranslatability of languages—as I will argue below—also reveals one's ethical position on cross-cultural interactions.

For Justin O'Brien, for instance, untranslatability is the highest virtue of a text, because this testifies to the text's unique quality: "The most convincing criterion of the quality of a work is the fact that it can only be translated with difficulty, for if it passes readily into another language without losing its essence, then it must have no particular essence or at least not one of the rarest."[13] Untranslatability may hence be perceived as the evidence of an insurmountable difference. At the other end of the spectrum, Octavio Paz has openly declared that he is offended by those who claim that poetry is untranslatable.[14] Translation is not just a marginal activity, but the very basic way humans understand and create in the world, which should testify for the postulate of universality.[15] He writes: "Although language is not universal, languages nevertheless form part of a universal society in which, once some difficulties have been overcome, all people can communicate with and understand each other."[16] Translatability may hence be perceived as a confirmation and guarantee of universality.

It was not solely literary writers and translators who entrusted translation with an intellectual responsibility. It cannot be a rare experience when we discover with a sense of discouragement that something resists fitting comfortably in the language, place, or medium where we want to put it. "It does not translate," we say, without perhaps paying enough attention to the implications of such a final judgment. When writers and architects discussed in this book hesitated over what can or cannot be borrowed from elsewhere, they exposed nothing but a concern over translatability. Chapter 1, "Modernism from Above: A Conviction about Its Own Translatability," argues that Kemalism in Turkey, which ruled the country after the foundation of the republic in 1923, can well be seen as demonstrating a confidence in the smooth translatability of Europeanness into Turkey—a program that the political elite did not hesitate to impose from above. Modernism itself may have had a certain conviction about its own translatability to the whole world so that its technical and social merits could be shared globally, a beautiful idea that nonetheless caused violent outcomes when it was pursued through paternalistic procedures. This chapter explains the official architectural program of Kemalism, and hence the translations of the garden city ideal and some formal aspects of modernism in architecture, by demonstrating how the garden city theory was transported from England to Turkey via Germany in order to guide both the new cities' master plans and new housing.

The premise of translatability has been the target of recent scrutiny, at least in language studies and philosophy. Let me present the dilemma over the theoretical possibility of translation into a longer conversation with the help of two authors. Untranslatability was a central argument in the work of Jacques Derrida, whose theory rendered humanist claims of translatability incontestably uncertain and made a lasting impact on translation studies after the mid-1980s. Derrida was responding to the structuralist and positivist theories of language, in which translatability had become both a major premise and a final destination, beginning around the end of the 1950s. The emerging theories in structuralist linguistics were used to reinforce the premise that an absolute and accurate translation is possible through a particular set of rules. Noam Chomsky is usually credited as one of the intellectual sources of these theories, even though he cautioned against employing his linguistic theory to analyze translation. Chomsky's theory—which sought to determine "abstract universals" that are common in all languages and to distinguish between the "universal deep structure," as opposed to the "surface-structures" that differ from language to language[17]—provided an appealing framework for a translation theory, since translation, after all, lies at the crux of the shared aspects and particular differences in languages.[18]

The traditional humanist notion of translation is predicated on the premise of universal communicability, a premise that gives confidence to translators that they can make foreign texts their own and represent the foreign comfortably in their own frame of reference.[19] For Derrida, however, no translation can or should be complete, because claiming that was possible would violently cover over the untranslatability of languages and the histories that produced them. Instead, the actual practice of translation ought to prove the inevitability of "incompletion, the impossibility of finishing, of totalizing, of saturating,"[20] or of assimilating another system of reference into one's own. Derrida treated translation as an indispensable but unattainable task not necessarily due to the essentially incommensurable differences between languages, but rather due to the indeterminacy of meaning within a single language: it is not possible to fix meaning within the source language itself,[21] not to mention the impossibility of the unproblematic translation of this "meaning" into another language. In "What Is 'Relevant' Translation?"—a title that "should remain forever untranslatable"[22]—Derrida applied to the word "relevance/relevante" (*relève*) the same irreducible ambivalence that he used for "difference/deference" in *Of Grammatology*.[23] How is it possible—or, rather, is it theoretically possible—to assess the "relevance" of translation, when the word *relève* itself is subject to an ongoing process of transformation, when it is perpetually unfixable and hence untranslatable?

Translatability is nothing but the premise of conventional philosophy for Derrida, because only when one claims that meaning and truth come before language can one argue that meaning can equivalently and universally be rephrased in any language. In Derrida's view that definitions of words themselves are constantly deferrable, translation of an indefinable word presents further difficulty.[24] Providing evidence for the untranslatability of languages is crucial because this confirms the failure of traditional philosophy itself, whose "origin," in Derrida's words, is nothing but the "thesis of translatability." Traditional philosophy "defines itself as the fixation of a certain concept and project of translation."[25] Deconstructing the trust in translatability, in turn, enables Derrida to contest the foundations of universal structures assigned to language and thereby to both the traditional and modernist premises of philosophy.

Is it still possible, may I ask, to envision a project of translatability, despite Derrida's convincing deconstruction of its assumptions? Why would we need such a project? Unlike Derrida, Walter Benjamin argued that a good text is one that is translatable.[26] "The Task of the Translator" (1923), originally written as an introduction to Benjamin's own translation of

Baudelaire's *Tableaux Parisiens*, has been a major reference for translation theories, inspiring multiple interpretations. Highly influenced by the German Romantics,[27] Benjamin treated translation as a historical necessity, an indispensable life support — a "medical injection," if you wish[28] — without which the originals would soon disappear into oblivion. Far more relevant here is Benjamin's multifaceted argument about "pure language" (*reine Sprache*). For him, the possibility of translation is evidence of the fact that "languages are not strangers to one another, but . . . interrelated in what they want to express."[29] The task of the translator is thus to find "the intended effect" in each text, which is the greater language, the "pure language" in which all different languages can be combined.[30] The test of a good text is its translatability, because this is the evidence of its proximity to the "pure language." This premise reveals Benjamin's traditional humanist aspirations, projected on the act of translating to demonstrate a universal bond between different languages. However, his theory is still not a conventional notion of translation that assumes languages are stable and finite systems into which foreign texts can be assimilated smoothly.[31] Translators must instead turn their own language into the foreign; they must allow their own language to be "powerfully affected," "expanded and deepened"[32] (*erweitern und vertiefen*) by foreign languages.

Rather than claiming the roots of Benjaminian "pure language" in Kabalistic thought,[33] a more productive interpretation for today, I suggest, is to consider it as an open-ended project. As long as "pure language" is interpreted as an aspiration for the future that is not yet defined, as long as it is conceived of as an ideal to which the task of the translator is directed, Benjamin's theory may acquire a newfound relevance for today's predicaments. Here, translatability must be seen as an aspiration, not necessarily a presupposition that can be sustained only by an unverifiable thesis about a preexisting universal bond between languages. For Benjamin, true translations take place only when translators broaden the limits of their own language through the use of texts in another language. The "pure language" may be envisioned as the utopian future, in which each language is broadened to such an extent that its incommensurable difference with other languages disappears. This is completely different from the notion that translators appropriate the foreign text in the closed boundaries of their own language. The Benjaminian translation calls for the expansion of languages so that they become compatible with other languages, not for their extension so that they assimilate others into their own.

In this conversation, Derrida's and Benjamin's ideas construct two different but equally innovative models of translation. Translation, for Derrida, is an unlikely but necessary task that allows for—but at the same time reveals the obstacles in—linguistic exchange. Translation therefore has a utopian dimension. Despite recognizing the impossibility of absolute translation, promoters of translation aspire toward the coexistence of incommensurable languages.[34] They prevent the exclusion of the foreign text from the local language, even though the foreign text should not be completely sustained within its norms. A utopian dimension, albeit a different kind, exists in the revised Benjaminian translation as well. Here, the translator's task is to construct the greater language that prepares a shared foundation for all languages. For Derrida, utopia is the dialogue between untranslatable languages. For Benjamin, it is the aspiration that all languages will be compatible with the "pure language," without being forced under one hegemonic language. The premise for Derrida is the irreducible heterogeneity of languages, whose radical alterity can only (and should not therefore) be obliterated through violence. The premise of Benjamin, on the other hand, is the future possibility of a shared framework, however abstract it may be. These two trajectories are both different from the premise of smooth translatability to be implemented from above. Chapter 1 of this book further introduces the potentials and limits of these three different positions on the theoretical possibility or impossibility of translation: the premise of translatability from above (the Kemalist project), untranslatability, and the aspiration for translatability from below.

Let me leave the indeterminable question on translatability unresolved. As Derrida pointedly asked, "How can one dare say that nothing is translatable, and by the same token, nothing is untranslatable" anyway?[35] The theoretical possibility or impossibility of translation will gain a new dimension after introducing the historical and geopolitical dimensions of an act of translation. In any event, this debate was meant to illustrate that translation is the very medium that exposes not only the formal but also the epistemological and ethical dimensions of cultural interactions. Is there anything untranslatable in architecture? What are the consequences of defending unbridgeable gaps between different artistic traditions? Conversely, what are the consequences of absolute translatability as a premise—that is, what would be the result of the belief that ideas and images can flow freely and smoothly between different places? These are questions worth exploring in order to understand global modernism, and I suggest that we try to answer them by enhancing the terminology of architectural translation.

APPROPRIATING AND FOREIGNIZING TRANSLATIONS

When you translate you should go as far as the untranslatable; then you catch sight of the foreign language and the foreign nation for the first time.
—JOHANN WOLFGANG VON GOETHE, *Maximen und Reflexionen* (trans. André Lefevere)

Good translation is demystifying: it manifests in its own language the foreignness of the foreign text. —LAWRENCE VENUTI, *The Scandals of Translation*

The Translation Office established in Turkey in 1938 was home to heated discussions about methods of translating foreign texts into Turkish. In a newspaper article titled "Türkçenin Eksikleri" (The gaps of Turkish), the novelist Reşat Nuri Güntekin complained about the untranslatability of European texts into Turkish due to the lack of appropriate concepts in the receiving language. He argued that the "poverty" of the Turkish language in expressing European ideas was particularly exposed during the act of translation.[36] Güntekin's views were by no means uncommon. During the early twentieth century, translation had become the arena in which the differences between Turkish and European languages were assessed and reconciled. For this reconciliation, Nurullah Ataç and Yunus Kazım Köni advocated two pointedly separate approaches in their responses to Güntekin's essay. Ataç argued that the alleged gap, which was not in the language but in the translator, could be filled by domesticating strategies that rephrased the meaning of an original sentence — not by using a word-for-word correspondence, but by rewriting it in Turkish.[37] This requires appropriating the foreign text within the norms of the Turkish language. In Ataç's own words, translated into English, "Someone who does not want to obey the rules and conventions of one's own language, someone who does not believe that one can convey ideas in that language has no right to write. The same is true for translation: someone who is translating from any language into Turkish needs to think of the Turkish norms before anything, even before the ideas in the original text, and must obey these norms."[38] Appropriations, changing words, and dividing or combining sentences are desirable for the sake of communicating meaning and making translations easily accessible to readers.

Conversely, Yunus Kazım Köni advocated what I will call foreignizing translations (a term coined by Lawrence Venuti),[39] which deliberately opened themselves to the foreign language even if this resulted in their own awkwardness.[40] Responsibility to translation required that translators enrich the receiving language with new concepts and forms, rather than freezing it within existing norms, as Ataç would argue. The difficulty of translation between any two languages need not indicate the gaps of the receiving language, as Güntekin claimed, but the contemporary distance between the two languages, which can and must be reduced through translation. This makes it all the more necessary to treat translation as a "medical injection on language,"[41] as a medium in which a language opens itself to another and "expands" (*genişletmek*) itself.[42] In Köni's eyes, foreignizing translations transcend the limits of Turkish and enrich it by exposing it to a different language. In his own words, translated into English, "the aim of a translation should not be to look like an original text written in the receiving language. This would mean that the translation had remained within the confines of the receiving language, which would be a limited benefit for this language."[43] Instead, a translation better "serves" (*hizmet*) its own language, even if it sounds awkward, when it "creates an acquaintance between languages, brings them closer, builds a 'change' in their relation, . . . [when] it earns on their behalf something they did not have."[44]

This debate over what I will call appropriating and foreignizing translations is indicative of a crucial concern in the practice of translation, which has not been limited to Turkey. When Friedrich Schleiermacher expressed the choice that had to be made between "moving the reader towards the writer as much as possible" and "moving the writer towards the reader as much as possible," he crystallized a very common dilemma among translators.[45] A similar choice repeatedly arises in architectural translations as well: should an architect appropriate the foreign in the local as much as possible in order to maintain continuity in the existing context, or intentionally preserve its foreignness as much as possible to implement a radical discontinuity? Throughout this book, I define *appropriating translation* as the tendency to assimilate or absorb a foreign idea or artifact into the local norms and *foreignizing translation* as the tendency to resist domestication, to expose the differences between two places, and to introduce a new idea, a discontinuity. Needless to say, every actual translation exists somewhere between these two ends of the spectrum.

How does one assess the results of this choice between the ends? Any moment of translation brings one face to face with what was previously considered the other, the foreign, the outside. Depending on the context and mode of transformation, a translation may move the world one step toward what might be called clonialism — the spread of sameness — under one hegemonic power; at other times, it may introduce a new and foreign idea to a given context, or strengthen the local norms at that given moment if the imported object is assimilated. On the one hand, the premise of absolute translatability may trigger the total assimilation of one place in another. On the other hand, the belief in untranslatability may draw sharp and fixed borders around places.

Rather than a predefined formulaic conclusion about the theoretical possibility of translation, or the choice between appropriating and foreignizing translations, I suggest that the evaluation ought to take ethical and political dimensions into account. As far as the history narrated in this book is concerned—that is, when we are curious about translations between one place deemed Western and another one deemed non-Western in a modern moment—we cannot disregard the unequal relations operating during this process. For instance, in the Ataç-Köni debate mentioned above, how can one disregard the perceived "poverty" of Turkish exposed in Güntekin's essay? Both literary and architectural translations establish contact zones where different locations interact with each other.[46] These are zones of exchange; but they are zones filled with uneven relations, geopolitical hierarchies, tensions and anxieties, which in turn foreclose translations' potential to be a prerequisite for a cosmopolitan ethics. Both the indeterminable dilemma between translatability and untranslatability and the choice between appropriating and foreignizing translations thus need to be contextualized in their geopolitical dimensions.

THE HISTORICAL UNEVENNESS OF TRANSLATION

> To rob a man of his language in the very name of language: this is the first step in all legal murders. — ROLAND BARTHES, *The Poetics of Imperialism* (trans. Eric Cheyfitz)

"I have to get used to the idea that I am made to torture myself and never be happy. This is why I am incapable of following today's absurd world.... In the last ten years, European products colonized Turkey. This destroyed Turkish art. If this continues, we will be completely absorbed by Europe.... Show Turkishness with pride. Don't take anything from Europe. It does not have to be beautiful for them."[47] One may not expect these words from Sedad Eldem, the sophisticated son of a privileged and modernized Ottoman family who spent most of his childhood in European cities, and who grew up to be one of the most influential architects of the twentieth century in Turkey. It may be easy to deride the guilelessness of these claims that a young architect scribbled in his diary during a study trip to Europe. Yet these melancholic inscriptions are indicative of a major tendency that needs to be theorized as part of the modern translation processes. In chapter 2, "Melancholy in Translation," I focus on the psychoanalytic and cultural concept of melancholy as a major tension that emerged in Turkey as a result of the translation policies discussed in chapter 1, and I trace the beginnings of the "Turkish house" discourse by pointing out the partially repressed melancholy in the texts of a number of intellectuals and architects in İstanbul. I will say more about melancholy in chapters 2 and 5 as a specific outcome of the Turkish elite's westernization policies, where I will argue that the paranoia of the subject of Orientalism produced the melancholy of the "object" of Orientalism.[48] Therefore, let me turn now to an undeniably integral dimension in any modern translation, of which melancholy is one manifestation.

Recent scholarship has amply demonstrated that translation served as one of the basic tools that the colonial powers used to construct and maintain their control over colonized populations. Words traveled, changing meaning with each translation in favor of Western hierarchies and reifying oppositions such as *civilized* and *savage*, *human* and *cannibal* with geographical and racial connotations.[49] Translation in a colonial context can hardly be considered a neutral exchange between two languages, since many translations maintained the superiority myth of the colonizer. Edward Fitzgerald's famous claim that Omar Khayyam's writing became poetry only when it was translated into English is one of the most overt examples.[50] Others include the metaphorical understanding of the colony and the non-West as a secondhand and inferior imitation of the Western original, and any statement that presents translation in this fashion relies not only on the mainstream perceptions of geopolitical affairs, but also on a supremacist definition of translation. Today these practices have acquired new forms under globalization through the institutions of translation, such as the representation of minority languages in unfairly small numbers, the relative lack of translations into English (which would have helped communicate ideas written in other languages around the world), the loss of languages, copyright laws, and publishing policies that treat translation as an inferior copy.[51]

This colonialist shadow throws into perspective the fragility of translation and invites us to reread translation theories. Drawing from her own experience as the translator of Derrida's *Of Grammatology* and Bengali poetry, Gayatri Spivak elaborated on the question of translating from and into non-Western texts (more specifically, those written by women). She criticized the translations from non-Western languages that fail to engage genuinely with the "rhetorical nature" of their originals.[52] More often than not, non-European literatures are treated in relation to English norms, overly assimilated to be made readily available to Western readers. A commitment to ethical translation instead requires the translator to surrender to the rhetoricity of the original. If one truly wants to translate a text by, say, a Bengali woman, if one genuinely engages with translation as the "most intimate act of reading,"[53] one would need to open oneself to the text so much that one can accept being transformed too. In Spivak's view, translations from non-European languages have hardly welcomed such surrender.[54]

A related question is Spivak's groundbreaking discussion about the representability of the subaltern, which I will rephrase in chapter 3 as the translatability of modernist mass housing models into the world of the global urban poor. In this chapter, titled "*Siedlung* in Subaltern Exile," I discuss a number of low- and middle-income *Siedlung* (residential settlement) projects in Germany and Turkey as their planners were confronted with not only geopolitical hierarchies, but also the difficulties of an economic system reliant on surplus values of real estate. Taking the history of collective housing from where we left off in chapter 1, chapter 3 traces the transformation of the prewar garden city ideals into the interwar *Siedlung* debate in Germany, and its simultaneous life in Turkey. The chapter juxtaposes the Marxist readings of the architectural historian Manfredo Tafuri and the postcolonial theories of Spivak in order to reveal the geopolitical and economic dimensions of residential architecture, especially as they expose themselves in the problems of low-income housing.

Throughout this book, I focus on historical conditions that can hardly be considered an unbiased exchange between equals. The traditional humanist supposition that translation provides an evenly balanced cultural exchange between languages would hardly tell the full story of world exchanges. Theories of postcolonial translation have significantly demystified the idea of translation as a neutral bridge between cultures and have meticulously discussed the contested nature of cultural exchange. I would like to pay particular tribute to the works of Venuti and Tejaswini Niranjana, in which they elaborated on a theory of translation that in each instance comes to terms with its geopolitical context.[55] Niranjana criticized translation studies for being oblivious to political consequences and asymmetrical relations of power operating in the process of translation, especially where non-Western languages are concerned. Any unproblematized translation suppresses the irreducible heterogeneity between cultures; it assimilates and domesticates the source language in the receiving language. Thus, the covering over of the impurities and impossibilities of translation is nothing but the suppression of the other in the name of the authority of the self. In recent scholarship, the premise of a transparent language, which would have made unproblematic translation possible, has also been challenged by demonstrating the diverse meanings of a word in the same language when different ethnic groups and genders use it.[56]

Niranjana, among others, also questioned the humanist notions of translation in anthropology and ethnography from a poststructuralist and postcolonial perspective. Talal Asad had observed in his influential essay "The Concept of Cultural Translation in British Social Anthropology," that since the 1950s, social anthropology had been popularly defined as the translation between cultures.[57] Many anthropologists, including Claude Lévi-Strauss and Edmund Leach, described their task as translating other cultures into their own, as bridging the gap between so-called primitive cultures and European ones. Lévi-Strauss famously said in *Myth and Meaning* that "to 'mean' means the ability of any kind of data to be translated in a different language."[58] However, the neutrality of this translation needs to be questioned, since it is the anthropologist or translator who has the power over the rules, and hence over true meaning.

Precisely because of this contested history, translation has also been a site of resistance and subversion for postcolonial studies, which critically assessed the assumption that the non-West is only a copy of the West and credited the translator with being an all-powerful reader, rather than a servant of the original.[59] With the scholarship of the last two decades, translation has moved from a discipline with autonomous linguistic concerns to a study that considers multiple issues of cultural and ideological contexts—a transformation observed as the "cultural turn" in translation studies, to use Susan Bassnett's term, which in turn inspires a "translation turn" in the studies of cultural artifacts.[60] The field is growing by situating translation in its sociological context, disclosing the role of translators as social actors and the influence of their habitus.[61]

German-Turkish translations in the early twentieth century were not operating in an officially colonized context, but they were nonetheless in the context of a third-world nation-building process emerging out of the decaying legacy of the Ottoman Empire. Moreover, the German-speaking professionals in Turkey were invited by the Turkish state itself, and some were exiles from Nazism—hence victims of history, rather than its victors. Yet none of these facts invalidated the tensions operating in the contact zone that I call translation, even if these tensions were not identical to the ones in colonial histories. The encounters of some German professionals in Turkey and the nationalism of some Turkish authorities were not totally devoid of what Susanne Zantop has characterized as "colonial fantasies" or "imperial imagination," which convinced both groups that they were playing a benevolent but paternalistic role in civilizing backward populations.[62] In the case of German-Turkish exchanges in the early twentieth century, the hierarchically defined divide between West and East continued to texture every case of translation, albeit in complex ways that involved not only familiar modes of stereotyping and hegemony, but also internalization and subversion. This exchange cannot be explained as a familiar account on colonialism, nor can it be fully understood by neglecting the history of latent imperial imagination. Any account of this history cannot disregard either the chauvinistic nationalism growing in Turkey or the Nazism that was on the rise in Germany.

Geographical categories such as Western and non-Western, which are then used as premises of exclusion, have historically been very common in architectural knowledge. However, such bipolarities not only maintain the ideology of an exaggerated difference between the West and its other, but they also disavow the differences within non-Western places. They undermine the centuries-long hybridizations between geographical regions, their intertwined histories, and the effects they had on each other's cultural imagination, as if a pure West and a pure East could exist. An understanding of modernization as translation subverts the category of the non-Western as the "civilization that clashes" with the West, even though West and East have been imagined as separate cultures and assigned different characters during many moments of this continuing hybridization process.[63]

THE UBIQUITY OF HYBRIDS AND THE
SCARCITY OF COSMOPOLITAN ETHICS

> No conclusion of peace shall be considered valid as such if it was made with a secret reservation of the material for a future war.
> —IMMANUEL KANT, "Perpetual Peace" (trans. Nisbet), 93

> All translation is a vivid demonstration of interdependency.
> —MICHAEL CRONIN, *Translation and Globalization*

Architects, architectural ideas, images, information, and technologies have been moving around the world for centuries, and this movement — this neither smooth nor egalitarian translation — has become an ordinary experience during modern times. An engineer might have lost sleep countless times before having the confidence to put iron in concrete based on the previous experiments of his foreign colleagues; an architectural student might have slept in run-down hostels for countless nights to observe what his peers had done with this new technology; and then a contractor might have searched around the world to find the proper insulation material, so that a flat roof terrace could be built even in a rainy and gloomy climate, making the rare sunny day remarkably more joyful. Thanks to the ubiquity of translation, there are architectural hybrids everywhere. As long as we define a *hybrid* as an artifact whose sources can be traced back to different places, there is hardly anything more common than an architectural hybrid. Coming back to the difference between linguistic and visual translation, linguistic creolization—in which a fusion tongue emerges from the mixing of existing languages—might be scarcer in history, but there has been no shortage of architectural hybridization.

Can we say that the same is true for cosmopolitan architecture? Neither of the countries discussed in this book were cosmopolitan, even though they were wide open to foreign influences, and even if some of their thinkers and artists vocally embraced the cosmopolitan ideal. The rise of Nazism in Germany—which, according to Hannah Arendt's early intuitions, was not unrelated to the racial concepts of imperialism[64]—and the irrefutable violence of Kemalism against the ethnic and religious minorities within Turkey should stand as a warning to those naive enough to think that hybridization and multicultural contexts would readily constitute a cosmopolitan ethics. Translation practices unlocked Turkey's borders to some countries, but they blocked those borders to others. The Kemalists translated extensively from European countries, but the same official program gave equal emphasis to erasing the influence of the Armenians, Kurds, Greeks, Arabs, and Persians who had shaped the Ottoman Empire. Translation alone is not a guaranteed antidote to separatist nationalism or ethnocentrism.

I would therefore like to differentiate the concept of a hybrid artifact from cosmopolitan ethics, which will be a pronounced theme in the last chapters of this book. I define a *hybrid* as a de facto product of modern times, in which there are no pure national or pure Western and pure Eastern artifacts, due to the constant translations between countries. However, being a hybrid in itself does not prevent the ideological separation between West and non-West, nor is it an antidote to chauvinistic nationalism. Chapter 4, "Convictions about Untranslatability," problematizes the concept of the original as the perceived untranslatable core of a culture and analyzes the rise of nationalist and purist anticosmopolitan ideologies, both in Germany and Turkey starting in the mid-1930s and throughout the 1940s. This chapter discusses texts and buildings that were obvious hybrids of multiple influences but that were paradoxically and mistakenly presented as products of nationalism. The hybrid only escapes its potential risk of maintaining chauvinism or ethnocentrism when it is coupled with a cosmopolitan ethics. Chapter 5, "Toward a Cosmopolitan Architecture," concludes the book with a detailed interpretation of the architect Bruno Taut's last theoretical statement, which, I suggest, aspired toward not only hybridity but also cosmopolitan ethics in the Kantian sense of the term—namely, a cosmopolitan ethical and political system that guarantees perpetual peace. In 1795 Immanuel Kant offered a list of regulations for cosmopolitan law and an ethics of hospitality to institute perpetual peace, a peace that annihilates the possibility of all future wars.[65] This was a cosmopolitanism predicated on the confidence that enlightened reason would accomplish the task of peace because, Kant argued, human rationality was universally shared and every human being was capable of acting in relation to universal maxims.

Cosmopolitan ethics is handled in this book as an ideal that has never been achieved in history, even though it has, as an aspiration, shaped the imagination of numerous citizens, writers, and artists in different ways. Historically, cosmopolitanism has been one of the most virtuous ideals that exposed the most unfortunate contradictions. It is an obvious irony that the Stoic philosopher and Roman emperor Marcus Aurelius meditated at night on the cosmopolitan city that embraced all of humanity, while during the day he led wars in the name of the Roman Empire.[66] This was an eerie link between imperialism and cosmopolitanism. Centuries later, August Wilhelm Schlegel distinguished between "workmanlike translations" and the ones that achieve a "higher poetic re-creation." The latter type of translation, he claimed, "is designed for nothing less than the unification of the best qualities of all nationalities, to enter fully into their thoughts and feelings, and thus to build a cosmopolitan centre for all humanity. Universality, cosmopolitanism is the truly distinctive German characteristic. . . . It is therefore, no mere sanguine optimism to suppose that the time is not distant when the German language will become the speaking voice of the civilized world."[67] It is hard to bear the gap between the nobility of an aspiration for peaceful humanity and the banality of an imperial linguistic imagination in such statements. Contrary to genealogies that trace a linear link from the Cynics and Stoics of the ancient world to Kant, cosmopolitanism has not been a Western concept alone. Translatable ideals that aspired to a type of cosmopolitan ethics existed in numerous teachings around the world.[68] Many of the non-Western historical moments attributed to cosmopolitanism were hardly without contradictions either. As Sami Zubaida remarks, the "nostalgia for this golden age [of Middle Eastern cosmopolitanism] conveniently forgets its imperial context."[69] Chapter 5 looks more closely at another historical example, an interpretation of the Kantian cosmopolitan ideal as it has arguably been an inspiration for the German architect Taut, then exiled in Turkey.

Although I will be exploring the allusion to cosmopolitan ethics in a specific historical context — namely, Weimar Germany and early republican Turkey — the term's relevance for today's globalizing world and rising religious or ethnic patriotism is also significant. Contemporary theorists of cosmopolitanism diverge in defining the term so that it would effectively help us think beyond nations without falling into the previous contradictions.[70] Jürgen Habermas, for example, has concentrated on the necessary transformations in the international legal orders, so that the Kantian project can be continued and so that all individuals can securely become abstract bearers of equal universal rights.[71] Martha Nussbaum has also argued for a Kantian, universal cosmopolitanism, now defined as the detachment from any type of "morally arbitrary boundaries," including national or ethnic bonds, in the name of solidarity with all of humanity.[72] For Sheldon Pollock, on the other hand, cosmopolitanism will be achieved through "attachment to the past," rather than detachment from cultural specificity in the name of universalism, and through "transformation from within communities themselves," rather than a top-down injection of universals.[73] Bruce Robbins defines a similar type of cosmopolitanism as "multiple attachment, or attachment at a distance," instead of "an ideal of detachment."[74] As another model, Kwame Anthony Appiah defines cosmopolitanism as admitting an obligation to "strangers" who might have disagreeably different values from "ours." Rather than assuming that reason and rationality are value free, or that economic inequalities are natural, Appiah calls for a definition of both moral and economic obligation, in which cosmopolitanism means a commitment to pluralism but not necessarily to universality.[75] Fuyuki Kurasawa questions both what he calls normative cosmopolitanism, which privileges abstract universalist commitments, and institutional cosmopolitanism, which concentrates on international laws and procedures, considering the two as projects from above. Adopting a phrase from Mary Kaldor,[76] Kurasawa highlights instead the existing practices of "cosmopolitanism from below" that remain continually a work in progress, where ordinary citizens and civic organizations perform solidarity without borders.[77] The term has also inspired the rewriting of modern art history through a perspective informed by postcolonial studies, most notably in Kobena Mercer's *Cosmopolitan Modernisms*.[78]

There are many, however, who define an existing place today or in the past as cosmopolitan. Although it is important to differentiate worldviews working toward cosmopolitanism from ones that defend national purism or ethnocentrism, and although there certainly have been individuals who were dedicated to cosmopolitan ideals, I would nevertheless hesitate to use the word *cosmopolitanism* as a synonym of *multiculturalism*. Adopting cosmopolitan ethics does not happen naturally by living in a multicultural society, by performing as part of a transnational group, or by being in the presence of hybrid artifacts, as the examples in this book also testify. As long as we define *cosmopolitan ethics* as that which is committed to solidarity with all of humanity and that which guarantees perpetual peace in an increasingly interconnected world, there will be little doubt that the productive debate over cosmopolitan ethics and legal order is still going on.

This book rephrases the unanswered questions of cosmopolitan ethics as questions of translation. The cosmopolitan ideal can be redefined in relation to the two approaches I distinguished by taking off from Derrida's and Spivak's, as well as Benjamin's and Köni's, ideas on translatability. According to the first approach, a true hospitality must be possible through a commitment to the untranslatability of cultures. Only through the realization of difference can one unconditionally open oneself to the other, rather than assimilating the other into one's own values in the name of universality. According to the second approach, cosmopolitanism is possible only through a commitment to the translatability of cultures, as long as these translations expand cultures from below rather than assume a metaphysical bond that combines all of them. A cosmopolitan ethics that is continually in the making—one translation at a time, if each place could be expanded toward another—might be comprehensible. In any event, translation is the antidote to the sedentary; the ubiquity of translations is evidence against the myth of a pure, authentic, and original culture. If it can be pursued without imperialist intentions, translation is the process through which each place is opened to and enriched by its outside; and if it can occur in multiple directions, rather than only from Europe and the United States to the rest of the world, translation is the prerequisite of a cosmopolitan ethics. Things do not get lost in translation, but they get multiplied through displacement and replacement. And based on the specific story of this transfer in each particular case, the places of departure and arrival of each transportation—which are both already constantly changing with the continuing translation processes—are connected to each other in a unique way. In this way, translations make history.

ONE | **Modernism from Above**

A Conviction about Its Own Translatability

The Turkish Republic, established in 1923, was initially antagonistic to both its Ottoman precedents and the French, British, and Italian forces against which the War of Independence had been fought. It should not be surprising then, that it chose its German-speaking allies as the visible model for its modernizing and Westernizing reforms. Among the German professionals invited to Turkey during the early republican era, it is worth mentioning such prominent figures as Ernst Reuter, later mayor of West Berlin; composers and literary critics such as Carl Ebert, Leo Spitzer, and Erich Auerbach; economists and lawyers such as Fritz Neumark, Gerhard Kessler, and Alexander Rüstow; doctors such as Rudolf Nissen and Philipp Schwartz; and architects, artists, and city planners such as Bruno Taut, Martin Wagner, Hermann Jansen, Gustav Oelsner, Paul Bonatz, Margarete Schütte-Lihotzky, Wilhelm Schütte, and Rudolf Belling. Many Turkish architects of the period received part of their professional education in Germany. For example, Sedad Eldem went to Germany on a study tour with a state fellowship in 1928; Seyfi Arkan studied architecture in Berlin and

Turkey, 1923 . . .

worked in Hans Poelzig's office from 1930 to 1933; Arif Hikmet Holtay studied in Stuttgart and Berlin from 1926 to 1930; Emin Onat studied in Zurich around 1933–34; and Emin Necip Uzman worked in the office of the Berlin-based architect Fritz August Breuhaus from 1937 to 1939. However, the republican elite refused to rely on Turkish talent, perhaps because many of the experienced architect-builders (*kalfa*) of the Ottoman Empire after the eighteenth century were members of the Armenian or Greek minority groups whose successors the last Ottoman sultans and the new Turkish state avoided working with, and perhaps because the newly educated Turkish architects seemed too young for the task, with notable exceptions who were associated with Ottoman revivalism.[1]

The Kemalist intellectuals in Turkey did indeed consider linguistic translation a crucial act of modernization. Just three years after the foundation of the Turkish Republic, a Copyright and Translation Committee (Telif ve Tercüme Heyeti) was created in the Parliament. In 1935 the philosopher Hilmi Ziya Ülken published *Uyanış Devirlerinde Tercümenin Rolü* (The role of translation during ages of reawakening), a book that associated reawakening (*uyanış*) with the growth of translation.[2] Drawing examples from a variety of places and historical periods, Ülken argued that the human mind owed the great intellectual and cultural leaps it made to translation. "Those who don't know how to open their doors wide to all influences cannot create anything new," he wrote. "Translation is that which gives the creative power to the eras of awakening."[3] In 1938, the first Turkish Publication Congress (Neşriyat Kongresi) decided to establish a Translation Office under the minister of education, then Hasan Ali Yücel.[4] Both the directors and the relatively autonomous authors who worked with this office had high hopes for translation.[5] They imagined themselves at the threshold of a new age, no matter how many works had been translated from Arabic and Persian by their predecessors during the Ottoman Empire, and from French after the Tanzimat reforms in 1839[6]—and no matter how broadly Ottoman thinkers such as Ahmet Mithat had contributed to translation practices and theories.[7]

Both Ülken and Yücel were convinced of the universality of civilization and hence of the translatability of languages. In the very first editorial of the office's journal, *Tercüme* (Translation), Yücel wrote: "Civilization is a whole [*Medeniyet bir bütündür*]. East and West, new and old worlds are the representations of the same whole with individual differences.... It is natural that a translator enriches the world of ideas in his own community by bringing in concepts from another."[8] When human civilization was perceived as one continuous evolution made possible by translation, the argument effortlessly followed that the new Turkish Republic, allegedly unlike the Ottoman Empire, had to join this world civilization primarily by translating world classics. This approach was not limited to literature alone. Translation could refer to a broad range of activities rather than simply conversion from one language to another. Cities and their houses could also be constructed through a translation process.

Studying the German-Turkish exchange in residential culture is a particularly informative way to explore the role of translation in shaping both modern Turkey and the globalizing world. The relationship between the two countries took specific turns throughout history. The diplomatic associations between the Ottoman and Prussian Empires intensified during the eighteenth century, as part of the modernization policies of the former and the pursuit of military alliances favorable to both. The Ottoman-Prussian Pact of Friendship was signed in 1761 and a military alliance in 1790, which triggered a period of intensified economic relations. During the industrialization period, Germany, competing against France and Britain, sought to find new resources and markets in Ottoman lands. The German-Ottoman Treaty of Commerce that gave extensive legal rights to German firms was signed in 1890, followed by the establishment of several German banks and schools in the Ottoman Empire. The construction of the Baghdad Railway across Ottoman territory, a battlefield of international rivalry since 1856, was exclusively handed to German firms in 1903, which decisively increased the accessibility of Ottoman resources and markets for the European power.[9] According to Rosa Luxemburg, the agreement was bound to be the destroyer of the Ottoman Empire because paying the money needed to support a railway system it could not maintain would ruin a country based on agriculture.[10] Faced with economic and political hardships, the Ottoman army increasingly relied on educational support from Germany during this period,[11] and the two countries remained allies during World War I.[12]

Historians have often argued that the German military and economic presence had a smaller impact on the cultural life of the Ottoman Empire than the presence of the French, British, and Italians.[13] For instance, the number of German schools was far smaller than the number of other European ones.[14] According to the census of 1850, there were around 1,000 German-speaking residents in İstanbul; in 1918 this number had only increased to 1,300. Nevertheless, toward the end of the Ottoman Empire, ten main German associations were functioning in İstanbul, including the Center for German-Speaking Residents (founded in 1847) and the German Women's Association of İstanbul (founded in 1856), in addition to the German schools of İstanbul in Pera, Haydarpaşa, Bebek, and Yedikule.[15] The newspaper *Osmanische Post* was first published in 1890 (it closed in 1895), and the legendary *Osmanischer Lloyd* in 1908.[16] The German-Turkish Friendship Association (Freundschaftshaus, Dostluk Cemiyeti), founded in 1914, sought to reinforce the cultural relations between the two countries. In the words of its charter, the association aimed to "inform the Turkish people about Germany and put an end to French cultural imperialism."[17] As part of its program, the association organized the German-Turkish House of Friendship architectural competition among Werkbund architects in 1916.[18]

This perceived lack of cultural interaction between Germany and Turkey changed significantly with the major transformations that followed World War I. The German-Turkish Treaty of Friendship, signed on March 3, 1924, restored the diplomatic and commercial relations between the two countries, which had been officially disrupted since 1918.[19] The newspaper *Türkische Post* started publication in 1926; the first German-Turkish dictionary using the Roman alphabet was published in 1931.

NEW CITY: TRAVELING GARDEN CITY

City planning and architecture were among the first fields to show the effects of the reinstated alliance between Germany and Turkey. On October 13, 1923, the Kemalist state declared Ankara to be the new capital of Turkey and, from the following year onward, employed German-speaking planners and architects to build it. Making Ankara the capital city was a significant political and cultural statement, announcing that İstanbul—the symbol of the Ottoman Empire and the quintessential multicultural city of the East—was no longer to serve as the country's administrative and political center. Rather, a minute and relatively undeveloped settlement in Anatolia, one that had been Turkey's military center during the War of Independence, would be built anew as the locus for the revolutionary changes the Kemalist revolution was yet to introduce. Constructing a new capital city for a new nation required not only a youthful, futuristic, and assertive enthusiasm, but also the erasure of the past and the fierce assimilation of Turkey's diverse ethnic groups under the purified umbrella of the nation.

Nineteenth-century travelers depicted Ankara as a poor, "melancholic and unkempt" settlement.[20] The census of the period documented an ethnically and religiously mixed population with a majority of Muslims and minorities of Greek Orthodox, Armenian Catholic, Jewish, and Protes-

1.1. "Ankara Construit" series in *La Turquie Kemaliste*.

tant people.²¹ Descriptions of the city from the 1930s, in contrast, stated over and over again that the republican revolution was building a totally new, modern, and grandiose Turkish town from scratch on the same land (fig. 1.1). The contrast between the prerepublican and republican Ankara has been exaggerated in the official historiography, which offered self-congratulatory praise for the achievements of the new nation-state.²² For famous novelists of the revolution—including Yakup Kadri Karaosman-oğlu, who wrote a book on the city²³—Ankara would be everything that İstanbul had lost, a symbol of Turkey's decolonization from Western forces that occupied the country after World War I (if not earlier) and its commitment to modernization through Westernization—namely, a new symbolic city that would simultaneously be anti-Western and Western, and as such an embodiment of the constant dilemma in the country's cultural production for many years to come.

Contemporary accounts suggest that the architecture of Ankara was seen as a test case of the young nation's ideological aspirations. In "Hülya Bu Ya" (Well, it is a fancy, 1921), Refik Halid [Karay] created a science-fiction story, narrated by a fascinated American tourist.²⁴ Here, the future

Ankara was a city with moving streets that made all vehicles and walking obsolete, a city with no roofs or glassed windows because the climate was regulated by a huge machine that protected the inhabitants from rain and snow, and excessive heat and cold. The machines of modernity also turned all nights into a perpetual day. "It's true," said the American tourist in the story, "these are only necessary in our backward cities of Europe and America."[25] This satirical story not only demonstrates the high expectations invested in Ankara by Mustafa Kemal's followers but also ridicules their blind admiration of Western technological progress. Here the success of the city was measured against the feelings of inferiority it could cause in a Westerner—revealing, in fact, the feeling of backwardness sensed by the Turkish rulers themselves.

As early as 1924, the Kemalist state asked the German planner Carl Lörcher to prepare a master plan for Ankara, trusting the foreign expert in the relatively new discipline of city planning to ensure the capital's hygienic, well-equipped, and controlled growth.[26] Designed to accommodate 150,000–200,000 inhabitants, Lörcher's plan did actually lay down the principles of the Governmental Complex (Regierungsstadt) that were followed by his successor, but it differed in policies for the old town's rehabilitation and new housing. For residential areas, Lörcher anticipated a very low density of one-to-two-story row houses with large private gardens, organized around big, common lawns and additionally bonded by a community center with a small mosque (fig. 1.2). Repeating a premise that was widely shared by his colleagues in Germany, Lörcher envisioned generous green spaces as a moral virtue and thus a major gift of modern city planning to humanity.[27]

The municipality of Ankara found Lörcher's rehabilitation plan for the old town financially unfeasible and his master plan for the new areas inadequate to respond to the growing demand for housing. Consequently, a new competition was organized between Hermann Jansen, Joseph Brix—both were from the Berlin-Charlottenburg Technical University, and they had shared the first prize for the Greater Berlin master plan competition in 1909—and Léon Jaussely, a professor of urban composition at the Paris Institut d'Urbanisme and the winner of Barcelona's master plan competition.[28] The contestants visited Ankara in July 1927 and submitted their proposals in November 1928. Six months later, on May 16, 1929, the jury, enforced by Atatürk's strong presence, gave Jansen the first prize and Jaussely the second.[29] The two had quite different approaches to the existing urban fabric and new housing. Jaussely suggested that the old city, the Citadel, needed to be completely reconstructed, whatever the cost.[30]

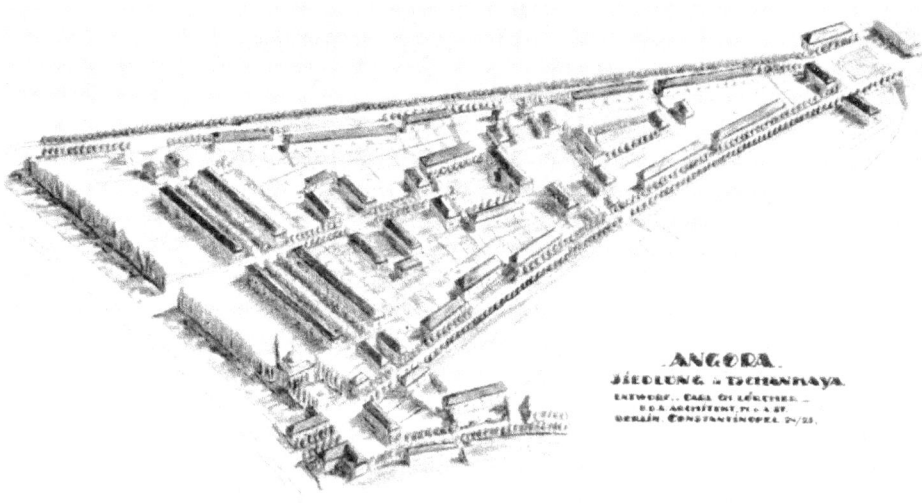

1.2. Carl Lörcher. Residential settlement, Ankara, 1925.

"Today Ankara really looks like a simple village rather than a central governmental city,"³¹ he said, presenting a long list of the city's additional shortcomings—such as its topographical limitations caused by the hilly landscape, its excessive climatic conditions, and the inadequacy of its soil for vegetation.³² Despite his brutally honest analysis of Ankara's inadequacies, Jaussely's plan was more ambitious than those of his competitors, suggesting wide, straight, monumental streets and promenades, ring avenues and boulevards, and large public squares with symbolic monuments and sculptures³³—decisions that were criticized for being too extravagant, unrealistic, and expensive in contemporary newspapers.³⁴ Jansen, on the other hand, invested a highly symbolic significance in Ankara's Citadel and the traditional houses of the old city, comparing them to Rome's Capitoline Hill and Pergamon's Acropolis.³⁵ Yet, wanting to avoid the costs that had caused the rejection of Lörcher's rehabilitation plan, he proposed deferring any significant work in this area. More important, Jansen proposed the garden city model, rather than one associated with denser, monumental, and axial European cities of the nineteenth century.

The difference between Jaussely and Jansen was revealed most clearly in their proposals for new housing. Jaussely distinguished between a "closed system" and an "open system": the former consisted of five-story building blocks surrounded by streets in the front and enclosed common courtyards at the back, while the latter referred to free-standing villas in a garden, for which Jaussely used the French word *banlieue*. The denser closed system, reminiscent of nineteenth-century European urbanism, would have characterized Ankara's center. The open system was suggested only for the peripheries.[36] Jansen, in contrast, forcefully condemned any residential texture that remotely resembled the nineteenth-century urban blocks: "In many European cities, the health of the city inhabitants was sacrificed to appearances. Boulevards on the front, but dim courtyards with dirty air on the back. This, accompanied with the lack of empty areas, caused the degeneration of many stratums of the masses"[37] — a statement that again attached health and moral virtue to city form. Jansen proposed instead to construct the new houses of the capital as a garden city.

The World, 1902...

The garden city ideal and its executions in different countries are the most evident examples of the power of translation in shaping world cities. The theory is usually credited as one of the founding ideas that led to the emergence of city planning as a modern discipline, and has usually been mentioned in modern architecture surveys.[38] The garden city was a frequently circulated model of the twentieth century, reemerging in different locations as *Gartenstadt, bahçeşehir, cité jardin, cuidad jardin, den-en toshi,* and *tuinstadt,* although each translation was considerably transformed in relation to the original. Germany, the United States, France, Belgium, Sweden, Denmark, Japan, Russia, Australia, and Turkey were all early destinations of the traveling garden city. The term and model was freely interpreted, often resulting in what would be more appropriately called a garden suburb, garden factory village, or simply collective housing with garden city principles. Unlike scholars who characterize these processes as mistranslations, maintaining the existence of a linear history in which the true modernization takes place in one place and any diversion from the "original" is perceived as distortion, I call them translations that make world history.[39] Following the idea's path from England to Turkey via Germany will reveal the history of one of these translations.

England, 1898–1902

The term *garden city* was launched in England in *Tomorrow! A Peaceful Path to Real Reform* (1898), by Ebenezer Howard (1850–1928), and it was popularized by the revised version, *Garden Cities of Tomorrow*, published in 1902.[40] Historians emphasize the possible impact of Howard's visits to the United States, in addition to the probable influence of thinkers such as Henry George, Edward Bellamy, and Peter Kropotkin and designers such as Frederick Law Olmstead and James Silk Buckingham on Howard.[41] The theory aimed to manage the impact of industrialization on human settlements and to redeem what Howard called the decay of rural

1.3. Ebenezer Howard. "The Three Magnets."

areas caused by the lack of social interaction as well as the decay of urban areas caused by the lack of interaction with nature. As Raymond Williams later explained in *The Country and the City*, the word *country* in the British literary context often symbolized a happier past, a natural and authentic existence, a melancholic resistance to and a thoughtful withdrawal from the ills of the new age at moments of big change—whereas the city, initially perceived as the locus of money or the source of turmoil, came to symbolize hopes in the future, progress, liberation, modernization, but also imperialism.[42] Howard also elaborated on the persistent and common lure of both the country and the city, the "two magnets" that drew people: the city was rich in "alluring social opportunities and places of amusement," but destitute in residential conditions because of high rents and excessive distance from work; and the country was the "source of life, of happiness, of wealth, and of power," but "dull for lack of society."[43] What Howard proposed was nothing less than a "third magnet," which he thought would rather effortlessly combine the charms of both country and city: a planned, self-sufficient, green, affordable new town, with a maximum population of 30,000 people, built from scratch on bare lands and surrounded by an agricultural belt (fig. 1.3).

Politically, Howard considered his model as the third way that invalidated the polarity between communism and individualism by safeguarding both the "well-being of the community" and "the freest and fullest opportunities for the individual."[44] In Peter Hall and Colin Ward's terms, this was "a vision of anarchist co-operation, to be achieved without large-scale state intervention."[45] Howard projected that the entire revenue would be derived from "rents" paid by "responsible gentlemen," which, he asserted, would also suffice for municipal undertakings and public purposes — a miscalculation (and optimism) that would significantly challenge the translation of the ideal to reality.[46] The proximity of the agricultural and urban land would make it possible for farmers to have easy access to markets, and for city dwellers to benefit from cheaper harvests. To convince his readers that the garden city ideal was not just a naive utopia but a plausible policy that would provide all economic classes with healthy and affordable housing, Howard focused extensively on the financial and administrative aspects, while limiting his architectural ideas to diagrams.

Howard's *Garden Cities of Tomorrow* was received cautiously but favorably in England. The English Garden City Association, founded on June 10, 1899, gave his ideas a chance by organizing numerous conferences (260 lectures in 1902–3 alone) and publishing promotional pamphlets. In 1903, Letchworth was chosen as the suitable site for the first garden city, and Barry Parker and Raymond Unwin were selected as its planners. Howard himself moved to the city in 1905, overseeing its rough journey to realization in relation to his principles. The theory of the garden city started circulating in Europe almost simultaneously with its reception in England.

Germany, 1902–1929

In its immediate translation to German as *Gartenstadt*, the meaning of the term *garden city* was transformed in a few ways. The German Garden City Society (Deutsche Gartenstadt-Gesellschaft e.v., or DGG) was founded in September 1902 in Berlin. Following the translation of Howard's book into German in 1907,[47] publications about garden cities poured out.[48] The instant acceptance of the theory was partly predicated on the pressing problems it was perceived able to resolve, such as the overcrowded rental barracks (*Mietskasernen*) that were considered responsible for what the critics called the unnatural lifestyle of the industrial age, the unhealthy living conditions of metropolitan residents, and the uncontrolled development of cities. Howard's idea was easily assimilated into the existing discussions in Germany, including those about the life-reform movement, mobilization of the "back to nature" motto, and factory towns. The garden city fulfilled two basic objectives that had already been key in Germany: to revive the city resident's relationship with nature and to respond to the urgent need for large quantities of affordable housing by establishing cooperatives (*Genossenschaft*). In the eyes of its promoters, the model also promised a healthy and hygienic life — especially for children, who needed light and air; a better quality of life for the workers' wives;[49] an effective way to struggle against alcoholism (this was one of the common themes in Germany as well as in Howard's book);[50] and the possibility of implementing a working infrastructure of water, central heating, and sewage.[51] Most important, it was perceived as the source of "spiritual regeneration," of not only physical but also mental health, of "higher cultural existence, of community (*Gemeinschaft*)."[52] "How can we hope for a healthy *spiritual life* [*gesundes Geistesleben*] when we put human beings into such an unhealthy existential condition as the one in the metropolis?" asked one proponent. "So much a small garden with its vegetables, flowers and fruits can do for all men, tired of the haste and troubles of the day," answered another.[53] It was assumed that living in gardens and engaging in garden-related activities would cure humanity.

DGG's first program, written in 1902, redefined the garden city as a settlement that mobilized inner colonization and decentralization[54] — two concepts that had been quite frequently used in Germany long before the arrival of the theory.[55] Decentralization connoted the necessity of spreading the nation's industrial, artistic, and intellectual activities among different regions, rather than crowding them together in one big city. The term *inner colonization* brings to mind an article by Victor Huber in 1845, among other works. Huber sought the improvement of agricultural living standards to avoid surplus migration to the city.[56] Huber was equally concerned with the notion of self-help and with motivating workers to establish cooperatives that combined their resources. In a way, the transportation of the garden city ideal to Germany was an example of an appropriating translation. The German professionals conceptualized the model by assimilating it into their own vocabulary.

Among the German translations of the garden city, prior to or after the publication of Howard's book, Theodor Fritsch's *Die Stadt der Zukunft* (The city of tomorrow, 1896) requires special emphasis due to its similarity to Hermann Jansen's applications.[57] Not long after, Fritsch wrote the anti-Semitic *Handbuch der Judenfrage* (Manual on the Jewish question, 1907), a fact that Jansen may have noticed. *Die Stadt der Zukunft*, which was regarded by the author's contemporaries as a theory of garden city *avant la lettre*,[58] theorized alternative definitions of urbanity to the one offered by the metropolis. Like Howard, Fritsch defended the planned development of new and contained cities and suggested self-sustaining settlements surrounded by large green belts. Nevertheless, his proposal was radically dissimilar to Howard's because of Fritsch's ideas on social and economic segregation, which also differentiated him from the socialist politics of many DGG members. Fritsch proposed to divide the city into seven different zones, placed as hierarchically organized belts radiating away from a central area that was reserved for monumental buildings. The belts were zoned in relation to social classes, moving from distinguished villas close to the center to workers' houses at the periphery, with fine houses and communal houses in between the two. The outer areas of the city were reserved for small workshops, factories, and public gardens, respectively. Finally, the whole city was surrounded by a green belt, sparsely occupied by summer and weekend houses (fig. 1.4).

Despite the frequent use of the term *Gartenstadt*, the German garden cities (with the possible exception of Hellerau) did not function economically as Howard's model proposed—namely, they were not self-sufficient, small towns that were financially independent from the bigger metropolis. Given that Howard had limited himself to diagrams, the architectural aspects of the garden city were created in Britain and Germany simultaneously. The variety of examples associated with the term *garden city* prompted further conceptual distinctions.[59] Hellerau in Dresden was identified as the first German *Gartenstadt* (garden city); Margarethenhöhe was named a *Gartensiedlung* (garden residential settlement); and Bruno Taut's Falkenberg in Berlin was called a *Gartenvorstadt* (garden suburb) in some publications (fig. 1.5; also see fig. 3.1).[60] In order to accommodate multiple interpretations of the term, DGG issued a second program in 1907:[61] "The establishment of housing settlements, suburbs, industrial colonies, and the extension of existing cities all belong to the definition of a garden city."[62] The term *garden city* thus came to signify both a new town, just as it was formulated in Howard's theory, and collective housing settlements in the extended borders of an existing city, indicating that a transformed meaning had emerged during the process of translation.

Ankara, 1929

When Hermann Jansen referred to his designs both for Ankara's master plan and its first cooperative housing as a garden city, he echoed this split of meaning in the German translation of the term. Let me take each meaning separately so as to trace its further translations in Turkey.

Berlin, 1904–1929

Despite the scholarly neglect of his career, Jansen (1869–1945) was an important figure in Berlin, where he moved in 1898 after receiving his

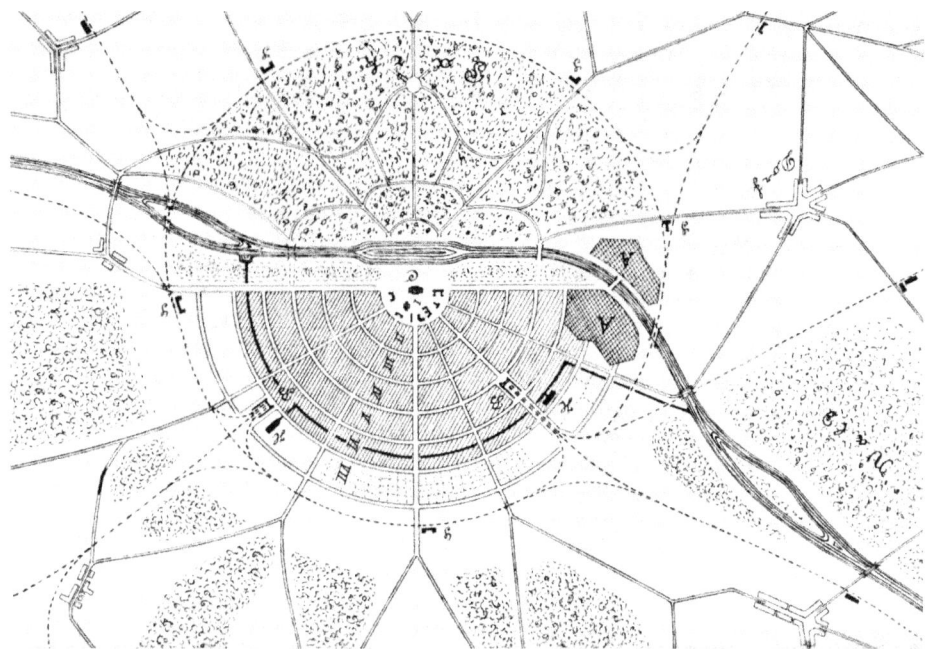

1.4. Theodor Fritsch. Diagram of ideal city, 1896.

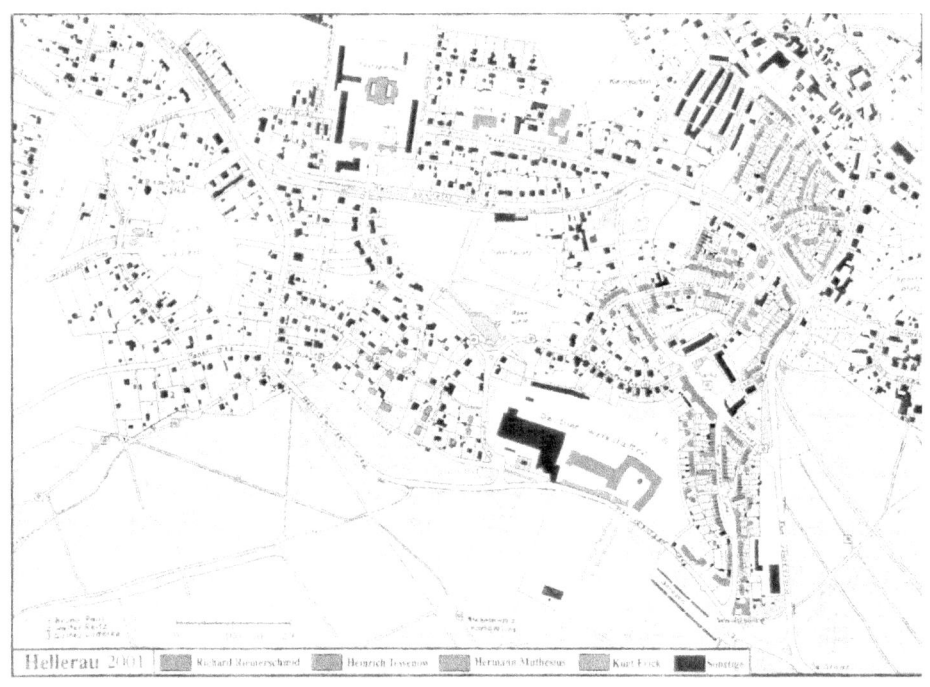

1.5. Richard Riemerschmid, Heinrich Tessenow, Hermann Muthesius, and Karl Frick. *Gartenstadt* Hellerau.

architecture degree from Aachen Technical University. He was the editor of and a frequent contributor to the influential architectural journal *Der Baumeister* (1904–30); he was a professor at Berlin-Charlottenburg Technical University from 1920 onward, where he taught with Heinrich Tessenow; and he designed numerous city plans and housing neighborhoods that informed his work in Turkey.[63]

As the editor of *Der Baumeister*, Jansen was very familiar with the values attached to single-family houses. Apart from numerous plans for *Landhäuser* (villas or single houses in gardens) published during his editorship, Jansen published a number of influential articles by Hermann Muthesius, who was one of the main advocates of the family values promoted by a single house with a garden, in *Der Baumeister*.[64] Jansen himself reviewed Muthesius's *Landhaus und Garten*, emphasizing the connections between German and English single-family houses.[65] In addition to his general editorials, Jansen was a cultural critic for *Der Baumeister*, writing on such varied topics as contemporary art and architecture exhibitions, competitions, new projects, and the work of influential architects.[66] He wrote extensively on residential types in both the city and the country, differentiating them in relation to size, height, composition, and location in the site.[67] Although he carefully discussed conceptual and architectural attributes of different residential types — such as the distinctions between *Einzelhaus* (single house) and *Massenhaus* (collective house); *Eigenhaus* (one's own house) and *Mietshaus* (rental building); *Landhaus* (country house), *Reihenhaus* (row house), and *Wohnbaublock* (residential building block) — affordable housing received hardly any attention in *Der Baumeister*, only appearing occasionally as part of Jansen's exhibition reviews.[68]

One of Jansen's main concerns was the lack of "artistic quality" in contemporary big cities, which prompted him to call for "artistic principles" in the city design (*Städtebau*) and housing. He particularly emphasized the necessity of harmony and unity in the urban environment. Aesthetic issues had to be addressed at the scale of the city or the neighborhood, rather than at that of the individual building. In this way, Jansen clearly allied his views with Camillo Sitte's principles, to which he must have been introduced during his education at Aachen Technical University under Karl Henrici.[69] Sitte's emphasis on tradition, the appropriation of the teachings of the past into modern requirements, and the unity and harmony to be reclaimed in the modern city found continuing echoes in Germany through the journal *Der Städtebau*, to which Jansen also contributed articles and projects.[70]

The quest for unity and harmony in the urban environment remained a governing principle for both the promoters of the early garden city ideals and the members of the Sitte school in Germany. Both groups believed that the city had to be a harmonious whole. As Jansen also insisted, big cities were growing spontaneously in a disorderly fashion because of the individualistic design of each housing block that did not take the whole street into account.[71] Instead, all buildings had to rise to the same height; the slopes of all roofs had to be aligned; all buildings had to surrender to the street line, and had to speak anonymously under the harmonizing (and homogenizing) rules of a building regulation; the windows on all walls had to create a unity; the green spaces had to be organized under a predefined plan. The modern chaotic metropolis, which grew arbitrarily and developed untidily, needed redemption through the creative and organized touch of the architect. And what were better opportunities to demonstrate how a built environment could be designed as a unified whole than new cities and large housing settlements built on bare lands?

Before his appointment as the planner of Ankara, Jansen was best known for his prizewinning project for the master plan of the greater Berlin area in 1909 (which was never executed since there was no official administrative basis for its implementation),[72] as well as his projects for Cologne, Trier, and Nürnberg in Germany; Bergen in Norway; and Bielitz in Poland.[73] All three competitors in the competition to design Ankara's master plan—Jansen and Brix, who shared the first prize in Berlin, and Jausseley—had also entered the competition for greater Berlin, and Ludwig Hoffmann, whom the Turkish bureaucrats had approached for advice, was on the jury.[74] Berlin was not a garden city to be designed from scratch, but a complex metropolis whose problems Jansen nevertheless proposed to fix with the German garden city and Sitte-esque principles. As an indication of the influence of garden city ideas, Jansen proposed to surround Berlin with "hundreds of green belts with forests and meadows" (fig. 1.6).[75] He put particular emphasis on the network of vehicular roads and the artistic design of streetscapes. His proposed interventions in Berlin's existing sections revealed his dedication to some of the ideals of the garden city and of the reform housing movements that offered the urban block with spacious inner gardens as an alternative to rental barracks.[76] Predictably criticizing the unhealthy living conditions in the narrow and tightly packed nineteenth-century tenement blocks, Jansen recommended the implementation of a special law (*Sondergesetz*) to reduce their urban density. In the ideal situation that he contrasted to the *Mietskasernen* by drawing an unambiguous plan diagram, narrow courtyards of the perimeter block were bounteously enlarged by eliminating their side and rear wings, and consequently abolishing the very concept of the rear house (*Hinterhaus*) that had no direct access to the front street (fig. 1.7). For new housing, Jansen made class-based distinctions, placing different income groups in different residential zones: workers' living quarters, composed of small dwellings, were planned near industrial zones, far away from the single-family houses reserved for the rich.[77] For upper-middle-income groups, he offered planned and unified neighborhoods with no shortage of large parks and generous green lawns, composed of two- or three-story row houses that encircled large private backyards in common courtyards, and that, he was convinced, would have given the residents the luxury of a "miniature villa" without the cost (fig. 1.8).[78] On the very outskirts, he proposed suburbs in the spirit of garden cities.[79] Having already designed the garden suburb of Dahlem in Berlin, Jansen was not a newcomer to the idea. In summary, two design principles, proximity to nature and low density housing — ideals that were quite akin to the garden city model — guided the project, which Jansen believed would help Berlin grow into a planned, healthy, and controlled modern city. These were the principles that he would loyally repeat in Ankara.

Ankara, 1929–1939

Ankara, a new city to be single-handedly planned almost from scratch, was a perfect opportunity for Jansen to demonstrate his design ideals. Following Howard's theory, Ankara was a new town, at least in the minds of its modern founders. Unlike traditional cities whose locations were determined by environmental attractions such as a river, lake or other natural resource, a garden city could be built practically anywhere. Just as the garden city represented an escape from the nineteenth-century metropolis, Ankara was an escape from İstanbul. The reason to flee the existing big city was not necessarily overcrowding, pollution, urban decay, or unhealthy living conditions due to unplanned development or rapid industrialization — as was often thought to be the case in England and Germany — but rather the political will of a new nation-state. Many of the financial measures in Howard's model were not compatible with Ankara either, since the garden city of Turkey was not to be built by private enterprise with socialist sensibilities, or residents pooling their resources in a cooperative, but rather by a single-party state. Unlike in England and Germany, where intense professional engagement in the garden city theory took the form of numerous publications and projects, in Turkey, the garden city was brought in from above by forceful state bureaucrats and their chosen architect.

After winning the competition in 1929, Jansen continued working on

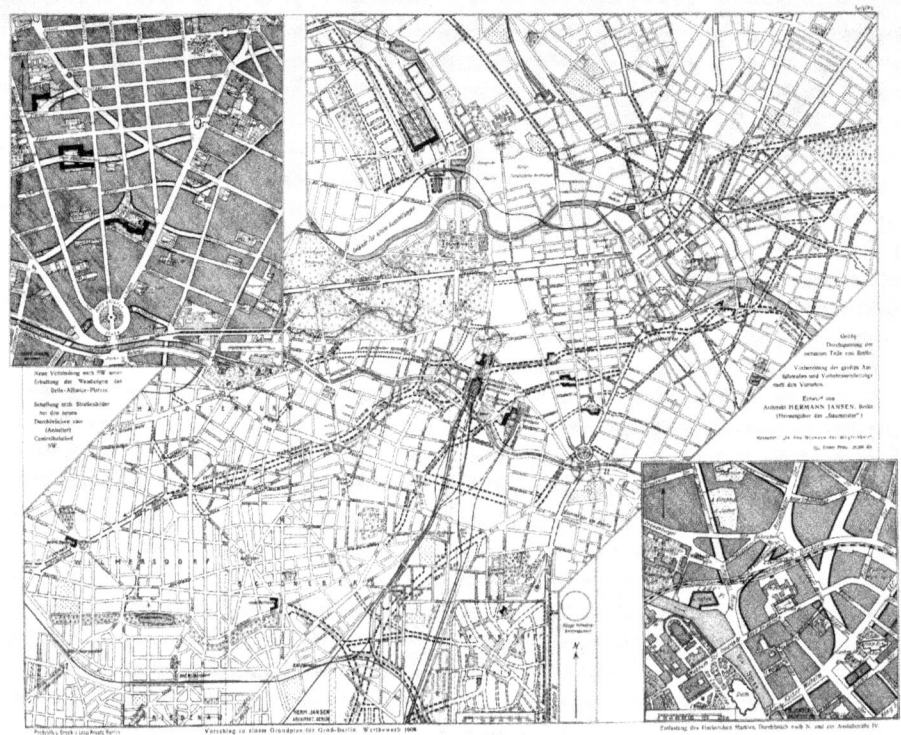

1.6. Hermann Jansen. Greater Berlin Master Plan Competition, 1909.

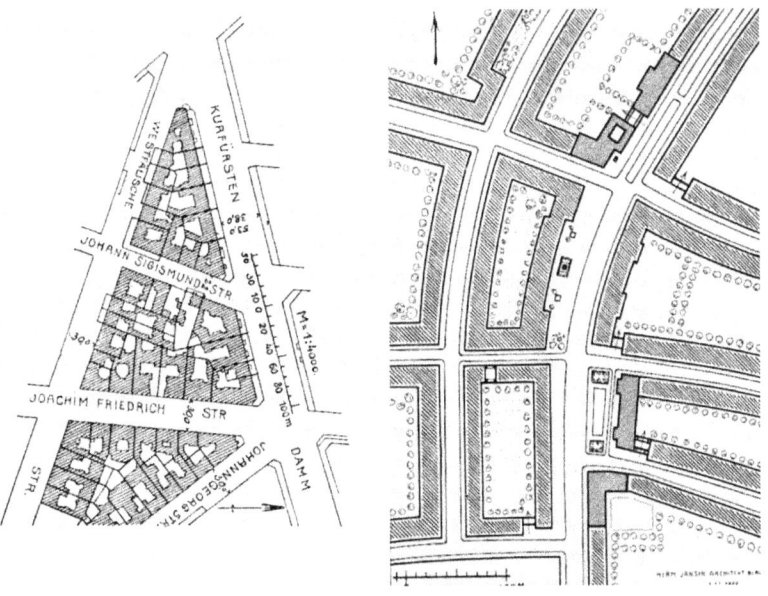

1.7. Hermann Jansen. Comparison of existing and ideal building blocks in Berlin.

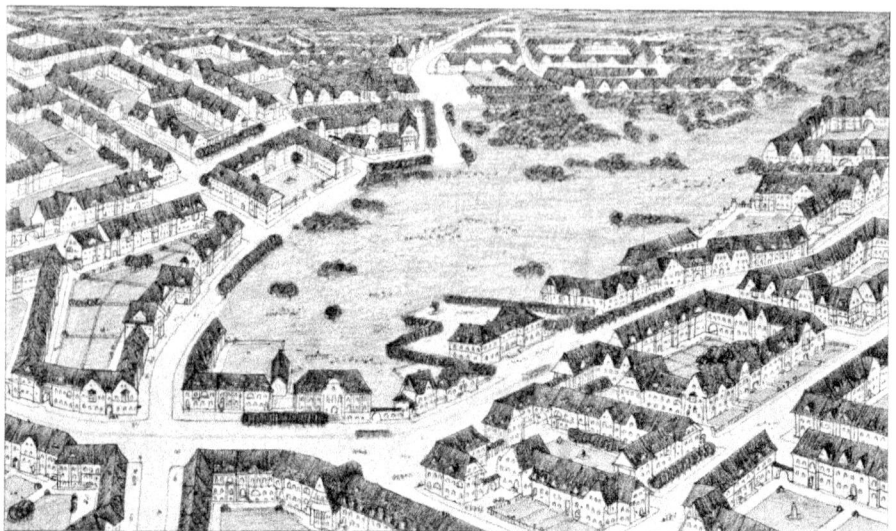

1.8. Hermann Jansen. *Kleinwohnungssiedlung* [residential settlement with small houses], Berlin, 1910.

Ankara's master plan until the project was put into practice on July 27, 1932. In 1934, another contract was issued, whose dates were eventually extended to 1939—the year Jansen's responsibilities and ties in Ankara came to a close. Jansen never moved to Turkey during his ten-year appointment, even though he visited the city at least once or twice a year, as required by his contract.[80] The countless letters between Jansen's office and Turkish bureaucrats were constantly translated (and mistranslated) between Turkish and German. Unlike the younger German architects who moved to Turkey after 1933, Jansen continued living in Berlin after the National Socialist (Nazi) takeover. In 1939, he received the Goethe Medallion for Arts and Sciences from the head and chancellor of the state, Adolf Hitler—a fact that historians have overlooked.[81] Alfred Cuda and Walther Bangert worked as Jansen's main employees for his projects in Turkey.[82] In Jansen's view, "while proximity to nature is the most important ideal in a governmental center, this should not deprive the city residents from the benefits of a big city. Only in this way can one approach the ideal contemporary organization of a city."[83] Explaining his ultimate aim for Ankara in these words, Jansen defended his plan for reconciling the two requirements of modern life noted above: proximity to nature

1.9. Hermann Jansen. Zoning in Master Plan of Ankara, 1928.

and benefits of an urban setting—namely, the country and the city. In this way, Jansen's Ankara was the third magnet in Howard's book: it combined the city and the country; it was the garden city.[84]

Jansen insisted that the city's population should not exceed 300,000 by any means, and he envisioned belts of green spaces separating the functional zones and the housing neighborhoods from each other (fig. 1.9). In his opinion, these "free" areas (*Freiflächen*), which would be filled in with places for recreational activities, were essential attributes of modern city design that distinguished planned cities from those that condemned their inhabitants to live in crowded and chaotic conditions.[85] These green areas continued inside the neighborhoods as narrow belts along the vehicular and pedestrian roads, but they also separated the residential zones for the rich and the poor (fig. 1.10).

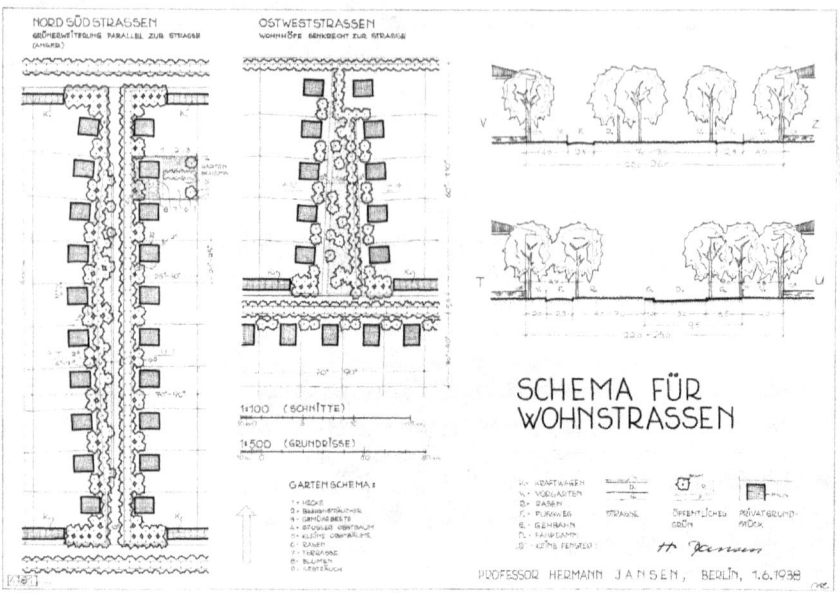

1.10. Hermann Jansen. Sections for residential streets, Ankara.

Unlike the densely woven urban fabric of İstanbul, where remnants from different historical periods stand side by side, Ankara was designed to have stark distinctions between the old and the new (fig. 1.11). The traditional houses in the Citadel were to be left as they were, without any rehabilitation. Jansen insisted that the old city should be isolated, covered with a "glass dome" if necessary.[86] And the Citadel did indeed remain in ruins, accommodating poorer families who continued their traditional living habits in the traditional houses deprived of any rehabilitation (fig. 1.12). Meanwhile, the new life of the Kemalist elite, with strikingly new buildings, open parks, private gardens, and wide streets, started in the new city (fig. 1.13).

"One goal of the modern city design is the single-family house," Jansen stated explicitly in his report on Ankara's new residential areas.[87] He laid down functionalist principles of orientation, envisioning a city with low-rise, low-density housing.[88] All houses were to have extensive front and rear gardens, and none was to have more than three stories. Jansen actually demanded that the fourth floors of the buildings that were built before his plan's permission be torn down, so that the existing urban density was reduced. In envisioning the new residential culture to serve as a model for the whole Turkey, he segregated residential areas in relation

1.11. Hermann Jansen. Perspective of a street with a view of the Citadel, 1933.

1.12. Photograph of houses in the Citadel of Ankara. Photo: Esra Akcan.

1.13. Şevki Balmumcu's Exhibition Hall as represented in *La Turquie Kemaliste*.

to class-based categories, separating them with large green areas. In this Jansen followed Fritsch's model, often referred to as the "German garden city theory," rather than Howard's or those of the socially oriented DDG members. Green, which was promoted to reunite the modern soul with nature, could thus easily be used as a vehicle for segregation.

Jansen assigned a different residential type for each income group. He reserved areas for free-standing single-family houses in private gardens on the southern hills of the city, and referred to them with the German word *Landhaus*. Many of the houses for Ankara's new statesmen were placed in this area, including Atatürk's Presidential Residence, for which Jansen used the German word "*Schloss*" (palace) (see figs. 1.21–1.26).[89] The rest of the city was to contain middle-income collective housing with ample garden space provided for each family. These *Gartenstadtsiedlung* projects, several of which Jansen designed himself, would be composed of *Einzelhous* (single-house), *Doppelhous* (double-house), and *Reihenhaus* (row-house) types (see figs. 1.43–1.47).[90] They would be organized around common amenities such as community and commercial centers, kindergartens, other schools, and, most important, large sports fields and public parks. And finally, far from the rich people's houses, Jansen proposed an *Arbeiterviertel* (a workers' quarter), specifying that workers would live in single-story double and row houses made of simple materials, with standardized doors and windows (fig. 1.14).[91] Although it would have

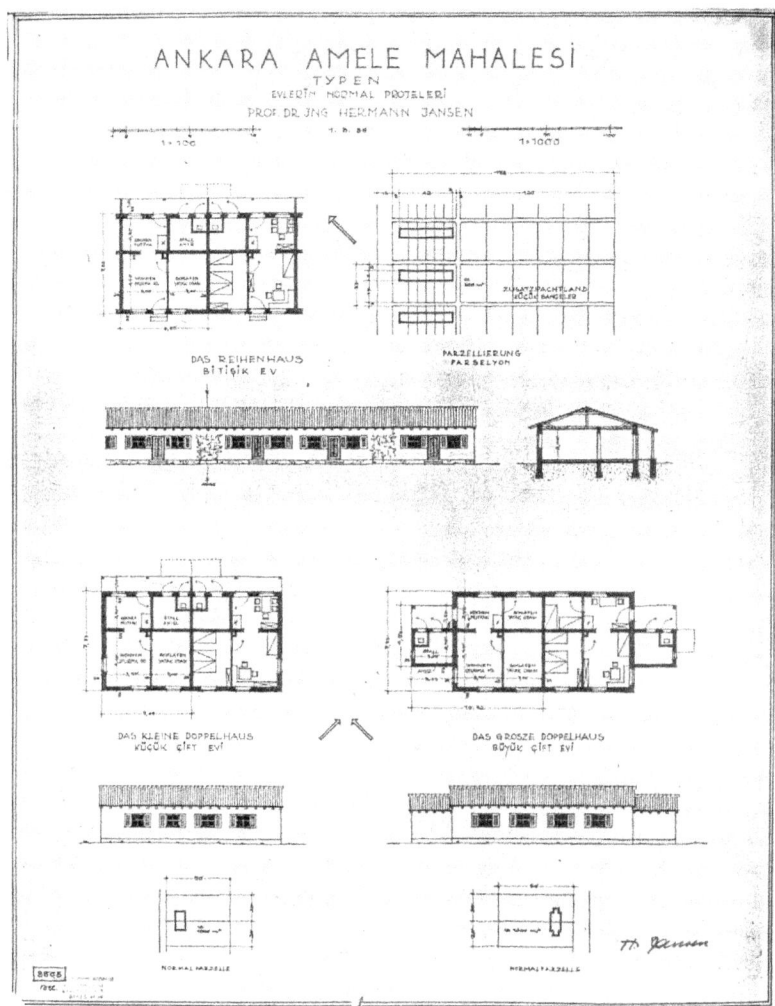

1.14. Hermann Jansen. Workers' housing, dwelling units, 1936.

been easy to make a case for the economic efficiency of other models for workers' housing already suggested at the time, such as the multifamily building blocks of Bruno Taut and Martin Wagner in Berlin, the ideas of Ernst May and his colleagues in Frankfurt, or the high-rise building blocks in Le Corbusier's *City of Tomorrow*, Jansen nonetheless followed the prewar garden city models.

Some of Jansen's decisions proved to be completely irrelevant for Turkey, such as the stable with an outdoor WC he proposed for workers' housing. This design was common in prewar German housing settlements, where the architects envisioned that the industrial workers would be engaged in agricultural activities, have barn animals, and even use what they collected in their own dry toilets to provide fertilizer for the agricultural activities in their backyards.[92] Well-known examples include *Siedlung* Törten in Dessau, designed by Walter Gropius, and *Kleinsiedlung* Friesland (near Emden), designed by Jansen himself.[93] Jansen's attempt to introduce this hybrid vision of rural and urban life had no appeal for the families of Ankara.

Jansen had only a brief moment of hesitation in settling these residential types. In a manuscript dated June 1929, he mentioned the climatic differences between Germany and Turkey, admitting that he was not "totally clear" whether all of the German "knowledge in hygienic city planning is applicable to oriental conditions."[94] He acknowledged that "bad European models" such as rental barracks (*Mietskasernen*) should be avoided, but he hesitated over the transfer of other standards. Looking for an alternative, Jansen mused: "One thus thinks here whether one must go back to the oriental house grouped around an inner courtyard [*Innerhof gruppierte orientalische Haus*] to which the living spaces are directed."[95] Nevertheless, this briefly considered option of courtyard houses did not eventually infiltrate Jansen's project, except for a marginal sketch (fig. 1.15).

The Ankara of the Kemalists and Jansen was a strong example of a foreignizing translation, whose impact on the lives of residents both of this city and — given the extension of Ankara's plans to the rest of the country — of Turkey as a whole was not small. There had been a couple of collective housing projects in İstanbul (such as Akaratler), but the main residential stock of the Ottoman cities previously had consisted of wooden or, in the southeast, stone houses commonly referred to as "old Turkish houses," and individual apartment blocks in İstanbul that were built as part of the late Ottoman Empire's modernization.[96] Some individual two- and three-story houses in gardens had already been built during the first years of the republic. Nevertheless, Jansen's plan was the first institutionalized attempt of the new nation-state to translate the modern European residential types to Turkey.

Jansen's decisions exemplify a translation with minute transformational adjustments. Even though Turkey had not experienced the problems associated with industrialization, which had motivated the garden city theory in the first place, Jansen and the Turkish authorities found this model appropriate. All of the residential types in the plan were thought of in German terms. That is, *Landhaus, Einzelhaus, Reihenhaus, Doppelhaus, Siedlung, Zeilenbau, Arbeiterviertel, Mietskasernen*, and of course

1.15. Hermann Jansen. Sketch for houses organized around courtyards.

Gartenstadt were concepts that were commonly used in Germany at the time but required the invention of new terms, or the alteration of existing ones, in Turkey. This was not just Jansen's preference. The Turkish bureaucrats rejected his occasional domesticating gestures and demanded more European-looking houses, as I will show below. There were some repressed opposition to and hesitations about Ankara's houses, and emerging alternatives (which I will discuss in following chapters), but according to the bureaucrats of Ankara at this moment, these foreign residential types of the new city embodied Turkish hopes for a new life — a new life not for themselves alone, but for the whole nation. This modern, westernized life was to be achieved by opening a nation — voluntarily or by force — to a foreign residential culture introduced through the medium of translation.

The Kemalist modernization process relied on the premise that Europeanness was smoothly translatable into Turkey, even if it had to be inserted from above. Modernism itself may have relied on the conviction that it was translatable throughout the world, so that its technological, social, and cultural merits could be shared globally — a beautiful yet unchecked idea when pursued with paternalistic means. I am not questioning the premise of translatability, and definitely not the very act of translation—quite the contrary—but I am questioning the top-down process through which it was executed. The actual houses built within the norms of Jansen's master plan and residential types illustrate the impacts as well as the complicated agents of this foreignizing translation, as I demonstrate below.

NEW HOUSE: REPRESENTATIVE AFFINITIES

Vienna, 1927

In his memoirs, the Austrian architect Clemens Holzmeister recalled the first time that Turkish officials approached him, in 1927. He was a professor at the Viennese Academy of Fine Arts. The Turkish ambassador to Austria, Hamdi Bey, met him in Vienna and requested the name of an architect specializing in the design of ministry buildings, particularly Ministry of Defense buildings. Holzmeister replied that he knew no such specialist, but "any architect with some courage and experience, and whom the Turkish Government can trust" would be fit for the job.[97] A few months later, Holzmeister received an invitation from the Turkish Ministry of Defense to speak about the site of the building. And so the governmental symbolism of the new Turkish Republic took its decisive turn (fig. 1.16). Although Jansen was the chief planner who made the urban planning decisions, Holzmeister and his former assistant Ernst Egli were the two main architects who determined the face of the institutional buildings in Ankara.[98]

Clemens Holzmeister (1886–1983) had studied at the Technical University in Vienna and had already established a successful practice in his home country.[99] In 1936, Joseph Gregor described him as one of the masters of Austrian architecture, along with Otto Wagner and Josef Hoffmann, but—unlike them—a designer who put a special emphasis on Baroque curves (*Barockbogen*).[100] The critic must have had the architect's churches and cathedrals in mind. Walter Koschatzky compared Holzmeister to the Romantic expressionists, in particular to Hans Poelzig, drawing attention to the theatrical and monumental aspect of his buildings.[101] Holzmeister had especially made his reputation with the Salzburg Theater in 1926, a commission that earned him the title of *Festspielarchitekt* (theater architect). In private houses and collective housing projects, Holzmeister usually restrained himself from excessive expression and was responsive to urban and natural contexts. For instance, in the country house for Hans Holzmeister in Innsbruck (1927–28), and in his own mountain house in Kitzbühel-Hahnenkamm (1930), he explored different materials and forms of expression while situating the buildings in

1.16. Clemens Holzmeister. Project for Governmental Complex, Ankara, 1927.

their different natural environments. Holzmeister also participated in the contemporary developments of social housing. Among these, special note should be given to the *Volkswohnhaus* (people's apartments) in Vienna (1924–26) and the project for the social housing block of Karl Marx Hof in the same city, which was eventually built by Karl Ehn (fig. 1.17). Both of these projects were part of the creation of a new urban and socialist residential culture in Austria, commonly referred to as Red Vienna. Eve Blau describes Holzmeister's rejected project for Karl Marx Hof as an "interiorized and disengaged" *Siedlung* that "turns its back on the area around it, and that the officials found "uninspiring."[102] Even though his scheme for Karl Marx Hof was not built, Holzmeister did successfully participate in the Werkbund Housing exhibition in Vienna (1932), along with Adolf Loos, Josef Frank, Margarete Schütte-Lihotzky, Andre Lurçat, and Gerrit Rietveld. He designed two double-story adjacent row houses.[103]

The other official architect of the new Ankara, Ernst Egli (1893–1974), also received his architectural diploma from the Viennese Technical University, in 1918; in addition, he earned a doctoral degree in 1925.[104] He had an architectural office in Vienna from 1919 until 1927, where he designed *Siedlung* Eden with Margarete Schütte-Lihotzky. Egli arrived in Turkey in 1927 and started working at the Ministry of Education in Ankara. After three years, he was also appointed as a professor at the Academy of Fine Arts in İstanbul, and he continued to travel between these two cities, two posts, and possibly two architectural positions.[105]

1.17. Clemens Holzmeister. *Volkswohnhaus* Urban apartments in Rottstrasse, Vienna, 1924–26.

Egli moved to Turkey and lived there for thirteen years (1927–40), reaching the heights and definitely the most productive stages of his career (he designed about thirty-three buildings and ten master plans in Turkey). However, Holzmeister continued to reside in Austria, only moving to Turkey in 1938 when the Nazis made their presence felt in Austria. He set up his office in a hotel in Tarabya, on the periphery of İstanbul, a building that became a refuge for many Austrian and German exiles during World War II.

The buildings of Holzmeister and Egli in Ankara would come to be known as "Viennese cubic architecture." Their influence exceeded the immediate physical space they filled in the city because they became the symbols of modernization that the residents and other architects, depending on their perspective, either looked up to or criticized.

Ankara, 1930–1935

In addition to Ankara's Governmental Complex, Holzmeister also designed the President Mustafa Kemal Atatürk's house in Çankaya, which still functions as the Presidential Residence. In his master plan for Ankara, Jansen reserved the southern hills of the city for the high-income families' villas, which he called *Landhäuser*. The contemporary novelist and thinker Ahmet Hamdi Tanpınar once described the president's life as an invisible newspaper that nobody ever saw, but whose content everybody knew perfectly.[106] This held true for the Presidential Residence and the other canonic houses commissioned by the regime, which were promoted as emblems of modernization and westernization, and whose photographs were showcased to demonstrate to the nation how to live the modern way, and to exhibit to the rest of the world how the Turkish bureaucrats had stripped off their Oriental habits. The lives of the official elite were meant to construct the ego ideals of the masses; their houses were to establish the new standards of taste.

During the last years of the War of Independence, Mustafa Kemal [Atatürk] resided in a room in the Agricultural School that was used as a military compound in Ankara. Following the foundation of the Turkish Parliament on April 23, 1920, he moved to a stone house that was commonly referred to as the Direksiyon building near the first railway station. Soon after his girlfriend Fikriye's arrival in the city, they moved to an abandoned farm house (*bağ evi*) on the slopes of Çankaya, whose original owners are still in dispute.[107] Most likely after Mustafa Kemal married his newfound companion Latife [Uşakki], an extension was constructed (1923–24). The architect Vedat [Tek] prepared the designs for the extension and made the changes that are still prominent in this house. He added a bay to the original building, an extension wing, and, most prominently, an octagonal tower with a noticeably steeply slanted roof. These decisions exposed the regime's ambivalence in residential symbolism at this stage (fig. 1.18). A second extension became necessary in 1930, which eventually culminated in the construction of the new Presidential Residence, designed by Holzmeister.

"I am not getting married just to get married. I have to set an example to create a totally new family life in our country," Mustafa Kemal is remembered to have said during a dinner with friends and colleagues.[108] The house in which this new model family would live was thus significant in the message it would convey to foreigners and the Turkish public. The symbolic importance of Holzmeister's design becomes most starkly evident when it is compared to the designs that were rejected. In 1927, a project signed by Fritz Hermann for the Berlin-based firm Lenz and Company proposed a vision that was most likely found inappropriate because of its Western classical symbolism (a symmetrical plan, raised first floor, traditional window proportions, and cornice) and its gigantic scale, which must have been associated with late Ottoman palaces (fig. 1.19).[109] In his report, the architect projected a lifestyle for Mustafa Kemal that he was trying to make Turkey leave behind. Had it been built, the residence would have been one of the most majestic palaces in Turkey, with wings that covered an area 106 meters long and 88 meters wide. It would

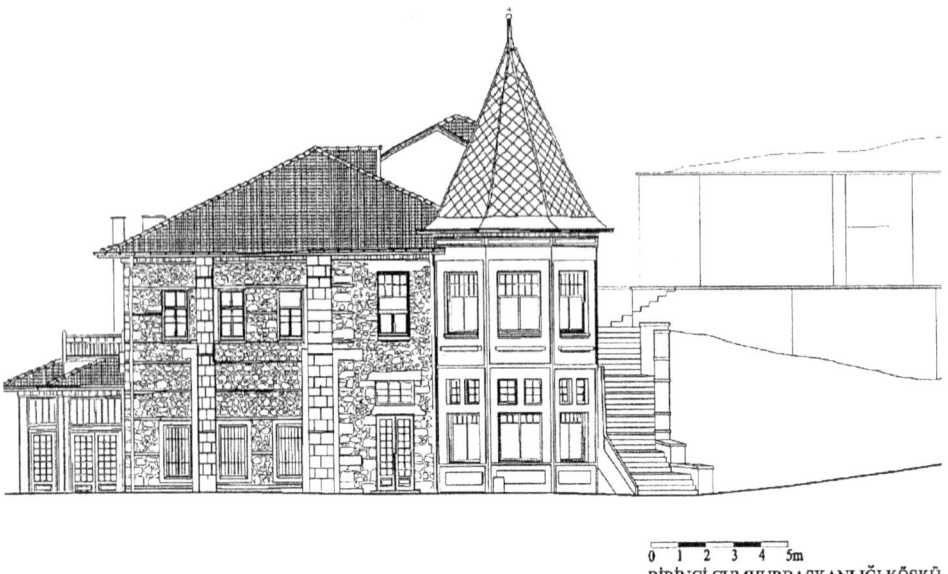

1.18. Vedat [Tek]'s renovation of Mustafa Kemal's house in Çankaya. Measured and drawn by Yıldırım Yavuz and Izzet Özkeresteci.

have contained an abundant number of rooms for guests and servants; a music room that could be turned into a big concert hall, with comprehensive backstage functions; and a segregated women's realm (*Harem*) — something that the new republic was determined to eliminate.

Two other rejected projects—one of which competed with Holzmeister's in 1930 and the other probably competed with Seyfi Arkan's for the president's vacation house—came from the Italian architect Giulio Mongeri, who had been living in Turkey and working as a professor at the Academy of Fine Arts in İstanbul since 1898. In the early years of the republic, Mongeri had become one of the few prominent architects in Ankara, and he had designed a number of buildings in the new center of the city, including the Ottoman Bank (1926), Agricultural Bank (1926–29) and İş Bank (1928), often acknowledged by historians as the exemplary pieces of the so-called First National Style.[110] These buildings were characterized by Ottoman revivalist elements on their façades, such as pointed arches, onion domes, and steep roofs. All this came to a close with Mustafa Kemal's rejection of Mongeri as the architect of his houses. Mongeri proposed to the president houses with massive stone walls, steep roofs, arched and colonnaded entrances, octagonal bay windows, decorated

1.19. Lenz and Company. Proposal for Mustafa Kemal's Palace, 1927.

chimneys, and towers reminiscent of grandiose mansions (fig. 1.20). The projects were eclectic in their sources but definitively revivalist in their representative choices. The defeat of Mongeri's project by Holzmeister's represented a turn in state-sponsored architecture. It was the end of an era, as two influential contemporary Turkish architects later stated.[111]

In contrast, Holzmeister's design for the president's house, which would come to be known for years as an example of Viennese cubic architecture, seemed more modest, with deliberately mixed private and public connotations (fig. 1.21).[112] It was situated away from the Governmental Complex, but it could easily be recognized as an integral, albeit displaced, part of it. Holzmeister used common aesthetic motifs—such as window proportions, accentuated lintels at the peripheries of windows, and projected boxes on the façade—so that the Presidential Residence looked like a continuation of the Governmental Complex, the two together marking the unquestionable arrival of cubic architecture in the city. It was crucial that this house represented the president with Western-inspired domestic spaces (fig. 1.22). It had to erase the memories of the war in which its owner fought against the Western forces, on the one hand, and of the common symbols of Oriental living associated with the Ottoman rulers, on the other hand. These two intentions were crystal clear to the contemporary Austrian ambassador, Norbert von Bischoff, when he—after a visit to the house in 1935—described it as a building that "unites the modern architectural notions of the West with the ancient cubism of the Asian Steppes." The ambassador could not help but notice the quite pointed elimination of war trophies and victory photographs, which had been re-

1.20. Giulio Mongeri. Proposal for Atatürk's vacation house, c.1927. Pierre de Gigord collection of photographs of the Ottoman Empire and the Republic of Turkey. Research Library, The Getty Research Institute, Los Angeles, California (96.R.14).

placed with "several eloquent pictures and art objects, a powerful library," and "the most distinguished and best European furniture." Most importantly, the ambassador praised Mustafa Kemal for being "the only head of the state in our times who wants and is able to live in a house that is free from the baroque and classical magnificence of earlier palaces."[113] All these points were well taken. Rather than the grandeur of historical styles, the Turkish president chose to represent his authority with modern monumentality. It was the hidden layers of classicism that differentiated this house from many other milestones of modern architecture.

Despite its flat roofs and exterior walls of undecorated stucco, the building relied on a classical plan. Symmetrical wings on each side and rooms with closed boundaries rather than an open plan were quite conventional architectural tools for representing order and authority (fig. 1.23). The house was organized around an inner courtyard that was complemented on one side with slender circular columns and galleries. This

1.21. Clemens Holzmeister. Presidential Palace, Ankara, 1930–32. Photo: Probably J. Scherb.

1.22. Clemens Holzmeister. Presidential Palace, interior, Ankara, 1930–32. Photo: Probably J. Scherb.

1.23. Clemens Holzmeister. Presidential Palace, floor plan, Ankara, 1930–32.

space has often been appreciated for hybridizing modern expression with elements from Anatolian houses, and hence for creating an agreeable, shaded, cooler microclimate in the hot summer days without sacrificing the intended allusions to Europe. Perforated roofs that covered the galleries surrounding the courtyard cast shadows on walls and floors just like traditional window screens, while figurative reliefs placed in the round niches of the arcade were most likely meant to remind the viewer of a European ambiance (fig. 1.24). For those who entered the house, the furniture and fixtures would have thrown the memories of the recent war and revolution into oblivion. Fikriye had decorated the previous wooden house with the cozy items available to her in Ankara; Latife [Uşakki] had brought expensive household goods from her parents' house in Izmir; but Holzmeister chose, purchased, and brought in from Vienna all of the furniture, lighting and bathroom fixtures, metal fittings, wallpaper and curtains, picture frames, carpets and ceramics of the new Presidential Residence.[114]

Two particular rooms in this house invite further discussion. First, a winter garden was placed between the entrance and the paved courtyard

1.24. Clemens Holzmeister. Presidential Palace, gallery and courtyard. Ankara, 1930–32. Photo: Probably J. Scherb.

1.25. Clemens Holzmeister. Presidential Palace, winter garden from the courtyard. Ankara, 1930–32. Photo: Probably J. Scherb.

1.26. Clemens Holzmeister. Presidential Palace, dining room. Ankara, 1930–32. Photo: Probably J. Scherb.

1.27. Bureaucrats concentrating on papers rather than their meals in the dining room of the Presidential Palace.

as if to proclaim the hopes and human will invested in the modernization project (fig. 1.25). A provincial city unnoticed by history, a city of uncultivated soil and unfavorable climate, would overcome its shortcomings with this winter garden, representing what could be achieved by the determined will of the new revolution. Professional architecture, with its advanced tools in taming nature, would come to the city's aid. Second, the dining room (fig. 1.26) hosted the legendary dinner and drinking parties of Mustafa Kemal, which were not simply social gatherings but important platforms for discussing state affairs, as illustrated by a photograph showing the bureaucrats concentrating on papers rather than food (fig. 1.27). One can easily imagine the official and social hierarchy acted out in this room when it was occupied by glancing at the grandiose table, ornamented roof, and elaborate chandeliers, which overshadow the plain modern furniture. Those who were frequent guests at this table enjoyed a potent self-confidence not only about their roles in governmental matters but also in daily life, while others who hoped every night to be invited contemplated on how they could improve their status. Where one sat and how close to the president at the dining table was another sign of the power ladder.[115]

Between 1932 and 1935, Holzmeister prepared the designs for almost a dozen houses for Kemalist bureaucrats, most of whom were usual guests at the president's dining table.[116] So did his former assistant Ernst Egli, who also designed the institutional buildings associated with Viennese cubic architecture—although the two architects had quite distinct personal styles, as the historian Bernd Nicolai has demonstrated.[117] The Fuat Bulca house (1935) by Egli, also constructed on the southern hills of Ankara, is a characteristic example of a cubic house (fig. 1.28). A childhood friend of Mustafa Kemal who fought beside him in the Gelibolu and Balkan Wars, Fuat Bulca was the president of the Turkish Aviation Institution (*Türk Teyyare Cemiyeti*) at the time.[118] In this building, Egli went beyond treating cubic architecture as a matter of façade. Thanks to new structural techniques, the living room, dining room, and sitting niches could flow into each other without solid walls in between. The framing of rooms as pictures to be viewed from other rooms together with level differences in the interior perspectives suggest a sophisticated understanding of space, reminiscent of Adolf Loos's *Raumplan* conception (fig. 1.29).

Berlin, 1930–1933

In addition to Holzmeister and Egli, Atatürk also trusted the Turkish architect Seyfi Arkan (1903–66) to create a new residential symbolism. In a city where the German-speaking architects designed literally all of the state-sponsored institutional buildings, Arkan stands out as an exception.[119] Arkan worked on these houses just after he returned from studying in Germany with Hans Poelzig for almost three years. Before departing for Germany with a state fellowship,[120] he had graduated from the Academy of Fine Arts in İstanbul in 1928. At the time, the teachers at the academy, such as Vedat [Tek] and Mongeri promoted a pedagogical approach that was inspired by the Beaux Arts tradition. In Germany, Arkan experienced a different type of education, as well as firsthand exposure to the development of the new building style.[121]

As a graduate student in Poelzig's studio, Arkan probably worked on the preliminary designs of all three houses that he later submitted to the Turkish government (fig. 1.30).[122] The nationalist context in Turkey that guided the final designs nevertheless gave totally novel meanings and functions to these houses. These houses are informative studies, illustrating the translation of a representational style from one context to another, as well as the impact of architecture schools in building cross-cultural connections. Berlin-Charlottenburg Technical University was the locus of important debates at the time. Heinrich Tessenow and Hans Poelzig were the influential teachers at the school, whose pedagogical methods (and eventually politics) were often contrasted by their contemporaries and students.[123] The fact that Jansen and Tessenow taught together at

1.28. Ernst Egli. Fuat Bulca House, Ankara, 1936.

1.29. Ernst Egli. Fuat Bulca House, interior perspectives, Ankara, 1936.

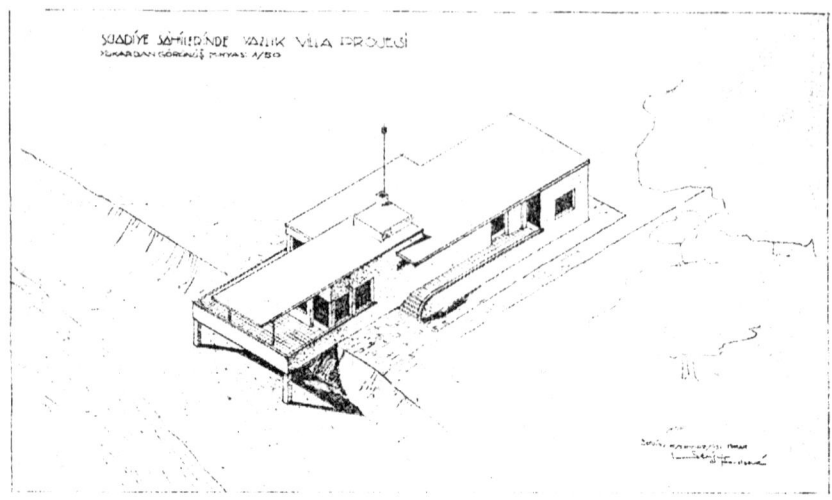

1.30. Seyfi Arkan. Waterfront House, student project in Germany, 1930–33.

similar times at the same school discloses the indirect reflections of the pedagogical split between Poelzig and Tessenow on Turkey.

Repetition, regularity, modesty, everyday experience, mediation between extremes and collective unity were considered great virtues in Tessenow's classes, yet it was individual creativity and extraordinary expression that were emphasized in Poelzig's. The German historian Julius Posener, who was a student of Poelzig at the school a few years before Arkan (1926–29), remembered him as an eccentric, inspiring, and bohemian teacher who "tried to guide every student to his 'self.'"[124] Many critics noted that Poelzig taught individual "creative power" to each student, rather than the rules of his own practice.[125] *Poelzig und seine Schüler*, the influential exhibition of Poelzig's students' work in the *Akademie der Künste* in which Arkan participated, stressed the differentiated character of each student. In his introductory text to the exhibition catalogue, Poelzig underlined his "nonformalist" approach, indicating a departure from the traditional formal canons, rather than a lack of a distinguishable position.[126] The Poelzig school, if there was one, was not a matter of form but of a "mentality of building" (*Baugesinnung*).

Hartmut Frank and Matthias Schirren have suggested that Poelzig's former master classes in Breslau were the first pedagogical steps toward what would come to be known as the revolutionary Bauhaus workshops.[127] Already in 1916, Poelzig was in close contact with Walter Gropius, advising him on the necessity of formulating a new pedagogical vision.¹²⁸ The overlaps between the early Bauhaus workshops and Poelzig's classes in Berlin, especially the emphasis of both on individual artistic creation, should not thus be regarded as a pure coincidence. However, despite the Bauhaus's increasing incorporation of new technologies, Poelzig remained critical of making technology an end in architecture. He insisted on the permanence of artistic values that he opposed to what he considered to be transitory utilitarian and technical matters.¹²⁹

Arkan's close contact with German architectural developments and debates for three years made him a crucial agent of translation between Turkey and Germany. During the 1930s, Arkan became one of the most outstanding Turkish architects following a modernist agenda. Apart from formal expressions of modernism, such as horizontal windows, white walls, and flat roofs, Arkan also explored the organization of the open plan, the dissolution of boundaries between the outside and the inside, and the functionalist standards of collective housing and minimal dwelling types. His teacher, Poelzig, was also invited to take up a position in Turkey in 1936, on the recommendation of Martin Wagner, yet Poelzig died just before he arrived, opening the post for Bruno Taut.¹³⁰ Poelzig's architectural approach that sought for the individual expression of an artist "genius" was a perfect match for the Kemalist clients' desires to represent themselves with exceptional houses.

Ankara, 1933–1936

The *Landhäuser* on Ankara's southern hills were designed as taste-making examples to disseminate visions of modern and European living in Turkey. Of these buildings, the Foreign Minister's Residence (1933–34) and the Makbule Atadan House (1935–36) for Atatürk's sister, both designed by Arkan, were two of the most memorable (figs. 1.31 and 1.32). Two graduate student projects that Arkan designed in Germany anticipate several features of these houses, including the long, horizontal roofs to shade out the sun, pergolas carried by slender circular columns, horizontal windows, an emphasis on transparency, and an open plan. Both houses embodied not only the living spaces of their owners, but also spaces for social gatherings of the Kemalist bureaucrats. Additionally, the Atadan House was envisioned as a symbol to display the face of a "civilized" Turkish woman. Makbule Atadan was a fairly close associate of her brother. When Mustafa Kemal tried to implement a multiparty system of democracy and asked his friends to found a new political party to compete against his own, she was one of the first to be made a member of this staged rival party.¹³¹ In one of her interviews, Atadan declared that one day she complained to her brother for not being allowed an education, to

1.31. Seyfi Arkan. Foreign Minister's Residence, Ankara, 1933–34.

1.32. Seyfi Arkan. Residence for Makbule Atadan, exterior perspective, Ankara, 1935–36.

which he responded by asking whether she needed money and gave her two houses as a gift.[132]

The liberating and yet equally paternalistic attitude of the Kemalist cultural program toward women is given an architectural expression in this house. Women's rights were one of the main paths to Western civilization in the eyes of the Kemalist reformists. The constitution granted Turkish women the right to vote and hold office as early as 1934, much earlier than many Western women, and the propagandist journals constructed the ideal of a new Turkish woman, unveiled, attending school, working as

1.33. Portrayal of the new women, Girl's Institute, designed by Ernst Egli.

a scientist or artist, and participating in Western sports (fig. 1.33). Atadan's house may be read as part of this cultural program, as is suggested by its portrayal in local and foreign magazines:[133]

> Both interiors and exterior show how far *Turkey has progressed in providing a setting for femininity*. It is amazing to see the rooms of this house and realize that they are in the same country, which accepted the *harem* in the Sultan's Palace at Constantinople as the right type of accommodation for ladies of the *elite*. In the old houses the intimates looked inwards and even upwards, but here the mistress of the house *looks outwards and far away. Openness*, and a sense of breath govern here.[134]

"A setting for femininity," displaying to the world how Turkey has stripped off her Oriental habits; a house where Islamic women were not enclosed behind the walls and screens of a traditional house or harem, but where they could look "outwards and far away" — Arkan hoped to achieve this goal by the repetitive use of large glazed surfaces and winter gardens. Rather than the outdoor spaces in traditional houses, such as courtyards or *sofas*, he chose winter gardens to mediate between the interior and the exterior. Suitably, the house was named the glass villa (*camlı köşk*) (see figs.

1.32 and 1.34). Arkan employed a foreignizing translation, a modern house with large glazed surfaces and an open plan to "open" the new women to the outside, and consequently the whole country to a new residential culture. Full transparency, an important value for the modernist movement, was transported from Europe to Turkey, now intended to signify the progress of Turkey "in providing a setting for femininity." The "unveiled" transparent house became a trope for the unveiled Islamic women.

However, a closer look at the interior organization and translucent surfaces reveals contradictory meanings (fig. 1.35). The interiors of this house created ambiguities between transparency and obscurity, displaying and hiding, being seen and being screened. What is striking here is the stark separation between the spaces of the public sphere and the spaces of privacy — namely, the division of large communal halls from the daily living spaces. The spaces for social gatherings were extraordinarily large for a house of a single woman. There was a spacious main hall (fig. 1.36), a music room separated from the main hall by movable glass partitions, a winter garden, and a more intimate sitting corner. These spaces of the public sphere, with their high ceilings, galleries, and large glazed surfaces, were the main points of attraction. Arkan fully explored the potentials of modern technology, using reinforced concrete and glass to create a space with fluid interior boundaries. A large service area with rooms for four maids supported these spaces for social gatherings.

The spaces of privacy, in contrast, were hidden from the spaces of social gatherings. The private rooms for Atatürk's sister and her guests were placed in these zones. There was a closed living room reserved specifically for women — ironically called the women's room in a house owned by a woman (fig. 1.37). These private spaces were always accessed indirectly. The door that leads to the sleeping and daily living rooms was hidden in one corner. In fact, it was much more practical to enter the private sections from the secondary entrance located at the back. It is as if two worlds existed simultaneously in the house: the spaces of privacy that were used continuously, and the spaces of the public sphere that were exhibited occasionally.

These distinctions were also gendered. The women's realm, including both Atadan's private spaces and the women's common living room, was separated from the spaces of the public sphere with glass screens and silk curtains. A glass partition divided the women's room from the main halls (see fig. 1.36); an aquarium divided Atadan's private rooms from the music room. Despite its modernist appearance, the semitransparent glass in the interior maintained a very traditional organizational principle in defining

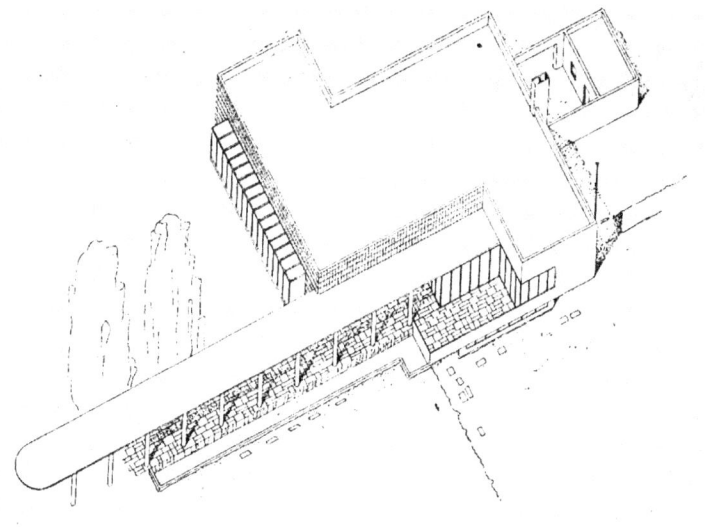

1.34. Seyfi Arkan. Residence for Makbule Atadan, early version, Ankara, 1935–36.

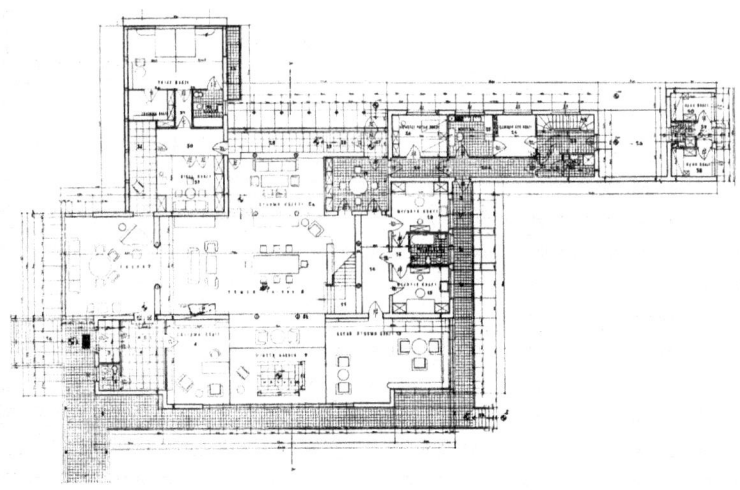

1.35. Seyfi Arkan. Residence for Makbule Atadan, plan, Ankara, 1935–36.

1.36. Seyfi Arkan. Residence for Makbule Atadan, main hall, Ankara, 1935–36.

1.37. Seyfi Arkan. Residence for Makbule Atadan, women's room, Ankara, 1935–36.

women's place in society. The women's sphere was implied and yet hidden; its existence was assured and yet made unreachable to the users of the main hall. The glass partitions with silk curtains functioned exactly like the semitransparent window screens in traditional houses, which separated women from the street. By dividing the women's realm from the main social gathering spaces, Arkan used a very common spatial tool to define and control women's place in society. Even though women were permitted to be voyeurs and occasional participants in the public sphere, their real place was implied to be behind the semitransparent screens.

Although the transparent exterior stood as a symbol of the Ottoman woman's "liberation from her dim traditional house,"[135] the treatment of translucent interior surfaces maintained the traditional hierarchies between genders. Glass, whose use on the exterior signified the unveiled Islamic women, veiled the women back with its elaboration in the interior.[136] Just as in Jansen's master plan, the Atadan House had the effect of a foreignizing translation, a translation in which the residents welcomed new residential norms by opening themselves to the foreign. A closer look, however, reveals an ambiguity: some patriarchal space-making tools were well maintained in the house on quite hidden levels through appropriating translations.

Though located at the periphery of İstanbul, Atatürk's vacation house in Florya, also designed by Arkan, was one of the rare number of houses built for the regime. In one of his favorite resort places, Atatürk decided to build a public beach and a house for himself. In choosing between Martin Wagner's proposal to turn Florya into a garden city while building a house for the president and Seyfi Arkan's delirious project that cheerfully offered to place the house literally on the sea, Atatürk preferred the latter because, according to the newspapers, Arkan understood his lifestyle and provided the right relationship between his house and the public beach.[137] Atatürk remained active in the realization of the project, visiting the construction site at least three times in one and a half months to give directions (fig. 1.38).[138]

İstanbul, 1935

The Florya house was meant to deliver the message to the masses that the new regime's rulers would do things differently than the Ottoman sultans. This was a house where the nation and the leader came together in their recreational time. It was a symbol to declare that the Ottoman aristocracy, and by extension the hierarchy between the ruler and the ruled, was over. Now the president could have his vacation a few feet in front of the masses: he could swim and row with them, wave his hand at them from the terrace of his shiplike building. Indeed, whenever Atatürk spent time in Florya, the newspapers of the next day published photographs of him mixing and mingling with young, cheerful men and women in their bathing suits. The propaganda captions typically said something like: "The most democratic president of the world, who cruises in a rowboat among the masses in Florya" (fig. 1.39).[139]

This house brought together visible analogies of modern architecture, such as the machine and the steamship, with a hidden, perhaps unintentional reference to the Ottoman waterbaths. The steamship, a metaphor for the Industrial Revolution, had already been noted as a basic inspiration for modern architectural form, most famously in Le Corbusier's *Vers une Architecture*. What was left unspoken, however, was the strong affiliation of the Florya house in the middle of the sea with the traditional Ottoman waterbaths — structures for swimming that used to float on the Bosphorus, but that had slowly disappeared with the decline of the Ottoman Empire (fig. 1.40).

Having lost the commission to Arkan, Wagner severely criticized the Florya house in a letter to Walter Gropius for putting a "mishmash of Le Corbusier and Mies" in the middle of the sea, and copying "functional houses" (*Funktionshaus*) from Europe while failing to understand the functional logic behind their creation.[140] Wagner himself failed to notice the connections of Arkan's design to the traditional İstanbul waterbaths. The Florya house confirms that the meaning of an architectural form may be significantly transformed during the process of translation from one context to another. A formal expression that usually stood against nationalism in the German context could well be used to symbolize the new nation-state's ruler in the Turkish one. A formal expression that symbolized industrial culture and socialist expectations of modernism — such as affordability, efficiency, and functionalism — could easily symbolize the state power in Turkey. There is no need to categorically denounce this process, as Wagner did, since architectural form is always partly the result of a representative aspiration. Rather, this example reaffirms the fact that architectural forms are never coupled with fixed ideologies but are almost always redefined in specific conditions. The exact meanings of forms are seldom transported from one context to another. The relatively free semantics of architectural form actually makes translation especially relevant in modern times.

The free-standing houses of the regime, five of which have been discussed here, were meant to represent the new Turkey's openness to foreign influences. These houses were intentionally estranging, but they were not

1.38. Seyfi Arkan. Atatürk's house at Florya, İstanbul, 1935. Photo: Esra Akcan.

1.39. Atatürk in front of the house at Florya.

1.40. İstanbul waterbaths of the Ottoman period. Anonymous photograph, circa 1885.

necessarily copies of their European counterparts. The architects transformed the European-inspired styles of expression by combining them with local features, whether this was an architectural element such as the courtyard in the Presidential Residence; or the wide, extending eaves in the Foreign Minister's Residence; a more implicit space-making principle that maintained the traditional values concerning women's place as in Atadan's House; or the legacy of a local architectural type, such as the Ottoman waterbath in the house at Florya. Apart from this last building, which was nevertheless a symbol of Ankara's rising power in İstanbul, these houses exemplified what Turkish garden cities could offer to their residents. Freely standing in gardens, extroverted, transparent, and clearly associated with Europe, albeit not without a pronounced Turkish identity, they were meant to build the ego ideals of a new nation.

NEW HOUSING: THE IDEAL LIFE

Ankara,
1934–1936

The new houses of middle-income Turkish families were also determined in relation to garden city principles, just as Jansen suggested in his master plan. The promotion of this lifestyle is perhaps nowhere better illustrated than in Yakup Kadri Karaosmanoğlu's (1889–1974) novel *Ankara*, written in 1934. The novel tells the story of Selma, the "new Turkish woman," whose three husbands and three different houses throughout the plot mirror the three residential types in the new Turkish capital. In the first part, Selma arrives in Ankara from İstanbul with great expectations, having heard all about the revolutionary spirit reflected in the new city. She is immediately disappointed however by the poor, "backward," and destitute living conditions in the traditional houses of the old Citadel (see fig. 1.12):

> She was frozen to death [*dehşetten donakaldı*]. She had to clean all the little filthy holes [in these walls] one by one in order to make this room and the house habitable. . . . The courtyard she shared with the landlord was the place where all the dirty labor was handled for both of the houses. The young woman remembered how disgusted she felt walking across this courtyard when she first arrived. It was still the same. A gutter greased with dishwater reached the street underneath the main door. Just across the door, the toilet that looked like a wooden security cottage was spreading out its filthy smell. Rows of diapers were hanging on the ropes. And there, just underneath those ropes, a man was beating a woman [*bir adam, bir kadını dövüyordu*].[141]

Selma's first husband soon becomes fed up with these living conditions in Ankara and returns to İstanbul. She stays, nonetheless. Even though her house represents everything that needs to be left behind after the revolution, she still prefers the "down-to-earth, pure, and sincere" life in Ankara to the "snobbish İstanbul." In the second part, Selma marries a former military commander who works with German engineers and professors, and who makes spectacular appearances with his modern and fashionably dressed wife at republican balls, where he flirts and dances with foreign women—and most important, who lives in the first "cubic house" of Ankara. In strong contrast to Selma's "old Turkish house," this second, European-style residence has corner windows, hidden electrical wires, and rooms that her husband proudly furnished by carefully examining "the pictures in the latest catalogs of modern furniture exhibitions in Berlin and Paris." With its "armchairs like dentist seats, sofas like surgery beds," "naked walls and naked floors," the house "glimmers like a cold clinic."[142]

While the first part of the novel represents in the author's mind the Ottoman period that the promoters of the Turkish republic, like himself, were determined to leave behind, the second part criticizes the corruption and blind Westernization of the new elite, which had become apparent to him by 1934. Karaosmanoğlu sarcastically depicts the ostentatious life in Ankara's "cubic houses," which, he writes, are pure and unornamented on the outside, but tastelessly decorated in the inside. He makes fun of both the sterile and modern bathrooms that alienate the residents, and the "Oriental Salons" (*Şark Salonu*) in the otherwise Westernized houses, which are furnished as isolated rooms separated with lattice curtains. Through the words of one of his favorite characters, the author describes these modern and Westernized houses as "phony and fake, makeshift and insincere [*sahte, yapmacıklı, iğreti ve uydurma*] things that one sees on the stage of an ugly theater."[143] Selma fits in well in her "cubic house," but she is unsatisfied with this lifestyle, her creator writes, where she has "lost touch with reality." "I don't want to live with this courtesan freedom that you have given to me, [*'courtisane' hürriyeti istemiyorum*],"[144] she says to her second husband and leaves her "cubic house."

Third part, third husband, third house: Selma now lives in cooperative housing. She is the representation of Karaosmanoğlu's ideal revolutionary woman. The writer referred to the third part as the unrealized utopia, the ideal future he depicted in 1934 for Ankara. This third house is located in an aesthetically and socially unified neighborhood with buildings that do not block each other's sun and view. Selma and her husband sit on their big, sunlit terrace, go to the sports fields rather than flamboyant parties, visit neighboring villages, and support cultural activities for the masses in the People's Houses.

Ankara was not just an idiosyncratic piece of fiction. An intense promotion of cooperative housing took place in Turkey during the mid-1930s. By 1935, Ankara's population had reached 122,721, as opposed to 74,553 in 1927, the year Jansen had entered the competition project for its master plan. Documents indicated that the number of people per house had increased to 7.06, signaling a housing crisis that raised doubts about whether Ankara was living up to Kemalist promises. The main concerns about the city were the lack of sufficient housing, expensive rents, forced nomadic lifestyle, and scattered individual houses that failed to contribute to the image of a well-planned modern city.[145] At this point, a group of state officials started promoting cooperatives based on European models to supply collective housing.[146]

It was in this context that Bahçelievler (houses with gardens) Housing Cooperative took shape: it was founded on January 26, 1935, the first cooperative housing in Turkey built to serve as a model settlement for the future,[147] initially designed by Jansen himself and subsequently appropriated by local professionals. The members of the Bahçelievler Housing Cooperative were well-positioned government officials who had the support of major state ministers, including İsmet İnönü, Celal Bayar, Şükrü Saraçoğlu and Şükrü Kaya—not members of the working class or the civil-service middle class—and who often quoted Atatürk's occasional comments on the importance of housing to seek popular and official recognition for their efforts. Gerhard Kessler, a German professor of political science whose ideas about the financing and organization of cooperatives were published in daily newspapers in Turkey, was a consultant for the project.[148] These newspapers had already been popularizing German developments in housing.[149]

Nusret Uzgören, the founder of the cooperative, was already well informed about European developments and regarded the garden city ideal as closest to his aspirations. "Rather than apartments, we must choose the garden city system," he stated explicitly in the pages of daily newspapers and professional magazines.[150] He denounced both the traditional wooden houses in Ankara's Citadel and the densely packed apartment blocks that had been built in the early years of modernization on the Citadel's slopes. He spoke about his unhappy childhood in these traditional houses, "the unplanned neighborhoods stacked with countless wooden houses that had windows with wooden lattices looking out on narrow and dirty streets, and dim rooms with cracked walls letting insects and bugs, scorpions, and even snakes straight into the bed."[151] He also recalled his disappointment on first arriving in Ankara after the establishment of the republic, when he discovered the high rents for the new, but gloomy apartments.[152] A third form of existence, unlike either the Ottoman traditions or the chaotic lifestyle of the modern metropolis, would need to be developed. This third way for Uzgören was nothing other than a new housing settlement planned as a garden city.

It was at this point in 1936 that the influential newspaper *Ulus* published an editorial including an extensive questionnaire about the ideal home.[153] The editorial emphasized the need for housing in the capital city:

A   Should houses for government officials be constructed as apartments or houses with a garden?
B   If garden houses are selected, would you prefer row houses in a garden or free-standing houses in a garden?[154]

The questionnaire, however, had already limited the readers to two options: Apartments or houses in a garden? At a moment when the apartments of the late Ottoman period were under continuous attack, the result was predictable. The questionnaire almost served as a staged support for the prewar garden city ideals of Europe, but it nevertheless illustrates the role of the new Turkish elite and governmental officials in choosing their residential spaces. What united those who cared to answer among the literate population (or whose answers were not rejected by the editorial board) was their feeling that a free-standing house in a private garden was superior. The answers to this questionnaire offer evidence that Turkish officials and intellectuals were well informed about urban developments in Europe, wary of repeating Europe's mistakes, and supportive of the import of reformative models to Ankara. Almost every respondent supported cooperative housing because of its potential affordability, shared infrastructure, and unified image. Influential bureaucrats of the time explicitly and confidently pointed to the garden city as the appropriate model.[155]

The rental barracks of Europe and their equivalents in İstanbul and Ankara received the toughest attacks. Many people commented on the increased level of sunlight and air, and therefore the possibility of sustaining better health in a single house with a garden;[156] some supported garden city housing because the vegetation would help temper the hot and arid climate of Ankara;[157] others brought up the common desire to make the recently founded city look bigger and more spread out, like a developed city, and therefore promoted dispersion with low-rise, low-density houses;[158] a few brought in the women's perspective, stating that it was essential for the children to play freely in a garden;[159] and the list goes on.[160] A few alternative voices that promoted denser neighborhoods and multifamily or row houses became inconsequential[161] because the strong advocates of the Kemalist regime presumed a direct connection between nationalism and the single-family house. According to Vedat Nedim Tör, for instance, an "apartment is a symbol of rootlessness [*köksüzlük*], temporariness [*geçicilik*], and almost a sort of modern nomadism [*modern göçebelik*]; a house in a garden on the other hand implies one's attachment to a life and a country [*hayata ve yurda bağlılık*], to cultivating roots [*kökleşme*] and continuity [*devamlılık*]."[162] And indeed, such a stimulation of nationalistic feelings was also Jansen's justification in his answer to *Ulus*'s questionnaire. The German architect advocated free-standing and row houses with private gardens as a better form of existence in modern times, because, he argued, the single-family house would establish "foundations of a happy family life" and, by extension, a national identity: "Those who live in houses with direct access to gardens are transformed into a whole different person and get attached to their fatherlands in a more intense way than the nomadlike people who spend their lives in a rental barrack."[163] The keystone in the formula for translating the garden city ideal to Kemalist Turkey had thus been invented: someone living in a single house with a garden was assumed to be a better patriot than someone living in an apartment.

Despite alternative voices, the media and official support campaigned for low-density settlements. Falih Rıfkı Atay, one of Atatürk's main men, a Minister in the Parliament, the editor in chief of *Ulus*, and long a supporter of Jansen,[164] praised the German architect in declaring the final results of the questionnaire. The majority, Atay said, "are against the apartment system that Professor Jansen refers to as rental barracks [*kira kışlaları*]. They are right. Because Hitler's Germany too has eventually given up these barracks and started building workers' housing in gardens, even in dense city of Berlin."[165]

Although the construction of single-family houses for low- and middle-income groups had started much earlier than Hitler's reign, Atay's reference to National Socialist Germany was not completely out of place. By 1936, the discourse on *Siedlung* in Germany had taken numerous turns. During the Weimar era, many residential types apart from single-family houses in private gardens had been developed, including multifamily housing that shared large parks and courtyards, row houses with higher density, and *Zeilenbau* blocks (parallel blocks oriented in the same direction). These were still seen as better alternatives that corrected the nineteenth-century urban tissue composed of *Mietskasernen*, but they were also promoted as residential types that met metropolitan requirements without necessarily promoting the single-family house as the only plausible form of healthy life. After 1933, some of the most important designers of Weimar housing—including Bruno Taut, Martin Wagner, and Margarete Schütte-Lihotzky—who were forced to leave Germany came to live in Turkey. Besides their political position, their design principles faced significant challenges in Germany, precisely because Hitler's regime promoted traditionalist single-family houses and took pride in increasing the number of families who had their own private gardens. Even though the garden city had initially attracted reformers from both sides of the political divide, after the mid-1930s, the Nazis increasingly adopted the model to reorganize a controlled territorial order and to promote the German village values fed by racial segregation.[166]

Berlin, 1914–1935

Designing collective housing was not a novel practice for Jansen. One of his earliest collective housing projects, the Streiffeld Worker's Colony on the outskirts of his hometown of Aachen, contained mostly two-story row houses for workers organized around front streets and backyard gardens, a smaller number of double and free-standing houses, and a square for communal buildings. Jansen held that a meaningful, hygienic, and healthy community life for the modern worker could and should be attained in the planned settlements outside the big city.[167] His prizewinning

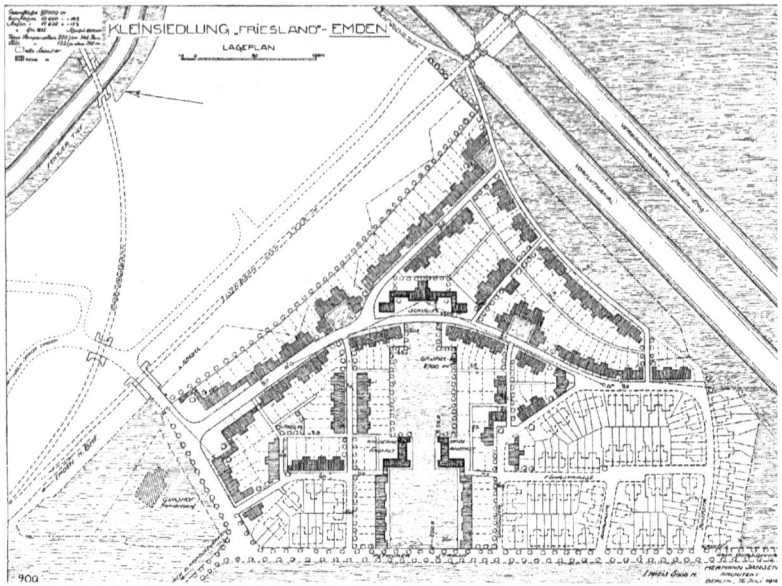

1.41. Hermann Jansen. *Kleinsiedlung* Friesland, Emden, site plan and perspective from common green areas, 1916.

competition submissions for *Kleinsiedlung* Friesland in Emden (1916), *Kriegerheim-Mustersiedlung* Bissingheim (1917), and *Kleinsiedlung* Johannisthal (1919) earned him further recognition as the designer of "nonartificial and plain" housing settlements that can provide the "ordinary man with the largest possible amount of sun and pleasure," to use the words that introduced him in *Wasmuths* in 1919.[168] Generously spaced row and double houses with vegetable gardens in the backyards, and large green lawns envisioned as gathering places of the inhabitants, can be seen in these projects. This environment was composed of houses with coordinated roof slopes and window and door frames; generous private gardens; carefully articulated gates at the neighborhood entrance (fig. 1.41).[169]

Siedlung Treptow (1914), a denser neighborhood, was designed as the

Mustersiedlung (model settlement) of Jansen's master plan for Berlin.[170] Here Jansen projected a variety of housing types, including single-family detached and row houses, as well as multifamily building blocks sharing common courtyards at the back. The important criterion was to avoid the *Hinterhaus*, the rear block of rental barracks, which could be accessed only from a narrow inner courtyard and which was criticized by twentieth-century architects for lacking adequate light, space, and view.[171] In line with his dedication to green spaces, Jansen provided large lawns in between clusters of housing, which, he thought, functioned as the breathing zones and piazzas for the modern citizen. As for aesthetics, he insisted that a designed urban environment as a whole would guarantee the much sought for harmony and unity.[172]

These principles informed Jansen's teaching at Berlin-Charlottenburg Technical University, where he worked as a professor of city design (*Städtebau*) from 1920 onward. He taught some classes with Heinrich Tessenow (an architect of the Hellerau garden city), and the two men criticized dense metropolitan living conditions, emphasizing instead small, plain houses with gardens. They shared design objectives such as modesty, restraint, and collective unity.[173] Jansen's students' projects at the university combined prewar garden city and Sitte-esque principles in *Siedlung* planning. "Jansen and his school" were introduced as the "pioneer of modern European city-design" (*Vorkämpfer des neuzeitlichen Städtebaues Europas*) in the pages of *Der Städtebau*.[174] His students (including Karl Schmidt, Otto Hodler, and Hans Haase) proposed housing settlements with free-standing and row houses in a garden, rather than with multi-family apartment blocks (fig. 1.42). Additionally, unlike the advocates of parallel blocks (*Zeilenbau*) that became increasingly common in Germany during the Weimar period, Jansen's students created unpredictable views and variable perspectives in the streets and public squares.

Ankara, 1935–1938

Soon after its foundation, the Bahçelievler Housing Cooperative purchased a site in the western part of Ankara, outside the boundaries of the original master plan. Located on the road connecting the train station to Atatürk's Forest Farm, this site was considered desirable for its reasonable price and proximity to recreational areas. The cooperative asked Jansen, who had already visited and approved the site before it was purchased, to prepare a master plan.[175] Just as *Siedlung Treptow* was envisioned as the exemplary housing of Berlin's master plan, Bahçelievler was charged with the significance of being the *Mustersiedlung* (model settlement) of Ankara (fig. 1.43).[176]

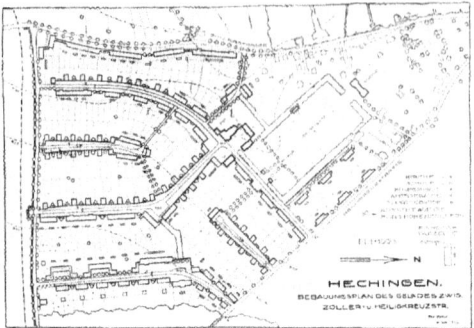
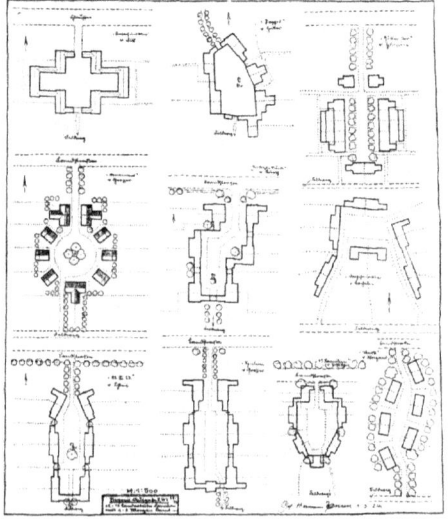

1.42. Student projects in Hermann Jansen's studio.

Bahçelievler went through so many transformations during its design and construction process, as well as the aftermath, that its story alone is sufficient to convince us of the extent to which world cities are shaped by translations.[177] The cooperative's requirements are significant because they demonstrate the agency of Turkish clients in shaping the garden city ideal's translation and in making their own history.[178] The families of the cooperative wanted separate rooms for different functions, rather than

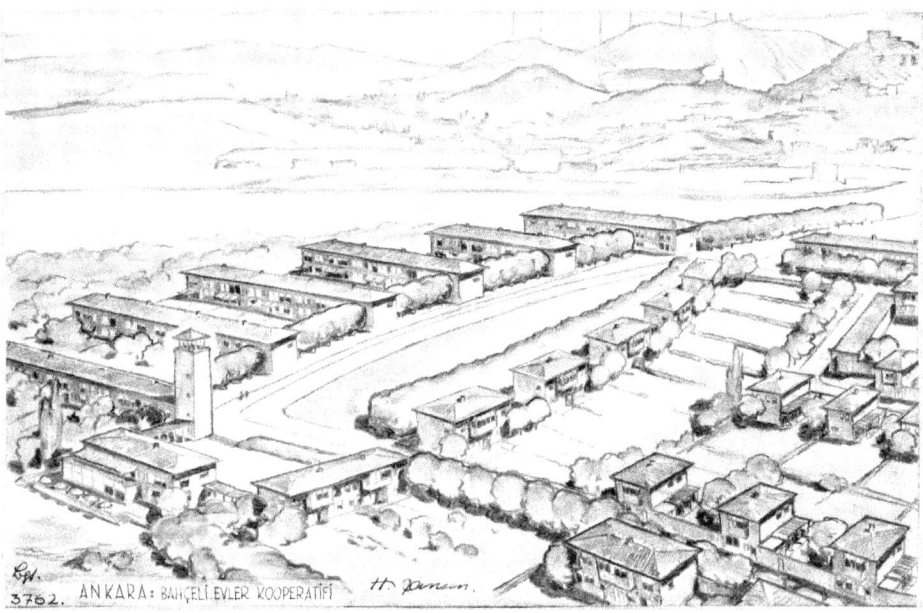

1.43. Hermann Jansen. Bahçelievler Housing Cooperative, aerial perspective, Ankara, 1935–36.

multipurpose ones as in traditional wooden houses, where living and sleeping activities were accommodated in the same space through the flexible organization of cochins [*minder*].[179] Most of them preferred to have a separate salon (usually used for guests), a living room for family gatherings, and a dining room. These rooms were furnished in Jansen's plans with European-style couches, armchairs, and fixed dining tables, not with traditional *divans*—multipurpose platforms—although this was not specified as a requirement in the letters. The families required open and big "balconies, terraces, and loggias" instead of closed courtyards, and toilets and kitchens placed inside the house, rather than in a courtyard. They wanted their houses to have "all the modern comforts such as electrical, gas, and telephone installation ... and central heating." There was no romanticism about a stove burning in the central hall, as in traditional houses. Nevertheless, they still wanted a Turkish toilet on the ground floor and a European toilet with a big bathtub on the upper floor. They also requested a maid's room and a place for a washing machine in each house (not a common laundry, as in European examples), as well as a garage for some houses. These last three requirements were rather unusual for Jansen, since cooperative housing in Germany was often meant for low- and middle-income families. The Bahçelievler Cooperative also required a school, a children's square, a marketplace (*Marktplatz*), a casino, and sports fields with two tennis courts and a swimming pool. These local requirements also implied a more luxurious and more Westernized vision than what Jansen had originally regarded suitable for Turkish families. Unlike in Europe, the first building cooperatives in Turkey were carried out by and for upper-income government officials who desired a luxurious, European lifestyle. It does not appear to be the case that Jansen, a German architect, "taught" a European lifestyle to a non-Western population, but rather that a certain segment of this population required this lifestyle, one that was official, upper middle class, and Western oriented.[180]

On January 16, 1936, Jansen submitted his architectural project, which would go through several revisions by himself and local architects, and, after its construction, by the property owners (fig. 1.44).[181] Jansen's first project was prepared according to the conventional norms of prewar garden city values. He defined three basic residential types to be repeated throughout the site: the free-standing (detached) house, double house, and row house, with variations ranging from three to six rooms. He emphasized the unity of the resulting environment, which he contrasted to cities without an overall plan. He defended the quiet, calm, and simple character of his design, as opposed to buildings adopting the latest "fashions."[182] Criticizing the contemporary buildings in Ankara that looked modern on the exterior, but failed to implement what he perceived to be truly modern values in the interior, he emphasized the functional aspects of his own design, such as each house's direct access to the garden, the correct orientation, efficient inner circulation patterns, and affordability and efficiency (*Verbilligung und Wirtschaftlichkeit*) resulting from serial production of windows and doors (fig. 1.45).[183]

Nevertheless, Jansen's intention to integrate some local architectural elements differentiated his project from its German counterparts. To attain a continuous street façade, he connected the neighboring free-standing houses with a garden wall one story high (fig. 1.46). This also provided a private courtyard (*Gartenhof*) for each house, reminiscent of the private courtyards in the wooden houses of Ankara's Citadel. Jansen's second step in the name of a domesticating translation was his use of extension bays (*çıkma*) on the upper floors overlooking the street. He also integrated a loggia into the double houses as a space reminiscent of an exterior *sofa* in the "old Turkish houses." He used extension bays in the row houses as well. In a second submission, he added a new residential

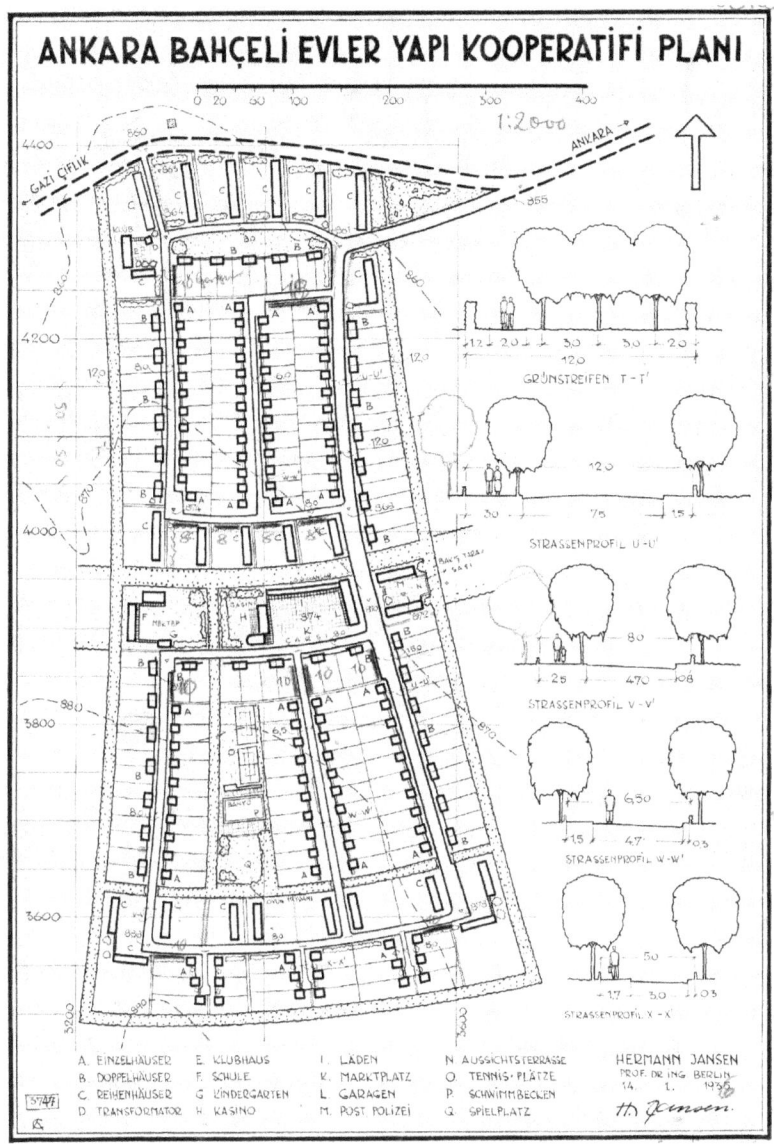

1.44. Hermann Jansen. Site plan for Bahçelievler Housing Cooperative, Ankara, 1935–36.

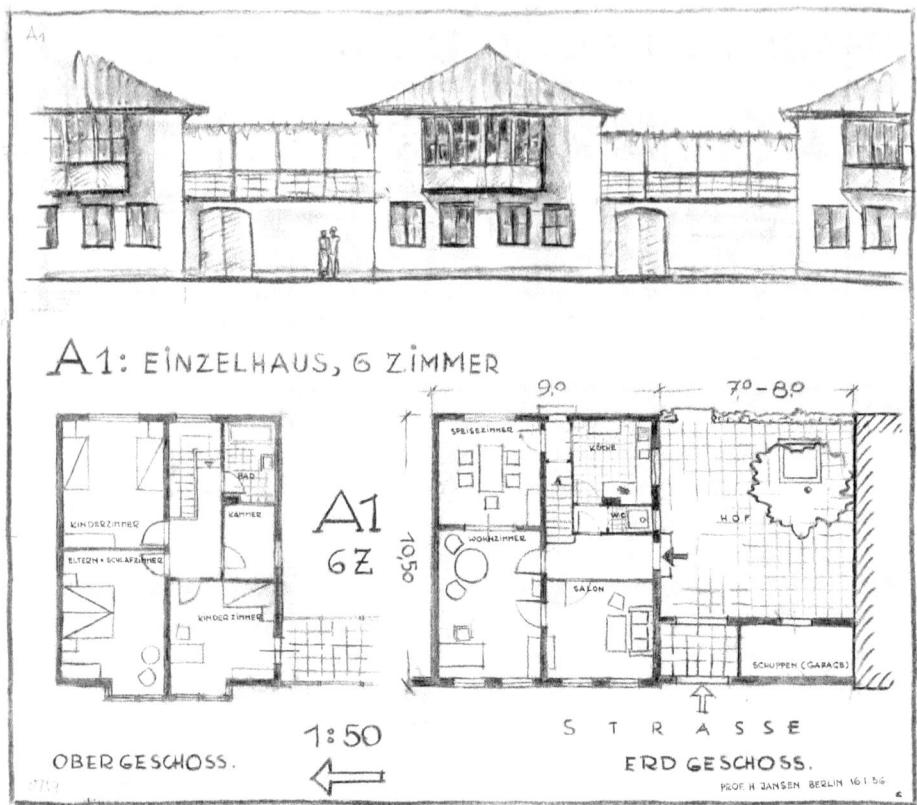

1.45. Hermann Jansen. Type A1 of Bahçelievler Housing Cooperative, Ankara, 1935–36.

type that integrated courtyards in between row houses (fig. 1.47). These were minor additional appropriations from the European experience to the residential types in Turkey.

Yet Jansen's occasional ideas for appropriating translation did not meet with much enthusiasm from his Turkish clients. On the contrary, the founders of the cooperative were critical of any overtly regionalist qualities:

> Dear Prof. Jansen, . . .
>
> A We do not want to build houses in traditional Turkish style, but only in modern style [*modernem Stil*]. When the outer façades of the houses are not of a modernized Oriental style, we prefer that they have a contemporary [*neuzeitlichen*] style corresponding to the building materials of our period.

1.46. Hermann Jansen. Perspective of a street with A-Type Houses, Ankara, 1935–36.

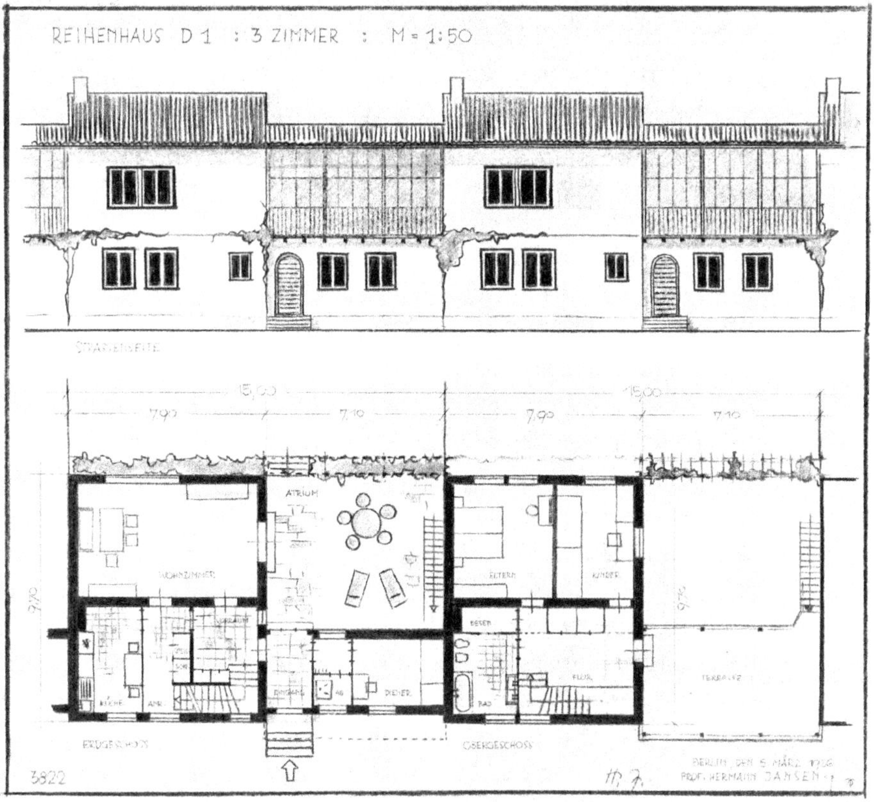

1.47. Hermann Jansen. Type D1 of Bahçelievler Housing Cooperative, Ankara, 1935–36.

B   We kindly ask you to give less of a countryside [*ländlichen*] look, but instead more of a metropolitan [*grossstädtischen*] character to the houses of the *Siedlung*.

C   For this reason, instead of oriental extension bays [*orientalischen Erker*] or small windows, we would like to have big and wide openings, and lots of terraces and balconies.[184]

Charged with being a traditionalist, Jansen immediately responded to the criticism, commenting on a subject that was new to him:

> Your interpretation that [the houses] are planned in traditional Turkish style is not true at all.... Modern building style [*Baustil*] is not at all indifferent to the location of the house, whether it is placed, say, in Germany, Italy, or Turkey. The more different the climatic factors and lifestyles [*Lebensgewohnheiten*] of the population are, the more different the organization will be. The commonplace/all-world style [*Allerweltstil*] that became common in Germany and other countries ten years ago, and in the manner of which many of the Turkish buildings are now designed, will disappear quickly within ten years, as is already happening now in Germany.[185]

This correspondence reveals multiple tensions operating in the contact zone of translation. First, the initial letter demonstrates openly that the cooperative was seeking a futurist image in Ankara, and a residential neighborhood with a "metropolitan character," not a suburban or a rural look. Although all of the members wanted private houses and private gardens dispersed throughout the site at a low density, and although most of them publicly advocated the garden city ideal, they still aspired to represent themselves with a metropolitan image. In other words, they must have seen little connection between congestion and the metropolis.

Second, the foreign architect and the local inhabitants adopted opposing roles in negotiating the degree of translation. It is usually assumed that local inhabitants tend to domesticate transported objects. Bahçelievler offers a counterexample. Here, it was Jansen who strove to assimilate some local elements into his European-inspired plans. However, he nevertheless rejected being called a traditionalist and argued that the response to different climates and lifestyles was part of the modernist agenda. For the local members of the cooperative, in contrast, Bahçelievler, just like Ankara, had to put an end to the "traditional Turkish style," making any historicist use of it unacceptable. For them, living in a Europeanized house was a matter of social status, a proof of their perceived superiority over the common people living in the "old Turkish houses."

Third, it is remarkable that Jansen claimed to represent the population more truly than the population itself could. Even though it was a segment of this population that asked him to erase regionalist references from the project, the architect continued to argue in favor of reflecting different lifestyles in architecture. In this, he followed a common type of Orientalism, in Edward Said's sense, that did not deem the non-West inferior, but that nevertheless sought to find an exotic difference in it. In Jansen's mind, the local habitants of the cooperative must have been unable to represent themselves, since their image of a modern house did not reflect the different lifestyles they were supposed to have. It would seem that Jansen thought he could speak in the name of a non-Western individual better than a non-Westerner himself. Nevertheless, in the case of Bahçelievler, the non-Western inhabitant did eventually have an impact on the end results. This is not at all to claim that this voice represented the majority of the population, however. On the contrary, the voice of those who were not directly related to the Kemalist circles remained unrepresented during the construction of Ankara.

And fourth, Jansen used recent developments in Germany under National Socialism as a justification for his architectural approach. He claimed that the *Allerweltstil* was disappearing in Germany under Nazi rule and predicted that it would do the same in Turkey, which was about ten years "behind" Europe. Not only does this view reaffirm Jansen's position in the 1930s on the side of the dominant German cultural politics, it also reveals his premise of linear history. Jansen's argument was predicated on the assumption that whatever happened in Europe would sooner or later resurface in other places of the world.

Eventually, a series of further negotiations prepared the resulting project. In March 1936, Jansen submitted his new plans, responding to some of the clients' requests.[186] Once the construction and administrative process started, the translation process continued, which resulted in considerably transformed site plan and housing units.[187] As more and more members made their selections of houses, some residential types were totally eliminated. The ones that remained underwent visible translations. Take Jansen's type for the free-standing single house, for instance. In the built version, many dimensions were changed: the winter garden was eliminated and its space was added to the living room; the wide pergola next to the winter garden was transformed into a narrower walkway beneath the slab of the upper terrace; a big covered balcony overlooking the backyard was added to the upper floor; and, most important, the one-story garden wall in Jansen's project, which gave a continuous façade to

1.48a. Bahçelievler as constructed, Ankara (c. 1940).

1.48b. Ernst Reuter's cooperative house in Bahçelievler.

the street and defined the private courtyard behind it, was lowered. This significantly changed the appearance of the neighborhood as a whole. Instead of giving a street a continuous boundary, the repeating individual houses now stood as autonomous units in space (figs. 1.48a and b). Similar transformations took place for all units.

Imagine the professionals in the cooperative's office redrawing Jansen's plans: putting their own tracing paper over his originals or starting from empty sheets; modifying his plans by moving one wall to the left, another to the right; canceling out some spaces and adding new ones; discreetly enlarging his window sizes; discussing, denouncing, or admiring his abilities; re-annotating his residential types; and transforming his projects in relation to the clients' requirements and their own decisions. The process for these professionals (whose existence was revealed through my archival study, but whose names could not be located) was a cross-cultural translation par excellence.

In this particular case, these translations were never in favor of traditional lifestyles. Many decisions resulted in the elimination of the local architectural elements that Jansen wanted to integrate into his design. The extension bays (*çıkma*) and loggias reminiscent of "old Turkish houses" were removed; so were the courtyards, because of the transformed dimensions. The local architects were not trying to appropriate an imported model into what they perceived to be authentic values, but to modify the design in relation to the requirements of a group of clients who were more European oriented than Jansen wanted to see. In Bahçelievler, the desires of the local clients were at times more foreign than what the foreign architect deemed suitable.

FROM ANKARA TO THE WHOLE NATION: TRANSLATABILITY FROM ABOVE AND BELOW

Despite the premise of smooth translatability, the translation processes described above during the early years of the Turkish Republic were hardly smooth themselves. The Kemalist revolution had created a major dilemma in the lives of Turkey's citizens: it was a project of modernization and westernization, yet building the Turkish nation-state simultaneously demanded the revival of what were perceived to be cultural roots. Translation was the contact zone where conflicts between westernization and nationalization were constantly negotiated. The ideas of the thinkers and professionals who desired to untie the knot between the two can thus be rephrased as theories of translation. Therefore, the early republican modernization presented an enigma about the continuities and disjunctions between westernization and nationalism, while attempts to achieve a synthesis between what were deemed the West and the Turkish never ceased. I would like to conclude this chapter by making a distinction between translatability from above and below, one of the conceptual subtleties of translation.

From the very outset, the Kemalist program intended to extend Ankara, as a cultural symbol, to the whole country. Between 1934 and 1938, Jansen prepared the master plans for six cities all over Turkey: İzmit, Adana, Ceyhan, Tarsus, Mersin, and Gaziantep.[188] Many of the principles

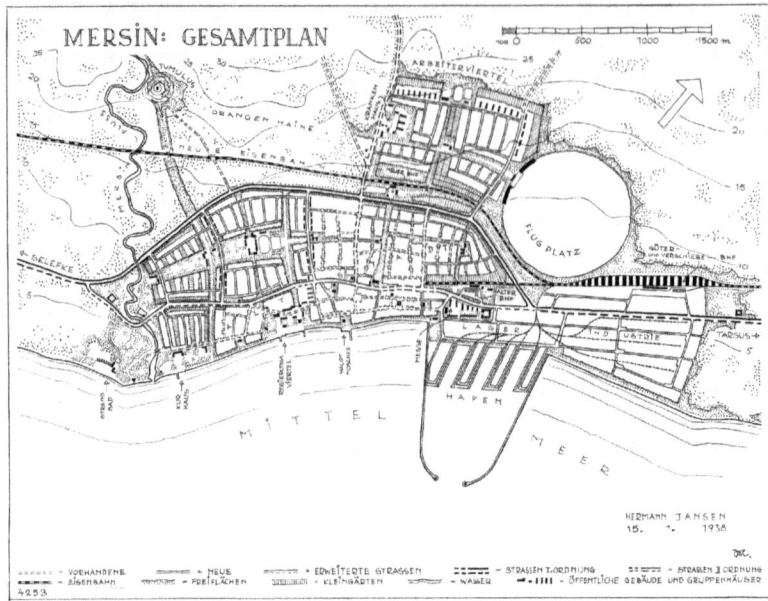

1.49. Hermann Jansen. Master plan of Mersin, 1938.

he had determined for Ankara were made into repeatable formulas for these subsequent developments (fig. 1.49).[189] Jansen differentiated among these cities according to their size (small to middle-size towns), climate, proximity to the sea, existing vernacular typology, and prominent economic function. However, these differences were reflected on the master plans as minor variations. He always proposed to maintain the distinction between old city and new city — namely, a sterile separation between what would connote the traditional and the modern, the Ottoman and the Turkish, the Eastern and the westernized zones of the cities. No new buildings would be built in the old sections, for which separate rehabilitation plans would be prepared only in the future, leaving them to a process of decay for the moment. Jansen designated two- or three-story single-family, free-standing, double, or row housing suitable for all these cities, just as he did for Ankara.[190] He thus envisioned an extremely low density and a sprawling urban development for Turkey as a whole. In regulating these residential types, Jansen assisted the Kemalist program, which was determined to collect the different ethnic and religious groups and various living patterns throughout the country under the unifying umbrella of the nation-state. Even cities out of the orbit of Jansen's contractual agreements were affected by his decisions, including new residential zones in the Asian side of İstanbul, which were developed according to a garden city conception.[191] By the time Jansen's contracts in Turkey came to a close in 1939, a translated garden city ideal had become the preferred model for modernizing and westernizing cities all across Turkey.[192]

The cubic architecture introduced in Ankara received widespread accolades as well. In *Modernism and Nation Building*, Sibel Bozdoğan illustrates how the cubic houses gained popularity in accommodating upper-income families in the early republican Turkey. These free-standing, one- to two-story houses, with unornamented white façades; flat roofs; and big, horizontal windows were promoted as the ideal homes for modern living in both professional and popular magazines of the 1930s and 1940s.[193] The influential intellectuals and art critics Celal Esad Arseven and İsmail Hakkı Baltacıoğlu advocated the new architecture as the appropriate container of the new life initiated by the republican revolution.[194] The popular magazine *Yedigün* published an example of an ideal cubic house in every issue, promoting its difference from both traditional houses and crowded İstanbul apartments.[195] "This home will be built in the middle of a small garden; and since it is reasonably cubic, it is beautiful," said one of the descriptions of cubic houses in this series.[196] Typically, these pages reproduced designs from foreign magazines and included photographs of recent buildings either outside of Turkey or in Ankara and İstanbul. However, these magazines often promoted houses beyond the financial reach of many Turkish families. The potential clients that the editors envisioned were couples escaping from the messy metropolis, upper-class families building a weekend house in the country, a poet living alone, and so on. The advertised "house for a middle-class family" with a garage, a large living room, a comfortably placed piano, and a separate study room was far removed from the reality of most middle-income families in Turkey.[197] Throughout the 1930s, cubic architecture became the mainstream representation of the modern and westernized elite home.

Bahçelievler Housing Cooperative, too, became a *Mustersiedlung* (model settlement) for upper-middle-class families, just as Jansen and the government officials had intended. By 1945, 50 building cooperatives had been founded in Turkey (22 in Ankara, 8 in İstanbul, and 20 altogether in Aydın, Adana, Antalya, Balıkesir, Burdur, Denizli, Diyarbakır, İzmir, and Tarsus); by 1952, this number had increased to 204.[198] These followed the same prewar garden city planning principles, although alternatives were explored in the organization of individual units. They were all composed of two-story free-standing houses in private gardens, organized around a network of hierarchically organized tree-lined streets and avenues. Abidin Mortaş, the coeditor of *Arkitekt* in the initial years, was especially committed to low- and middle-income cooperative housing.[199] Many of the milestones of collective housing in Turkey, including the 14 Mayıs Housing (1951–52), Subay Houses (1951–53), and Emek Cooperative Housing (1951–54) in Ankara, as well as the First Levent Housing (1947–52) in İstanbul, followed this typology.[200]

The aftermath of these projects puts into question the decisions taken during the process of translation itself. Jansen's master plan for Ankara was prepared for a maximum population of 300,000 people, which had already been surpassed by 1950.[201] Just as in Howard's ideal, Jansen envisioned Ankara as a controlled and contained city, whose maximum population should never be exceeded. He demanded radical measures, if necessary, to keep the city below its maximum size in order to maintain its "habitability."[202] In Howard's vision, the moment a garden city exceeded its population, another garden city, separated by agricultural land, should be planned next to it—quite a luxurious solution for a country like Turkey that had to struggle to maintain economic growth throughout the twentieth century. This rule was hardly followed in Ankara, and the city's population grew in an accelerated fashion, just as was the case in many other big cities in modernizing countries. The "free" green belts separating the built zones in Jansen's plan were gradually filled in with buildings. The failure of Ankara's planning cannot be explained solely as the inability of a non-Western country to sustain a Western model, since the question of overpopulation was one of the major problems in Howard's theory in the first place. Rather, we can ask: how appropriate was the garden city as a model for developing countries—which had to cope with rapid urbanization and vast population increases—during their early years of modernization?

The original houses built in Bahçelievler are hardly in existence any longer. İlhan Tekeli and Selim İlkin followed the transformation and eventually the disappearance of the settlement after it was completed. As each member applied to the municipality to add a room or two to their individual houses and, more important, as the zoning laws were extended and the building height limit was raised to four and five floors with the master plan of 1957, the density of the area increased almost sixteenfold. Many families were seduced by the idea of financial profits into tearing down their houses and gardens and replacing them with taller and bigger multifamily apartment blocks (fig. 1.50).[203] Karaosmanoğlu, who had supported cooperative housing in *Ankara*, later criticized the opportunistic drives of real estate speculators in his novel *Panorama* to express his dis-

1.50. Bahçelievler c. 2000. Photo: G. Çizgen.

appointment with the experience. Less than three decades after construction, the houses of Bahçelievler had evaporated into cash. The traditional historiography of Turkey has condemned the later republican periods for lacking the administrative and political rigor to preserve Bahçelievler and similar cooperative housing settlements in Ankara. Although this is definitely valid, it is also necessary to question the potential of the original model to live up to the requirements of a developing and rapidly urbanizing country in the second half of the twentieth century. Bahçelievler's disappearance reveals the limits of low-density garden city housing in metropolitan conditions in such countries. Even though contemporary professionals such as Burhan Arif, Martin Wagner, and Zeki Sayar warned against the dangers of low density; and even though the shortcomings of the prewar garden city standards had by then been internationally recognized (see chapter 3), Jansen and the Turkish bureaucrats continued to promote it. There is no good excuse for Bahçelievler's obliteration, but the question remains: what would have happened if the low-density garden city that was initiated as a model for future development could have been sustained? Today Ankara is a city of more than 4.5 million inhabitants. Under these circumstances, the choice was between endless sprawl or destruction of the garden city. In Ankara, history decided in favor of the second option.

The "failure" of the garden city both as a city and as a housing settlement raises questions about the theory itself in hindsight. In many countries, the garden city increasingly served antimetropolitan ideas, turning out to be a model that was meant to protect modern individuals from the big city itself, even though the shift from the country to the city was admittedly unavoidable—a model that presented itself as a solution to large waves of immigration to the city, but one that offered to decrease the density. In Turkey, the garden city was attached to a modernist agenda and aesthetics; but regardless of representative style, the unresolved problems of overpopulation and low density signal a similar antimetropolitan tendency. In that regard, the garden city theory may be inherently nonsustainable for economically disadvantaged countries that had to industrialize quickly and cope with vast numbers of migrants from the country to the city.

The translations of the garden city also raise questions about the link between planning and social control. Is a garden city at the hands of a powerful state a perfect example of a panopticon in Michel Foucault's sense,[204] a necessary tool of modernization that creates livable cities with proper infrastructure, transportation services, and social networks, but one that simultaneously controls where and how people live, plans future growth, sets limits to a city's expansion and thereby disciplines the future? Historically, at least in Turkey, the garden city was implemented through the interventions of a strong state that was determined to modernize the population, with force if necessary. I have emphasized the role of both European and Turkish agents in making this history. Who speaks and who cannot speak during the process of translation? In this particular case, all of the European architects who were invited by the Kemalist state were influential speakers. But so were their Turkish clients. The Kemalist elites decisively shaped the modern residential culture in Turkey, not only by inviting German and Austrian architects and city planners to build Turkish cities from scratch, but also by making consequential selections in representing themselves, as was the case in the choice of Holzmeister, Egli, and Arkan. Bahçelievler's upper-middle-income government officials were also influential agents, effectively transforming the German architect's original designs during the process of translation. However, there were large groups of the population in Turkey whose lives were significantly changed by these translation processes but who were given almost no chance to speak in shaping this history. An account that credits full agency only to European professionals would be ungrounded, but so would be the assumption that this was the local people's voice as a whole.

Rather than taking a stance against translation due to its contested history, as those promoting anticosmopolitan nationalist ideologies would have done, is it possible to differentiate among alternative modes of translation? It is after all translation that makes it possible for a population to be enriched by what was its outside, rather than being consumed in its own claims of national superiority. In order to discuss translation modes that offer alternatives to the top-down modernization programs, is it possible to envision a project of translatability from below? The modernization and westernization program during this period was appreciated by a considerable segment of the population who did not necessarily have direct ties to the official ideology, but who nevertheless did try to add their own voice and transform some of the decisions — a process that can be named as an aspiration for translation from below. This was evidently not without contradictions and painful doubts either. The following chapter looks at one such translation, albeit still carried out by a privileged section of the population, and interprets the melancholic responses to Ankara's residential program as an example of a tension rising during the moment of translation.

In mourning the world becomes poor and empty,
in melancholia it is the ego itself.

                SIGMUND FREUD, "Mourning and Melancholia"

Every effort is made to bring the colonized person to admit
the inferiority of his culture... the confused and imperfect character
of his own biological structure.

                FRANTZ FANON, *The Wretched of the Earth*

TWO | Melancholy in Translation

The new life in Ankara resonated with a melancholic tune in İstanbul.

In an article discussing the state of the "non-Western" architecture of the 1980s, the architect Romi Khosla spoke about an "Oriental complex," caused by Orientalism itself and the superiority myth of the "West." He asserted that the "Oriental" believed in this myth himself, which took over his own design process.[1] In his classic book *The Wretched of the Earth*, Frantz Fanon, a psychoanalyst, articulated the feeling of insecurity resulting from the cultural politics of colonization that made every attempt to convince the colonized subject of the "inferiority of his culture." In one of the most chilling cases of mental disorder that he analyzed, an Algerian husband who could not perform sexually with his wife after her rape by a French soldier said, "she tasted the French."[2] The situation in Turkey was not identical to that in countries officially colonized by the West. Nevertheless, in a completely different political context than the ones in Fanon's and Khosla's minds, there was a similar glorification of Western culture in Turkey during the early republican years of modernization. One may look at the pages of both official and popular periodicals such as *La Turquie Kemaliste* and *Yeni Hayat* (New life) to see how being blond and having blue eyes, holding one's body in the Western way, and living and working in Western-looking houses and institutional buildings were promoted as signs of modernity and were thus constructed as the ego ideal of the nation's upper and middle classes. In his three-part essay "Aşağılık Duygusu" (The feeling of inferiority), written during this period, the Turkish writer Tahsin Banguoğlu described the nation's insecurity in terms quite similar to those of Fanon and Khosla.[3]

The fragility caused by translation from above is perhaps nowhere better exposed than in the reception of the Kemalist regime's residential program outside the circles of the bureaucratic elite. What about the houses in the old towns where the population used to live before the arrival of modern master plans, houses in Ankara that Jansen proposed to abandon to natural decay, or those in İstanbul that respected exiles such as Martin Wagner, Wilhelm Schütte, and Ernst Egli proposed to tear down and replace with what Wagner called the German *Siedlung* system (see chapter 3)?

The devaluation of the "old Turkish house" (*eski Türk evi*, as it was commonly called at the time, and which should always be read in distancing quotation marks in this book for reasons that will be clear below) during the modern era produced a melancholic echo in İstanbul, a city known for these houses (figs. 2.1 and 2.2). İstanbul's wooden fabric was left to decay slowly. Old neighborhoods had long been perishing due to the extensive fires that would wipe out a whole group of houses in one night;[4] and the legendary waterfront houses were abandoned in republican times to be used for storing coal. The official decay of the city produced a literature of resistant melancholy among early republican writers and architects, who portrayed İstanbul as the precious last remnant of a lost civilization. In the words of the renowned Turkish novelist and essayist Ahmet Hamdi Tanpınar, the Orient died with the burning houses of İstanbul (fig. 2.3):

> "What you call civilization resembles this old mansion [*İşte medeniyet dediğin bu eski konağa benzer*]. . . . Then, there comes a moment when the mansion burns down. Now, we resemble those bodies that we see in the rubble. Tons of trash, blackened columns, rotten iron, smoke burning here and there, smuts and mud. . . . Now, you can try to make something out of this trash as much as you like, you can love our old songs and our old world, live attached to it as you like, but once the magical breath has vanished, what can possibly come out of this wasteland?" The whole of İstan-

2.1. Guillaume Berggren. Wooden houses and Topkapı gate, circa 1885. Pierre de Gigord collection of photographs of the Ottoman Empire and the Republic of Turkey. Research Library, The Getty Research Institute, Los Angeles, California (96.R.14).

bul ... seemed to her to share the fate of this orphan whose secret was just disclosed. The Orient was dead [*Şark ölmüştü*].⁵

Something that crushes the lives of one generation may seem trivial to the members of another. It may be difficult for an outsider to empathize with the laconic feelings that seem unreasonable to him or her. Yet a sorrowful mood will touch each generation in one way or another, even if the reasons for it appear to others unlikely to produce such insecurities. Understanding a period necessitates understanding its melancholy, however remote this may seem to those who have accepted the challenge of looking at it. Ideologies of Eurocentrism traveling to the "Orient" caused the perception of the Western (which itself varies, should not be standardized, and should be read with distancing quotation marks just as with the word *non-Western*) as the ideal norm for humanity, with its cultural productions seen as universal expressions. What happens when the ideal is socially constructed as unreachable in the dominant cultural politics—that is, what happens when the ideal is constructed through the hierarchy of the West and the non-West? How does this reflect on the psyche of the

2.2. Guillaume Berggren. Wooden houses near the aqueduct, circa 1885. Pierre de Gigord collection of photographs of the Ottoman Empire and the Republic of Turkey. Research Library, The Getty Research Institute, Los Angeles, California (96.R.14).

non-Western, whose ideal is perceived to be something belonging to the West while she or he is excluded from the West in the first place? What exactly is this "Oriental complex"? Is it possible to discuss it through a theoretical framework offered by decades of thinking about melancholy?

Since antiquity, melancholy has been a topic of interest for numerous writers and physicians, including Aristotle, Ibn'Sina, Al'Kindi, Marsillo Ficino, Robert Burton, Sigmund Freud, Walter Benjamin, Melanie Klein, and Julia Kristeva, to name just a few.[6] Although the persistence of the

2.3. Photomontage by İstanbul Fire Department showing how to stop fire, circa 1890. Pierre de Gigord collection of photographs of the Ottoman Empire and the Republic of Turkey. Research Library, The Getty Research Institute, Los Angeles, California (96.R.14).

term is significant, its definition has not stayed the same over the course of history, nor have the distinctive features that differentiate melancholy (a common emotion) from melancholia (a mental disorder). Over the years, melancholy has usually been associated with sadness, suffering, and depression, but also with creative energy, brilliance, and thoughtfulness — and, in some cases, with idleness. Many writers have characterized it as the swing between opposite emotions such as joy and grief, cheerfulness and despair, love and hate, overconfidence and unjustified fear. In accounts from different periods, the causes of melancholy have ranged from disorders in black bile to demonic manipulation, from overeducation to loss of a loved one. In one of the earliest accounts on the subject, Aristotle associated melancholy with both brilliance and fluctuations between confidence and fear, joy and grief, and he explained its cause in terms of the vacillating temperature of the black bile.[7] Medieval Middle Eastern scientists, including Al'Kindi and Ibn'Sina, offered similar characterizations and more detailed explanations of melancholy as a disorder of the black bile.[8] It is a well-known fact that the Middle Eastern body of knowledge influenced the Italian writers of the Renaissance, such as Marcillo Ficino, whose writings on melancholy[9] Robert Burton paid homage to in the decisive work of the seventeenth century on the topic, *The Anatomy of Melancholy*. In this three-volume magnum opus, Burton associated melancholy with causes as diverse and at times contradictory as idleness, imagination, sorrow and fear, shame and disgrace, emulation, hatred and the desire for revenge, anger, discontent, self-love, pride, love of learning, education, loss of liberty, poverty and want, death of friends, and unfortunate marriage.[10]

Freud's "Mourning and Melancholia" arguably had the greatest impact on the modern interpretations of the concept. Although current scholarship in psychoanalysis has moved well beyond Freud, challenging many of his accounts of pathological conditions and proposed therapies, his basic definitions still serve to structure the starting points in a discussion of melancholy. Freud differentiated *mourning* from *melancholia*, defining the first as a normal, and the second as a pathological, reaction to loss. Loss and deprivation had traditionally been associated with melancholy, but it was Freud who singled them out as the main cause of melancholia. Usually in mourning, the subject overcomes the feeling of loss after a period of grief; however, in melancholia, he or she resists confronting the loss and preserves the lost object, person, or ideal in the shelter of his or her ego. In mourning, "reality passes its verdict that the object no longer exists";[11] in melancholia, the intense attachment of the ego to the lost object eventually leads to the lost object's internalization. Now, it is no longer the world that seems empty, it is the self. Although Freud emphasized loss, he continued to use some of the common characterizations of melancholy, such as the swing between different moods, especially the grieving subject's love-hate relationship with the lost object. Melancholia is "complicated by the conflict of ambivalence . . . countless single conflicts in which love and hate wrestle together,"[12] which is then reflected on the self. Melancholic subjects swing between narcissism and self-hate, between feelings of self-adulation and inferiority.

At this point, we need to ask how much Freud's models for normalization would work for subjects who are excluded from the definition of the *normal* in the first place, and to criticize the strictly pathological borders he drew for melancholia. In his text, Freud implied but did not pursue the consequences of his gendered reading: "A good, capable, conscientious woman will speak no better of herself after she develops melancholia than one who is actually worthless; indeed, the first is more likely to fall ill of the disease than the other, of whom we too should have nothing good to say."[13]

Leaving Freud's categories of good and bad women aside, this statement implies that the more "the good woman" is conscious, the more she realizes her distance from the ideal and the more she becomes melancholic. When we consider the Eurocentric definitions of the *normal*, the *universal*, or the *ideal*, we can replace "the good woman" in this quotation with "the non-Western." It is nothing but the construction of the ideal as Western (which is simultaneously perceived as unreachable) that produces melancholy[14] in the non-Western subject. This melancholy is no longer caused by the loss of something previously possessed, but rather by exclusion from or the lack of a possible perfection.[15] In a world where modernization is defined as the universal processes guided by the West, the others who are excluded from this definition of *universality* live through a loss or the lack of a natural right. This is the natural right of belonging to the process of modernization that is conceived as the inevitable universal achievement. Orientalism and Eurocentrism, which have dominated the history of translation, stretch the distance between this subject and his or her ego ideal. As Edward Said has put it, "psychologically, Orientalism is a form of *paranoia*"[16] that dreads the invasion of "our" (Western) boundaries by "them" (Orientals). When Orientalism and Eurocentrism travel outside the West through practices of translation, I suggest that the paranoia of the subject of Orientalism constructs the melancholy of the "object" of Orientalism.

THE MELANCHOLY OF İSTANBUL

With the republican revolution, the old Turkish houses came to be seen as something belonging to the past, even though almost the whole population still lived in them. Nowhere is this verdict as blatantly stated as in Yakup Kadri Karaosmanoğlu's novel *Kiralık Konak* (Mansion to rent).[17]

İstanbul, 1923–1951

The houses depicted in this novel mirror the personalities of its leading characters. Naim Efendi, the grandfather, lives in an old, traditional mansion in İstanbul and is steeped in traditional customs, unwilling and unable to adjust to the new times; he refuses to move out of the mansion into a new, westernized apartment with his family and continues to live alone in the decaying ruins of the big house, where the only sounds resonating between the rotten walls are his own cries. Mr. Servet, the son-in-law, is fascinated by the European apartments and furniture, detests the old mansion, proudly moves to a modern and fully equipped apartment in Şişli, on the European side of İstanbul, loves the entertainment business, and often comes home late and drunk. He is an enthralled follower of the new times, but the author treats harshly those who favor the foreign over the national and who, in his eyes, are blindly pro-Western. Karaosmanoğlu's choice of a Şişli apartment as the metaphor of Ottoman modernization was quite typical. İstanbul had developed toward Şişli, extending the famous Western symbolic urban axis, the Galata apartments (fig. 2.4) and the Grand Rue of Pera—today, Istiklal Avenue—(fig. 2.5) toward the north with solid apartment buildings and straight wide avenues.[18] The traditional wooden houses and irregular streets of the historical peninsula were often contrasted with the westernized neighborhoods on the European side, while the waters of the Golden Horn separated the two. Seniha, the granddaughter in the novel, rebels against her elderly grandfather and the old mansion she feels trapped in, runs away from home to Europe, but has to come back when her finances dry up. She loves her new, fashionably furnished room in the Şişli apartment, but something nevertheless makes her feel guilty and conflicted. And finally, Hakkı Celis—the writer's favorite character, Seniha's platonic lover who is enamored of the charming smell of her modern room in the Şişli apartment—feels uncomfortable with both the "snobs imitating the West" and the nostalgic people stuck in Ottoman times; he respects the grandfather but holds him responsible for failing to restore the mansion; he joins Mustafa Kemal's movement and dies in the War of Independence. The generation gap between three age groups demonstrates three types of İstanbulite: the anachronistic Ottoman, the westernized snob, and the nationalist Turk. The mansion, the traditional Turkish house, around which the plot revolves, is a contested zone of modernization par excellence. Seniha treats her grandfather's mansion as the symbol of her own imprisonment.

> Do you think I will stay in a house like this for the rest of my life? . . . No! Grandfather, I am not a girl with such a primitive soul [*basit ruhlu bir*

2.4. Guillaume Berggren. Galata apartments, circa 1885. Pierre de Gigord collection of photographs of the Ottoman Empire and the Republic of Turkey. Research Library, The Getty Research Institute, Los Angeles, California (96.R.14).

kız].... You assume that I will accept growing old in this mansion just like my mother lived and grew old with you here. But I want to live my own life.[19] ... This gloomy and sunken garden is my grave.[20]

Not all writers agreed with Karaosmanoğlu's depiction of the old houses through the eyes of his unappreciative characters, but this was without doubt the voice of the victor during the early republican years. The victor's voice was mirrored by a literature of resistant melancholy outside the official circles, even by those who were not at all against modern-

2.5. Guillaume Berggren. Pera apartments, circa 1885. Pierre de Gigord collection of photographs of the Ottoman Empire and the Republic of Turkey. Research Library, The Getty Research Institute, Los Angeles, California (96.R.14).

ization or westernization per se. During the twentieth century, melancholy was a fairly common term in everyday language as well as prominent novels, poems, and cultural magazines in Turkey,[21] which in turn shaped the next generation — whose members grew up in the 1950s and 1960s. One of them, Orhan Pamuk, described the role of melancholy in his autobiography.[22] For example, *Varlık*, the foremost journal of literary and cultural criticism in Turkey at that time, started publishing short stories and memoirs on these houses as early as 1933. In his story "Kanlıca'nın Bir Yalısında" (In a waterfront house in Kanlıca), Nahit Sırrı described his fascination as an eleven-year-old with the Bahaeddin Molla waterfront house, interiors of which he could never enter despite his countless smart and earnest attempts; the windows of which he could never count on its pinkish façade; and the legendarily large *sofas* of which he could never play in. When he returned to the site thirty-five years later, the writer was astonished to see that the house was being used to store coal, just like many

2.6. Antoine Ignace Melling. Engraving of İstanbul's waterfront houses. *Voyage pittoresque de Constantinople et des rives du Bosphore*, 1819. Research Library, The Getty Research Institute, Los Angeles, California.

others that he had observed on his way, and that not much had remained except an ash-covered skeleton that could barely stand in the middle of the coal-black landscape.[23]

Abdülhak Şinasi Hisar (1888–1963) published works in the same journal with a similar tone, describing his childhood memories of different houses: a *köşk* in Çamlıca, a waterfront house in Kanlıca, and a mansion in the Princes Islands.[24] As part of the same series, Hisar criticized the decisions on Ankara's urbanization, suggesting instead that the value of old Turkish houses should have been acknowledged.[25] Hisar gave detailed descriptions of each house — not only their visual characteristics and spatial organizations, but also the smell of each neighborhood (Rumeli smells of the sea, Princes Islands of pine, Çamlıca of thyme),[26] the sound of cicadas and birds outside, the different textures of the wood when it was dry and humid, levels of sunlight reflecting in the rooms and on water, the colors of the houses on the streets whose shades changed with the light, the *sedirs* that could be transformed throughout the day from a bed to a couch, the trees in the gardens, and so on. The people described in these memoirs were almost always anonymous. Instead the houses were personalized: a

2.7. Gülmez Frères. Panorama of Bosphorus, circa 1885. Pierre de Gigord collection of photographs of the Ottoman Empire and the Republic of

round one resembled the writer's fat aunt; the roof of another reminded him of his uncle with curled hair; the one with distorted towers looked like a porter;[27] the buildings spoke[28] and cried for help as they were being pulled down.[29] Hisar claimed to describe his memories as a child, but his remarks were unusually sensitive and nostalgic for a child. The grown-ups were "too materialist and realist," he said; they could not appreciate the "contemplative," sophisticated, and slow pace of life in these houses, the "accumulated silence" that left room for envisioning a "second, more valuable life."[30]

Within a decade of these publications, Hisar wrote a book, *Boğaziçi Mehtapları* (The full moons of the Bosphorus) — a eulogy to the decaying Bosphorus houses.[31] This book can be read as a textual Bosphorus panorama. It verbalized the memory of what might be called a panoramic look at the Bosphorus that was constructed through the engravings of Antoine Ignace Melling (fig. 2.6), and most notably the nineteenth-century photographs of Abdullah Frères, Pascal Sebah, and Gülmez Frères. A specific visualization paradigm had developed in these Bosphorus photographs, despite both the Western Orientalist and the local disciplinary gaze that created a tension regarding Ottoman photography. While both traveling and local photographers shot staged photographs of stereotypical men and women for the Orientalist market, Sultan Abdülhamid II (ruled 1876–1909) employed this medium systematically for a conscious fight against Orientalism, on the one hand, and as a tool to control the lands and populations under his reign, on the other hand.[32] Architecture and cityscape had been favorite topics for almost all of the prominent

Turkey. Research Library, The Getty Research Institute, Los Angeles, California (96.R.14).

early photographers since the 1850s, and the deceptively benign nature of these photographs attracted audiences as diverse as tourists, occupying military forces, members of the Ottoman court, and present and future residents. Bosphorus photographs opened up a specific genre that constructed a distinct way of looking at the city. I use the term *panoramic city photographs* not because they were necessarily panoramas in the technical sense — that is, images composed of two or more prints attached to each other — although these certainly existed. The panoramas of the historical peninsula from the Galata tower were among the most widely circulated images. This panoramic view was applied to the Bosphorus as well, both in the form of an actual panorama — as in the exceptional Bosphorus panorama of Gülmez Frères that pans the Bebek bay and its environs — and in the form of panoramic city albums (fig. 2.7). I am not using the term *panoramic* because these photographs necessarily reproduced an aerial gaze from a high point, even though this was also common. Rather, I use the term because they constructed a specific perception that marked the city as panoramic. Rather than staging a monument in a carefully constructed frame that froze its image, as in most travelers' guides and pictorial traditions, these photographs represent buildings in a slice of the Bosphorus. This visualization invites the viewer to expand the actual frame of the photograph to its outside, to imagine the sea and the city outside of the frame, to locate the object in the context of the city and then to complement the view by imagining the continuity of the Bosphorus. It was a cognitive mapping that gave meaning to these photographs, that made them "a way of 'getting a grip' on things that surrounds and seizes the whole, and that now demands completion," to use Stephan Oettermann's definition of a panoramic vision (figs. 2.8 and 2.9).[33]

İstanbul's writers in the early twentieth century politicized the visual memory carried in these photographs through a resistant melancholy, precisely because the city's urban fabric was put under threat. Hisar's book, for example, is a translation of the Bosphorus panorama into words. There is no plot in this book, no notable character, not even a single short conversation between any two people, no story line or dramatic incident that was consequential for others, no chronological logic to the presentation of occasional events — only pure description of life in the old waterfront houses. Word after word, sentence after sentence, almost nothing happens in this book, which is really a description that lasts for a tightly condensed 195 pages. It requires the reader to freeze time and meditate on descriptions without expecting a thrilling mystery, pathos, or even an emerging character. It calls the reader to contemplate the described world and accompany the writer in his endless but quite intentional repetitions, mourning, missing, and perhaps protesting against the disappearance of İstanbul's old houses. Hisar wrote: "The Bosphorous has an effective and melancholic beauty like a full moon [*mehtap gibi tesirli ve hüzünlü bir güzellik*].... I cannot believe this past has been wasted.... The Bosphorous is the most beautiful part of the unmatched İstanbul, and yet, like all subtle and gracious things, it has a sad beauty [*mahsun bir güzellik*]."[34]

Hisar was not alone in associating beauty with sadness. Most notably, Charles Baudelaire described beautiful as "something intense and sad, ... and a desire for life together with a bitterness, which flows back upon them as if from a sense of deprivation and hopelessness." He then continued: "Melancholy may be called her illustrious spouse, so much so that I can scarcely conceive a type of beauty which has nothing to do with sorrow."[35] Like Baudelaire, Hisar also treated beauty as "something sad," and melancholy as something inherent in the urban landscape — in this case, of the Bosphorus — rather than in the eye of the beholder looking at the object. For Hisar, it was the "beautiful" waterfront houses, "a poetry that lasts for kilometers," that aroused the melancholic mood.[36] For both writers, melancholy is no longer something internal to an individual, but an attribute of the object. It is not a single individual who is melancholic, but the city's landscape (*manzara*), the beautiful object, that elicits the feeling of melancholy as a collective emotion. Melancholy thus goes beyond the isolated individual and infiltrates the city and its houses.

Another legendary testament on the city coming out of the mid-1940s was Ahmet Hamdi Tanpınar's *İstanbul*.[37] Its first sentence is "İstanbul has

Vue prise de Roumeli Hissar (Bosphore) Château des Ambassadeurs. Les 7 Tours.

2.8. Abdullah Frères. Rumelihisar, Bosphorus, İstanbul, circa 1870. Pierre de Gigord collection of photographs of the Ottoman Empire and the Republic of Turkey. Research Library, The Getty Research Institute, Los Angeles, California (96.R.14).

2.9. Abdullah Frères. Waterfront houses on the Bosphorus, İstanbul, circa 1885.

a peculiarity; even those who come from elsewhere miss the city."[38] The preeminent novelist and essayist—who was also a professor of aesthetics at the Academy of Fine Arts, where architecture students also took his classes—used the past tense in most of the book to depict the city he lived in. Between the revolutions of 1908 and 1923, he said, the residents of İstanbul witnessed a sudden transformation that was much more intense than the one that crushed Western poets, who "remember their home towns with a sense of melancholy"[39]—including Baudelaire, to give one of Tanpınar's favorite examples. It was this anachronistic "old İstanbul" that Tanpınar narrated in detail in his text, although he never once nostalgically proposed returning to the old days. He was rather bothered by the shallowness of what was left behind after the disappearance of old İstanbul:

> No, what I am looking for is neither them, nor the times of their existence. . . . No, we do not love the old things themselves. What attracts us to them is the void they left behind [*Bizi onlara doğru çeken bıraktıkları boşluğun kendisidir*]. Whether there is a hint of it or not, we search in them for something about us that we believe we have lost during our inner struggles.[40]

Tanpınar searched for traces of this unnamed lost thing in the physical remnants of old İstanbul. Architecture, the bearer of these clues, thus frequently becomes the subject of the text. There is a long section on Ottoman monumental buildings such as Sinan's mosques, but there are also equally comprehensive passages on the old Turkish houses, trees, coffeehouses, Beyoğlu's night life, and the Bosphorus's waterfront houses, coupled with the writer's own memories, depictions of Yahya Kemal Beyatlı, Dede, Nedim, Melling, Gérard de Nerval, and Théophile Gautier, and their legendary stories. Needless to say, a sense of deprivation permeated the passages on the old houses, because "hardly any examples of this architecture have been left behind."[41]

In his majestic and idiosyncratic *İstanbul Ansiklopedisi* (Encyclopedia of İstanbul), Reşad Ekrem Koçu (1905–75) also gave special emphasis on İstanbul's decaying wooden houses (fig. 2.10).[42] Published between 1944 and 1951, Koçu's encyclopedia is enough to make Borges and Foucault envious of its choice of subjects. The ambitious list of contents printed at the beginning of every volume promised to cover a vast and eccentric set of topics, including "all buildings in İstanbul"—not only monumental mosques, churches, and palaces, but also private houses, coffeehouses, and brothels; "all celebrities"—not only politicians, scientists, teachers,

2.10. Reşad Ekrem Koçu. *İstanbul Ansiklopedisi*, 1st ed. Cover.

and artists, but also thieves, beggars, drunks, gamblers, vagabonds, and young boys Koçu met on interesting occasions (a category that appeared frequently); "all streets, neighborhoods, and districts, fires, epidemics, earthquakes, riots, revolutions, murders, and legendary love affairs." The opulently illustrated pages contained sketches of houses, technical architectural drawings of monuments, and maps of neighborhoods. Apart from the entries on every single street and neighborhood, there were items on the mansions of politicians and celebrities, modest houses of people that the writers met in the street, houses from Greek and Jewish neighborhoods (fig. 2.11), houses where Koçu and his friends had interesting experiences, a house with a tree in its garden planted by a certain poet, houses haunted by mythic characters — and the list goes on. So many anonymous houses were mentioned that sometimes they were not even given a proper name or address, but simply identified with colloquial directions (for example, "the wooden house on the Akbıyık street near the railway bridge").[43] In a special entry on the "Wooden Building" (Ahşab Yapı), Koçu defined the wooden houses as what made "İstanbul itself," and quoted lengthy passages from writers who described the old Turk-

2.11. C. Biseo. Drawing of wooden houses in a Jewish neighborhood as it appeared in *İstanbul Ansiklopedisi*.

2.12. Abdullah Tomruk. Drawing of the Köprülü Amcazade Hüseyin Paşa waterfront house as it appeared in *İstanbul Ansiklopedisi*.

ish house. Yet he also patiently recorded the history of their loss: fires that burned them down, families that abandoned them, owners who used them to store coal.[44] The entries on specific streets always noted houses that had recently been demolished and the ones that were about to collapse: "it won't be long before we see that another old Turkish house of İstanbul will perish, only a few examples of which have survived until today."[45] Some streets had totally disappeared even though their names were included in the encyclopedia.[46] Documenting the Köprülü Amcazade Hüseyin Paşa waterfront house (fig. 2.12), Koçu bitterly stated: "This is a priceless artwork on the Bosphorous, a testament to the Turkish art of wooden construction in İstanbul, a golden-decorated marvelous ruin that is about to collapse due to a terrifying, a sad and tragic negligence and ignorance [*hazin bir ihmal ve gaflet*]."[47]

In the midst of this wide-ranging and labor-intensive task, Koçu had completed the letter A and just reached the letter B when the series stopped publication in 1951. Koçu's impossibly extensive, obsessively antiquarian, bravely antisystematic, and not surprisingly unfinished encyclopedia was like the last energetic effort of a compassionate and melancholic collector. This documentation was meant to be a full testimony of a past that was sadly passing, compiled by a set of writers who were unwilling to let it go and perhaps unable to learn how to lose — writers who had a deep affection for each historical corner, every anonymous house, each resident of the city, whether or not they were recognized by the modern institutions that produced the new master plans and buildings.

Perhaps no other person was as comprehensive, devoted, and productive as the internationally recognized architect Sedad Eldem in documenting these disappearing old Turkish houses and in bringing them back to life with his own architectural *oeuvre*. Strikingly, Eldem's path to what he often called the "modern Turkish house style" was the result of a translation process that took place partly in Europe, and one that also revealed melancholy.

A JOURNEY TO THE WEST

Born into a wealthy and well-known Ottoman family, Sedad Eldem (1908–88) spent much of his childhood in Nice, Geneva, Zurich, and Munich, where his father had been sent to represent the Ottoman state. Most of his primary education took place in a Gymnasium in Munich, where he recalled watching the craft-based construction process of a building in Bogenhausen with great admiration for the artisans of stone.[48] Having be-

Turkey, 1924–1928

come fluent in German and French during his life abroad, Eldem returned to Turkey in 1924, shortly after the establishment of the Turkish Republic. The same year he entered the Academy of Fine Arts in İstanbul, hoping to become an architect. When his teacher asked the students to draw classical column capitals with fine, clean, and exact lines, Eldem recalls running away to sketch the Topkapı Palace, patterns for textiles and carpets, and especially İstanbul's wooden houses. As a summer intern at the construction sites of the buildings designed for the Kemalist regime, he spent many hours after work in Ankara's Citadel, sketching the wooden houses with a passion that his peers perceived as a youthful yet misguided enthusiasm. Years later, Eldem recalled:

> These houses were exceptionally beautiful, more so than I had ever seen in a Turkish town before. Most of their ornaments had been preserved with their brightest colors. I memorized all the streets and slopes. There were narrow pathways passing in between high garden walls and underneath colorful extension bays [*çıkma*]. Sometimes the streets were fully covered with houses on top of them. The greenery of the courtyards behind the walls, poplars rising in between, green roof tiles covered with moss, walls filled in with golden-yellow bricks...[49]

Eldem's sketchbooks from 1926 to 1928, when he was still a student, are full of drawings of these houses, showing their construction details, extension bays, and overhanging eaves. These sketches bear witness not only to a young architect's curiosity about existing houses, but also to his first steps in revising them according to a modernist taste. For instance, in a sketch that he enigmatically entitled "Landhaus bei Angora," Eldem repeatedly drew a wooden house that must have been located in a village near Ankara. In each version, he transformed the sketch by adding horizontal windows, corner glazing, a balcony, a recent-model European car, and a city dweller with a pipe, envisioning a different context, use, and lifestyle than that of a typical house in an Anatolian village (fig. 2.13). This process of redrawing with modernizing modifications suggests that Eldem's motivation was to find an architectural guide for the design of new buildings. His drawings no longer attempted to represent reality on a sketchpad but decontextualized the real, transforming it in the imaginary modern world of his creation.

During the last years of his studies in Turkey, Eldem started working on watercolors that depicted new houses designed for hypothetical sites in Anatolian landscapes.[50] He referred to these drawings as the "result of his research in İstanbul and Anatolia."[51] With a couple of exceptions

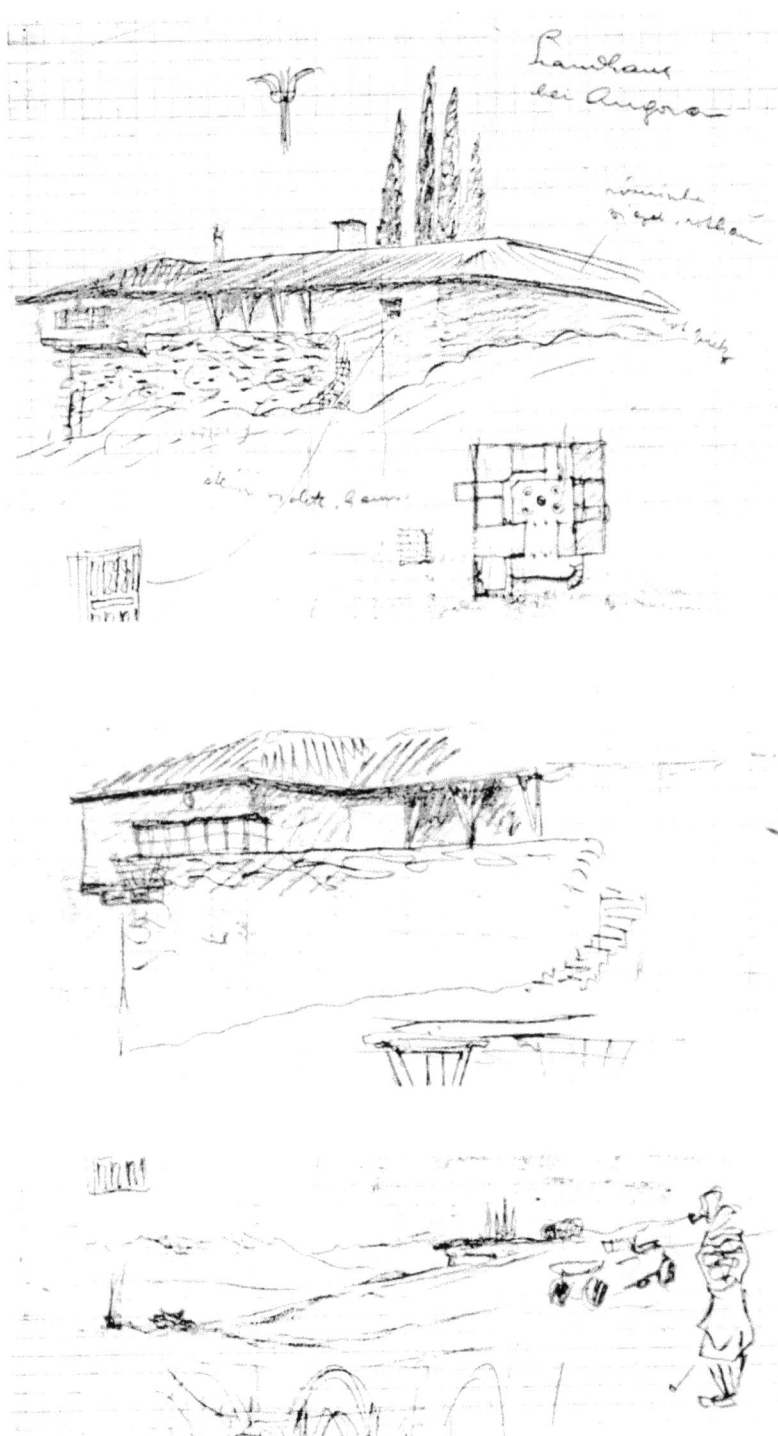

2.13. Sedad Eldem. "Landhaus bei Angora," circa 1927.

2.14. Sedad Eldem. Watercolor of a Turkish house, 1927–29.

showing flat roofs and white façades that imply a similarity to Mediterranean buildings,[52] most of these colored drawings depict free-standing houses with exaggeratedly pitched roofs and long extending eaves (fig. 2.14). Some are organized around a central *sofa* (treated as the main outdoor or indoor living space), a space that would become another subject of fascination for him. After graduating from the Academy of Fine Arts in 1928, Eldem received a state fellowship for postgraduate research in Europe, and he started his journey to the West at the age of twenty.[53] During this trip to Europe between 1928 and 1931, Eldem visited Greece, Italy, Britain, France, and Germany and studied the works of Erich Mendelsohn, Paul Schultze-Naumburg, W. M. Dudok, Auguste Perret, and Le Corbusier — an ideologically diverse and aesthetically competing group of architects. Eldem's diaries and travel sketchbooks during his journey to the West reveal an incessant anxiety about his own identity and his swings between admiration of and distaste for both European modern architecture and Ottoman houses.

France, August 1928– June 1929

At the beginning of his journey to the West, Eldem posed big questions about the state of architecture. After being deeply moved by the works of Greek antiquity in Athens, he went to France and asked himself: "Where are we now? We have thirty years of effort behind us. Which path is the correct one? We have the cubics, the rustics, Corbusiers, Perrets, Schools of Beaux Arts."[54] He had similar hesitations about his own watercolors of Turkish houses. In Paris in 1929, he wrote in his diary:

> I almost finished my collection of Turkish houses, I had too much of it anyway. It is a shame for the amount of time I spent on it. I will leave the colors and study lines and volumes. I am fed up with drawing fancy perspectives, too. All this that exhausts me is almost for good, since this proves that I have an honest nature, and that all complications and lies disgust me. I will try to represent the true me [*me montrer tel que je suis*]. Besides, I can pretty much say that I don't have the right to be ashamed of myself....
>
> But what if I will not show them? Then I should be free to paint them [*Alors je suis libre de les faire*]. Because I see my own house in the middle of nature.
>
> I will now design the city house, with unbelievable purity and severity.[55]

Drawing colored perspectives of anonymous houses in Anatolian landscapes was wrong, based on what Eldem learned in his trip to Paris. His own renderings of this type were "complicated" and "untruthful," whereas geometrical drawings, city houses with "purity and severity," were "honest" and modern. Eldem's willingness to be stimulated by the contemporary European architectural milieu impelled him to disapprove of his own work, at least momentarily — on second reflection, he felt uncomfortable with this self-denial as well. What if he continued working on such perspectives, as long as he hid them from the eyes that decided right from wrong, he wondered. What if he designed pure and severe city houses, although his own house was meant to be "in . . . nature" just like the ones he had painted before he got to Europe? Shouldn't he be allowed to continue exploring the Turkish house as long as he kept it in his personal sketchbook?

When Eldem says in the passage above, "I will try to represent the true me. Besides, I can pretty much say that I don't have the right to be ashamed of myself," the very slippery nature of the phrase *true me* is indicative of my point. At the moment this sentence appears in the passage, Eldem is asserting that his own drawings of Turkish houses were untrue to his nature, implying that he was concealing his true self behind these colored perspectives. However, a few lines below, he says he sees his own true house in the middle of nature, like the ones he drew before his trip to Europe. The last sentence implies that he now had to conceal his true self behind the pure and severe city houses. The true self that the architect tells himself not to be ashamed of shifts from one to the other in just a few lines in the diary.

Eldem's openness to Europe on the one hand, and his heartfelt anxiety over being suppressed by Westernization on the other, are apparent in countless other sentences. Compare, for instance, the previous quotation written in French in the diary with the following one written in Turkish: "Show ... Turkishness with pride. Don't take anything from Europe — it does not have to be beautiful for them."[56] In a sentence that he later crossed out, Eldem continued: "In the last ten years, European products colonized Turkey [*istila etti*]. This destroyed Turkish art. If this continues, we will be completely absorbed by Europe [*Avrupa'nın eline geçeceğiz*]."[57]

Instead of dismissing these conflicting statements as the self-contradictions of a confused soul, we may take them as a sincere young architect's hesitant and uncertain response to the dissemination of European modernism in Turkey. This dilemma is provoked by the insecurity of living in a place deemed non-Western, and the simultaneous sense of excitement and loss brought about by westernization — that is, the melancholy resulting from translation. It rises at the moment when the translator realizes the perceived inequality between the languages to be translated from and into. This is the moment when one intuits less of a cultural exchange and more of a cultural monologue in the process of translation. This melancholy bears witness to the fact that cultural hierarchies can be as upsetting as political ones. The process of translation always runs the risk of self-annihilation — of being overcome by the perceived supremacy of one place — and thus it is not surprising to observe an architect having simultaneous feelings of admiration and revolt.

It was not only the old Turkish houses that Eldem contemplated while studying European architecture. On the state of modern architecture in Europe itself, he wrote in his diary:

> Every epoch has an architecture that characterizes [*personnifie*] itself. Yet to make this possible, the epoch should have already formed a "character" [*personnalité*]. . . . Art realizes that what it produces is outmoded and no longer of the times. . . . We realize suddenly that after having searched with meaningless forms, industry that is not occupied with these forms but is under a more direct influence of the times has created an "art" that at least represents the epoch (silos, bridges, autos, standardized furniture . . .).[58]

During his trip to France, Eldem often persuaded himself to overcome what he described as his own "romanticism," by deprecating some of his own designs as "middle-age like," "invaluable," and "disastrous."[59] One comes across various statements that reveal Eldem's swings between insecurity and confidence. "How is it that I trust my work so much, whereas I am so unsure of myself in life?"⁶⁰ he wondered on a spring day in 1929 in Paris. And a month later, he wrote:

> Life is no longer gay [*La vie n'est pas plus gaie*], it seems to me. I have to get used to the idea that I am made to torture myself all the time and never be happy. . . . This is why I am incapable of following today's absurd world. A house should be an object that reveals no effort or artistic volition . . . like a tennis court or a trunk. . . . Let's not forget that a ship or an airplane has nothing to do with a house, and that our houses are still fixed, composed of walls and openings like before, but we, we believe that we have to live in an ambiance of radio [?] and factory.⁶¹

The comparison of these two passages — the first one written in Font-Romeu in August 1928 and the second in Paris in April 1929 — shows that Eldem had doubts about modernist architecture in Europe. The earlier passage indicates that he was quite familiar with contemporary European architectural movements yet considered most of them "meaningless forms," trying to catch up with the speed of the times. At this point, he agreed with Le Corbusier's arguments in *Vers une Architecture* that the art (or style) of the times was already hinted at in industrial landscapes.⁶² Yet, writing in his diary a year later in Paris, Eldem had changed his mind about Le Corbusier's fascination with industrial artifacts. He was now suspicious of the "absurdity" of Le Corbusier's *machine à habiter*: now, a ship or an airplane, a radio or a factory should have had nothing to do with a house.

Just as he had in Turkey, Eldem designed imaginary houses during his stay in Europe. In Paris, he drew several two- or three-story houses, emphasizing their exposed structure of reinforced concrete that was filled in with textured aggregate and linear windows. Some of these sketches bear a notable resemblance to the work of Auguste Perret, whom Eldem met in Paris (fig. 2.15). Years later, the architect recalled (or rationalized) that he had felt a similarity between the construction logic in Perret's buildings and that in the old Turkish houses. He noted that he "dreamt of the infill walls colored as they were in Ankara, Kastamonu, and Amasya" when he realized that "the beautiful concrete framework had to be visible without any concealment."⁶³ The other formal possibility that Eldem saw in the use of reinforced concrete was liberating the mass from the structural limits of masonry, and thus carving out large outdoor balconies. He may have found similarities between these outdoor spaces and the outdoor *sofas* he had drawn in his colorful perspectives back in Turkey. Just as he equated the exposed reinforced concrete with the wooden framework of

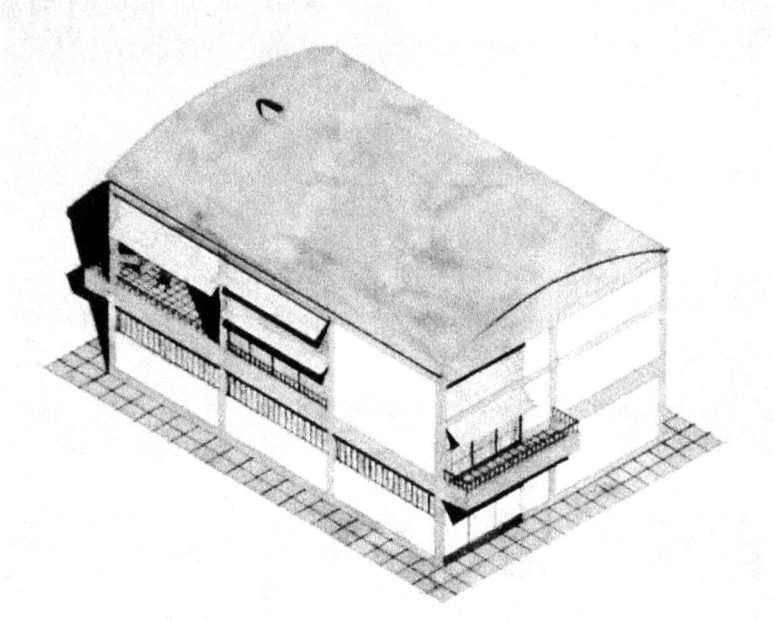

2.15. Sedad Eldem. Sketch for individual houses, France, August 1928–June 1929.

Ottoman houses, he might have conceived of the large, carved-out balconies as modernized and technologically advanced versions of *sofas*.

Britain,
July 1929

Eldem spent July 1929 in the British cities of Glasgow, Chester, Lanark, Liverpool, and London. His opinion of London, which he was visiting for the second time, was highly favorable, and he wrote adoringly about it as "the most lovable and the most civilized part of England."[64] However, Eldem did not have similar words for the rest of the country. He described the "misery" of industrial towns as opposed to the "prettiness" of traditional ones,[65] portraying the workers' life in Glasgow in quite dramatic words. Still using French, he wrote:

> [Glasgow] is a miserable city with one million workers. As I was leaving the city, [I saw] the mines with their sticky and red coal, the never-ending raucous row houses, and groups of men with their caps [*casquettes*] all alike on the street.... They are the humanity, workers' labor; they don't have an individual personality.... Their misery is their whole life, which is completely tied up with those mines. Those miserable neighborhoods are for them, to my surprise, the day, the light, the free time after work.[66]

These words summarized half a century of industrial experience, specifically of the residential condition of industrial workers. Disappointment would be an understatement. Eldem was sadly shocked to observe the housing conditions offered by modernity. The twenty-one-year-old member of an Ottoman elite family continued in his sketchbook: "And me... I moan because of my little miseries. Yes, but they, they do not have little miseries, they have their big misery, which is their lives, and they don't revolt! I have fantastic ideas of an immense rebellion, an unparalleled upheaval; an infinite desire to equalize the people's different ways of life, by humiliating today's better-off."[67]

Eldem would not make such socialist ideals public at any point in his life. Why did the son of a wealthy, well-known Ottoman family identify himself with the working class and desire to "humiliate" the "better-off" at this moment? Might it be that he sympathized with the workers due to his own perceived powerlessness in the face of European architects? Is it too unthinkable that the categories of class and geography slipped into each other in Eldem's mind?

Germany, August 1929–1930

Observing the industrial towns in Britain motivated Eldem to shift some of his attention to the problem of social housing for the workers during the rest of his journey, which consisted of a brief stay in Paris and then travels in Germany. Germany was one of the best places to think about this topic at the end of the 1920s. The *Siedlungen* of the Weimar period that were being produced in Frankfurt and Berlin were two of the finest achievements of modern housing in the world (see chapter 3). Just a month after his visit to England, Eldem was working on a project for affordable housing that he intended to present to the Turkish government. "Our country needs a great number of houses," he wrote. "The important thing is to construct them as economically as possible. The only solution is to standardize and use local materials. Local labor."[68] In his four-step social housing program, he first suggested using local materials, such as brick, stone, wood, adobe, Kütahya mosaics, and tiles, and importing only reinforced concrete. Predictably, he called for research on rural houses to explore the construction possibilities of wood. Second, he insisted on using local labor, additionally noting that Turkish construction workers were still inexperienced to build overly elaborate structures, and thus proposing to simplify the unit plans and details. Third, he proposed to standardize not only plans, but also building parts such as windows, doors, toilets, and sinks. And finally, in an unexpected move, Eldem proposed to eliminate the private architect as the middle man. The typical plans should be prepared in an office of the municipality in order to remove the fees of the individual freelance architect.[69] "The architects should be anonymous and forget their individual ego," this architect wrote in Berlin, probably echoing the words of Hannes Meyer.[70] "In this way, we will finally be emancipated from foreign oppression and we can speak of Turkish architecture as a work,"[71] Eldem wrote in his sketchbook—and then crossed the sentence out. Fairly so, as all the principles he had been considering—including standardization, simplicity, unity, and affordability were possibly inspired by the German debates that he observed in Europe. His regionalism was therefore hardly an antimodern or anti-Western reaction. It was the result of an aspiration toward economical and efficient housing, a concept that was equally relevant for German modernism at the time.

His sketches in Germany indicate that Eldem was interested in a number of issues, including the weekend house, a familiar topic in Germany at the time,[72] and industrialized furniture made with tubular steel (a new occupation most notably carried out by Marcel Breuer in the Bauhaus since 1925, and by Le Corbusier, Pierre Jeanneret, and Charlotte Perriand, who exhibited the *chaise longue* that appeared in Eldem's sketches at the Salon d'Automne in Paris in 1929). Nevertheless, Eldem remained ambivalent about industrialized housing production and the anonymity of the architect that he entertained as part of a social housing program. In Munich, he wrote an ironic science-fiction story that depicted the future of industrialized housing production in the period 1950–2000, where families chose their dwellings from a range of brand names such as "Erika's rural houses," "Mercedes's office and row houses," "Parthenon 1960," or "XI Louis." Judging from the tone of this story, Eldem was quite skeptical about this hyperindustrial and consumer culture. This text alone conveys the variety of ideas that Eldem was exposed to during his journey in Europe, and his unresolved responses to each. The removal of the individual architect's signature from the industrial production of houses echoes Hannes Meyer, while the critique of the all-authoring architect ignoring the wishes of the client sounds similar to Adolf Loos's satires of *Gesamtkunstwerk*, elaborated in texts such as "The Poor Little Rich Man." Eldem spoke about a "vain question" as a reference to the *Dachkrieg* (roof wars) that took over the German architectural debate throughout the 1920s. And finally, he referred to the machine to live in as an obvious reference to Le Corbusier, albeit a disapproving one.[73]

In Germany Eldem also explored the multistory and multifamily urban block. Drawn in an urban setting, possibly envisioned as blocks of

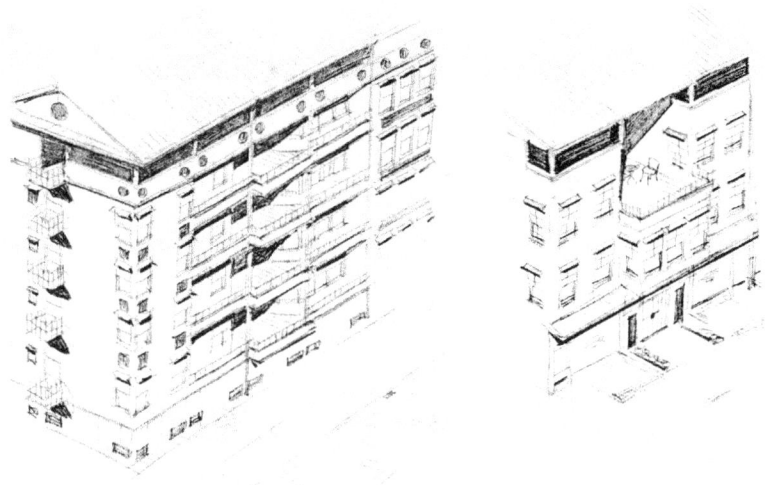

2.16. Sedad Eldem. Sketches for urban apartments, Germany, August 1929–30.

a *Siedlung*, his sketches were important steps in his confrontation with the metropolitan requirements to which he had been resistant at the beginning of his trip. The emphasis on large balconies and terraces imply that Eldem, not unlike the architects of the German *Siedlungen*, wanted to provide spaces—in his case, modernized *sofas*—where the urban residents' relationship with nature could be reclaimed (fig. 2.16).

Since his days as an architectural student, Eldem had been exploring multiple stylistic preferences. He drew countless sketches with dramatic linear windows and dynamic masses, some of which were obviously inspired by those of the German architect Erich Mendelsohn, which had been published in *Wasmuths Monatshefte für Baukunst* in 1924 (fig. 2.17).[74] Accompanying Eldem's Mendelsohn-inspired sketches in the adjacent pages are drawings with steeply pitched roofs, buttresses, and smaller arched windows, some of which significantly resemble Paul Schultze-Naumburg's Cecilienhof in Potsdam (fig. 2.18). It was as if Eldem, trying to find a way that would help him modernize the old Turkish houses, was fluctuating between the two competing expressions that were already the focus of a harsh debate in Germany. Eventually, the emphasis on horizontality in Mendelsohn and the large eaves of the pitched roofs in the old Turkish houses were combined, leading to a formal expression that would become Eldem's signature for almost all of the rest of his career (fig. 2.19).

2.17. Sedad Eldem. Sketches inspired by Erich Mendelsohn, circa 1927.

2.18. Sedad Eldem. Sketch inspired by Paul Schultze-Naumburg, circa 1927.

None of these may have been as determinative as Eldem's exposure to Frank Lloyd Wright's work in the pages of *Wasmuth Monatshefte für Baukunst* in Berlin. Later, Eldem recalled his experience of "discovering" Wright's prairie houses as follows:

> I believe I had discovered some important elements of the Turkish house of the future in these designs. The long low lines, the rows of windows,

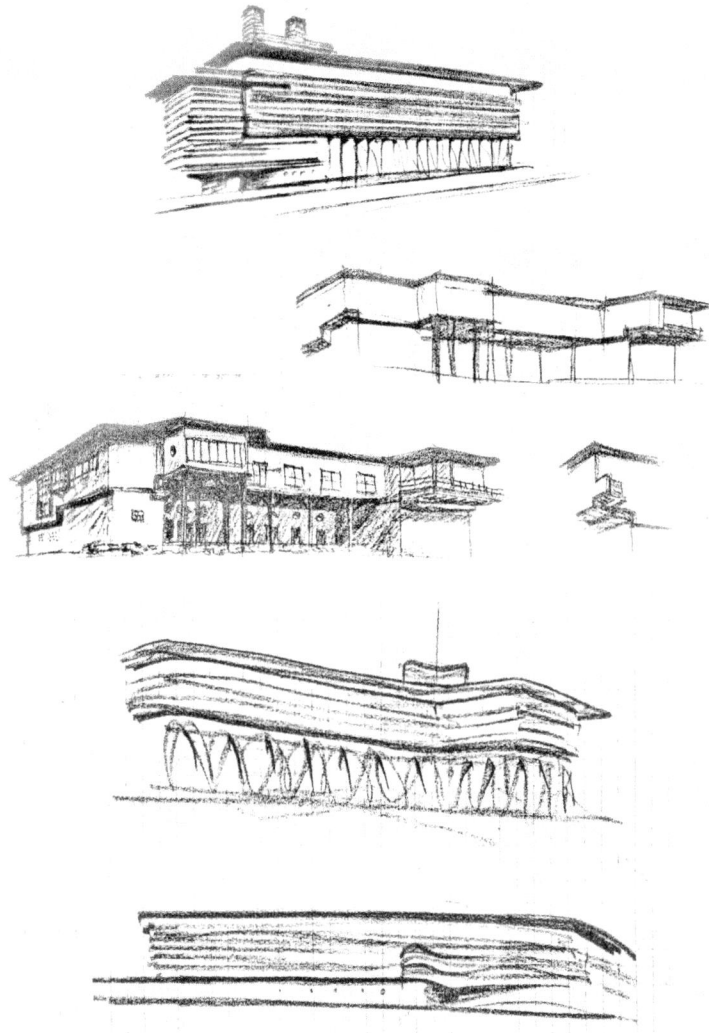

2.19. Sedad Eldem. Sketches suggesting hybridization between the "old Turkish houses" and modernism.

the wide eaves, and the shape of the roofs were very much like the Turkish house in my mind. But how had Wright arrived at these forms?... Wright's sources were not in America but in Asia and, "prairie" was merely a metaphor for his horizontal linearity.[75]

Although Eldem did not explicitly mention Wright in the travel diaries, his sketches in Berlin confirm this statement, and they also bear striking simi-

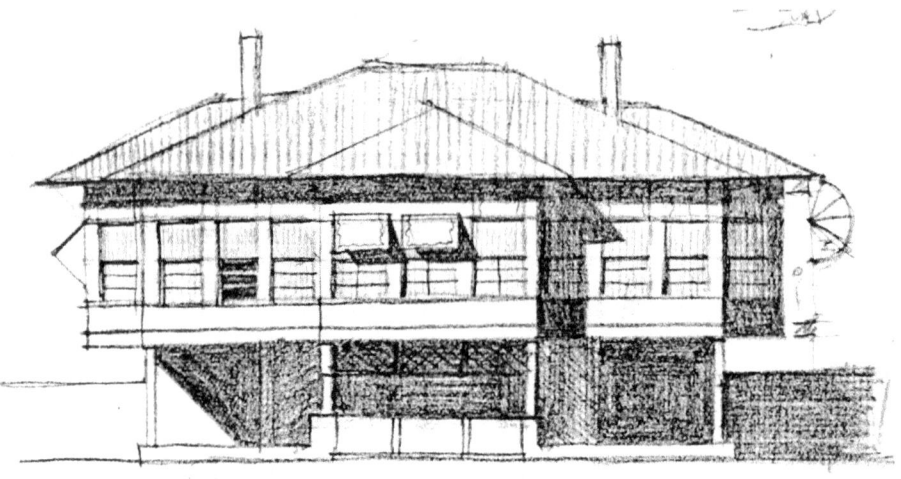

2.20. Sedad Eldem. Sketch possibly inspired by Frank Lloyd Wright, Germany, August 1929–30.

larities to Eldem's future work (fig. 2.20). His discovery in Germany of an American architect and the belief that the sources of Wright's prairie houses were the anonymous houses of Asia may have given Eldem the courage to search for the roots of modern masters in places other than the West, and subsequently, the roots of old Turkish houses in places other than Turkey.

Eldem's approach to Wright was in fact no different than his reception of many other architects associated with modernism. Whatever the architect defined as the old Turkish house, he usually liked to justify it by comparing it to a well-known building in Europe or the United States. Modular and exposed structural framework with infill in the old Turkish houses was similar to the exposed reinforced concrete of August Perret; long horizontal lines were reminiscent of Wright's buildings.[76] Eldem continued to find similarities between old Turkish houses and European modernism after returning to Turkey. In his mind, both city and country houses in Turkey established a strong connection to the outside, and hence they predated the garden city ideals that sought to remedy the congested rental apartments in the European metropolis: "The Turkish city is essentially a garden city [*La ville turque est essentiellement une cité jardin*].... Here are all the advantages known, recognized, and adapted by the modern urbanists, especially the English and the German."[77] It is surprising that Eldem felt less empathy toward Le Corbusier during his trip, but had he been aware of the latter's *Voyage d'Orient*, he would have probably reconsidered his reception of Le Corbusier. Eldem later suggested an affinity between old Turkish houses and Le Corbusier's houses. The former's separation of the served and service spaces and the location of the served spaces almost always on the semi-open ground floor was similar to Le Corbusian *pilotis*.[78] It was Eldem's travel diaries that anticipated the architect's continuing validation of the old Turkish houses by their perceived modernness. In dealing with the dilemma of being modern without "being absorbed" or "colonized by Europe" — to use the words in Eldem's diary — the old Turkish house acted as a perfect peacemaker.

THE BIRTH OF THE "MODERN TURKISH HOUSE"

After returning to Turkey from his trip abroad, Eldem's approach led him to a fruitful career. Despite his justification of the old Turkish houses through the tenets of European modernism, Eldem's own architectural sensibilities were transformed during this trip, as is manifest in a comparison between his drawings before and after (see fig. 2.14). As a matter of fact, he had worked on the preliminary sketches of his most important early buildings during his trip to Europe, including the Ağaoğlu House (1936), Tahsin Güner waterfront house (1938–44), and Taşlık Coffeehouse (1945–47) in İstanbul (figs. 2.21 to 2.25).[79] On the exterior of the Ağaoğlu House, Eldem used familiar elements from İstanbul's houses such as the *cumba* (extension bays) and widely extending eaves, defamiliarizing them with linear windows and nonornamented, painted stucco surfaces (figs. 2.22 and 2.23). Eldem's use of a T-shaped plan is also noteworthy in the Taşlık Coffeehouse (fig. 2.24) and a couple of houses he designed in the early 1930s.[80] A T-shaped plan opens the interior to a maximum panoramic view of the Bosphorus, enabling the person inside to look in not just one but three directions, and also provides cross ventilation. The Köprülü Amcazade Hüseyin Paşa waterfront house was a very well-known example and an explicit source for Eldem (see fig. 2.12). One can observe the emphasis on the panoramic vision in both Eldem's sketches of old Turkish houses and his designs for new houses with accentuated horizontal windows encircling the *sofas* (see fig. 2.25).

Turkey, 1931–1945

By the mid-1930s, a heartfelt melancholic appreciation of Ottoman mansions and waterfront houses, coupled with a harsh critique of the cubic houses that were associated with Europe, extended beyond the pages of professional magazines into daily newspapers. Peyami Safa (1899–1961), a literary writer, denounced the practice of cubic buildings in Turkey as the work of the "uneducated builder, tasteless carpenter, cata-

2.21. Sedad Eldem. Sketch that would probably inspire the Ağaoğlu House, 1927–29.

2.22. Sedad Eldem. The Ağaoğlu House, İstanbul, 1936.

logue lover copy-cat architect, and talent-less painter," who produced "distorted, short and flat apartments built out of cheap cement with low ceilings and narrow rooms":[81]

> We have to put a stop to this epidemic of cubism, arming ourselves with our pure hatred [*en halis nefretlerimizle silahlanalım*]; otherwise it seems capable of becoming a much bigger trouble than expected, a much more

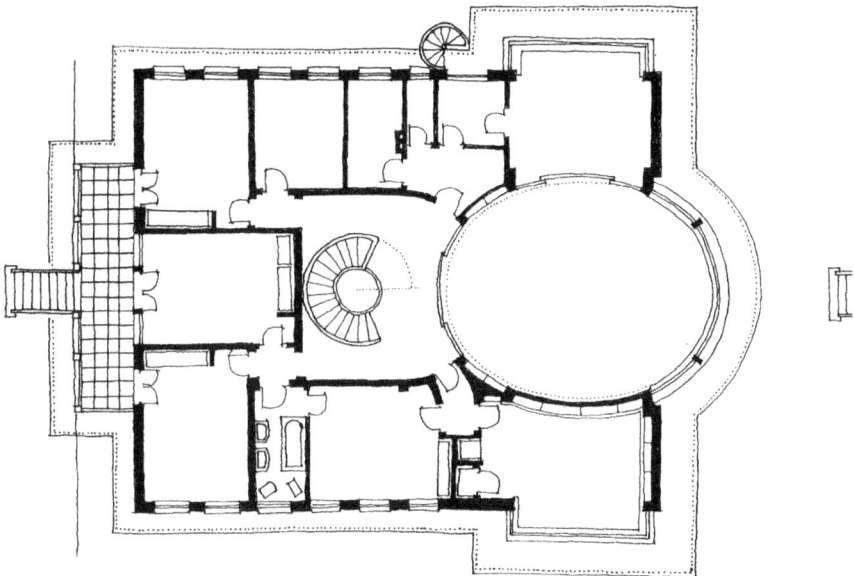

2.23. Sedad Eldem. The Ağaoğlu House, plan with oval *sofa*, İstanbul, 1936.

dangerous one in burning up our taste and philosophy than the famous fires that burned down İstanbul's wooden houses.[82]

In his radio speech titled "Kübik Yapı ve Konfor" (Cubic building and comfort), the architectural historian Behçet Ünsal (1912–2006) carried his critique of cubic architecture to a popular audience:

> However our cubic buildings are not like the ones that come out of the social transformations in the world. Our cubic architecture is a caricature that we all find demeaning. . . . There is no sunlight in [these buildings]. Their infrastructure does not work. Greenery and flowers can only grow in the pots placed in front of the windows. . . . The rooms of such a building are like a box . . . , the walls in between the neighbors are made out of half-sized bricks. Besides, there are dirty patterns on the walls left by the water leaks. If you walk a little fast or if you dance, the downstairs neighbor will complain, because the floor is made out of the thinnest concrete slab. No running hot water, broken central heating, small boxy [*sefertası*] rooms and the laughter of your neighbors ringing in your ears. . . . The Mr. is cranky [*asabi*] coming from work every afternoon. You can't say a thing. Well, one naturally gets cranky climbing ninety-five stairs, [making one] breathless after a tiring day.[83]

2.24. Sedad Eldem. The Taşlık Coffeehouse, İstanbul, 1945–47.

2.25. Sedad Eldem. Sketch of an interior showing a panoramic vision that would probably inspire the Taşlık Coffeehouse.

On another front, Sermet Muhtar Alus (1887–1952) started his series "Eski Konaklar Bize Neler Anlatıyor" (What do old mansions tell us?) in the daily newspaper *Tan* in 1936.[84] Alus had already made a name for himself with his texts and caricatures, which he had been regularly publishing since 1931 in such publications as *Akşam*, *Yedi Gün*, *Tan*, and *Yeni Mecmua*.[85] These vividly portrayed İstanbul's everyday life, famous characters, streets, and buildings. His series on old mansions and waterfront houses in *Tan* often described their architectural features, as well as the flamboyant life of their owners and anecdotes about the events that had taken place there. Toward the end of the series in 1936, an anonymous writer published a manifesto in the same newspaper, claiming that "the old Turkish house must set an example for today's Turkish house" and that people must stop "copying" European houses:

> What kind of houses are we living in now? How were we living in the past? It is a shame that the residential architecture we import from Europe, just because it is contemporary [*asri*] becomes totally tasteless, spiritless, and meaningless [*zevksiz, ruhsuz, ve manasız*] in practice. Before all, we would like to tell and remind you that the "Turkish house" is a totally complete and excellent being.... We would like to reveal this fact and call the uneducated mimics to conscience.[86]

The old Turkish house was thus seen as a much superior alternative to cubic architecture, at least in some İstanbul circles, outside the core group of Kemalists around Ankara. What is striking about many of the houses designed during this period is the extensive, interchangeable, and slightly ambiguous use of the word *sofa* or *hol* (Turkish version of the word *hall*, which is the usual English translation of *sofa*). In one of his first projects published in the architectural magazine *Mimar*, Abidin [Mortaş] (1904–63) designed a big central hall inside the house, which he called *sofa* on the second but *hol* on the entrance floor. Though this space is not designed as a living space, it is a spacious and important area at the heart of the plan.[87] *Mimar* was founded in 1931 by the first generation of republican architects, most notably Zeki Sayar (1905–2001) and Abidin Mortaş, both 1928 graduates from the İstanbul Academy of Fine Arts. The young generation decided to launch this journal to give themselves a public face, to inform Turkish architects about the architectural movements elsewhere in the world, and to gain the attention of the Turkish state that they criticized for commissioning projects from foreign architects alone.[88] (The editors were forced by the state to find a Turkish name for the journal, and they changed the title to *Arkitekt* in 1935.) Mortaş used a *sofa* in

2.26. Abidin Mortaş. Single-family house, 1931.

three houses whose plans he published in 1931 (fig. 2.26).[89] Of these, a single-story house is particularly interesting because it was designed as a small dwelling but included a relatively large *sofa* as a circulation space.[90] Dozens of similar examples appeared in the pages of professional magazines during this period. There was an extensive yet ambiguous use of the word *sofa* in these plans. Whether the house is roofed[91] or cubic,[92] with a traditional or new appearance, a large *sofa* (hall) prevails.[93] Usually this space is designed for circulation to connect different rooms, yet there are examples that use it for living purposes, too.[94] Sometimes the word *sofa* is used to designate the space connecting the bedrooms and *hol* the space connecting the living spaces (such as the guest rooms and living and dining halls); sometimes the opposite is true. Sometimes the word *sofa* or *hol* is used for spaces with minimal circulation purposes; sometimes these spaces are designed as very large and inefficiently spacious. Last but not least, in several projects by Arif Hikmet Holtay (fig. 2.27), Zeki Sayar, and Behçet Sabri, the large and spacious *sofa* (or *hol*) is used both as the space that gives access to other rooms and as the main living space of the family.[95] Even though these architects were inspired by the modernist style of contemporary European architects for the exterior appearance of their houses, they were not equally enthusiastic about modernist interior

2.27. Arif Hikmet [Holtay]. Mansion in garden, 1933.

plans. Rather, they continued to organize their plans around a space called *sofa*. In many of these examples, the architects did not refer to the word *sofa* as a conscious or deliberate gesture to integrate an element of an old Turkish house. Instead they seem to employ it out of habit. The use of *sofa* at this point seems to be more determined by a spontaneous collective memory than a conscious and intended gesture of symbolism.

In Eldem's work, the *sofa* moved from being used as a habit to a message. Starting in 1931, the architect published perspectives that were designed as "clean, calm, and cozy Turkish corners that nevertheless fulfill civilized comfort standards [*medeni komfor*]" by bringing in some elements of the old Turkish house such as the *sofa*, T-shaped plan, *divan*, and *çıkma*.⁹⁶ Eldem declared that he introduced these projects as "experiments in an attempt to offer our new houses the *national character* that obviously existed in the past, rather than the late buildings *without character*."⁹⁷ In 1931, Eldem published a trilogy of villas differentiated in relation to climatic conditions.⁹⁸ A summer house had a closed *sofa* at the center; a year-round city residence had a closed peripheral *sofa* along its façades; a city house in a hot and arid climate had open *sofas* and terraces on every floor. Whatever the climate, some form of *sofa* could mediate between the interior and exterior, between the private bedroom and semiprivate meet-

2.28. Sedad Eldem. Indian Embassy, Ankara, 1965.

ing place of the family. In the interior organization of the houses he designed during the 1930s, each room was allocated a specific function, such as bedroom, living room, or dining room, rather than the multifunctional rooms of traditional houses; the rooms were designed for stable, Western-style furniture, rather than the flexible *divans* of Ottoman houses. Despite this anticipation of a transformed life associated with modernism, Eldem did not follow either Le Corbusier's *plan libre* or Loos's *Raumplan* conceptions. Rather, he organized the houses around a central and highly symbolic space called *sofa*, as was most explicitly shown in the oval space of the Ağaoğlu House (see fig. 2.23). Eldem very vocally argued that the *sofa*, a lifelong obsession for him, was the main distinguishing characteristic of the old Turkish houses (see chapter 4).

Quite different from Jansen's and Arkan's foreignizing translations, Eldem's were appropriating translations. Nevertheless, it was his claim of the modernness of the Turkish house and the Turkishness of the modern achievements in Europe and the United States that helped him resolve the dilemma of modernization in Turkey. This dilemma was initiated by the simultaneous desire to be part of the "Western civilization" (*Batı medeniyeti*), as it was commonly called in Turkey, and to establish an identity that would avoid being "absorbed by the West." Eldem must have made himself believe that the old Turkish houses were not incompatible with the ideals of Western modernism. Long after Eldem developed these ideas, scholars independently traced Le Corbusier's and Wright's sources to the examples they observed during their trips to the East, making some of Eldem's claims conceivable[99] — but this is not my point. As much as Eldem's formulation may appear to us today as a naive understanding of both European modernism and the wooden anonymous houses in Turkey, or an anguished failure to confront the discontinuities between the two, we have to admit its productivity for him at the time. Perhaps this was a tactic to subvert the perceived inequalities between places, the inequalities that obstruct the humanist aspirations of translation. The shield of the humanist ideal — that is, the faith in the universality of cultures — enabled Eldem to avoid both exoticist conclusions that would have searched for the essential difference in the East and cultural supremacist ones that would have unproblematically extended European modernism to Turkey. The shield of the humanist ideal thus helped the architect work through melancholy toward a more productive overcoming of a sense of loss (fig. 2.28).

This melancholic and yet productive tension has to be differentiated from the nostalgic longing for a lost past. Here the lost object causing melancholy is not only, or not even necessarily, the decaying traces of an older world that is made anachronistic by the forces of progress. The cultural milieu of the early years of Kemalism, of which Eldem was also a part, was more futurist than historicist, more enthusiastic about progress than nostalgic. What distinguishes this melancholy is rather the aspiration to be the subject of one's own history. Here the lost object that melancholy is predicated on is the natural right to be part of modernism and, by extension, of universality — since modernism was promoted as a placeless and transnational pursuit.

In his three-part essay on "Aşağılık Duygusu" (The feeling of inferiority), the author Tahsin Banguoğlu, one of Eldem's contemporaries, writes:

> The feeling of inferiority makes people either timid or audacious [*pısırık ya da atak*].... Like a pendulum, they swing between a fear of inferiority and a claim to superiority.[100]
>
> Just like individuals, the feeling of inferiority reveals itself as timidness or audaciousness in nations as well.... Insecure nations look down on their national history, deny their national power. They start humiliating their own national culture, and relapse into a blind admiration and imitation of the foreign [*körükörüne yabancı hayranlığı ve taklitçilik*].... National audaciousness is the counterpart of this feeling. Some nations with a feeling of inferiority come out with a claim to superiority [*üstünlük iddiası*].

They exaggerate their national history, inflate their national power. They even embark on a claim to racial superiority [*ırk üstünlüğü*] and insult their neighboring countries for being "of an inferior race"! As a result they fall into a blind xenophobia [*yabancı düşmanlığı*]. . . . Both audaciousness and timidness carry nations into a disaster.[101]

Coincidentally, Fanon made the same observations and outlined two basic outcomes of the colonized individual's perceived "inferiority of his culture." The colonized subject either "takes every opportunity of unfavorably criticizing his own national culture, or else takes refuge in setting out and substantiating the claims of that culture in a way that is passionate but rapidly becomes unproductive."[102] In other words, there is a swing between self-love and self-hatred or between hidden envy of and resistance toward the West. Both approaches, as Fanon immediately added, lead to "impossible contradictions."

Can it be that these two repeating patterns are, in fact, the two faces of melancholy in which the non-Western individual swings between fascination and resistance toward the West — a West from which the individual is excluded by definition, a West that is lost to the individual who is defined as the West's other, or the non-Western? Can we say that, in both cases, there is a melancholic attachment to a lost ideal, and an aspiration toward finding the lost ideal back in one of its representations? In the phase of fascination, there is an attachment to the architectural artifacts associated with the West as a substitute for the denial of the right to be part of modernization's history. In the phase of resistance, there is a reaction against the West or the universal history that it supposedly embodies, and an attachment to the traditional architectural artifacts as a substitute for the lost glory days of the past, which are perceived as not being tainted by the feeling of being peripheral. The oscillation between fascination and resistance, or the swing between admiration of and reaction against the West, is similar to the "countless single conflicts in which love and hate wrestle together," in Freud's terms. As it has been defined over the centuries by writers including Aristotle, Ibn'Sina, Burton, and Freud, melancholy is a fluctuation between sorrow and anger, joy and grief, love and hate, and, I add, fascination and resistance. The internalization of the Western ideal, the lost object, results in the oscillation between cultural narcissism and denounced self-image. Rather than explaining this condition as a conflict between, say, regionalism and modernism in architecture, or as a dialectical struggle between two groups with opposite positions, it is more helpful to conceive of it as a dilemma, a tension that exists simultaneously in one person or a group of individuals. In other words, fascination and resistance are two faces of the same condition — a condition that is permeated by melancholy. Even though melancholy is not, of course, the only tension operating in the contested zone of translation, it is the one that infiltrated into İstanbul during the Turkish era of modernization.

Ever since Aristotle associated melancholy with "brilliance and achievement" of the thoughtful being, this meaning has scarcely left the connotation of the term, although it has usually remained in the background.[103] Melancholy is characterized as a sadness that nevertheless has charm, like a desirable tune. This appealing sorrow has also been the retreat of the individual who wants to be disassociated from the dominant process of history, where "there is no document of civilization which is not at the same time a document of barbarism," to quote Walter Benjamin.[104] The melancholy of the non-West is sorrowful at one moment, angry at the next, and content at not being part of the dominating and oppressing powers at another.

To summarize, the making of a geographical other — that is, the separation of the categories of West and East with an explicitly inscribed hierarchy between the two — causes melancholy in a non-Western individual. As long as the historical process of modernization is defined as a Western one, a process whose torch is carried by the West, this inscribed ideal becomes an unattainable lost ideal for the subject who is categorized as non-Western in the first place. The internalization of the Western ideal, and the resulting definition of the *non-Western* as one longing for the Western ideal, and the inevitable loss of this ideal to the non-Western who is excluded from it in the first place causes this melancholy. It is a melancholy predicated on the perceived distance of a non-Western individual from the ego ideal. It is the condition in which the attachment to the denied right to be a subject of the inevitable path of history creates a dilemma that fluctuates between fascination with and resistance to the West.

THREE | *Siedlung* in Subaltern Exile

The year 1933 opened up a new phase in German-Turkish relations. Until then, many of the German-speaking architects like Carl Lörcher, Hermann Jansen, and Clemens Holzmeister designed their projects for Turkey while they remained based in their home country, communicating with the Turks through translated letters. Following the National Socialist takeover in Germany in 1933, many Jewish and socialist professionals were forced into exile to avoid much severer consequences. These Germans included Leo Spitzer and Erich Auerbach, whose work in exile has been acknowledged in scholarly studies. The architects and city planners Bruno Taut, Martin Wagner, Ernst Reuter, Margarete Schütte-Lihotzky, Wilhelm Schütte, Franz Hillinger, and Gustav Oelsner came to Turkey after 1933.

Transformations within Turkey also contributed to making the year 1933 a milestone. On August 1, the sign in Arabic letters at the gate of the Darülfünun was replaced by a new sign in Roman letters: "İstanbul Üniversitesi" (İstanbul University). The German exiles took a significant part in this uni-

1933 . . .

versity reform and the restructuring of the pedagogical programs that terminated the Ottoman *Medrese* system. Approximately 180 professors and assistants were invited to universities to offer education in fields equivalent to the modern European disciplines, leaving a mark on the Turkish educational system that endured well beyond the period of their sojourns in Turkey.[1] German educators had already been influential in the modernization of the Ottoman Empire's army.[2] After the 1908 reforms, Turkish students were sent on fellowships to Germany; the group included Cevat Dursunoğlu, a student of Georg Simmel[3] and a good friend of Taut, who later became the inspector of Turkish students in Berlin (1930–35) and was influential in choosing the foreign architects invited to work on projects in Turkey. The university reform opened a new phase in these academic encounters. Philipp Schwartz, the founder of *Notgemeinschaft deutscher Wissenschaftler im Ausland* (Emergency society of German scientists in foreign countries) was invited to Ankara in 1933. After a seven-hour meeting, Schwartz later recalled suggesting about thirty exiled professors for employment in new university departments in Turkey.[4] The İstanbul University came to be known as Emigré Universität, where ninety-eight German exiles taught between 1933 and 1945.[5]

Meanwhile, the National Socialist takeover in Germany also had an immediate impact on the German community in İstanbul.[6] Within months of the regime change, the German school and the German official organizations in Turkey started disseminating the National Socialist mission. The German newspaper *Türkische Post* closely followed the change of power in Europe, working almost as a propaganda tool for Hitler: it printed large pictures of him, celebrated his birthday and political programs, and published articles on the German *Heimat*. National Socialist organizations and youth groups were founded and organized annual Nazi festivals. The German radio station in Turkey broadcasted in Turkish for fifteen minutes per day during World War II. According to the research of Johannes Glasneck and Anne Dietrich, the German media in Turkey and the German school were significantly altered due to the change of regime, employing teachers and reporters who were part of Nazi organizations.[7] German officials at times put pressure on the Turkish government to replace Jewish professors with those from a German list of suggestions.[8] The architect Paul Bonatz visited Turkey in 1943 to bring the National Socialist propaganda exhibition; he stayed until 1954.

German-speaking individuals in İstanbul thus occupied an array of intellectual and political positions. For the most part, the professors working in the Turkish universities, who had themselves fled the Nazi regime in their country, fought against its propaganda in Turkey. There were a few organizations to help the Jewish and refugee communities, as well as associations representing the German-speaking professors, in İstanbul at the time.[9] Some émigrés, including the Schütte couple and Herbert Eichholzer, were part of a circle of left-wing intellectuals in İstanbul that included the archaeologist Halet Çambel, with whom they kept in touch throughout their lives.[10] Eichholzer had established the Foreign Branch of the Austrian Communist Party, which had branches in Belgium, France, the Soviet Union, Yugoslavia, and Switzerland, and which also established links with the illegal Communist Party of Turkey, banned since 1926.[11] Schütte-Lihotzky joined the Communist Party in 1939 while in İstanbul. Gerhard Kessler was involved in the founding of the Turkish Workers' Syndicate. These German academics were commonly known as actively antifascist even if they officially fell under the jurisdiction of the German Embassy in Turkey.[12]

Most of the German professors gave their classes in German, with a Turkish translator. However, some learned Turkish — including Ernst Reuter, Fritz Neumark, and Leo Spitzer who also wrote an article titled "Learning Turkish" with a humanist message that Emily Apter has recently interpreted as one of the beginnings of a form of comparative literature.[13] Due to the relative lack of qualified German translators in some fields at the time, the German professors sometimes shifted to French in their classes.[14] In their memoirs and personal letters, many of the exiles like Reuter, Schwartz, Neumark, and Ernst Hirsch indicated that they admired the Turkish enthusiasm for modernization and for the most part were glad to be part of Turkey's programs, despite the country's lack of technical and financial resources.[15] For others like Martin Wagner, "the Orient was too poor," "the Turks (and possibly all Asians) in front of the machines and capital were like a child playing with a dangerous cigarette lighter."[16] Many literary scholars are familiar with Auerbach's laconic postscript about the alleged lack of a sufficient library, which both impaired and enabled the writing of *Mimesis* during his exile in İstanbul (1933–45) — a passage that had important repercussions about the possibility of comparative literature in a postcolonial world.[17] In a letter to Walter Benjamin in 1937, Auerbach singled out a fascination in Turkey with the "technological modernization in the European sense, in order to triumph against a hated yet admired Europe with its own weapons," which ended in "fanatic non-traditionalist nationalism"[18] — an observation not unlike the situation I described as one face of melancholy, albeit a non-empathetic one.

On August 2, 1944, Turkey broke all ties with Nazi Germany, declared its neutrality for the rest of World War II, and ordered the Nazi-associated Germans to leave the country. The German residents who wanted to stay were required to refrain from any political activity and become Turkish citizens, although some professors such as Reuter were exempted from this rule. Some German residents were subject to internment in Kırşehir, Yozgat, and Çorum until the end of the war.[19] Meanwhile, the German exiles created underground organizations to develop ideas for building a post-Nazi Germany. For example, Thomas Mann and Reuter wrote numerous letters to each other throughout 1943, envisioning a new Germany after the war.[20]

The German professors in Turkey usually kept in close social contact with each other. Their children's education presented a problem, since most of the professors refused to send their children to the German School, given the prevalence of the Nazi propaganda there. Some children had private lessons (mostly taught by Leyla Kudret Erkönen, if the children lived in Ankara), while others went to the British or Turkish schools.[21] For instance, Reuter, who lived in Bahçelievler in Ankara with his family, often mentioned his concerns about his children's solitude, since they were neither Turks nor Germans, but belonged to a small group of political refugees. Nevertheless, his children came to have Turkish friends and became successful academics and businessmen: his son Edzard, for one, wrote appreciatively in his memoirs about growing up in Turkey. He recalled his father's long discussions in İstanbul with Bruno Taut and Martin Wagner on the importance of city design (*Städtebau*), a memory he kept coming back to while working with Renzo Piano, Richard Rogers, and others on the reconstruction of the Potsdamer Platz after the unification of Germany.[22]

SIEDLUNG AND THE METROPOLIS

Berlin, 1924–1933

Between 1924 and 1933, the garden city movement in Germany was transformed into what might be called the Weimar *Siedlung* movement.[23] This transformation can best be demonstrated in the professional careers of Bruno Taut and Martin Wagner in Berlin, and Ernst May and his colleagues Margarete Schütte-Lihotzky and Wilhelm Schütte shortly before they took refuge in Turkey. Although they shared with prewar garden city promoters certain design principles — such as proximity to nature and organized, collective housing — they differed significantly in their approaches to metropolitan living, urban density, the integration of indus-

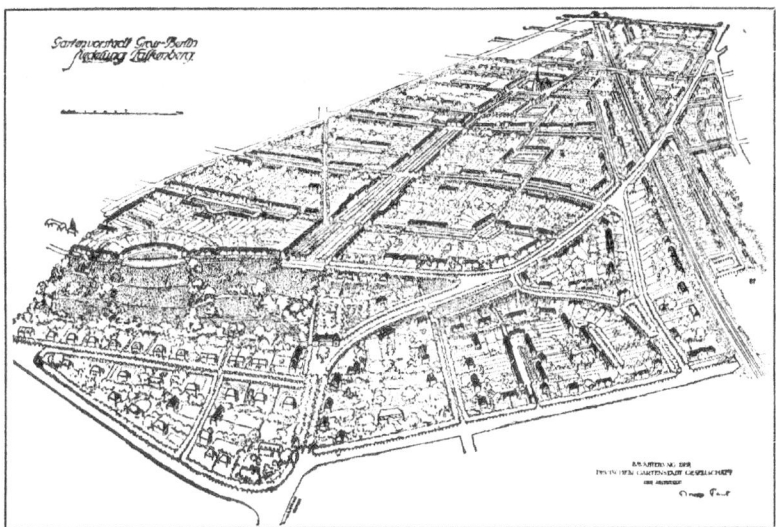

3.1. Bruno Taut. *Gartenstadt* Falkenberg, Berlin, 1913.

trial technologies, governmental responsibility, and aesthetic values. This chapter traces both the transformation of the prewar garden city ideals into the interwar *Siedlung* debate in Germany, and its simultaneous translations in Turkey. I also discuss the problems of mass housing both in an economic system reliant on surplus values of real estate, and in a global cultural milieu that limited subaltern populations' opportunity to participate in the decisions shaping their own residential conditions. Let me take a look at *Siedlung*'s urban, architectural, and economic aspects.

As a young architect, Bruno Taut (1880–1938) was already immersed in the theory of the garden city. In August 1910, he joined a study tour of English garden cities; two years later, he worked for Heinrich Tessenow on *Gartenstadt* Hellerau.[24] He also worked as the chief designer of *Gartenstadt* Falkenberg (1913), on the outskirts of Berlin, and reform housing in Magdeburg, commissioned by the Garden City Association.[25] Falkenberg was close enough to Berlin to function as a garden suburb (fig. 3.1), rather than as a city planned from scratch.[26] English garden city models admittedly guided the site plan, but what made Falkenberg memorable was the daring use of bright, primary colors in order to "give some life" to standardized and typical housing, as Taut phrased it.[27]

During and immediately after World War I, Taut promoted revolutionary visions of land settlement in a number of utopian books. *Die Stadtkrone* (The city crown), written during the war (1916–18) and published in 1919, was the depiction of an ideal modern settlement that had some similarities with Ebenezer Howard's garden city, to which Taut referred in the book.[28] Both were represented with circular diagrams; both found it necessary to limit a city's population (the maximum was 30,000 for Howard and 300,000–500,000 for Taut); both had a separate industrial belt; and both were surrounded by a green belt. The most significant difference between Taut's and Howard's schemes was in their visions for the city center. While Howard placed a big community garden at the focal point of his scheme, Taut envisioned a center for public buildings, including an opera, library, and theater, crowned with a crystal house.[29] In his influential texts written immediately after World War I, Taut continued to promote a revolutionary program for settling in the countryside.[30] In "A Program for Architecture" (1918), he wrote: "They [people's houses] cannot stand in the metropolis because the latter, being rotten in itself, will disappear along with the old power. The future lies on the newly developed land, which will feed itself."[31] In the face of the food crisis after the war, Taut advocated decentralization as a way for Germany to "feed its population."[32] The ideal settlement depicted in *Die Auflösung der Städte* (Dissolution of cities) was composed of small clusters of houses, dispersed loosely on the surface of the earth as a delicate latticework with no dominant hierarchy (fig. 3.2). Taut envisioned communities of like-minded individuals living there, growing their own vegetables and other food in their gardens, working in their chosen professions, and exchanging what they produced with each other in communal organizations. In the words of the architectural historian Rosemarie Bletter, this was composed of "centralized cells of human habitation within a larger decentralized context."[33] Not unlike the early garden city promoters, Taut believed his ideal settlement would have shaped the character of individuals living in it. Their bodies and souls would have been in harmony because they would have spent half of each day working with machinery and the other half with nature; they would have been "more subtle," more "hospitable" to others; they would have had "strong individual existences," living far apart from each other, but they would have also appreciated a qualified community life. Boundaries would have been impossible in this settlement; states would have disappeared, and with them the violence of states; a new form of human relationship would have developed, "supremely prophylactic but no longer organizational and dictatorial."[34] These social utopian books were unique translations of the garden city ideal. Even though Taut started from principles similar to those of Howard, he radicalized the garden city until it turned into an anarchic and decentralized vision of land

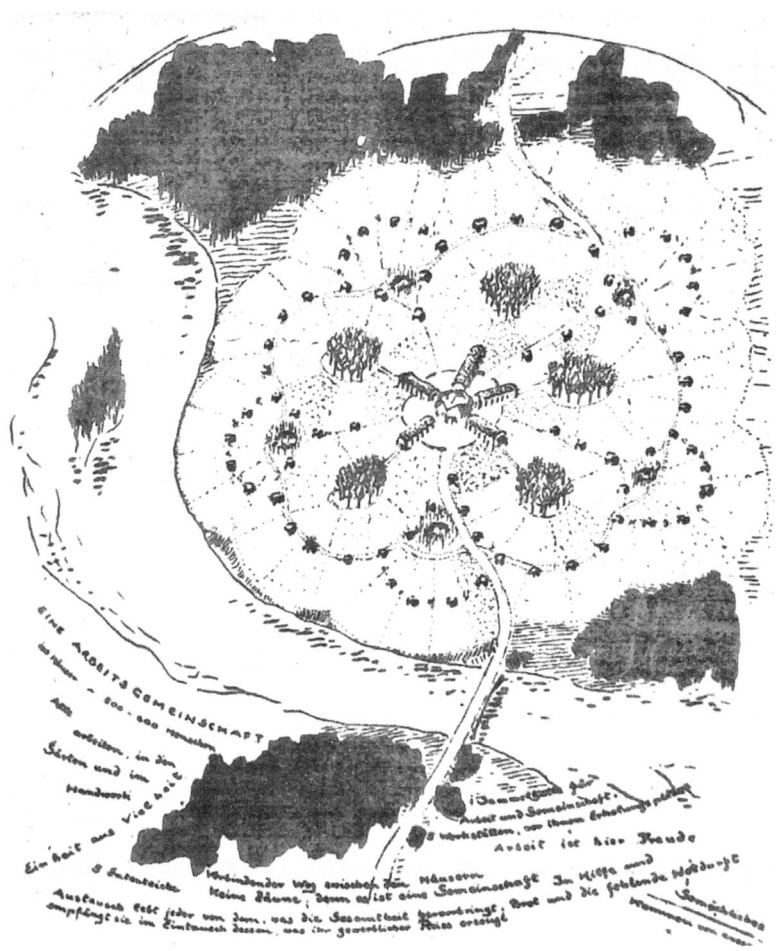

3.2. Bruno Taut. Views of the site in *Dissolution of Cities*, 1920.

settlement, which would, in his expectations, generate a social transformation.[35]

In 1924, Taut was appointed as the consulting architect of Gemeinnützige Heimstätten A.G. (GEHAG), a building cooperative that produced many of the most innovative social housing projects in history.[36] This began a new phase in his career, which radically changed his low opinion of the metropolis. The German housing law of March 1918, the Weimar Constitution that endowed every citizen with the "right to a sound dwelling," and the tax revenues that were directed to social housing after 1924 prepared the necessary legal and financial background for this ambitious, low-cost housing program, more than 70 percent of whose support came from public funds.[37] Between 1924 and 1932, Taut (with Martin Wagner) was responsible for the design of about 10,000 units in almost twenty different housing settlements all over Berlin, which are illustrated in this book with photographs by the photographer Arthur Köster, a contemporary of Taut. Taut also used Köster's photographs to represent his work during his retrospective exhibition at the Academy of Fine Arts in İstanbul, and hence many of these photographs must have reached the Turkish audience by 1938 (see fig. 5.10).[38] Taut — an architect who had hitherto been cultivating his utopian visionary side in fantastical projects, delirious colors, functionless and defiant buildings — was capable of instantly adapting to one of the most economically and institutionally restraining situations in architecture, which stimulated his practical and functionalist side.

The transformation from the early garden city ideals into metropolitan housing was possible with the unique collaboration of a group of architects working for GEHAG. On March 14, 1924, Taut, Richard Linneke, and Martin Wagner founded the Deutsche Wohnungsfürsoge A.G. für Beamte (DEWOG), a research organization dedicated to the improvement of collective housing projects, with the periodical *Wohnungswirtschaft* (1924–32) as its mouthpiece (fig. 3.3).[39] The DEWOG circle shared many motivations with the garden city movement. They also searched for alternatives to *Mietskasernen* (fig. 3.4) and struggled to resolve the housing shortage for the urban poor, to revive the city resident's relationship with nature, and to create a community life. However, the GEHAG *Siedlungen* were no longer composed merely of single-family row and detached houses in private gardens, but of a mixture of these and multifamily building blocks, as in Onkel Toms Hütte (1926–31) (fig. 3.5) and *Siedlung* Britz (1925–31). Large buildings were arranged to create varying outdoor spaces, including linear green areas between parallel blocks, large courtyards, parks, and long urban streets. In addition to the different income groups and family sizes that would be accommodated in such a plan, Taut experimented with a different relationship between the outdoor garden and the residential type in each *Siedlung*. For instance, in *Siedlung* Britz alone, there were different types of row houses. Some had three stories, others two; some had a small front garden facing the public street and a big backyard, while others had only a big garden in the front. Some encircled large urban playgrounds (fig. 3.6). This diversity in residential types had much broader implications for the abandonment of the garden city ideal and signified a new confrontation with the big city.

In 1925–26, Wagner published three articles on the garden city theory

3.3. Cover of *Wohnungs-wirtschaft*, February 1, 1931.

in which he sharply distinguished between the early garden city and the GEHAG *Siedlungen*.⁴⁰ Born in Königsberg, Martin Wagner (1885–1957) had studied architecture in Berlin and had worked in Hermann Muthesius's office in 1908–9. Before 1924, he had published an impressive number of articles in which he developed ideas about reducing production costs in housing.⁴¹ Apart from his theoretical contributions, he had designed the Small Housing Colony in Rüstringen (1914), created the development plan for *Siedlung* Lindenhorf (1918), and participated in *Siedlung* Eichkamp (1922).⁴² Acknowledging the important steps of the garden city movement for the rationalization of housing production, Wagner nevertheless stated: "But Germany does not build garden cities. . . . To prove the complete efficiency of the low-rise *Siedlung*—that is our most urgent and important task."⁴³ He also wrote: "These impending sentimental feelings about the 'garden city' with its small houses and gardens actually prevent the further development of the real idea of the garden city. The ideas of Howard, rooted in the bourgeois interpretation of the garden city, have long been dead."⁴⁴ Wagner had several objections to the

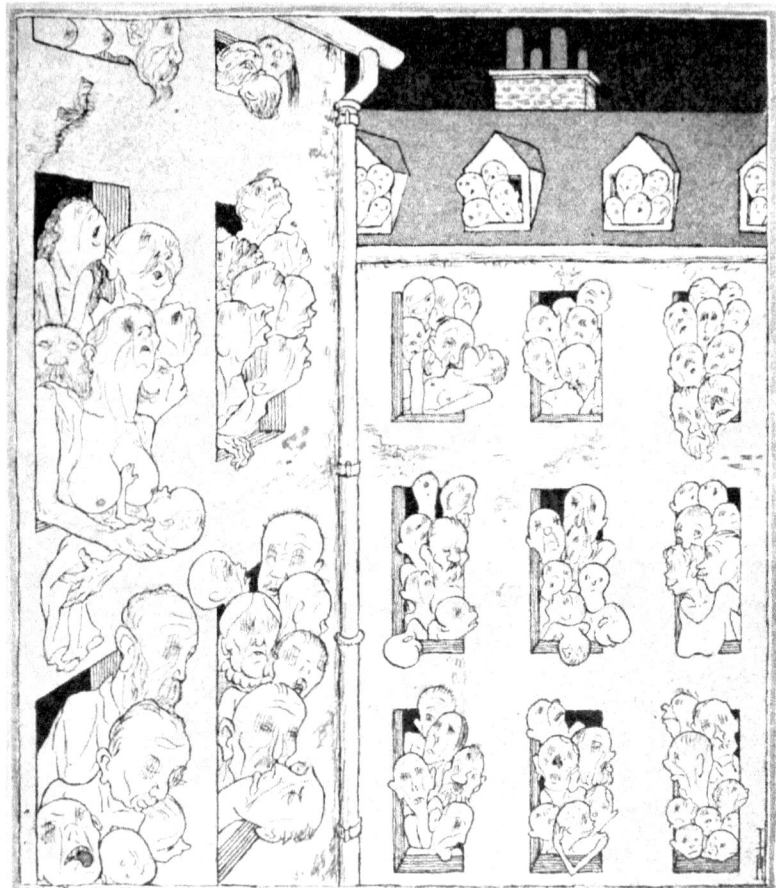

3.4. Th. Heine. Caricature of *Mietskasernen*.

"pure" garden city theory. One was its relative failure in responding to the housing demand of the masses as a whole, especially the most financially challenged people. Related was his second objection to the miscalculations of a garden city's financial benefits: "The small house with its private garden cannot compete with the rental block housing, because the profitability of dwellings in rental blocks [*Mietskasernenwohnung*] is supported by the distribution of parks, leisure places, hospitals, asylums, and so on, throughout the city."[45] The financial strength of the garden city in competing with the cheap but congested rental barracks depended on the low cost of land far from the city center. However, these semiautonomous garden cities had to be provided with communal services in order to make them true cities (and of course there was the cost of transportation when

3.5. Bruno Taut. *Siedlung* Onkel Toms Hütte, Berlin, 1926–31. Photo: Arthur Köster, c. 1931 (exhibited in İstanbul in Taut's retrospective exhibition).

3.6. Bruno Taut and Martin Wagner. *Siedlung* Britz, playground surrounded by row houses, Berlin, 1925–31. Photo: Arthur Köster, c. 1931.

they were garden suburbs). Therefore, Wagner's consideration of municipal services in the financial equation made an important point. In a way, "pure" garden cities following the English model required that the individual residents in a cooperative subsidize the common city services for which the state or municipality should have been responsible. In contrast, the profitability of the *Siedlungen* within the borders of the big city, in a welfare state, could be calculated by taking into account their ability to make use of the common city services.

Wagner's promotion of the multifamily building block had a financial justification, but it also meant that the DEWOG circle was prepared to confront metropolitan conditions with a more committed enthusiasm than the previous generation had shown. As Wagner explicitly argued, "the friends of the garden city should direct all their attention to the *regeneration of existing cities*," rather than the "creation of new cities."[46] In short, he placed the emphasis on the city, rather than the country, in order to regenerate Howard's theory of the garden city. As Berlin's *Stadtbaurat*—director of the city's Department of Urban Planning and Development—Wagner was also active in proposing projects and organizing competitions for the city center renewal, improving traffic and transportation, and developing metropolitan plazas, including Alexanderplatz, Platz der Republik, Potsdamerplatz, and Leipzigerplatz.[47]

Taut, who had been closely connected to the garden city movement and its decentralist principles before and immediately after World War I, also adjusted some of his ideas to the changing conditions after 1924 and joined Wagner in explaining the incompatibility of Howard's garden city theory with contemporary German conditions.[48] The world had changed. Now, individual gardens no longer served as private land where families could grow their own food; they were no longer "everyone's bread-maker," to use a phrase Migge and Taut liked. Now that there was no need to enclose gardens with fences all around them, green spaces could be shared by many families; they could be transformed into large, semiprivate parks to be used by all residents. The relation between the individual and the community could be redefined as well. Now that women worked outside the house, new arrangements—such as common laundries, dining halls, and kindergartens—were welcome. Taut was not too keen on the aesthetic ideals of the prewar garden cities either, which he described as "pretty" small cottages with pitched roofs and small windows:

> With all due respect to the idea of harmonizing with nature and the trees already growing on the site, ought not the actual idea of a communal dwell-

ing be guided by considerations of quite another order? Prettiness may very soon, perhaps even in less than a generation, come to be regarded as the greatest mistake from the practical point of view; people will soon get tired of small windows and the consequent lack of daylight in their rooms, once more houses have been built on modern lines.[49]

The metropolitan resident could, or rather ought to, enjoy the benefits of being in the country, but not at the expense of leaving the metropolis for a small settlement far away. The integration of nature into the city dweller's life provided a productive principle that Taut and his colleagues used in designing the most memorable site plans for metropolitan mass housing. In an article titled "Außenwohnraum" (outdoor living room), Taut reflected on the characters of a "living room on the outside," which would not only be a private garden, balcony, or loggia, but also a totally new type of outdoor city space.[50] In *Siedlung* Britz and *Siedlung* Freie Scholle (1925–32), Taut designed two of the most memorable of these outdoor living rooms, which functioned not only as the gardens for the apartments surrounding the open space, but also as green spaces open to the public (Wagner was the codesigner, and Leberecht Migge designed the landscaping in Britz).[51] While the horseshoe block in Britz was open to pedestrians (fig. 3.7), a quiet vehicular road circled around the one in Freie Scholle, connecting the row and double houses on one side to the multifamily blocks and neighborhood center on the other side (fig. 3.8). While semiprivate gardens and living spaces faced the green outdoor room in Britz (fig. 3.9), block entrances were placed in the common garden of Frei Scholle. Private gardens of the prewar garden cities were now turned into impressive public parks for the city, green piazzas for the modern residents who were welcomed in through carefully designed paths.

The actual site of GEHAG's *Siedlungen* in relation to the city was another factor in the transformation of the garden city ideals. This was most explicitly addressed in two *Siedlungen* in Prenzlauerberg, including *Siedlung* Carl Legien (1928–30) (figs. 3.10 and 3.11). Unlike prewar garden cities, and unlike some of GEHAG's own *Siedlungen* (such as Onkel Toms Hütte, which was far from the city center), these were close to the center of Berlin. Because of the projects' location in the city, Taut explained that he did not design single-family houses but only small apartments in multifamily building blocks:[52] "Front house, rear house, side panel, transverse building belong to the past [*Vorderhaus, Hinterhaus, Seitenflügel, Quergebäude gehören der Vergangenheit an*]. Now, everything is front house! The smallest house, just like the biggest, has a share in the light, air, and

3.7. Bruno Taut and Martin Wagner. *Siedlung* Britz, horseshoe block, Berlin, 1925–31. Photo: Arthur Köster, c. 1931.

3.8. Bruno Taut. *Siedlung* Freie Scholle, Berlin, 1925–32.

3.9. Bruno Taut and Martin Wagner. *Siedlung* Britz, horseshoe block, Berlin, 1925–31. Photograph published by Taut in Turkey.

the cultural facilities of the neighborhood."[53] The DEWOG circle considered *Siedlung* Carl Legien a metropolitan rental building, like those of the nineteenth century, but not at the expense of light, air, and nature, and not by creating inequality among citizens (at least as far as architecture could help foster social equality). GEHAG also built housing blocks that were inserted into the existing city fabric, such as the blocks in Neukölln (1927–28) (fig. 3.12), Prenzlauerberg (1927–28), and Weißensee (1928–30). In all, the urban residents' proximity to nature was ensured by the use of large and shared green areas, as well as by private outdoor living spaces— the balconies (fig. 3.13).

Unlike many of his colleagues who designed mass housing, Taut was particularly concerned with the quality and variation of these outdoor spaces. The *Zeilenbau* principle—which dictated perfectly parallel building blocks, usually aligned in the East-West direction and providing the same orientation and equal sunlight for each house—was slowly becoming a norm in the Weimar era. It was suggested as the most hygienic solution and the ultimate rationalization of site planning, employed in such well-known projects as *Siedlung* Westhausen in Frankfurt (see fig.

3.10. Bruno Taut. *Siedlung* Carl Legien, Berlin, 1928–30. Photo: Arthur Köster, c. 1930.

3.11. Bruno Taut. *Siedlung* Carl Legien, Berlin, 1928–30. Photo: Arthur Köster, c. 1930 (exhibited in İstanbul in Taut's retrospective exhibition).

3.12. Bruno Taut. *Siedlung* Neukölln, Berlin, 1927–28. Photograph published by Taut in Turkey.

3.13. Bruno Taut. *Siedlung* Onkel Toms Hütte, Berlin, 1926–31. Photo: Arthur Köster, c. 1931.

3.14. Bruno Taut and Martin Wagner. *Siedlung* Britz, street with row houses, Berlin, 1925–31. Photo: Arthur Köster, c. 1931.

3.28), by Ernst May and his colleagues, and Walter Gropius's *Siedlung* Dammerstock. Taut, on the other hand, criticized the architects who were fixated on the *Zeilenbau* principle.[54] The hygienic doctrine that dictated the orientation of all houses in the same direction created an awkward social situation according to him, because the living spaces of one family faced the private and service spaces of its neighbor. Taut alerted his readers to the drawbacks of housing types employed by other programs. The *Korridorhaus* (units placed around a corridor) and *Laubenganghaus* (units placed around a deck) were not appropriate for families with children, because they left little opportunity to place private rooms with windows on the sides of the corridors and decks.[55] Instead, Taut preferred to create lively environments in which the rooms of adjacent houses faced a common park, with playgrounds and common activities placed in this shared outdoor space; he carefully designed vistas in a Sitte-esque manner, with surprising twists and turns (fig. 3.14).[56] Many of the memorable outdoor living rooms (*Außenwohnraum*), including the horseshoe block in Britz, could be created only by abandoning the *Zeilenbau* principle.

During the Weimar period, the metropolis—which many had previously considered to be the cause of social and economic turmoil, a place of alienated, unkempt, and chaotic life—became an inspiring and productive topic for many more intellectuals and artists. To cite a few examples, Walter Benjamin wrote *A Berlin Chronicle* and *One-Way Street*, Siegfried Kracauer published essays on the streets and buildings of Berlin, and Harold Nicolson wrote "The Charm of Berlin."[57] In the architectural historian Manfredo Tafuri's eyes, the historical avant-gardes were distinctive precisely because they had managed to confront the metropolitan "dialectic of modernism"—the dialectic between order and chaos, between the cool rationality and efficiency of capitalist production and management systems on the one hand, and the constantly stimulated senses and the rapidly changing dynamism of the metropolis on the other hand.[58] The replacement of the prewar garden city ideals with metropolitan housing was part of this growing enthusiasm for the big city. Unlike the early garden city, the Weimar-era *Siedlung* was neither a village nor a full city, nor even a residential neighborhood with a small-town image. It was metropolitan housing. Unlike the previous generation of architects, those of the DEWOG circle confronted the complexity and chaos of the modern metropolis by defining their own task as providing solutions to the problems of the big city, rather than escaping to a new small town. The legacy of Howard continued to guide some of the site planning principles, but the architects of the GEHAG *Siedlungen* in the Weimar period increasingly defined the architectural expression of metropolitan living by designing housing at the inner periphery or, at times, in the center of the city, hoping to foster a strong sense of public life. They captured Howard's initial idea of uniting the city and the country, the city and nature, not by building new towns in the country, but by bringing the country into the city.

Gustav Oelsner (1879–1956)—an architect who was educated at Berlin-Charlottenburg Technical University (1896–1904), worked on city planning and housing in Breslau and Hamburg, and immigrated to Turkey in 1939—wrote:

İstanbul, 1931–1945

> *Siedlung*. We need *Siedlung*. Yes, but these should not be constructed as a collection of primitive villas, or totally formless new villages. On the contrary, we must build such *Siedlungen*, such residential estates [*ikamet bölgeleri*], so that they are the result of economic considerations; their means must be efficient.[59]

> In the modern residential districts [*semt*], namely in the *Siedlungen*, the biggest room of each house is the garden. . . . The nice old concept of the English "garden city" has now been replaced by *Siedlung*. . . .
> Now, I would like to give you one last piece of advice before I finish

my talk. Find a Turkish translation for this essential conception of city planning! [*Şehirciliğin şu asıl mevhumuna Türkçe karşılık bulunuz!*] In my country they call it *Siedlung*.⁶⁰

These words were by no means rare advice given by a German professor to Turkish architects. Taut gave a seminar on *Siedlung* at the Academy of Fine Arts, following several lectures in Japan on the German garden city and *Siedlung* projects, as well as a design of *Siedlung* Ikomaberg in Japan that advocated localizing translation.⁶¹ Wagner and Wilhelm Schütte wrote numerous articles that will be discussed below; Reuter, Ernst Egli, and Oelsner delivered lectures; Theodor Fischer's and Adolf Behne's articles were translated into Turkish.⁶² Well before the German exiles arrived in Turkey, *Arkitekt* had started publishing pieces on the German developments in collective housing, particularly the articles of Burhan Arif and Zeki Sayar.⁶³

The shift from the garden city type of houses to multifamily metropolitan housing did not take place in Turkey until at least a decade after World War II, and that shift can best be illustrated by the difference between the 1st Levent and 4th Levent housing in İstanbul, both designed by Kemal Ahmet Aru, a student of Taut and Oelsner. While the former (designed with Rebi Gorbon, 1947–52) followed the prewar garden city principles,⁶⁴ the 4th Levent housing (1956–60), in contrast, offered tall, multifamily blocks that stood separately on large open spaces (fig. 3.15).⁶⁵ Aru paid homage to Taut's *Siedlung* seminar in designing mixed-income neighborhoods with different family sizes and multiple residential types, although he translated the Weimar-era *Siedlung* ideals into postwar housing developments and adapted them to Turkey's own circumstances.⁶⁶ Planned for 1,800 people, the three-, five-, and ten-story blocks contained units with diverse types that ranged from 56 to 167 square meters, with almost a dozen different options. The blocks—with large, glazed surfaces; horizontal lines; and carved in or jutting out repetitive balconies—contributed to the making of a postwar international style in Turkey.⁶⁷

The application of Weimar metropolitan ideals to Turkish cities during the early republican era, however, was not without problems. Wagner, Berlin's former *Stadtbaurat*, who arrived in Turkey in 1935 as an expert of city planning for the İstanbul Municipality, directed his energy to large-scale city and regional planning, as well as to a detailed study of İstanbul's transportation systems.⁶⁸ As in Berlin, Wagner was interested in the "regeneration of existing cities," rather than in escaping to new towns. Although he acknowledged Howard's garden city as a forerunner of con-

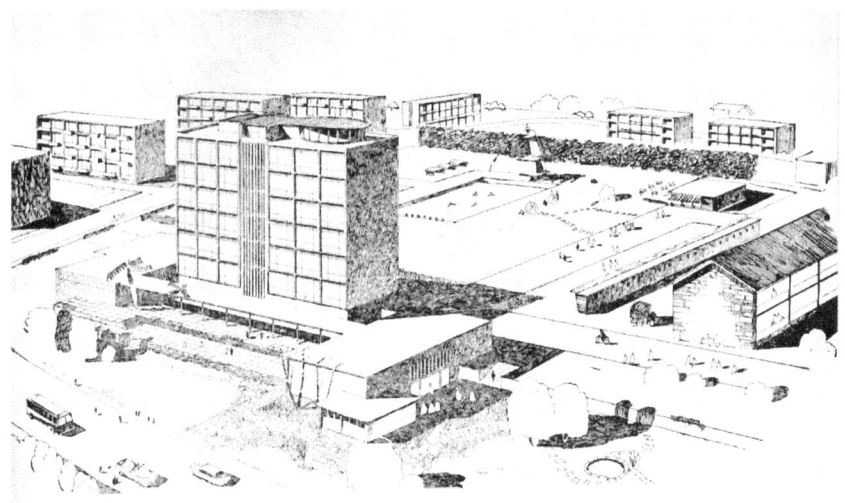

3.15. Kemal Ahmet Aru, 4th Levent housing, İstanbul, 1956–60.

temporary city planning, it was now time to "win over the big city exactly with the charms of the big city itself."[69] In İstanbul, Wagner focused his attention on the creation of an effective land policy, city planning regulations, and tax laws,[70] which followed his values in Berlin word for word, although he seemed to support taking Turkey's conditions into account before employing European methods.[71] When his fragmented articles are pieced together, one can conclude that Wagner proposed no less than restructuring İstanbul as a whole according to what he found to be the rational, hygienic, and civilized *Siedlung* model. İstanbul had two basic shortcomings, in Wagner's view, which could both be redeemed with German planning values.

First, Wagner was concerned about İstanbul's growing transportation problems due to the increasing distance people had to commute.[72] The broad differences in the urban densities were also alarming: neither the congested areas in the historical center, where residents lived in the manner of medieval guildsmen, nor the sparse areas along the Bosphorus for the wealthy were healthy or efficient.[73] Therefore, Wagner argued, İstanbul needed a total restructuring according to a "rational" master plan, which would relocate the city's population according to a new "*Siedlung* model."[74] This model would be "composed of houses with large gardens, which do not exceed two, three or four floors," so that İstanbul's "wonderful landscape and topography" would be preserved.[75] This was indeed the same argument Wagner had used to justify his theories in Germany.

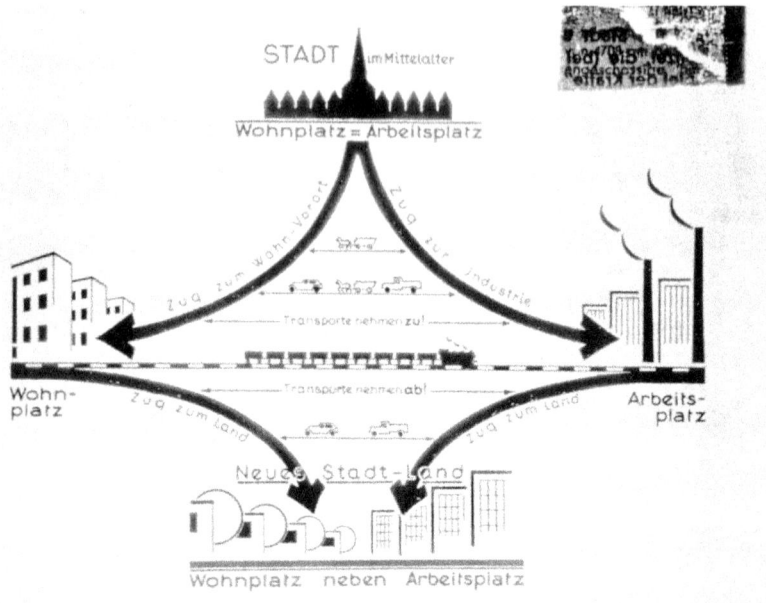

3.16. Martin Wagner. Scheme for new city land, 1932.

In his scheme published in *Das Neue Frankfurt*, he had distinguished between the city of the Middle Ages, that of the nineteenth century, and his own proposal with regard to the adjacency of professional and residential zones (fig. 3.16). In the Middle Ages, the working and living places were practically the same, a condition that changed with the Industrial Revolution when long commuting hours became the norm for the modern citizen. Wagner proposed instead "the new city land," based on the "*Siedlung* system," where the work and living space were neither synonymous as in the Middle Ages, nor separated, but situated adjacently.[76]

Second, Wagner disapproved of what was referred to as İstanbul's old Turkish houses:

> "The new life cannot be built unless the old one dies!" [*"Eskisi ölmedikçe yeni hayat kurulamaz!"*] This is really the truth. New forms can be created only when the old is destroyed during the struggle to make the city more useful [*daha iyi işe yaramak*]. There is no other way of repairing a city than by nibbling away at it [*içerden kemirmek*] to construct competent new cities of the highest economic measures, the highest civilization, and the highest culture [*en yüksek ekonomi, en yüksek sivilizasyon ve en yüksek kültür*].... Besides, this is quite natural! There is no growth, no rejuvenation

in nature that is not simultaneously at the expense of another. Therefore, it is essential eventually to admit that the big city as we know it must die and make space for a new life.⁷⁷

Wagner defended his demolition proposal on financial grounds. The experience of Europe, he said, demonstrated unequivocally that the financial capital necessary to restore the old was two or three times more than building the new, a claim that by now has been falsified.⁷⁸ He also criticized the use of private capital for land speculation as the main setback for İstanbul in constructing a collective housing program:

> An İstanbulite who admires the beauty and decency of the streets in German cities has to keep in mind that it is possible for him to feel the same admiration and respect [*hayranlık ve takdir*] for his own İstanbul. But, under one condition: İstanbul should benefit from the high land speculation [*toprak rantı*] for the sake of beautiful streets. . . . Instead, a few landowners are profiting from this speculation today without having to work.⁷⁹

For the sake of this economic and efficient new life based on the *Siedlung* model, Wagner thought it was justifiable to restructure the historical peninsula by "removing its narrow streets and providing large boulevards that would be convenient for all transportation needs," and subsequently by "demolishing small buildings that had thick walls, small rooms, and replacing them with modern buildings."⁸⁰ Concentrating on the Golden Horn area between the Galata Bridge and Eyüp as a case study, he proposed a municipality-supported rational rehabilitation plan to be executed by a semiautonomous financing organization in the form of a cooperative. Having eight years of experience in GEHAG, Wagner was well prepared to make a case for the efficiency of such a solution.

During his stay in Turkey, Wagner dutifully reported on his European experience, sincerely researched Turkish problems, and formulated extensive proposals. However, there was the paradox in Wagner's career in Turkey. He enthusiastically promoted a localizing translation, but his proposals were so radically foreign that they almost lost touch with the local common sense. Wagner advocated following European norms in İstanbul for their economic benefits, even if this led to the total destruction of the old city's wooden fabric, with the exception of a few landmarks from the Byzantine and Ottoman period.

Wagner was not alone in his proposals to restructure İstanbul as a whole by demolishing its wooden fabric. During the academic year of 1931–32, before his arrival, a group in Ernst Egli's design studio at the Academy of

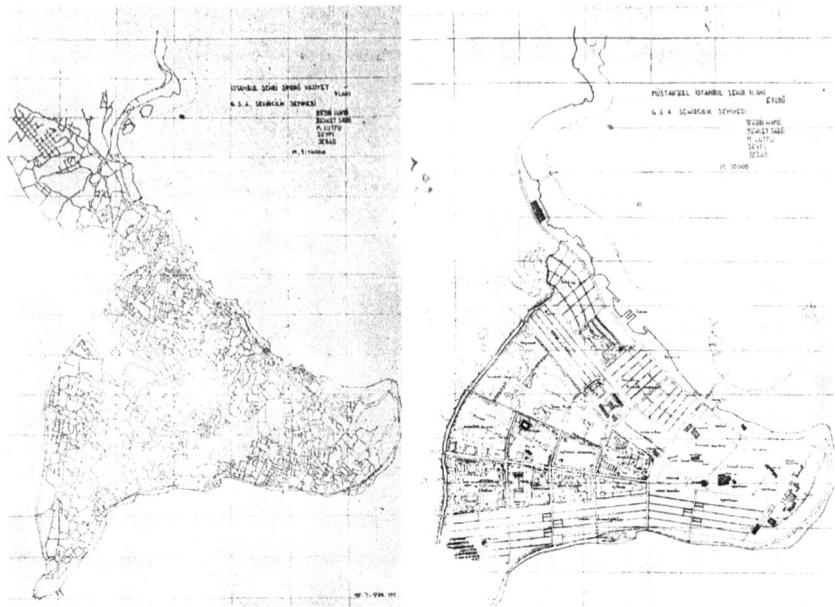

3.17. Work by students at Ernst Egli's Studio at the Academy. Rehabilitation of İstanbul's historical peninsula, 1931–32. Left: existing plan. Right: proposed plan.

Fine Arts had also proposed the total destruction of the wooden houses in İstanbul's historical peninsula (fig. 3.17). Preserving only monumental landmarks, such as the Topkapı Palace and Hagia Sophia, the project wiped out the urban fabric, replacing the existing streets with a grid plan, an allegedly rational and hygienic solution, a symbol of "civilization."[81] The south of the peninsula toward the Marmara Sea was reserved for the new residential neighborhoods, the northern periphery along the Golden Horn for industries and workers' housing. In between these zones, the peninsula was envisioned as a green space with parks, zoos, open-air auditoriums, and stadiums. Had this project been realized, nothing would have remained of the historical İstanbul except its highlights; the city's wooden houses in its narrow and curved streets would have been razed, not unlike the frequent fires that usually burned them down; the congested urban life rising out of these streets and their cultural reminiscences would have been abandoned; a new city would have been built on these ruins with modern buildings, spacious open areas, uncrowded parks, and straight streets that would have cut each other perpendicularly.

During his residency in Turkey, Ernst Egli swung between two poles of preservation. In a lecture in 1936, he called attention to the difference between the "modern cities in the European sense" that were composed of orthogonal road patterns and continuous axes on the one hand, and the Anatolian ones with "nonorthogonal," one-way streets and "irregular organic shapes" on the other: "If one imposes a grid plan or a radial plan on these Anatolian cities, nothing will be left behind from the old city.... We must find such a system that somehow integrates the existing irregular one-way streets into the main transportation network to be constructed."[82] Although in this lecture he expressed his hesitations over importing European city planning norms to Turkey, Egli supported demolition and displacement measures in his next talk in the same series. He suggested that the old and "bad" be torn down, new wide streets be opened, new residential blocks be constructed, and new residents in these blocks be prevented from "carrying their old living habits in their earlier dirty spaces" into the new modern settlements.[83]

Another German exile, Wilhelm Schütte, also commented on the rehabilitation of old İstanbul in relation to the *Siedlung* debate. Schütte (1900–1968) had studied building engineering in Darmstadt and then worked under Theodor Fischer at the Technical University of Munich, graduating in 1923. Beginning in 1925, Schütte worked in the housing program known as Das Neue Frankfurt with Ernst May (1886–1970), who was responsible for the housing, and Martin Elsaesser (1884–1957), who was responsible for public buildings.[84] Schütte contributed mainly to the school buildings. This was where he met and married Margarete Lihotzky, the designer of the legendary Frankfurt kitchen. The couple went to the Soviet Union with Ernst May from 1930 to 1934, continued to be involved in regional planning there until 1937, and ended up in Turkey in 1938 after a brief stay in Paris.[85] Schütte worked as a professor at the Academy of Fine Arts in İstanbul. In addition to his articles on housing, he also published on postearthquake reconstruction in Turkey, architectural education, and Theodor Fischer, Adolf Loos, and Karl Friedrich Schinkel.[86]

In "Sefalet Mahalleleri" (Miserable neighborhoods), Schütte implied a comparison between İstanbul's anonymous fabric and Germany's *Mietskasernen*: "'Atrium Houses' . . . continue to exist with all their charm especially in countries under the influence of Islamic culture. However, narrow houses that face the narrowest streets cannot be provided with the necessary amount of light and air according to our contemporary approaches to hygiene [*bugünkü sıhhi görüşlerimiz*]."[87] The wooden houses that the local intellectuals and artists melancholically appreciated as the most valuable cultural heritage under the threat of oblivion appeared to Schütte as dirty slums where evil originated: "These are antisocial. Masses of murderers come from here [*Cani sürüleri bunlar arasından çıkmaktadır*]. With their choked and pinched [*kargacık burgacık*] houses and courtyards, uncontrolled entrances, and undefined areas, these are the spaces where the big city's dark life finds ambush."[88]

Maintaining a common architectural determinist conviction about direct links between human character and building form, and subsequently the power of the modernizing architect's clean hand to remove the dirt, Schütte's proposal was to remove these buildings. More cautious than Wagner in his demolition suggestions for İstanbul's historical peninsula, Schütte elaborated on several degrees of rehabilitation that paid more attention to details and that varied from complete to fragmentary demolition, rather than unconditional destruction.[89] The population would eventually be relocated in new, healthy, and functional settlements based on the *Siedlung* model. "The contemporary building regulations have to be formulated so that they prevent the emergence of miserable neighborhoods in the future," he wrote. "The new buildings should be spaced with such adequate distance, the courtyards and gardens should be filled with so much air that they will permanently prevent the emergence of the conditions that arose in European cities at the end of the nineteenth century."[90] Illustrating the transformation from *Mietskasernen* to *Zeilenbau* blocks (translated *sıra sıra yapı tarzı*) (fig. 3.18), he explained that big metropolitan green areas now satisfied the old garden city ideal; hygienic building blocks replaced the lifestyle promoted in private houses with gardens.[91]

The ideas of Wagner, Schütte, Oelsner, and, to a large extent, Egli were predicated on a conviction about the smooth translatability of European norms in Turkey: the argument must have been that modernism was a universally applicable ideal that would sooner or later penetrate the whole world. Their localizing suggestions remained for the most part on the level of minimal transformations. The *Siedlungen* of Weimar Germany, among others, inspired many of the most important housing projects in Turkey after the 1950s, but they did not serve as commensurable models for the rehabilitation of the historical city sections during this period. While İstanbul's writers and architects were trying to persuade the officials of the worth of the old wooden houses, as discussed in chapter 2, these German exiles or immigrants were urging that the houses be razed in order to create a tabula rasa for the modern city. Demolition, radical or cautious, total or fragmented, ruled their proposals. In the blunt words of Oelsner: "Here is our manifesto: The old will be preserved only on the condition that it represents high culture! . . . We will build new and exemplary neighborhoods [*mahalle*], construct *Siedlungen* surrounded by green areas, and

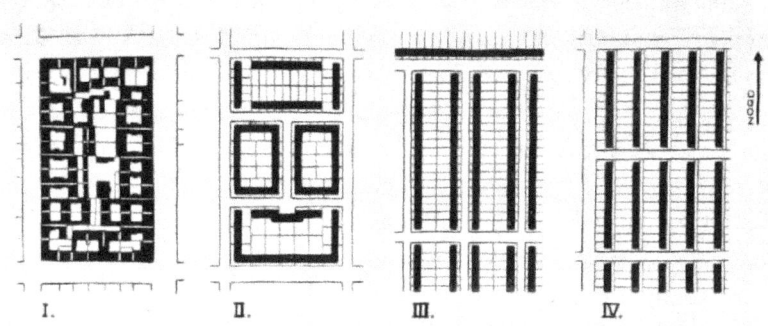

3.18. Wilhelm Schütte. From *Mietskasernen* to *Zeilenbau*.

adorned with gardens. In that way, the future generations will be unconditionally grateful to us [*medyumu şükran olacak*]."[92]

Many local architects did not easily surrender to these demolition proposals. Sedad Eldem had voiced his reservations about Berlin's preservation norms in 1931, and he continued to be a vocal opponent of the demolition of the wooden urban fabric in Turkey.[93] Although the two need not have been mutually exclusive, the *Siedlung* model and old Turkish houses were constructed as contrasting urban structures in the minds of many architects. Yet this was not necessarily an opposition between local and foreign architects. The German exiles Bruno Taut and Margarete Schütte-Lihotzky did not comment substantially on preservation, but they were more appreciative of the city's anonymous fabric (see below). Moreover, it was the Turkish students in Egli's studio who suggested the most radical demolition project for İstanbul's historical peninsula.

The fixation on German *Siedlung* principles, such as large green areas between parallel residential blocks and a uniform orientation for each dwelling, had stark consequences for the cultural significance of İstanbul's historical remnants. This was because of the premise of an unproblematic commensurability between the two distinct places — that is, the ideology of absolute and smooth translatability. There was no place for melancholy in modern times, according to the German architects discussed in this section; no place for the melancholy that motivated İstanbul's writers and artists in cherishing the city's ruins as their inspiration. Translation practices usually liberate a city from its previously restricted norms; but they can instead, as in this case, try to erase all that makes a city, and replace it with another set of standards whose superiority is hardly anything but a European myth.

Ankara,
1935–1945

The Weimar *Siedlung* debate nonetheless made a major contribution to the birth of city planning as a modern discipline in Turkey. Perhaps no German exile was as enthusiastic, committed, and productive as Ernst Reuter (1889–1953) in the establishment of a strong city planning department and in the structuring of modern municipalities.[94] After leaving Turkey, Reuter would become the first mayor of postwar West Berlin, where he is now commemorated with a public square. Before his arrival in Turkey, he had studied history, geography, and German at the Universities of Marburg, Munich, and Münster. He had been a member of the Social Democratic Party since 1912 and was secretary of the German Communist Party in 1919–21. He worked as a member of Berlin's town administration from 1926 to 1931 and served as the mayor of Magdeburg from 1931 to 1933. Reuter had spent 1916–18 in Russia as a prisoner of war and was put in a Nazi concentration camp in 1933, from where he escaped and went to Turkey via Holland and London in 1935. In Ankara he was appointed as an expert in the Ministry of Finance.[95] In the academic year of 1936–37, Martin Wagner gave three influential lectures on city planning at the School of Political Sciences (*Mülkiye*) in Ankara, which prompted the dean to establish a department of city planning. On Wagner's recommendation, Reuter was appointed as the department chair.[96] Immediately learning Turkish, he soon held his classes in this language.[97] During his stay in Turkey—he left in 1946—Reuter accumulated a long list of publications and lectures, through which he shaped the theories of collective housing in Turkey. His work acted as a bridge between architects, political scientists, and government officials, since he published for a multidisciplinary audience. His influence extended well beyond İstanbul and Ankara and reached even small Anatolian towns.

Reuter's book *Komün Bilgisi: Şehirciliğe Giriş* (Knowledge of communes: introduction to city planning)[98] was published after a series of lectures under the title *komün bilgisi* (1935–36) that was organized by another German exile, the economist Fritz Neumark, at İstanbul University.[99] The speakers in this series informed their audience about the recent Western developments in the field and designated hygiene, orientation in relation to the sun, proper ventilation, efficiency, sanitation, and infrastructure as modern residential principles to be followed in Turkey.[100] Reuter explained that he proposed the concept *Kommunalwissenschaft* instead of the French word *urbanisme* in order to deemphasize the formal aspects in city planning, and to stress instead financial, legislative, and organizational knowledge.[101] The urban designer as the giver of form to streets and squares had to be replaced by an institution that could act on not only formal but also administrative, technical, financial, and legal policy.[102]

Reuter did not consider city planning a matter of scale, but one of principle. Smaller settlements, towns, even villages should not have been deprived of it just because they were not cities. On the contrary, city planning—which he defined as the pursuit of an organized, harmonious, clean, and green settlement—was relevant for any scale.[103] Reuter made a case for city planning, thus seen almost as a synonym of modernization, as the indispensable discipline for the new Turkish Republic. Collective housing, which he exemplified with Berlin's *Siedlungen* Britz and Siemensstadt, was at the center of his concerns—a modern invention that he justifiably considered integral to urban structure and made possible by city planning. Like many of his colleagues, Reuter criticized the unplanned and unhealthy growth of cities in the nineteenth century; explained the need to formulate a new strategy for the production of housing; referred to Howard's garden city as the model that motivated discussions; emphasized the need for a master plan for the development of modern cities; criticized land speculation; and praised open spaces and parks between housing blocks.[104]

Reuter also headlined the absolute necessity of state support for the production of collective housing, and the removal of private property owners from the equation.[105] In their battle against land speculation, he proposed that the municipalities employ socialist precautions including property tax laws, extended expropriation rights, government control over building materials, and, most important, the authority to purchase cheap land for housing production. He often justified his proposals by asserting that "all European municipalities gradually took this road," especially Berlin and Magdeburg, where he had worked.[106] What Turkey needed was a "central organization that made use of the experience and practice of collective housing in other countries."[107]

Such an organization was nothing but the modern municipality with an ample budget and power. Apart from his teaching, Reuter also devoted extensive energy to institutionalizing municipalities for Turkish cities, regardless of their size. He advised the launching and editorial policies of *Belediyeler Dergisi* (Journal of municipalities)[108] and published many articles in it.[109] His contributions to other journals often raised the importance of municipalities for land settlements of any size.[110] Not satisfied with the fraction reserved for local municipalities within the government's overall budget, especially with the fact that this was only one fifth of the German ratio,[111] he proposed to raise this ratio and to employ the German decentralization model (spreading out the industrial and cultural resources across the country, as opposed to concentrating them in a couple of main cities). Reuter himself took posts in small towns all across Turkey: he was a jury member in the competition for the master plan of Ödemiş (1944); he prepared a development report for Yozgat with Wilhelm Schütte (1944); and he delivered lectures for educating the lieutenants of small settlements after 1941 (*Kaymakamlık Kursu* [courses for lieutenants]).

The evolution of municipalities in Turkey is not our subject, yet one could hardly miss the issues of translation operating in Reuter's analogy between the socialist European municipalities and the Ottoman system of *waqf*.[112] Reuter based his analogy on the two institutions' comparable responsibility to regulate public services and to reserve financial capital for the public good. *Waqf* was the act of unconditionally donating the benefit of one's durable property for the sake of the Muslim poor. During the Ottoman times, many mosques, schools, *hans* (temporary accommodating places), fountains, aqueducts, streets, and hospitals were built with the funds obtained through *waqf*. In Reuter's words, "the main difference between the European and Islamic countries is not that there are no *waqfs* in Europe, but that the European *waqfs* have been founded on different legal principles."[113] Despite this dissimilarity, the responsibilities of the European socialist municipalities, such as the ones in Germany where Reuter drew most of his examples from, were very similar to the Ottoman *waqfs*. In his writing, Reuter reviewed the history of German municipalities, frequently using the term *waqf*, translating the concept into his own conceptualization of the Weimar experience. In a way, Reuter designated the Ottoman *waqf* system as a socialist political structure *avant la lettre*. This must have given him sufficient confidence to advocate socialist strategies in the School of Political Sciences, where his long-lasting impact helped construct a strong foundation for social democratic ideals in Turkey. When he was addressing architects, Reuter argued strongly that it was the municipality's responsibility to participate in the production of social housing by buying cheap land and building on it.[114] The tax revenues had to be allocated to housing for the segments of the population that could not rely on private enterprises. The analogy between the Ottoman *waqf* system and the German municipalities during the Weimar period did indeed help Reuter in translating the details of an administrative system from his home country to the land of his exile. In his mind, Turkish society was already attuned to the social ideals of Weimar Germany. In the contemporary Turkish legal system, the municipalities claimed land whose owner could not be determined, and this, in his mind, could have provided a perfect opportunity for producing affordable housing.[115] He must have assumed that there would be extensive commitment to the production of social housing in Turkey.

However, Reuter was utterly mistaken in this prediction. Despite the seeming support for the ideals of social housing, and despite the cooperative housing produced for upper-middle-income families and governmental officials in Ankara, the state failed to produce large quantities of lower-middle-income housing, a surprising result given that many of the masterminds of European social housing were exiled in Turkey and educating the Turkish architects. Neither German nor Turkish architects seem to have had the power to persuade the subsequent governments to increase the production of housing for the lower middle class, and after the 1950s the lack of an effective housing program was exposed when illegal settlements and developer apartments became the two paradigmatic residential types in Turkish cities. In 1946, the editor of *Arkitekt*, Zeki Sayar, who became a leading critic of these housing practices, dissected the official policy apart in a two-part essay titled "*Mesken Davası*" (Dwelling battle). The construction of a few fancy cooperative neighborhoods demonstrated nothing more than the evasion of the actual housing problem.[116]

SIEDLUNG AND THE GENERIC RATIONAL DWELLING

The modern invention of collective housing was caught in a quandary of modernism. On the one hand, the industrial age standardized the modern dwelling, made it identical and repeatable, and used architectural elements that were industrially reproducible; on the other hand, the Enlightenment ideal cherished the idea of an individual who was liberated from any transcendent power and thus in full control of his or her own life, an individual who could make his or her own decisions and shape his or her own future. Perhaps the hardest quandary that modern collective housing presented to some architects was how to reconcile the standardizing impact of industrialization that made mass housing possible in the first place with the modern ethics that put the free individual on a pedestal. This quandary suggests itself when one briefly reflects on the dual meaning of the word *rational*—a word that was synonymous with efficiency, economy, and reproducibility when used in relation to dwelling and that, in other contexts, connoted the individual who could think on his or her own behalf, who did not surrender to any source but his or her own mind, who "dared to know," as Immanuel Kant once put it.[117] This quandary may

Berlin, 1924–1933

never have been resolved in the case of *Siedlungen*; nonetheless, the architects' struggles to reconcile the rationality of mass production and of the individual mind bear witness to the challenges it presented.

Even in the first decade of the twentieth century, Karl Scheffler had advocated the uniformity of the metropolis. As more and more city inhabitants would move into randomly chosen but identical apartments, as more and more identical floor plans would result in identical façades, the whole street would become a "coherent façade," the entire urban district and eventually the entire metropolis would "stand in architectural harmony" and "noble uniformity."[118] Scheffler's ideas were not idiosyncratic in Berlin's circles. Walter Curt Behrendt, Otto March, and the Viennese architect Otto Wagner commented on the future uniformity of the metropolis, an idea that influenced many architects in the competition for the greater Berlin master plan, including Hermann Jansen.[119]

The industrial production of housing not only confirmed but also intensified this prediction. In his essay "The Work of Art in the Age of Mechanical Reproduction," Walter Benjamin famously identified mechanical reproducibility as the main epochal change that differentiated modern artworks from earlier ones. Art could now be reproduced and shared by the masses rather than just a privileged few, but at the expense of its originality, its uniqueness and authenticity—in other words, its aura.[120] In the case of architecture, nowhere was this transformation in modern reproduction techniques more visible than the design of a *Siedlung*. Now, the collective production of hundreds, sometimes thousands, of housing units made it possible for architects to design dwellings for the masses, rather than only a small number of bourgeois clients. *Siedlung* Britz (in its Weimar phase) contained 1,000 housing units; *Siedlung* Onkel Toms Hütte, 1,271; and *Siedlung* Carl Legien, 1,145. In the *Siedlungen* designed according to the *Zeilenbau* principle, all housing units were identical; they faced the same direction and had equal exposure to sun and wind as if they had been mechanically reproduced in a factory. As the architectural historian Manfredo Tafuri theorized, such a *Siedlung* concept in its highest order would have transformed the relation between the architectonic object and urban organization. The aura of a single house with its particular and unique design in its own property would have been replaced by a total urban structure conceived of as repetitive housing units.[121]

Collective housing, whether it was in a garden city or a Weimar-era *Siedlung*, instigated the idea of generic design for unspecified dwellers. While designing the units, architects did not communicate directly with the thousand or so families expected to live in the settlement. To be financially viable, collective housing had to benefit from the potentials of industrialization and mass production, making serial building the focus of debates. In Wagner's words: "From our experience in the industrial production of schools, cars, engines, and so on, we know that an effective reduction of the production cost can be achieved only through serial building (*Serienbau*)."[122]

In this context, the task of the architect was transformed into designing carefully the most efficient, economic, functional, and reproducible housing unit, the most "rational dwelling" — to use the term of its proponents — which would then be repeated all over the *Siedlung*. Rationalization penetrated into the design process on a number of levels, including repetition in site plans, use of minimal floor plans, standardization of building parts, and mass production of materials. As Taut described in his memoirs, the ground plans of dwellings that he and his colleagues produced for GEHAG were copied by other organizations all over Berlin, whether the overall design of the *Siedlung* belonged to them or not.[123] At times, *Wohnungswirtschaft* published unit designs without necessarily placing them in an overall *Siedlung*. Architect-designed Berlin dwellings were becoming identical and generic; housing units were now considered consumer goods just like the industrial objects produced in sheer numbers under the logic of mass production.

Productively challenged by the quandary of modernism between industrialized production and individualist values, between standardization and uniqueness, between mass and aura, Taut was doubtful of the uniformity of the metropolis. It is not too improbable that his reluctance to unconditionally accept the *Zeilenbau* principle and, consequently, his alternative site plans in the *Siedlungen* were attempts to recover aura in the age of mechanical reproduction. In his designs for common urban spaces and parks, Taut searched for a unique and memorable dimension, which was nevertheless conditioned by the new reproduction methods. The horseshoe block in *Siedlung* Britz takes its architectural power from its unrepeatable character, even though the dwellings that make up the whole are repetitive. Any attempt to repeat the horseshoe block would render the repetition a copy and reaffirm its originality. In his attempts to recover individuality in mass production, Taut significantly differed from his colleagues Ludwig Hilberseimer and Hannes Meyer, whose commitment to socialism and the "posthumanist subject" — to use Michael Hays's term — made such concerns irrelevant.[124]

This quandary of modernism resulted in Taut's specific theory of "type" in the age of industrial production, which he developed in two books and a series of articles written after 1924. The "beauty" of this new architectural expression depended on the "clear logic" of mass production that would compose environments from a limited number of repeating elements, yet standardization did not have to mean a lack of variety.[125] Just as he rejected the view that the *Zeilenbau* principle was the only true form of hygienic site planning, Taut sought difference in the design of individual houses: "Serial building does not mean boredom [*Langeweile*] at all, residential streets with similar types of houses do not have to be dull passage ways.... Out of variations and numerous different solutions, a new artistic tradition must grow, which will lead to a truly modern formal convention."[126] In order to distinguish individual houses in masses of row housing, Taut painted each with a different color and meticulously worked on different color schemes for window frames and doors, establishing the act of painting as the individual touch on the standardized building production. Unlike Wagner, who focused on the design of the perfect model to be reproduced in sheer numbers, Taut used the word *type* (*Typ*) for the study of dwelling units. Type was "not a fixed and finished single form [*Einzelform*]," but "the expression of a certain relationship or a manner" of plan organization.[127] Adamantly rejecting the study of types as some sort of "mathematical problem" that could be easily produced in bulk at the factory,[128] Taut emphasized the role of the artist-architect, who would finalize abstract ideas in concrete designs for each specific condition.

Ein Wohnhaus—a book of 116 pages, 104 photographs, and 72 drawings—patiently explained and illustrated the features of Taut's own house in Dahlewitz, including the garden (designed by Leberecht Migge);[129] the functionalist organization of the plan; the kitchen (fig. 3.19); the character of each room; the choice of every single color; the use of every single piece of furniture; the placement of windows, large glass surfaces, and the balcony specifically designed to watch the view and the setting sun; the details of lighting; the dining table; the telephone; the paper-rolling machine on the work table; the storage area for potatoes; the closet; the bathroom; the washing machine; the ironing table; the heating and sewage system; the ventilation; and the indispensable flat roof. Taut insisted that he displayed this house in such meticulous detail not because it was a unique, precious, or unrepeatable example, but because it could be abstracted as a type, from the study of which one could infer principles of a new architecture based on rationalization and industrialization.[130] Similarly, units in a *Siedlung* depended on the unique design of an architect, who would build a new architecture culture through the study of "countless and nameless

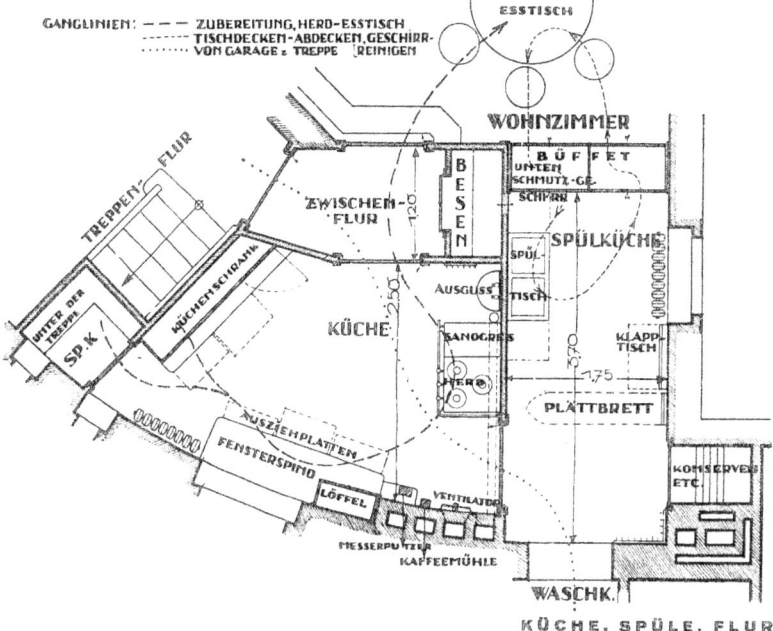

3.19. Bruno Taut. Own house at Dahlewitz, kitchen, 1926–27.

types [*zahl- und namenlosen Typen*]."[131] The plan of units needed to be adjusted in relation to their placement on the site, or their access from the public and semipublic spaces (street, deck, corridor, garden, courtyard, or outdoor living space) (fig. 3.20).

The examples of GEHAG dwellings illustrated in *Wohnungswirtschaft* varied from forty-eight to sixty-five square meters and from one and a half to three rooms (two full and two half rooms [*Kammer*]), slightly bigger than the Frankfurt program. This provided for flexible use of each room, either as a bedroom and living room (see fig. 3.22). The units usually had a separate kitchen rather than a *Wohnküche* (living kitchen), as had usually been the case in the prewar German garden cities. All of them, without exception, had a balcony or a loggia overlooking the common green area of the *Siedlung*, even though there was no fixed rule for the placement of this private open space within the inner organization of the unit's plan. Taut provided a separate entrance and staircase for every two apartments per floor, rather than connecting units with a horizontal circulation route such as a corridor or deck. Even though this increased the number, and subsequently the cost, of stairs, it allowed him to place living spaces on both sides of a housing unit. The DEWOG circle paid particular

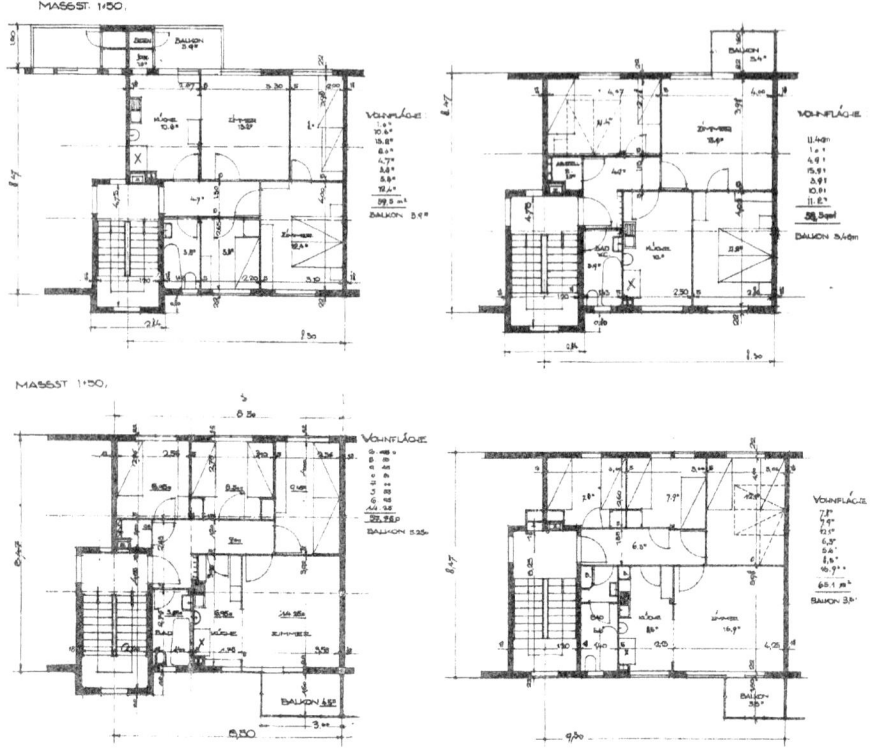

3.20. Bruno Taut. Variations of "type."

attention to the flexible use of each room based on each family's choices within the limits of their small dwellings, which went well beyond using flexible furniture like folding beds and tabletops. For instance, Jakobus Goettel studied possible ways of using and furnishing GEHAG dwellings (fig. 3.21), which could accommodate individual perspectives and different lifestyles.[132]

Taut's *Die Neue Wohnung: Die Frau als Schöpferin* (The new house: woman as creator) was one of the most engaging texts of the period to lay down the principles of a modern dwelling.[133] The book made the following unambiguous declarations: Women were the designers of the modern house. There was no longer any place for those who confused a house with an antiquity museum, those who still longed to live in the artistic (*künstlerische*), homely (*traut*), and sweet (*hübsch*) rooms of the nineteenth century, jammed with ornaments, objects, furniture, conventional paintings on figurative wallpapers, obsolete symbols, and memories.[134] These extravagances would have to be filtered out for the sake of

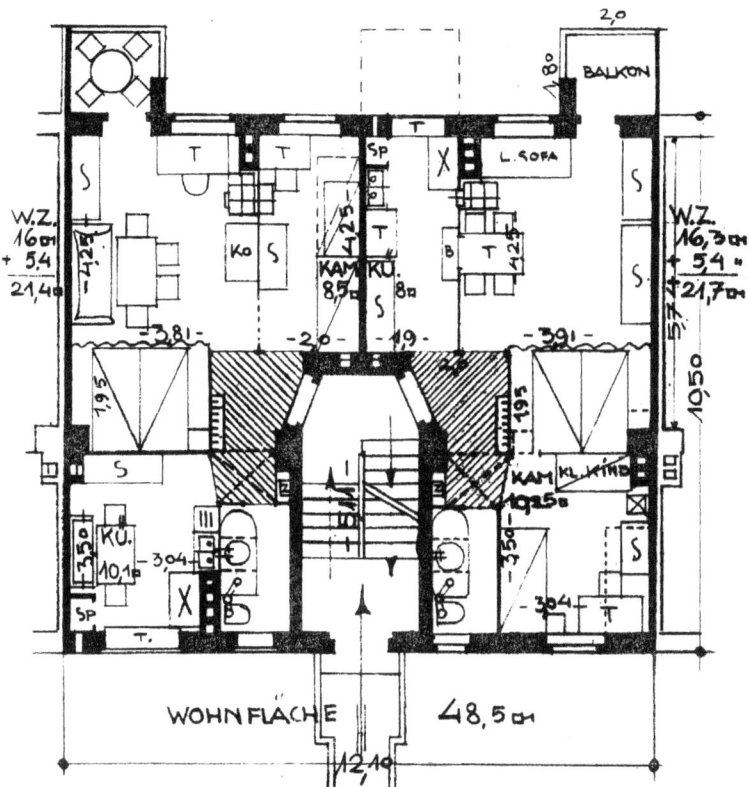

3.21. Jakobus Goettel. Variation for furnishing a housing unit, 1930.

functional, economic, efficient, practical, and plain houses. If the goal was the abandonment of the superfluous, who else but women could distinguish necessity from excess? Women would eliminate the aging curtains, dusty carpets, unused household goods, and traditional decorations. The revolutionary cry to "end her slavery"[135] would challenge anyone who regarded her house as a junkshop (*Trödelladen*), warehouse (*Speicher*), or a museum.[136] Taut continued that men's duty, accordingly, was to quit their old conformist habits and make the transition to this new residential culture.[137] The place of Taut's book in the evolution of feminism in architecture requires more discussion here, partly because he maintained the conventional gendered designation of the house as women's sphere — but in his mind, at least, this modernization process had broader social implications. It was easy to clean the modern dwelling, which would eventually eliminate the concept of having servants and strip the modern families of their bourgeois tendencies in favor of plain domestic spaces (fig. 3.22).[138]

3.22. Bruno Taut. Interior of a unit in *Siedlung* Onkel Toms Hütte, Berlin, 1926–31. Photo: Arthur Köster, c. 1931.

The revolution started in the kitchen (fig. 3.23), from where it expanded to the whole dwelling, building block, and *Siedlung*. To make a claim for the efficiency and functionality of his designs, Taut contrasted the older floor plans with his own schemes by using circulation diagrams that were inspired from the study of rational kitchens, the Taylorist principles of Christine Frederick, and most notably the Frankfurt kitchen designed by Schütte-Lihotzky, who also took refuge in Turkey after the National Socialist takeover of Germany (see fig. 3.19).[139]

Turkey, 1931–1945

Taut transformed his practice in Turkey to adapt to new conditions (chapter 5). Nonetheless, the rational dwelling that he contributed had a fragmented though widespread impact in Turkey. Even in the first issue of *Mimar* (renamed *Arkitekt* after 1935), the editor Zeki [Sayar] promoted standardization as the paradigm of the new era:

> The industrial life has disseminated to the whole world like a flowing river, and it has now reached every sphere. . . . The essential aspect of this new spirit and muse [*ilham*] is "serial" production [*seri inşaat*] and "standardization." . . . In the "standardized" construction, the plans are idealized. They have a rational and general form [*mantıki ve umumi şekil*], whose

3.23. Bruno Taut. Kitchen of a unit in *Siedlung* Britz, Berlin, 1925–31. Photo: Arthur Köster, c. 1931.

labor intensity [*işçilik miktarı*] has been minimized. . . . Just like an automobile factory that produces thousands of the same part, a framing factory produces numerous doors and windows of the same type."[140]

Although the Turkish house and the cubic house stood out as the two main models among architects in Turkey at this time, there was also a desire for a rational house, which would apply the effects of industrialization to the modern dwelling. Many architects considered social housing as the main locus of modernization. In Behçet Ünsal's words, "the goal of our times is to match the rational and economic methods used for dwellings with an aesthetic expression. In its most general sense, the new architecture is characterized as 'people's architecture' [*Halk mimarlığı*]. The old architecture started with a monument, a palace, a fortress. . . . The focus of new architecture is the 'house.'"[141] During the early republican period, Burhan Arif, Egli, and Schütte delivered lectures and published articles on the design of a standardized, efficient, repeatable, affordable, and minimal dwelling.[142] Taut gave a seminar on *Siedlung* at the İstanbul Academy of Fine Arts in 1936.[143] In his studio, the students designed four hundred units for a governmental housing project in Ankara whose actual

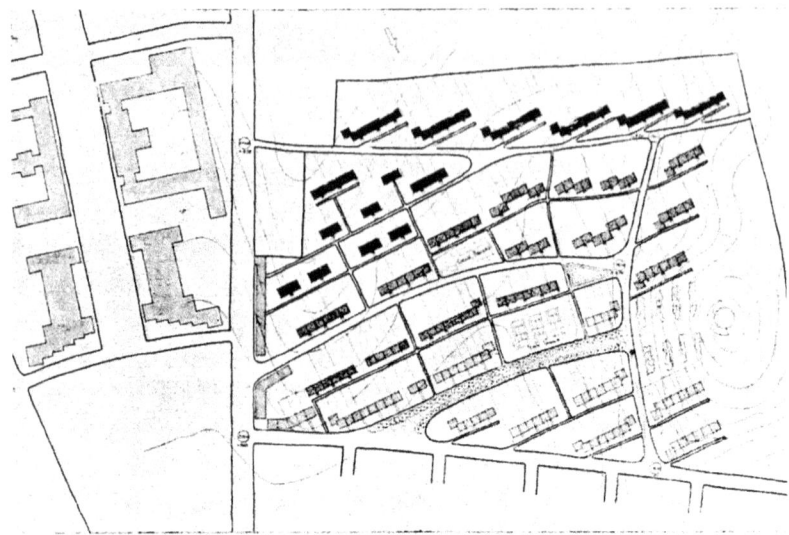

3.24. Student project for a *Siedlung* in Ankara in Bruno Taut's studio at the Academy of Fine Arts. Site plan of Kemal Ahmet Aru, 1937.

commission would eventually be handed over to Paul Bonatz a decade later. The students followed familiar norms of *Siedlung* design, including large, public green spaces; private balconies; a mixture of row houses and multifamily blocks with different circulation patterns, including some blocks with multiple entrances and cores and others with decks; the southern exposure of living rooms; multiple dwelling types with ample variations (Taut asked students to provide nine different types, with one and a half, two, and three rooms); the standardization of building materials; and modern kitchens, bathrooms, and heating systems. The students were also expected to calculate the cost of their projects and determine the monthly rents in order to make a case for affordability (fig. 3.24).

The most visible impact of the idea of industrial housing in Turkey may not have been the mass housing projects, only a couple of which were realized before the 1950s, but the principle of rationalization itself. Projects abound that were designed to be functional, efficient, small, and rational even in the context of wealthier family homes. Abidin Mortaş proposed an "affordable and hygienic small dwelling" (1931) that was designed for a family with two children, divided into served and service zones by a space that he called a *sofa*—an indication of translation. Mortaş emphasized the flexible boundaries between the living and dining spaces, the lack of ornamentation, and the large windows in the living spaces.[144] Nine months later, he produced a typological study of "affordable small houses," differentiated in relation to the placement of the *sofa* (fig. 3.25).[145] The same year, Sedad Eldem published a project on minimalist dwellings for row housing, which he offered as an alternative to traditional İstanbul apartments.[146] Legitimizing his case with English and German examples, Eldem argued that the modern citizen did not need to be imprisoned in apartments, just because they were cheaper than houses. Minimal and affordable, but also individual, houses could well have been produced as collective ensembles. Bekir Ihsan's "Projects for Minimal Houses" (1933) for the employees of the State's Railroad Department stand out as other important examples.[147] Kemal Ahmet Aru wrote an article on the calculation of minimal housing units that would be appropriate for Turkish lifestyles.[148] Ünsal elaborated on the idea of minimal housing adjusted to the "modern Turkish character" in two projects that were organized around a "spacious and breezy [space] just like the large *sofas* of the [traditional] Turkish houses." Nevertheless, Ünsal emphasized that the rest of the plans were designed so that there would be "no loss of space."[149] The abandonment of unnecessary space that justifiably guided the functionalist designs of minimalist and affordable housing also infiltrated wealthier homes. Abdullah Ziya Kozanoğlu, who designed a double house in Adana (1932), proudly explained how he economized on the cost of the stairs by designing a vertical circulation core that served both of the dwellings but was squeezed into an area necessary for one staircase only (fig. 3.26).[150] The Himayei Etfal Community organized an architectural competition for a multifamily apartment block in Ankara (1934), where all entries unanimously repeated the same principle — "to gain maximum efficiency with minimum cost" — and the jury declared it had selected the project by Nizamettin Hüsnü for achieving the best results according to exactly this criterion.[151]

The struggle for individual difference in generic housing in Germany resonated in Turkey as the search for cultural difference, putting the universality of the rational into question. While many architects sought to create industrial, functional, and efficient houses, they simultaneously looked for minimalist existence in the traditions found in Turkey. These examples, most of which remained on paper, demonstrate the aspiration for minimal, standardized, and industrial housing, but they also expose the lack of administrative support for their implementation, not to mention the relative lack of industrialized production itself.

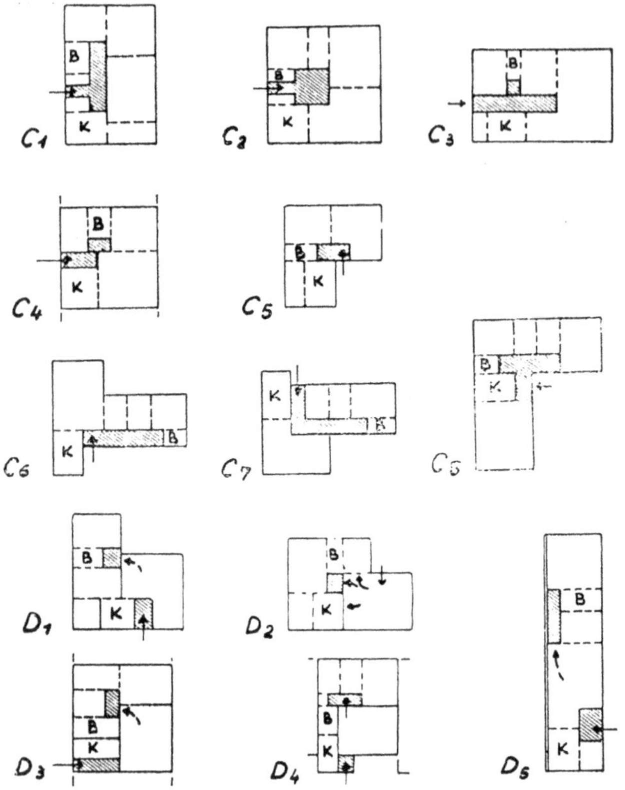

3.25. Abidin Mortaş. Typological study of small houses, 1931.

3.26. Abdullah Ziya [Kozanoğlu]. Double house in Adana, 1932.

No architect deserves more credit than Margarete Schütte-Lihotzky (1897–2000) for the revolution that started in the kitchen of the Weimar *Siedlung*.[152] The idea of a minimal, efficient, machine-like kitchen not only reshaped German dwellings during the Weimar period, but it also reentered European households in the Cold War era (usually called the American or Swedish kitchen) without paying due acknowledgment to her.[153] Schütte-Lihotzky was educated as the first woman architect in the Viennese *Kunstgewerbeschule* (School of Arts and Crafts), during 1915–20. After a brief stay in Holland, she became an active figure in Viennese social housing, working with Adolf Loos and Ernst Egli. In 1926, she moved to Frankfurt to participate in Das Neue Frankfurt, the extensive social housing program under the direction of May and Elsaesser, described above. There she gained her reputation as the designer of the Frankfurt kitchen and married Wilhelm Schütte. In 1930, the architect couple moved from Frankfurt to the Soviet Union with May's group of seventeen architects to embark on more social housing projects. Following seven years of practice in the Soviet Union with May's circle (May left in 1933) and a brief stay in Paris, the couple fled to Turkey (accepting an invitation from Taut) after the National Socialist regime in Germany came to power and made its impact felt in Schütte-Lihotzky's homeland, Austria.

Frankfurt, 1926–1930

Schütte-Lihotzky contributed her ideas in journals edited by May from 1921 onward, starting with her articles in *Schlesisches Heim* and continuing with the ones in *Das Neue Frankfurt*.[154] The Frankfurt housing program also sought to provide rationally designed, efficient, and functional housing for the working and middle-income groups. May had been trained according to the garden city principles by Barry Parker and Raymond Unwin, but he later participated in the transformation of the *Siedlung* conception from an environment with private houses to one with urban blocks. The Frankfurt housing program differed from Berlin's in a number of ways. May's *Siedlungen* made a name for their flat roofs and white surfaces, which must explain the relatively greater attention they have received in the history of modern architecture. However, the Frankfurt *Siedlungen* were distributed throughout the empty lands on the periphery of the city, following the principle of *Trabatenstadt* (city of satellites), in contrast to the increasing emphasis on the inner metropolis in Berlin's program. Although Taut openly distanced himself from monotonous site plans, there was a gradual move toward the *Zeilenbau* principle for its perceived rationality in Frankfurt, as is manifest when the memorable zigzag blocks of the earlier *Seidlung* Niederrad (1926–27) (fig. 3.27) and the circular streets and surprising vistas of *Siedlung* Römerstadt (1927–28) are compared to the perfectly parallel and nonhierarchical blocks of the late *Siedlung* Westhausen (1929–30) (fig. 3.28). The *Existenzminimum* (minimal existence) studies in Frankfurt ended in much smaller units than the ones in Berlin, where bigger rooms allowed for flexible use to accommodate individual differences.[155] This individual freedom and difference so important to Taut was dissimilar to May's functionalism, which was another "project of emancipation," as Hilde Heynen put it: "The term *Existenzminimum* no longer implied dwellings that reduced housing to its essentials; instead what was discussed was a choice between two evils. It was better to have too-small houses for many people than 'good' homes for the few."[156] These dissimilarities in site plans and unit designs suggest subtle differences between Taut, a representative of more individualist values, and May, an architect leaning more toward socialism — though both were operating in a social democracy.

Schütte-Lihotzky envisioned her design of the Frankfurt kitchen as an efficient domestic machine that could literally be brought in and installed inside the house (fig. 3.29). The new kitchen was designed in contrast to the *Wohnküche* in previous collective housing settlements, where dining, living, and cooking were combined. Taking "the rationalization of the household" (*Rationalisierung im Haushalt*) as her motto and paying homage to the day she read Christine Frederick's *The New Housekeeping* (1913), Schütte-Lihotzky proposed a kitchen 1.90 meters wide and 3.40 meters long that minimized the women's unnecessary movement during household activities by organizing necessary appliances according to storing, preparing, cooking, eating, and cleaning. When it was compared to the traditional kitchens, she calculated that the scientifically designed Frankfurt kitchen reduced the walking distance from 19 to 8 meters. The appliances were made out of easy-to-use and hygienic materials (for example, there were garbage disposals and aluminum drawers); the swivel chair and cupboards were designed according to ergonomic considerations; and the pantry could be ventilated. Between 1926 and 1930, the Frankfurt kitchen was installed in every dwelling of the Das Neue Frankfurt program, culminating in approximately 10,000 units (fig. 3.30).[157]

Schütte-Lihotzky's future practice in Turkey also confirms that she was far from seeing women's place as the kitchen, instead envisioning that the timesaving methods of the Frankfurt kitchen would expedite women's liberation and help them take part in professional life.[158] The historians Mary Nolan and Susan Henderson have pointed out the irony in Schütte-Lihotzky's career, given that she responded to women's needs within the

3.27. Ernst May et al. *Siedlung* Niederrad, Frankfurt, 1926–27.

3.28. Ernst May et al. *Siedlung* Westhausen, Frankfurt, 1929–30.

broader political context of Germany. Despite the fact that her kitchens liberated women from excessive housework, the emphasis on the kitchen as a female sphere nevertheless was partly responsible for middle-class women's redomestication in Germany instead of leading them to a more equal participation in professional life.[159] Toward the end of her Frankfurt years, Schütte-Lihotzky herself became uncomfortable with her reputation as the designer of women's realm in the house—a role that

3.29. Margarete Schütte-Lihotzky. Frankfurt kitchen, Frankfurt, 1926.

3.30. Margarete Schütte-Lihotzky. *Lehrküche* [kitchen class], Frankfurt, 1929.

she felt marginalized her as a professional architect.¹⁶⁰ She must have felt so strongly limited that she agreed to leave for the Soviet Union with Ernst May's circle only on the condition that she would no longer design kitchens. Later she would admit that cooking and feminism are hardly related.¹⁶¹

Three architects from Das Neue Frankfurt program came to Turkey. Martin Elsaesser, who stayed in Germany and paid only occasional visits to Turkey, designed governmental buildings in Ankara¹⁶² and an unbuilt collective housing commissioned by a group of government officials who split from the Bahçelievler Housing Cooperative.¹⁶³ Margarete Schütte-Lihotzky and her husband Wilhelm Schütte accepted an invitation from Bruno Taut in March 1938.¹⁶⁴ In her official post for the Turkish Ministry of Education, Schütte-Lihotzky designed a high school for girls in Ankara as an extension to that city's Girls' Lycee, temporary monuments for governmental ceremonies, and plans for elementary schools in Anatolian villages. In addition to her government employment, she also taught classes at the İstanbul Academy of Fine Arts and maintained her own private practice (fig. 3.31).¹⁶⁵

Ankara, 1928–1947

Schütte-Lihotzky's ideas on the modern kitchen had arrived in Turkey before she did. Drawings similar to the Frankfurt kitchen circulated in middle-class domestic life magazines;¹⁶⁶ women took lessons in modern cooking and rationalization of the household in Girl's Institutes. The Girl's Institutes were founded in major Turkish cities starting in 1928, at the suggestion of professionals such as the American progressive educator John Dewey, who was invited to Turkey for consultation. By 1940, there were thirty-five Girl's Institutes all around the country, and evening schools in small towns and villages with some 16,500 women students enrolled altogether.¹⁶⁷ The state's educational program of these institutes sought to transform the Eastern and traditional Ottoman housewives into westernized and modernized Turkish ones.

Women took lessons in modern cooking and rationalization of the household in these institutes in classrooms similar to Schütte-Lihotzky's kitchen class (*Lehrküche*) in Frankfurt (fig. 3.32; see fig. 3.30). The institutes published yearbooks advising women on how to become a modern housewife. The teachers published textbooks on the rationalization of household, including Süheyla Altunç's *Ev İdaresi* (Organization of the household) and Süheyla Arel's *Taylorisme*.¹⁶⁸ Arel's book was full of explicit references to Christine Frederick, who elaborated on Catherine Beecher's ideas from the 1840s about the rational household in scientific

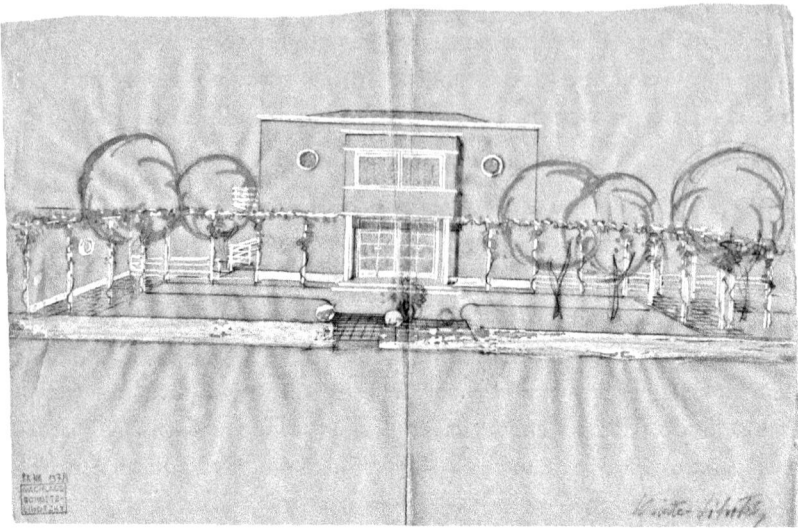

3.31. Margarete Schütte-Lihotzky. House for Kemal Ozan, İstanbul, 1939.

and Taylorist terms, in order to achieve the most efficient, timesaving, and economic results. Echoing this aspiration for rationalization, Altunç defined the modern household as follows: "A housewife is a woman with qualities of womanhood who knows how to organize the house. The household is the type of knowledge that shows the methods of organizing a house according to the principles of health, order, and economy."[169] Altunç conveyed modern and scientific knowledge in her textbook on topics including personal hygiene, laundry, ironing, sewing, moving, cleaning, the maintenance of heating and lighting amenities, cooking, and washing dishes.

The modern rational kitchen was one of the most pertinent subjects in these textbooks. What makes the Turkish debate on modern kitchens distinctive was how the proponents of Kemalism posed a rigid polarization between the old, traditional, Eastern, Ottoman cooking places and the new, modern, westernized Turkish kitchens. The Girl's Institutes were unavoidably part of the Kemalist state's modernization and westernization project, even if women involved in the institutes sought to find their own unique voices.[170] By coupling the traditional Ottoman domestic spaces with the patriarchic family structure, it was also possible to claim that the new technological Western amenities and the scientific household would liberate Turkish women from men's oppression. In her book, Altunç, the home economics teacher, described the new Turkish kitchen with the

3.32. Cooking classes in Turkish Girl's Institutes, c. 1935.

modernist architectural principles that she shared with her Western colleagues: "The kitchen and the storage must face north. . . . The kitchen must be spacious, bright, and cool during summer . . . it must let the air and light come in through wide windows. . . . The kitchenware must be practical and simple. There must be nothing but the most necessary equipment."[171] Altunç continued with details, such as the height of the tiles covering the kitchen walls for easy cleaning; fine points about washing dishes, including ten different types of equipment to be used; necessary closets for multiple categories of storage; and varieties of kitchenware and their appropriateness for different tasks. These details were not necessarily a direct transfer from Western sources. They combined the local necessities with Western debates, as can be observed in her explanations of storing homemade jam and her categorization of the kitchenware suitable for Turkish meals. Nevertheless, the Girl's Institutes explicitly created a hierarchical distinction between the Ottoman and the republican housewives.

This distinction was unavoidably generational. It was common to see depictions that constructed a polarity between a generation of women that was allegedly oppressed by the traditional customs and architectural spaces, as opposed to their daughters, who were allegedly liberated by the Kemalist revolution and, by extension, their modern kitchens and rational and scientific household methods. Interviewing the women of the Girl's Institutes years later in the 1990s, Yael Navaro-Yaşın exposed the cross-generational dialogues and negotiations that were initiated by this perceived polarity: "As long as the Turkish girls were taught to denounce their mothers' methods for being 'non-scientific,' 'unorganized,' and 'traditional,' the girls entered into daily disputes with their mothers on 'modern' household methods."[172]

Although the new women sought to contest the traditional methods of their mothers and grandmothers, it is hard to claim that they achieved to subvert the very traditional role of women in the society. Looking more closely, one can detect a tension that exposes this predicament in the textbooks of the Girl's Institutes. For example, after discussing the timesaving modern kitchen at length, Altunç reserved an equal number of pages to document the new customs of the dining table:

> The tablecloth is not put directly on the table. . . . The tablecloth must first be stretched well, then the plates must be placed 8–10 centimeters away from the table edge. . . . The distance between the plates of two people must be at least 70 centimeters. The knife is placed to the right, fork to the left of the plate. The spoon is placed to the right of the knife. They must be placed so that the inner edge of the fork and spoon can be seen. . . . Nicely folded napkins are put on the plate . . . the glasses should be organized as follows.[173]

Altunç explained in the utmost detail the norms of table organization for different occasions, such as family dining, dining with casual guests, and dining with important guests. She also specified how the housewives should serve their husbands and guests at the dinner table: "The service at the dinner table must be performed fast with a sweet and firm haste. . . . Once one of the courses is finished, the plates should immediately be changed and the other course must be served."[174] These dining table norms depicted a new lifestyle that may have been different from the traditional ways in the rural areas. It is hard to claim, however, that they transformed bourgeois women's status and role in the house. Despite their Taylorist principles of rational and efficient household that would save women time and energy, the textbooks of home economics nevertheless kept the traditional gender roles in Turkey intact. They still concentrated on ways of being a good, serving housewife, a comforting and pleasing helpmate to the husband, even if the new housewife would have been transformed into a new Western body. The paradoxes of the home economists have to be conceptualized within the context of the tension between feminism for women's sake and for the Kemalists' sake.

By the mid-1940s, the discussion on the rational kitchens in the Girl's

Institutes had reached the professional architectural circles. Lami Eser wrote a dissertation in the architecture department of İstanbul Technical University (it was entitled "Modern Residential Kitchens," published in 1952).[175] Eser brought in information from a variety of sources from Germany, Sweden, France, and the United States. Schütte-Lihotzky's Frankfurt kitchen received an appreciative reference as well.[176] Eser concentrated on the architectural details of preparing food, cooking, and washing the dishes; illustrated linear, parallel, L-shaped, and U-shaped kitchens; and advised on the technical matters of waste management, ventilation, lighting, modern equipment, and building materials. However, the kitchen remained the women's realm throughout Eser's dissertation: "In the design and construction of the residential buildings, little care has unfortunately been spent on the workspace of woman, namely the kitchen. . . . It is undisputable that there is a need for a deep and detailed study on the space where housewives spend approximately five hours a day."[177]

Perhaps this explains why Schütte-Lihotzky did not participate in the kitchen debate taking place in the Girl's Institutes in Turkey as enthusiastically as one might have expected, although she prepared the architectural project for an extension building for the Girls' Lycee in Ankara, whose original building was designed by her Austrian colleague Ernst Egli. In Turkey, Schütte-Lihotzky shifted her attention to designing village schools and teachers' accommodations in Anatolia, a practice that aspired to open space for subaltern participation.

SIEDLUNG AND THE SUBALTERN

I have differentiated modernization practices from above (those of the Kemalist state) and what might be called from below (translation practices without the entitlement to official authority), but the agents of transformation that I have analyzed so far were the privileged individuals, not the subaltern. Inspired by Antonio Gramsci's use of the term *subaltern* as the nondominant, nonhegemonic, nonelite groups of history, Gayatri Spivak and the subaltern studies group—including Ranajit Guha, Dipesh Chakrabarty, and Partha Chatterjee—have pointed out the necessity of writing history by acknowledging the subaltern, while many of them also exposed the very problems of the subaltern's representability.[178] In the following pages, I will also use the term *subaltern* to designate groups on whose exploitation the operating systems of power depend, both economically and geopolitically. The question becomes particularly crucial in analyzing mass housing, since after all *Siedlung* projects were visions of how the subaltern would or should reside in the metropolis, while they were created by professional architects who hardly belonged to the subaltern class themselves. The question remains: Is the voice of the subaltern translatable in architecture, particularly in *Siedlungen* that were envisioned for the subaltern? Subalterns of history emerge on a few levels. Although the subaltern in Germany was the working class, because of its economic exploitation, the subaltern in Turkey was dominated both geopolitically and economically.

Germany, 1929–1932

A similar question — albeit in other terms — occupied the architectural historian Manfredo Tafuri, who came to be known for challenging the very possibility of critical practice in architecture.[179] Tafuri explained in quite certain terms that capitalism made the working class the absolute other of Architecture. A profession that consumes so many of a country's resources and constitutes such a large portion of its capitalist production, one that is so dependent on institutional and political decisions, and one that so desperately needs wealthy and powerful clients could never make space for the working class. Tafuri reached this conclusion largely through a critical analysis of the Weimar *Siedlungen*.

"Private property has made us so stupid and one-sided that an object is only ours when we have it — when it exists for us as capital, or when it is directly possessed, eaten, drunk, worn by us."[180] Karl Marx's loud cries against private property and its consequences as land speculation were heard clearly in the Weimar *Siedlung* circles. As a perfect illustration of Marx's differentiation between capitalist and benign circulation, land speculation was a major target of criticism in order to achieve a "positive transcendence of private property."[181] The mouthpieces most favorable to housing reforms in Frankfurt and Berlin, *Das Neue Frankfurt* and *Wohnungswirtschaft*, often published articles that advocated resistance to free economy and capitalist production, as well as texts underlining the necessity of a restructured housing program for the poor.[182]

With the background of a loaded intellectual history of the relationship between property and inequality, it is not surprising that Tafuri searched for the architecture of equality in places where profits from individual property could be minimized. Even if he eventually judged them as "failures," he regarded May's housing estates in Frankfurt, and Wagner's and Taut's in Berlin, as "the most important chapters in the history of modern urban planning," "the constructed utopias" kept isolated from the urban reality of capitalist production, "the oases" on the margins of the metropolis that otherwise perpetuated contradictory spaces and uneven development.[183] Yet, he immediately added that these niches of social production fell well short in affecting the larger urban reality whose "contradictions would soon appear more vital than the tools established by the architectural milieu to control them."[184] Hence, Tafuri concluded that "there can never be an . . . architecture of class, but only a class critique of . . . architecture," a motto that has since then provoked many architects' and critics' belief that critical practice is impossible.[185]

In explaining the *Siedlung* experience, Tafuri explicitly opposed the *Trabantenprinzip* (the idea that a city should be divided into semiautonomous nuclei) to the capitalist metropolis (a city vulnerable to unlimited sprawl and land speculation). *Trabantenprinzip* empowered May and Wagner as the responsible agents for the entire building industry in an autonomous, limited, but large segment of the city.[186] Wagner often commented on the transformation of the institutional role of the architect, who could no longer sustain the status of an individual and detached artist, but who had to reinvent himself as an organizer with an understanding of the operating economical structure.[187] The *Trabantenprinzip* was possible only through the emergence of this "city as a sector" as opposed to the private sector.[188] These semiautonomous regions had to be delicately preserved from the dynamics of capitalist growth, making them "islands of rationality," "metaphors of liberated work," "image[s] of the city of work," in Tafuri's half-heartedly supportive words.[189] Despite their brief existence outside the capitalist production cycle, the Weimar *Siedlungen* were doomed to failure, according to Tafuri, because of reasons he listed in diverse texts: First, the selection of housing as the main function applicable to *Trabantenprinzip* ignored the other functions of the city and thus failed to provide a major economic transformation. Second, it made it difficult to integrate these housing districts with the rest of the city or to have any effect on the overall organization of land use. Third, rationalization, prefabrication, and standardization were still vulnerable to the free play of the market because the fluctuation in the prices of building materials destabilized the calculation costs—no matter how minimal, standardized, or rational the design was. The rationalization of building production or studies of *Existenzminimum* came to a close because the rents ended up being too high for the working class, due to the simultaneous rise in the cost of building materials or uncontrolled credits. Hence, Tafuri concluded: "Here was the proof that a reform in one sector, isolated from a complex of institutional reforms coordinated in a coherent political strategy, is doomed to failure even in that particular sector."[190]

In his article "Gegen den Strom" (Against the trend), written after *Die Wohnung für das Existenzminimum* (The dwelling for minimalist existence) exhibition in Frankfurt in 1929, Taut had admitted a similar failure.[191] It may have been during this exhibition in 1929, when architects from all over Europe shared the results of their research on mass housing, that the inherent problems were also becoming clear to them. Quite different from a heroic self-assurance, Taut's tone in discussing minimalist existence was bleak. What use was research on the minimalist dwelling unless the state's housing program controlled overcrowding? Architects' efforts were in vain if the units were used by larger families than intended. One-third of apartments in Berlin were "wretched" (*schäbig*), with only one room and a kitchen. But could this situation ever come to an end, given the low salaries of the workers? Despite architects' efforts, the situation was ruled by political systems beyond their control.

According to established historiography, the rise of the National Socialist regime in Germany in 1933 is usually considered to have terminated the social housing programs of the Weimar period. Yet Tafuri's analysis and Taut's implications suggest an inherent structural problem that would sooner or later have exposed the impossibility of sustaining housing programs for the subaltern population under capitalist production.

Nonetheless, Tafuri's condemnation of social housing and his subsequent conclusions about the impossibility of critical architectural practice call for questioning. These *Siedlungen* did not eventually achieve "the positive transcendence of private property," but weren't they temporary "enclaves of social transition"?[192] Tafuri considered the final destination of a positive avant-gardist project (the predecessor of the Weimar housing) as the total destruction of the architectonic object within the city structure, achieved only in two unrealized and unrealizable projects: Hilberseimer's *Großstadt* and Le Corbusier's plan for Algiers. Only these two projects conceived of the entire city as a single unity, a social machine with elementary cells building up the urban organism as a whole, where aura has dissolved into mass; bourgeois, free-standing building into mass produced housing; architecture into planning; author into producer; architect into organizer; and private enterprise into property-free existence.[193] However, this preference for total architecture over the *Siedlung* model should be evaluated in relation to Tafuri's own choices between architecture and planning in the context of the 1960s, when questioning the relationship between politics and architecture convinced many young students that the answer lay in moving architecture into planning.[194] The finest achievements of social housing in world history that managed to accommodate a large proportion of the subaltern population at least temporarily would seem to be failures only to those who are committed to this very specific agenda. Others could still see them as critical practice.

There was also an ethical arbitrariness in Tafuri's class critique, which exposes the geopolitical dimensions of the subaltern question in social housing. Why does the exploitation of working-class labor get priority in this analysis, instead of the exploitation of domestic labor, colonized labor, or animal labor? In exposing the oppressions due to class-based categories, it is not unfair to say that Tafuri often overlooked categories based on geography, gender and race, or ethnicity. The historian's silence on the overtly colonialist implications of Le Corbusier's Algiers project is a case in point. For Tafuri, Le Corbusier's urban plan for Algiers was the "most advanced" and unsurpassed project of modern urban planning because it grasped the whole city, the entire landscape, in its unifying gesture.[195] However, Tafuri failed to see the oppression of the casbah's North African and Muslim population in this project, the segregation of the city into colonizer and colonized, the cutting off of the local residents from the sea. Preoccupied with the *telos* of total architecture, he excused urban apartheid.[196]

Zonguldak, 1934–1936

This ethical arbitrariness, historically quite symptomatic of critical theory, may be further discussed through a subaltern mass housing project in Turkey. Ernst Reuter often pointed out the need for new residential towns to accommodate industrial workers, so that they would settle in their jobs rather than feel themselves to be perpetual nomads. He insisted that these mass housing projects had to be real residential places, where workers could live with their families and engage in communal activities. Following the early garden city models, Reuter proposed a hybrid of urban and rural life: he envisioned private double houses with private gardens, where workers would grow their own food and use dry toilets to produce fertilizer for agricultural activities.[197]

Although the German professionals spent most of their time publishing and teaching theories of mass housing, it was Seyfi Arkan who designed working-class settlements in Zonguldak, a town in northern Turkey along the Black Sea. The workers' conditions in the Zonguldak coal mines had remained a problem since 1848. During the Ottoman Empire, these mines were under the management of British, French, German, and Russian firms. Soon after the Industrial Revolution, the rich mines had become a significant source of fuel for European factories. As early as 1848, the Ottoman Empire had left the management of the Zonguldak mines to a group of English businessmen who had founded the Coal Commercial Firm (*Kömür Kumpanyası*). During the nineteenth century and into the early twentieth, the mines' management had been handed over to various foreign and occasionally local groups, and French forces had finally occupied the region during the Turkish War of Independence. In the eyes of the Kemalists, the fact that the French army agreed to withdraw from the region on June 21, 1921, symbolized not only a military victory for Mustafa Kemal's army, but also the end to the capitulations during the Ottoman times that had jeopardized the region's economic independence. In the same year that Arkan started designing the housing settlements, Ahmet Naim wrote a book on Zonguldak's semicolonization from the perspective of Turkish nationalism. Unsurprisingly, he stressed the importance of the Kemalist revolution in liberating the Turkish economy from Western countries.[198]

Modern infrastructure had been implemented in Zonguldak as a consequence of these financial and organizational arrangements. One example was the railway constructed by the British to facilitate the transport of coal, especially during the Crimean War (1853–56), when the region was handed over to Britain to supply the material for the benefit of the allies. Another icon of modernization, the Zonguldak port, had been designed during a period of French control by an architect referred to as "Yanko."[199] The foreign firms had provided railways, ports, and new technologies to support the coal mines, and yet they had been criticized for employing workers with rules that were partly capitalist and partly feudal and that offered few benefits and little guarantee of timely payment. An account of a peasant worker in a French-owned mine may serve as testimony: "When I was nine years old in 1905, I left my village with my father. This was the first time I was going out of my village. We walked from the village until Kozlu. . . . Our work hours were not defined. Nobody had a watch anyway. Whenever the chief said it was enough for today, we left the mine. Sometimes we stayed in the mine for 16–17 hours. Often . . . we would see the sunlight once every 7–8 days."[200] A segregated French neighborhood was built during these times in Zonguldak. Naim described the French living district in 1934 as follows:

> Ereğli Company built up a neighborhood with the most beautiful and luxurious buildings at the most beautiful part of the town; they placed a church in the middle of the neighborhood and established two religious schools. This neighborhood was no different than a French colony. . . . [T]hey also brought missionaries who were specialists in propaganda techniques for

the African population. These missionaries tried to disseminate the culture of imperialism and the ideology of dependence [*bağımlılık ideolojisi*] among the workers and the peasants.[201]

This was how the Kemalist nationalists criticized the European control of Zonguldak's coal mines, but their own revolution did not improve the workers' conditions. Between 1927 and 1932, 282 workers were killed and 3,109 were injured during working hours.[202] Insufficient and substandard housing was one of the primary causes of the workers' destitute living conditions under both European and Turkish control. Despite occasional regulations designed to ameliorate these conditions, the workers kept sleeping outside or in barracks they built themselves, away from their families. The Dilaver Paşa Regulation of 1867 called for the implementation of more-rationalized planning to increase the workforce's efficiency, and for the production of dormitories. A law passed on September 10, 1921, mandated that coal miners and employers be provided with sleeping pavilions, dining halls, and bathing facilities. It forbid forcing peasants to work (which was common practice) and employing workers who were younger than eighteen years old; it defined several rights for health benefits and minimum salaries. However, many of these regulations were not implemented, and workers responded with extensive strikes in 1923.[203]

Interviews with miners of the early republican period in Zonguldak give some insights into their housing conditions:

> I was so thin that you could see the light passing through my ears [*kulaklarımdan ışık gözükürdü, ışık. Zayıflıktan*]. I was eighteen years old. Thin and flimsy. They gave me a big shovel. I could not hold it still [*Elimde dönerdi kürek*]. I was too weak. . . . They beat us like crazy [*Dayak nasıl. Tekme tokat*].[204]
>
> In those times [1937] there were no pavilions. No family or kids, only workers. We slept on top of each other in barracks. There were a few houses but these were for foreigners [*bunlar dışardan gelenlerindi*].[205]
>
> We worked sixteen hours a day in the mines. There was no place to sleep. No bathroom. We went to bed the same way we worked in the mines, without changing. In cold weather we slept in the mines. We had to invent our own ways of bathing. . . . We slept on the ground, on *sayvan* (canopy), with a wooden support in place of a pillow. . . . Where would you find a blanket? [*Yorgan nerde?*][206]

Arkan's designs for Türkiş and Kömüriş workers' housing, which sought to modernize the coal miner's living conditions, were thus a mat-

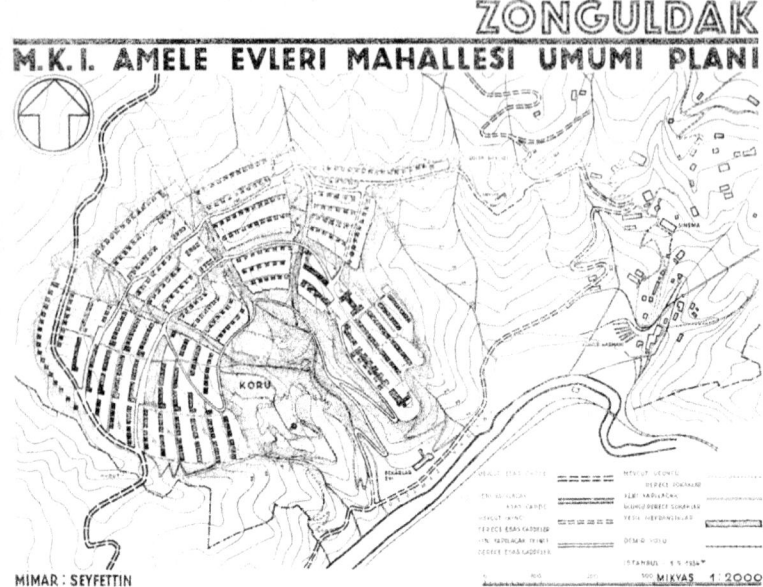

3.33. Seyfi Arkan. Türkiş workers' housing, site plan, Zonguldak, 1935.

ter of national pride and a symbol of economic independence (fig. 3.33).[207] It could have empowered the workers' movement, although I will argue that this was hardly the case. It was indeed similar living conditions that had motivated new solutions for modern social housing, some of which Arkan had had the chance to observe during his student years in Berlin (chapter 1). In Germany, Arkan had designed two affordable housing projects for Ankara that he named *Kleinhaussiedlung* (*Siedlung* with small houses).[208] Returning to Turkey, he repeated the tone of common nationalist speeches and presented the Zonguldak projects as Turkish architects' "duty."[209] The projects contained not only dormitories for single workers but also houses for families. Arkan suggested common dining halls, laundries, and showers, as well as a primary school for the workers' children in the Türkiş settlement. The developers must have anticipated that the workers would be living with their families, which indicates their attempt to organize permanent solutions rather than temporary ones.

Arkan's housing projects for Zonguldak were contemporaneous with the Bahçelievler Housing Cooperative in Ankara (1935–38), designed by Hermann Jansen (chapter 1). Although both projects translated European social housing models for the Turkish context, Bahçelievler was designed for middle- and upper-income bureaucrats, in contrast to the

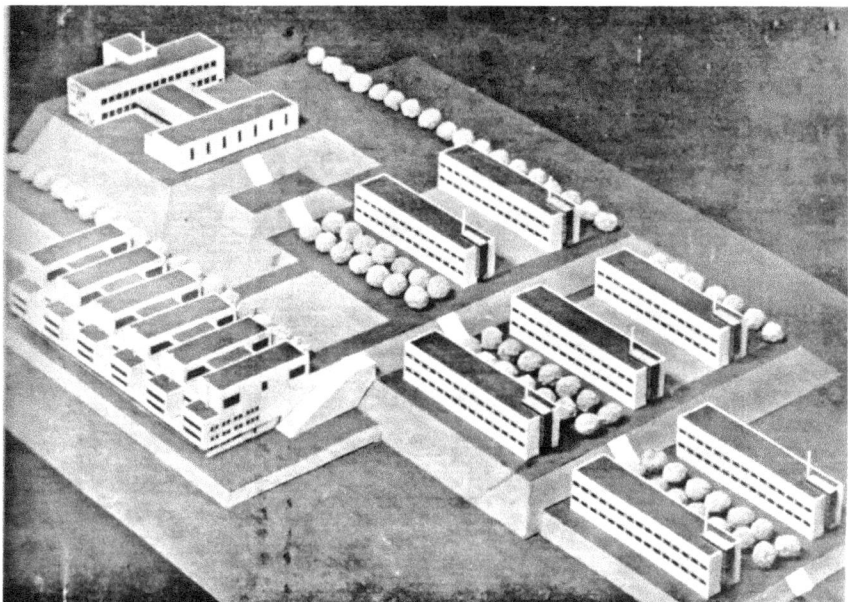

3.34. Seyfi Arkan. Türkiş workers' housing, blocks in the *Zeilenbau* model, Zonguldak, 1935.

Zonguldak housing for miners and engineers. Bahçelievler was based on prewar garden city models, often rejecting the developments undertaken during the interwar period. In contrast, the parallel urban blocks with white-washed walls, flat roofs, and horizontal windows in Arkan's project were in dialogue with Weimar *Siedlungen* and the Bauhaus, rather than the traditional *Heimatstil* (the name for the style inspired by traditional German houses). A variety of housing types were employed, including free-standing single-family houses in a garden and multifamily housing blocks in the *Zeilenbau* model (fig. 3.34). In parts of the Türkiş housing, Arkan gave up the *Zeilenbau* principle to provide all houses with a view of the valley and to use the land's slope efficiently. Free-standing houses in the Türkiş housing were even smaller than the ones produced as part of the Frankfurt *Existenzminimum* research. However, the houses stood as free-standing blocks on big plots of land, forsaking the efficiency of row housing that would have reduced the cost of land use and construction. The dormitories and multifamily housing blocks were placed parallel to each other with a specific emphasis on orientation, to get southwestern and northeastern sun.

Arkan not only provided houses for former peasants, but he also de-

3.35. Seyfi Arkan. Kömüriş workers' housing, director's and engineers' houses, Zonguldak, 1936.

fined a new lifestyle that was meant to transform a traditional peasant into an industrial working-class citizen. Community living was emphasized, common service spaces were provided, and identical units were standardized and reproducible. The project was seen as rationalizing the use of space by creating efficient, economic, and functional units that provided only the minimum amount of space necessary for modern living. These living units were no longer the vernacular houses built by the village mason or carpenter. They were defined and standardized by the city architect for the modern worker whom he had never met.

These projects explicitly defined new class distinctions in the built environment. The houses for the director, engineers, and workers were designed with different amenities reflecting their social ranks. Arkan separated the director's and engineers' houses from the workers' — a spatial strategy not too different from the one in the French neighborhood during the previous era. The director's house, the largest residence, stood out on top of the hill above the engineers' houses (fig. 3.35). In Arkan's mind, these class distinctions also implied cultural segregations, which were to be kept intact. He wrote: "Peasants have a great value for humanity's health and strength, and yet their appearance, outfits, status, and work have a different structure."[210]

Arkan adopted one of the most common strategies of the Turkish republican elite in confronting the West. This was a translation of the Western models of modernization in order to contest Western imperialism itself. Arkan's descriptions underscore this seemingly inconsistent and yet strategic relationship:

> The Turkish architect, who works as much as the foreigners on urban matters and who is accustomed to foreign science and technology, is trying to live up to the revolution [*Türk mimarı devrime layık olmaya çalışıyor*]. Until the Republic, our coal mines and workers were in the hands of the foreigners satisfying their own interests [*hep yabancı çıkarına yarayan*]. This part of the country was neglected and deprived of the Turkish culture and character.[211]

In Arkan's eyes, undoing the neglect, giving the worker back an environment that corresponded to "the Turkish culture and character," and eliminating foreign domination would have been possible by using "foreign [that is, Western] science and technology." The Turkish nationalists of the early republican period considered the economic and working conditions in Zonguldak as one of the most overt examples of Western semicolonization during the Ottoman Empire.[212] In their eyes, improving these conditions was a matter of national pride as well as a testimony to the new regime's success in terminating Western hegemony. Arkan's projects exemplify a common strategy of the republican elite that translated Western models of modernization while trying to contest some of the established Western hierarchies. However, the example of Zonguldak also alludes to one of the biggest paradoxes of postcolonial modernization and nationalization around the world. The voices of the former peasants and workers of a new industrializing nation were seldom represented because they were pressed between Western power and nationalist control.

The subaltern studies group has proposed the use of the word *subaltern* to differentiate the peasants and working classes in India from the dominant groups in the country, including both the British colonizers and the Indian nationalist elite that fought against colonization. For them, the subaltern should be one of the main focuses of postcolonial studies because the subaltern was dominated not only by the forces of colonization but also by the forces of its opponent, nationalism. Each force had an instrumental interest in using the subaltern as part of its ideological project.[213] This definition of the subaltern is perhaps the best description for the Zonguldak workers. Despite the shift of power from the European firms to the Turkish Republic, the situation of the coal miners remained unimproved. In the eyes of the workers themselves, both the foreign capitalists and the nationalist elite abused their production.[214] Given the competing interests of two dominant forces, their own voices went unheard — something that confirms Spivak's theory on the problems inherent in subaltern representation.

One of the objectives underlying the modernist housing settlements was to make the masses the subjects of built environment. Architects saw themselves as no longer merely building monuments to power or villas for the elite, but providing collective housing for the masses. However, both in Germany and Turkey, the mass housing experience can hardly be disassociated from the heroic self-assurance and patronizing tones of the professional and political elite, who — however well-intentioned — sought to change the lives of the masses by a top-down civilizing process. The architects of mass housing were deeply committed to the masses, but only from a distance.

Anatolia, 1938–1940

In Turkey, Margarete Schütte-Lihotzky tried to open up a different model than the ones discussed above with her ideas on participation. Schütte-Lihotzky began her book *Erinnerungen aus dem Widerstand* (Memoirs from the resistance) with a poem by Nazım Hikmet and ended it with another one, by Pablo Neruda.[215] What she shared with these Turkish and Chilean poets was imprisonment and exile because of her socialist beliefs. The year Schütte-Lihotzky arrived in Turkey as a political exile, the Turkish poet Hikmet had been sentenced to twenty-eight years for advocating communism. Two years later, she would find herself similarly accused and locked away for the rest of the war.[216]

After her arrival in Turkey in 1938, Schütte-Lihotzky designed types of village schools and teachers' accommodations all over Anatolia, as part of the state's modernization program for rural areas. European *Siedlung* and mass housing principles were also implemented in villages and rural immigrant settlements in Turkey. Starting in 1934, the Kemalist regime built a few villages to accommodate immigrants to Turkey during the exchange of populations with the neighboring countries. This exchange of populations was often executed through violent methods after the creation of new nation-states in the Balkans due to the dissolution of the Ottoman Empire. A new village with 10,500 houses was constructed in Thrace (1938) to settle some 80,000 immigrants from Bulgaria, Rumania, and Yugoslavia, who were expected to engage in agricultural activities (fig. 3.36).[217] The *Siedlung*, now functioning as a civilizing tool, was used to construct rapid new villages from scratch and to create new homes for the ethnic groups who had to leave their houses after borders were drawn between the new nations in the area. These new villages were often constructed with standardized houses placed according to a grid plan.

3.36. The immigrant village in Thrace.

Village schools and teachers' accommodations were also parts of the program for the countryside. In 1941, the Ministry of Education organized an architectural competition for standardized designs of village schools with respect to hot, moderate, and cold climates.[218] Three years later, a similar competition was organized for the typical houses of village teachers, who, assuming the heroic posture of the Kemalist elite, took posts in the remotest villages to educate the new generation of the nation under a centralized pedagogical program.[219] Although these studies were not meant for collective housing, they still involved a standardization of sorts. All of the houses and schools in the Turkish villages, including the ones in the remotest settlements, would be determined in relation to a standard plan, and different regions would be unified under a nationalist umbrella.

These village schools and teachers' houses were not industrially produced, regardless of the fact that the very idea of a planned and standardized village had emerged in response to the effects of industrialization. Despite the architects' call for being attentive to the local lifestyle and needs, the standardization of village houses as part of the state's building program was a patronizing extension of the urban mind into the rural surroundings. This missionary attitude toward the countryside characterized literary works as well. Reşat Nuri Güntekin's influential classic novel,

Çalıkuşu, for example, depicted a woman teacher from İstanbul who decides to spend the rest of her life educating children in the Anatolian villages. In the novel, the heart-broken heroine leaves what the author deems as her corrupt and arrogant metropolitan life behind and travels to the countryside to share her knowledge with the uneducated common people. While she teaches village children about the latest advances of civilization, village life in turn teaches her about her true self. This type of Anatolian romanticism, a discourse idealizing the countryside as the Anatolian heaven (*cennet Anadolu*) and the hidden source of the nation's "true" virtues, characterized other literary and intellectual works of the period. However, it prevented a more realist and productive confrontation with the pressing issue of poverty in the countryside.[220]

Architects who had participated in the discussions about Germany's residential culture over the previous fifty years, including Schütte-Lihotzky, had a great affinity with similar ideas. The healing power of the countryside, proximity to nature, and engagement in agricultural or gardening activities had indeed been advocated by the German life reform and garden city movements since the end of the nineteenth century. Ernst May's Frankfurt social housing program, in which Schütte-Lihotzky had participated for five productive years, had partially emerged out of this legacy.

Although Anatolian romanticism painted the rural areas of Turkey in similar strokes, the Turkish leftist intellectuals, such as Nazım Hikmet to whom Schütte-Lihotzky paid homage, openly resisted this type of idealization. In the same period, Nazım Hikmet represented Anatolian villages by stressing instead their poverty and destitution caused by negligence and colonization:

> An old peasant
> > more like death
> > than his old mare
> > > near us
>
> not near us
> > but within
> > our burning veins.
>
> Shoulders without thick capes
> hands without whips;
> without horses, without carts
> > without village police
>
> we have traveled through
> villages like bear dens

> muddy towns,
> over bald hills.
> This is how we crossed that land!
> ...
> We have not traveled
> as though in a dream,
> oh no!
> from one rubbish heap we reached another.[221]

Rather than describing Anatolian rural life as an uncorrupted source of humanity and a locus of spiritual wealth, Hikmet focused on the physical destitution of the villages, explaining that the political deprivation and ignorance of the countryside caused this poverty. Hikmet's criticism of the European Orientalist gaze in Turkey followed similar lines. In 1925, the poet elaborated on this point, attacking Pierre Loti for the romantic idealization and exoticism of his depictions of İstanbul:

> Opium!
> Submission!
> Kismet!
> Lattice-work, caravanserai, han
> fountain
> a sultan dancing on a silver tray!
> ...
> *This* is the Orient the French poet sees.
> ...
> But...
> An Orient like this
> never existed
> and never will.
> Orient!
> The soil on which
> naked slaves
> die of hunger.
> The common property of everyone
> except those born on it.
> The land where hunger itself
> perishes with famine!
> But the silos are full to the brim,
> full of grain—
> only for Europe.[222]

As someone who was close to the socialist intellectual life in Turkey and who had an intimate knowledge of Hikmet's critical poetry, it is likely that Schütte-Lihotzky began to sense the gap between nationalist Anatolian romanticism and the growing socialist opposition taking root in the country.

Schütte-Lihotzky's designs for the Turkish government inevitably embody the paradoxes in the life of an architect who is critical of the establishment while simultaneously bound to work for it. She was actively engaged in the European anti-Fascist movements and criticized the Turkish government's oppressive practices toward her Greek and Armenian colleagues at the ministry, who were deprived of equal professional rights with the Turkish architects.[223] However, the village schools and teachers' accommodations that she designed were bound to be part of the state-sponsored program that sought to define a new life for the rural areas. It is thus important to understand how the architect handled her designs within this context.

In her report to the Ministry of Education on the village schools and teachers' accommodations, Schütte-Lihotzky acknowledged the importance of educating and civilizing the countryside. "The villagers are rightly proud of their schools that represent the great progress,"[224] she wrote, sharing the government's position. Her experience in trying to improve women and children's living conditions in Frankfurt informed her work. She made sure that all classrooms and the teachers' accommodations faced south, no living space had direct fenestration to the north, and light entered rooms from the left of children's desks, because that was considered better for writing unless the child was left-handed.[225] She designed special spaces for integrating home economics classes into the schools and reserved ample space for vegetable and flower gardens—a residue of German modernism that sought physical and mental health through activities related to the soil. In many of the village school types, Schütte-Lihotzky was asked by the government to integrate the teacher's dwelling into the school building, resembling the living space of the urban teacher, Çalıkuşu, in Güntekin's novel. Having participated in the research on *Existenzminimum* in Frankfurt, she used her experience in designing such small dwellings, without forgetting to include a separate garden for the teacher's individual use (fig. 3.37).

However, it would be a mistake to see Schütte-Lihotzky as a heroic Westerner, a missionary seeking to civilize the rural inhabitants on the premise of smooth translatability. In her report for the village schools, she firmly opposed the idea of importing building materials from other

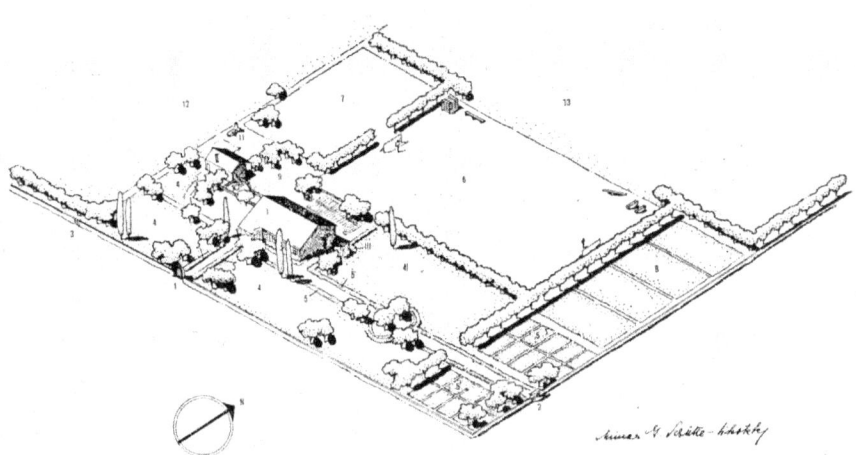

3.37. Margarete Schütte-Lihotzky. Site plan of a village school in Anatolia.

countries: "It is not possible to utilize examples from other countries. It is necessary that the construction of village schools in Turkey rely on local life and local labor."[226] Schütte-Lihotzky explicitly argued against the use of ready-made industrial materials or industrial techniques because the village buildings had to be built by the local people, not technologically advanced construction workers: "The projects and technical details need to be as simple as possible, so that they can be constructed without qualified workers. The types of the village schools have to be completely different from each other, depending on their location, climate, site, local construction materials, and finally the size of the village or the town."[227] To that end, she defined forty-nine possible permutations for the schools depending on the number of students, accommodation of the teacher, climatic circumstances, and construction materials. She anticipated that villagers would choose the type that suited them best and then construct the building themselves. After categorizing the types of schools according to climate and local materials, she stressed how important it was to use traditional colors and ornaments for the buildings' façades. To explain the colored perspective drawn for the project,[228] she wrote:

> The architecture of the village school must be in harmony with the whole landscape, environment and the overall silhouette of the village. . . . Not only the form, roof, and the façade but also, and above all, the building color play a role in this. Naturally, the color has to be different in each

different landscape. A school's color in the yellow-brown-green steppes of Anatolia will be different from another one in the middle of a rich coastal vegetation. . . . The interiors must also have friendly colors, for which one has to go back to the colors, paintings, and crafts that were customary in the past.[229]

These comments indicate that Schütte-Lihotzky wanted to give the villagers a chance to represent themselves and participate in the decisions guiding their lives. Instead of letting the central government define and construct the schools as a standardized project, she tried to open a space for the voice of the villager in the decision-making and construction process. She expected villagers to choose from the forty-nine permutations of types, construct the building, and adjust it according to their customs. The architect must have interpreted the schools as the work of villagers themselves, assisted by the state and, by extension, herself as an expert in consulting for the design, rather than single-handedly defining it. In a way, Schütte-Lihotzky advocated the agency of the subaltern in shaping the environment. Additionally, her intentional withdrawal from using advanced industrial materials and production processes, unlike her practice in Frankfurt, may also be interpreted as a conscious nonuse of technology, again hoping to make the subaltern an active participant in the choice of which technology to import, and how. By hesitating to impose the latest industrial technologies from Europe on the Anatolian villager, Schütte-Lihotzky may have desired to contribute to the definition of a more appropriate way of engaging with modern technology in Turkish villages. This would have made the Anatolian rural inhabitants active agents in their own environment, rather than passive recipients of a lifestyle imposed on them by the government.

Schütte-Lihotzky must have sincerely believed in the pedagogical missions of the Kemalist state in cultivating the youth in the countryside. Yet while the government invested in the village schools for nationalist reasons, she must have shared the unresolved Marxist question of how the peasant class would represent itself by legitimizing its class interest. She could not entirely avoid being part of the state's modernization program for the rural areas. This, to be sure, has to be evaluated by taking into account the restrictions of someone in her situation: her options were clearly limited as she was an exile from Germany and an immigrant in Turkey, in the country on the condition of her appointment as the architect of the Ministry of Education. This chapter does not discuss how the Turkish government realized her suggestions, or how the real users responded to them, because the point here is to show how Schütte-Lihotzky configured the subaltern as an active agent rather than a submissive recipient of Western architecture.

It is not possible, however, to conclude that a participatory model would have achieved the construction of problem-free social housing, as it was confirmed by future trials after the 1960s. The question remains whether participation brings democracy in architecture, or ignorance of architectural expertise; the dominance of bureaucracy on both architecture and the people; or an invitation for mediocrity. Nonetheless, Schütte-Lihotzky's position in Turkey stands out as an exception in the context of housing practices of the early twentieth century that usually did not reflect on the question of participation or subaltern representability.

Schütte-Lihotzky did not have the opportunity of explaining or theorizing her architectural choices in Turkish publications. Yet, given her participation in the socialist intellectual life in İstanbul, I argue that her deliberately regionalist taste differed from nationalist tones.[230] In 1940, Schütte-Lihotzky left Turkey to help her sister, who had fallen sick in Vienna. Schütte-Lihotzky was hoping to return to Turkey shortly, but she was caught by the Gestapo and imprisoned for five years until the end of the war. Had she been able to continue her work in Turkey, she might have helped to initiate a separate discourse on social housing.

> We have to distinguish between two things. On the one hand, there is the need for the development of the society [*sosyal kalkınma*]. This can be achieved by thinking about the society's realities and by changing them. Of course, İstanbul will not forever remain a city where we grow lettuce. A program of action is necessary for İstanbul and for every corner of the country.... The second is our world of likes and dislikes [*zevk dünyamız*]. In short, the world of ours [*Kısaca dünyamız*]. I am not an esthete of collapse [*Ben bir çöküşün esteti değilim*]. Perhaps I am looking for things alive in this collapse.
>
> AHMET HAMDI TANPINAR, *Huzur*

FOUR | Convictions about Untranslatability

UNTRANSLATABLE CULTURE AND TRANSLATABLE CIVILIZATION

When Mümtaz, the leading character of Ahmet Hamdi Tanpınar's novel *Huzur* [*A Mind at Peace*], distinguished between "development" and the "the world of ours," he was reproducing a very common conceptual duality in the dilemmas of Turkish modernization. The official program of the early Turkish Republic relied on a conviction about translatability, but building a nation-state simultaneously necessitated the production of nationalist myths. In such a context, some claims to untranslatability emerged as radically chauvinistic nationalism that opposed any foreign infiltration — a position against translation per se. A more common reaction was to distinguish what I would like to call the translatable from the untranslatable, as Ziya Gökalp, one of the intellectual founders of Kemalism, did. Gökalp differentiated civilization (*medeniyet*) and culture (*hars*), defining the first as the scientific and technological progress that could be borrowed from the West and the second as a nation's authentic values. By distinguishing the untranslatable culture of a nation from the translatable civilization, by distilling out those attributes that would not

Turkey, 1923...

fit well in any other context, he thought that one could specify the allegedly essential values that should always be preserved by the nation.[1] According to a Gökalpian theory of art and architecture, Turkish architects could translate as much Western science and technology as needed, as much civilization as possible, as long as they preserved the untranslatable essence of Turkishness. This type of essentialism based on a conviction about untranslatability also became common in Turkey during the early Republic.

Just like many other intellectuals and professionals, the Turkish architects who contributed to *Arkitekt* (edited by Zeki Sayar and Abidin Mortaş) were quite conflicted about translation. While opening themselves enthusiastically to the architectural movements in foreign countries, in Europe in particular, they sought to create a uniquely nationalist expression. On the one hand, they increasingly protested the fact that foreign architects in Turkey got all of the state commissions, at times using criticism that bordered on chauvinism.[2] On the other hand, they were eager to learn and follow the zeitgeist, for which they looked unhesitatingly to the West. Each issue of *Arkitekt* recorded news from not only Germany, France, and Britain, but also Rumania, Hungary, and Czechoslovakia. Finding an architectural expression that would be both modern and national thus became the paradigmatic question for the *Arkitekt* generation (fig. 4.1). Samih Akkaynak (1904–71), a 1928 graduate of the Academy of Fine Arts in İstanbul and one of the five architects who launched the journal, wrote articles on the principles of "new" architecture in both *Muhit* and *Mimar* (later *Arkitekt*) soon after his graduation.[3] Abdullah Ziya Kozanoğlu, another founder, who graduated in 1929, was also a supporter of a movement commonly referred to as new art in the first years of his career. "The nineteenth-century architect who imitates is dead. Today a new art is born,"[4] he wrote. Yet he criticized "imitating Europe" [*Avrupayı taklit etmek*] for the sake of catching up with the zeitgeist: "We must create a new Turkish architecture."[5]

Copying architectural forms from Europe was not deemed appropriate, nor was imitating Ottoman monuments. In a typical editorial statement in 1933, *Mimar* (later *Arkitekt*) denounced the "early nationalist architectural style" of the 1920s as "a big mistake."[6] The same sentiment infiltrated essays by the art historians Behçet [Ünsal] and Bedrettin [Hamdi] during the early 1930s.[7] Enthusiastically supporting the recent movements in Europe and the United States, the writers were simultaneously cautious about constructing the same type of building in every region (*muhit*). "Regional art is both rational and national," they wrote in an assured tone,

4.1. Cover of *Arkitekt*, no. 1, 1937.

a conviction that was predicated on the neat isolation between two different spheres of architecture.[8] Making the Gökalpian distinction between the "technical and material" attributes of architecture as opposed to its "emotional, creative, and intuitive" ones, they associated the former with international values and the latter with national ones.[9] The magic synthesis between the "rational and national," between the "modern and Turkish" architecture would thus have been possible by translating the European "civilization," while simultaneously cultivating the untranslatable "culture." What also distinguished the *Arkitekt* group from their peers was their search for culture in the anonymous houses in Turkey, rather than the institutional monuments of Ottoman architecture:

> The architecture of the Turkish Revolution will be different from the old Ottoman architecture. That architecture has become *history* [*o mimari ... tarih olmuştur*] with its domes, plastered windows, forms, and life. There is no return on the road of progress [*Terrakki yolunda geri dönmek yoktur*]. Stopping means staying behind. Our experience over the years has shown us that old elements, Seljuk and Ottoman motifs are now not valuable. . . .

Those who want to narrate us something about the past: rather than repeating the name of the well-known Architect Sinan . . . , [they should tell us that] there is also the *architecture of the common people* [*halk mimarisi*]. Why don't they see this? Since the Turkish spirit is more plain and simple in these ordinary or modest works, it would be easier to understand and explain it.[10]

Although the monumental Ottoman architecture was perceived as "history" — used in a pejorative sense in many texts of the period to connote obsoleteness — the everyday architecture of the "common people" could still have relevance. The old Turkish house was thus celebrated for being authentically Turkish by virtue of its being built by the common people. This characterization was consistent with the theories of Gökalp, who also argued that members of the Ottoman elite had already been alienated from "Turkish culture" since they had gone too far in adopting the "Eastern civilization," while the "authentic Turkish culture" could be found in the products of the common people. This meant that the Turkish elite could translate Western civilization from Europe and carry it to the people, while learning Turkish culture from them in return.

The argument about untranslatability — which observes that things may resist fitting comfortably in the language, place, or medium we want to put them in — has taken multiple forms in history, up until today when Derrida and Spivak are defending it to inspiring ends (see the introduction). In this chapter, I introduce only one form and episode of this complex history, when untranslatability was perceived as the evidence of an incomparable difference, and when it had severe essentialist motivations in complete opposition to the recent poststructuralist debates. The search for the untranslatable culture was indeed a search for the origin, that authentic attribute that made an artwork Turkish and that allegedly unchanging core one was supposed to find after peeling off the civilization.

"THE ORIGINAL"

Turkey, 1912 . . .

Nothing was perceived as so appropriate for the role of this "origin" as the commonly named old Turkish house, whose typological study occupied the most productive architects of the period, including Sedad Eldem and Ernst Egli. Juxtaposing some of the competing theories on the original house would indeed reveal the perceived objectivity of this category itself.[11] As I hope to have already made clear, the definition and status of the original in conventional linguistic translation and in architectural translation are quite different. In the case of architecture, the source of translation (ideas, form-making principles, styles, or technologies that get transformed in the process of transportation) is undetectable and multiple; whereas a myth of the original in the receiving culture is operative, managing the effects of translation itself. The original is a construction, and it is the history of this construction that this chapter records. What is important here is not the true definition of the Turkish house or the German house, or whether or not one could analyze all these houses under the name of a residential type and study them typologically, but rather their definition for the architects of this period and, more pointedly, their role in German-Turkish relations. I intentionally do not define the original Turkish house or the original German house myself, but rather point to the history and consequences of their definitions during the interwar period.

The very categorization of anonymous houses under the name of the Turkish house was itself a significant appropriation of history into the nationalist ideals of the period. It is with this appropriation that the house of the Turk was given a higher status than those of the other ethnic and religious groups of the Ottoman Empire — the Armenians, Greeks, Jews, Kurds, and Alawites. It is with this appropriation that the hybrid culture that created these houses and terms of coexistence was concealed for the sake of a nation-building program. *Turkish* thus became an all-encompassing category referring to the entirety of residential buildings coming out of the Ottoman period. Although this assimilation raised the national consciousness as a guard against the disappearance of these houses during modernization, it erased the very multiculturalism of the former period. One of the goals of the art historians of the early Republic was thus to establish, in Sibel Bozdoğan's words, "the latent Turkishness of Ottoman architecture."[12] Carel Bertram suggests that the category of the Turkish house, with its specific ideological association, was created in 1912, in a public lecture at the Turkish Hearth Society (Türk Ocağı), where Hamdullah Suphi [Tanrıöver] designated these houses as a carrier of Turkish identity and cautioned against their distortion by Western infiltration.[13] The architect Arif Hikmet [Koyunoğlu?] later wrote an article to draw a similar attention to the anonymous houses in Ankara's Citadel, which he characterized as exemplary old Turkish houses.[14]

Visual and literary representations of these houses in engravings, travelers' drawings, and literature, as well as art historical studies of them, existed well before the foundation of the Republic. For instance, in Ger-

Germany, 1909

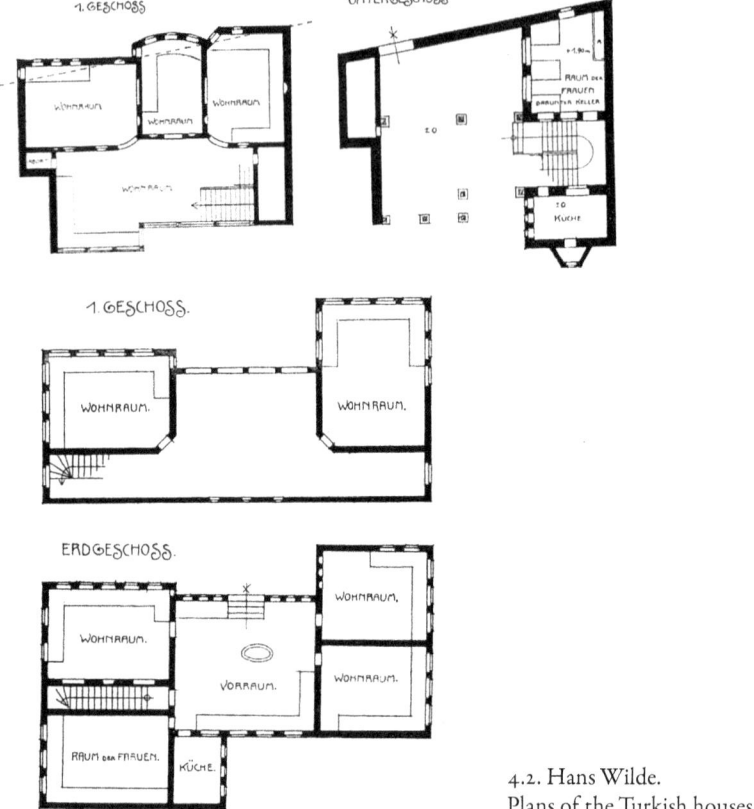

4.2. Hans Wilde.
Plans of the Turkish houses.

many, Hans Wilde published a book in 1909 on the former Ottoman capital Bursa, as part of a series edited by the architectural historian Cornelius Gurlitt.[15] Wilde devoted a comprehensive chapter to residential architecture (*Der Wohnhausbau*),[16] describing the wooden construction of these houses; the ornamentation of their doors, windows, and ceilings; and the patterns of the streets around them. Wilde explicitly used the category of the Turkish house (*Türkisches Wohnhaus*) in this study, and he was especially drawn to its difference from what was familiar to him. These features that seemed radically different to him were the separation of the *harem* (women's section) from the rest of the house, the scarcity of furniture, the multipurpose rooms that could be used both as bedrooms and living rooms, and the colorfully painted built-in closets and ceiling patterns. He also included a fairly extensive number of floor plans for one- to six-room houses, which must have been drawn for the book because no such drawings were used by the carpenters who made these houses (fig. 4.2).

The category of the Turkish house also appeared, somewhat hesitantly, in Celal Esad [Arseven]'s book *Constantinople: De Byzance à Stamboul* (Constantinople: from Byzantine to Istanbul), published in French in 1909 and in Turkish as *Eski İstanbul* in 1912.[17] Arseven (1875-1971), a painter, novelist, editor, playwright, filmmaker, and art historian, had grown up in İstanbul in one of these mansions himself; worked as a writer and editor at the newspaper *Kalem* at the turn of the century; lived in Paris, Vienna, Berlin and Munich, where he produced the German movie *Die Tote Wacht*; and then became a professor at the Academy of Fine Arts in İstanbul (circa 1920). He wrote numerous books, dictionaries, and encyclopedias, including *Constantinople*, *Türk Sanatı* (Turkish art, also published in French as *L'art Turc*), *Yeni Mimari* (New architecture), *Şehircilik* (Urbanism), and *Türkler'de Mimari* (Architecture of the Turkish people).[18] In *Constantinople*, Celal Esad [Arseven] introduced Turkish art as a category distinct from Arabic and Persian art—an attempt that was resisted by contemporary European historians, as he complained.[19] He criticized the "prejudgment" about the lack of a "Turkish art": "So many exclusively Turkish artworks have been unjustly considered as belonging to the Arabs and the Persians! It is often pretended that the nomadic people like Turks cannot have an art. [*On prétendait souvent qu'un people nomade comme les Turcs ne pouvait avoir un art*]."[20] Like many art historians who sought the "latent Turkishness of Ottoman architecture," Arseven set himself the task of proving the "purity of the ethnically constructed genealogy" on the one hand, and of responding to the biases of Orientalist European scholarship, on the other hand.[21]

Constantinople moved chronologically from the Byzantine to the Ottoman architecture and had a section on houses from both periods. According to Arseven, the Byzantine houses, of which few had survived into the twentieth century, were distinguished by their balconies, cornices, and stone construction. Analyzing the residential architecture in the Ottoman times, he shifted somewhat imprecisely between the categories "*les habitations muslumanes*" (Islamic houses) "*konak*" (mansion, left untranslated from the Turkish), and "*maison turque*" (Turkish house). He explained that the most distinguishing characteristics of these houses were the separation of the men's and women's realms (*selamlık* and *harem*); abundance of windows; *cafesses* that provided sun shading and prevented women from being seen from the street; wooden construction materials; multipurpose rooms and flexible furniture that could be used both as beds and sofas; overhanging eaves (*saçak*); and ornamentation.

However, Arseven seldom used the phrase *Turkish art* in *Constanti-*

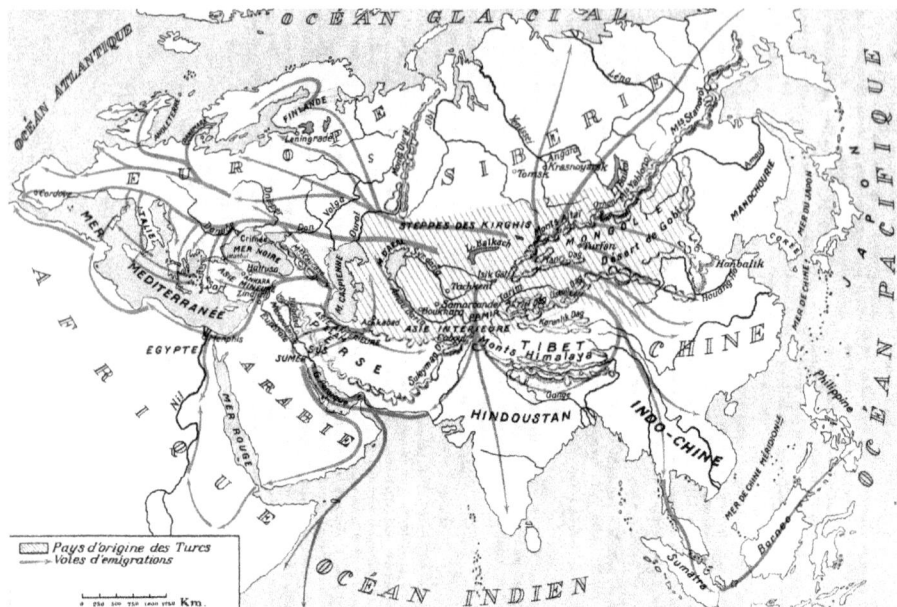

4.3. Celal Esad Arseven. Map showing the alleged immigration of Turkish tribes and influence of Turkish art.

nople, except in the introduction, where he declared it to exist, preferring instead the term *Ottoman art*. He more firmly established the first category two decades later with his comprehensive book *Türk Sanatı*, which he revised for the French version *L'art Turc* by using some of the research done at the National Architecture Seminar under Eldem and Egli.[22] Arseven's main thesis in this book was to trace the origin of Turkish art to Central Asia, and to develop art historical categories that established chains of influence from the ancient Turkish tribes to the present (fig. 4.3). This was an extension of the nationalist Turkish history thesis that claimed there were Turkish roots in early Anatolian settlements, as well as in parts of Asia and Europe. Arseven must have relied on the additional disciplinary support of the Austrian art historian Josef Strzygowski, whose book *Altai-Iran und Volkerwanderung* (Altai-Iran and migration of peoples, 1917) had already bestowed a relatively heightened role to the Turks in Islamic art. At the First Turkish History Congress in 1932, where he was invited most likely due to the resemblance of his ideas to Atatürk's historical accounts, Strzygowski ridiculed the perception of Turkish art through the lens of the distinction between civilized and barbaric.[23] Moreover, Arseven praised nomadic cultures and suggested that the original form of dwelling must have been the tent, which then must have evolved into Anatolian houses. Unsurprisingly, he called for more research that would demonstrate the historical evolution of the Turkish house from the Hittites (the ancient people of Anatolia) to the present.[24]

Against this background, Ernst Egli and Sedad Eldem, one of his assistants, initiated the *Milli Mimarlık Semineri* (National Architecture Seminar) at the Academy of Fine Arts in 1933, a research project with students that documented the anonymous houses in İstanbul and all over Anatolia. Eldem explained that the demolition of yet another memorable example of these houses, the Köprülü Amcazade Hüseyin Paşa waterfront house (see fig. 2.12), motivated them to launch this research project.[25] Egli's other assistant, Arif Hikmet Holtay, joined them after graduating from the Stuttgart Technical University in 1927, where Paul Bonatz and Paul Schmitthenner were the leading teachers.[26]

İstanbul, 1933–1940

Ernst Egli (1893–1974) had received his architectural diploma from the Viennese Technical University in 1918 and had won a doctoral degree with his dissertation on "Criticism of Protestant Churches" in 1925.[27] After working in Vienna from 1919 until 1927, he moved to Turkey to start work at the Ministry of Education in Ankara and, three years later, as a professor at the Academy of Fine Arts in İstanbul. Together with Holzmeister, whose assistant he had been in Vienna, Egli was the chief Austrian architect designing Ankara's institutional buildings.[28] During his thirteen years in Turkey (1927–40), Egli designed about thirty-three buildings and master plans for ten towns. In 1940, he left Turkey for Switzerland (his post at the Academy was taken by Bruno Taut in 1936), where he worked as a professor at the Eidgenössische Technische Hochschule (ETH) in Zurich until his retirement, except for a brief intermission during 1947–51 when he held posts in Lebanon. He returned to Turkey for an extensive tour from 1953 to 1955 to prepare a report on housing conditions.[29] He wrote various books, including *Climate and Town Districts, Sinan, Şehirciliğin ve Memleket Planlamasının Esasları* (Principles of city and country planning), and *Geschichte des Städtebau* (History of city design).[30]

Throughout the 1930s Egli's name was frequently associated with cubic architecture (see figs. 1.28 and 1.29),[31] while he seemed surprisingly committed to regionalism in his published texts. In "Mimari Muhit" (Region and architecture), he called for a regionally specific modern architecture, which he found more relevant than racial or national specificity.[32] Egli made a distinction between two types of human beings, those who were attached to their regions and the "metropolitan people" who were shaped by international values. The latter's intellect, Egli claimed, "is not under the influence of the region. This intellect creates civilization. But at the same time it destroys itself."³³ Egli did not deny the necessity of "civilization" and "international architecture," which he associated with Renaissance, Baroque, and modern periods. But he asserted that this technically and scientifically oriented architecture had to be complemented with regional concerns. Otherwise, the result would have been the "so-called modern" houses in Ankara that "copied European villas" but "had nothing to do with modern architecture" or "their region."³⁴ This distinction between *civilizational*, or translatable values, and *regional*, or untranslatable ones, must have sounded to the Turkish ears similar to Gökalp's division of civilization and culture. At the end of his article, Egli suggested that the "old Anatolian house" (*eski Anadolu evi*) could guide a new modern movement in Turkey.³⁵ He thus continued by developing a theory about the origin of these houses, which he had observed not only in İstanbul and Ankara, where he lived or worked, but also in İzmir, Denizli, Balıkesir, and Edirne where he visited between 1936 and 1939, and Tokat, where he went on a professional tour after a big earthquake hit the region in 1939.³⁶

Three years after the foundation of the National Architecture Seminar, Egli published "Das Türkische Wohnhaus" (The Turkish house) in *La Turquie Kemaliste*—the state's propaganda journal that had often used photographs of his institutional buildings as a testimony of modern Ankara's construction.³⁷ Egli's argument was predicated on the existence of a "pure" (*rein*) and "original" (*ursprünglich*) archetype of the Turkish house, which belonged to the "ancient Turkish people." This, he claimed, could best be observed in the houses of the early Ottoman period, such as the one in Edirne on which he based his theory, and in the anonymous houses of the Anatolian villages, rather than the houses in İstanbul that had been diluted with foreign influences.³⁸ In defining this allegedly pure and authentic original Turkish house, Egli used a climate-based categorization. He differentiated residential types in relation to their geographical locations on the globe, such as the northern houses of Saxony as opposed to the southern houses of Iraq, and he suggested that the Turkish house was in the middle of these poles, shaped by the moderate and "friendly climate." For this reason, Egli continued, the Turkish house stood out on account of its direct relation with nature (an important modernist ideal in Germany), in contrast to the northern and southern residential types, which had to protect the interior from either excessive cold or heat. He added that the ensemble of these houses created a unique Anatolian city design (*Städtebau*), which he unsurprisingly concluded could inspire the creation of a modern Turkish city.[39]

After moving to Zurich in 1940, Egli elaborated on his previous ideas as a full-fledged theory on the origin and historical evolution of world houses, including the German and the Turkish. At the ETH, Egli taught courses on Turkish architecture, the architect Sinan, and İstanbul during the academic years of 1941–44. After 1943, he started teaching the history and theory of city design, integrating examples from Turkey into his lectures. These eventually culminated in his books *Climate and Town Districts*, which explained cities in relation to climatic zones, and his magnum opus, *Geschichte des Städtebau*.[40] He also gave lectures about Turkey,[41] started translating the poetry of Mevlana Celalettin Rumi into German,[42] and wrote a manuscript for a novel that took place in Venice, İstanbul, and Vienna.[43]

Zurich, 1940–1951

In a lecture in front of a Swiss audience that was translated and published in the Turkish magazine *Ülkü* in 1941,[44] Egli offered a comparative diagram of the evolution of the Turkish, Roman, Greek, and Lower Saxon houses (fig. 4.4). He suggested that all human houses must have come from the farmhouse (*Bauernhaus*) — namely, all must have established a boundary on earth, a closed frontier that must have marked the property of not only a house, but also a farm. Consequently, rooms, arcades, and courtyards must have been created taking account of climatic concerns inside the original boundaries. Egli specified the wall, the garden, and the pavilion as the three primary architectural elements that made up the Turkish house. Just as he did for the Roman, Greek, and Lower Saxon houses, he speculated that the builders of the original Turkish house must have first marked a boundary on earth, and then, unlike what must have happened for the other three, the Turks must have enclosed the zone with a wall and placed a garden inside. Maintaining that nomadism was the identity of Turkishness, Egli asserted that this was a peculiarity in nomadic cultures. The Turks must have then placed tents in this enclosed garden, he continued; they must have differentiated the women's and men's tents; these tents must have then evolved into pavilions, and then into *köşks* with extension bays, and eventually into *sofas*, when the area in between must have been covered with a roof (fig. 4.5).[45]

In speculating about the original house that must have informed all subsequent episodes in architectural history, Egli's intentions were similar to those of the primitive hut theorists. But unlike Semper's or Laugier's theories of the primitive hut, which assumed a universal relevance, Egli's

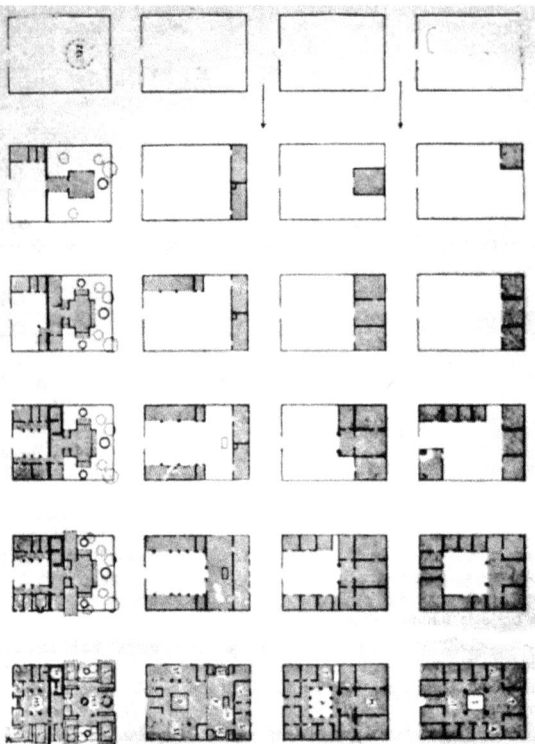

4.4. Ernst Egli. Comparison of the evolution of Turkish, Saxon, Greek, and Roman houses, 1941.

theory presumed different original houses coming out of different climatic zones. Another set of precedents for Egli must have been the studies on the origin and historical evolution of the German house, which had been a common topic since the late nineteenth century. Egli's tracing of the origins of all world houses to the farmhouse was an unprecedented argument for the Turkish house, and quite an unusual one for the Roman and Greek houses. However, it fit well with contemporary theories on the origin of houses in Lower Saxony. This was indeed a common argument in German-speaking countries, where Rudolf Henning, Rudolf Meringer, Bruno Schmidt, Kurt Junge, and Erich Wolfrom, among others, sought to find the origin of the German house in the *Bauernhaus* (farmhouse).[46] In his book *Das deutsche Haus in seiner historischen Entwicklung* (The German house in its historical development), Henning, in particular, differentiated between residential types in relation to the constructed regions of Europe (fig. 4.6). The rectangular schemes in Egli's comparative diagram drawn to speculate on the stages of the Lower Saxon *Bauernhaus* with a stove burning in the hall (*Diele*) was quite similar to the diagram

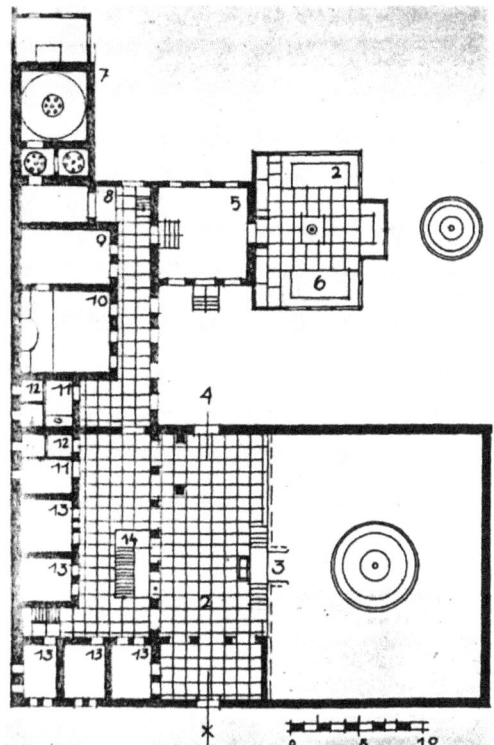

4.5. Waterfront house in Bebek that Ernst Egli used to illustrate his theory.

of a "Saxon Farm-House" in Henning's book, and in Meringer's. The same diagram appeared as a "North German farmhouse" in Schmidt's book and a "lower Saxon house" in Junge's book. In other words, Egli's hypothesis about the original Turkish house was in harmony with the theories about the original German house and extended some of the methodological and conceptual tools that had become commonplace in Europe to the rest of the world. This was a universalist theory that traced the origin of world habitation in the rectangular *Bauernhaus*, while defining climate-based differences. Bracketing the paradox of tracing the origin of nomadic cultures in the farmhouse, Egli overassimilated the other into his preconceived notions of self, in order to justify the universality of his own theory of history.

In his lectures at the ETH, Egli used his findings in the National Architecture Seminar and reiterated his theory on the original farmhouse and its evolution into German, Greek, Latin, Saxon, and Turkish houses.[47] He specified the architectural features of Turkish houses in terms similar to the existing descriptions of the other houses, such as their wooden

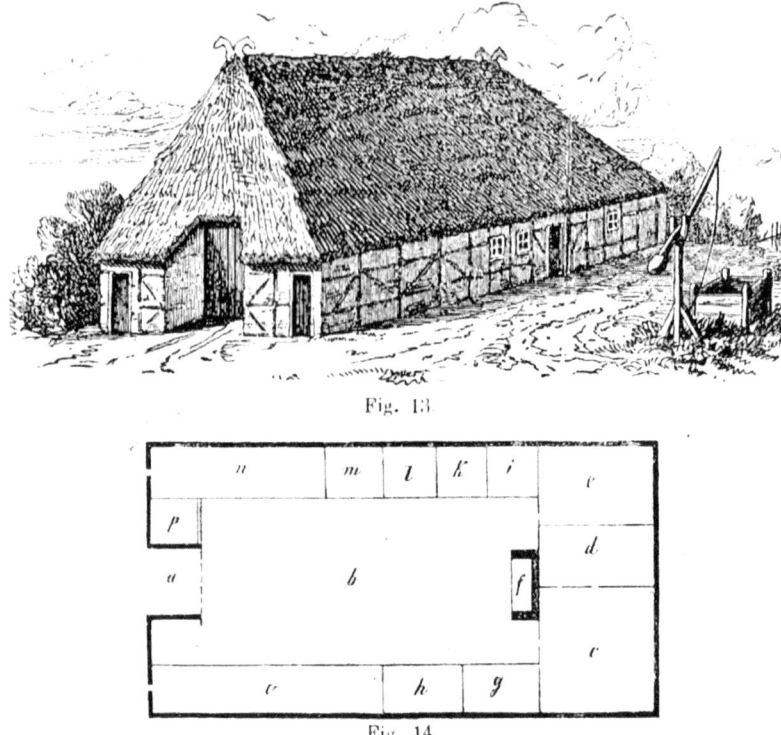

4.6. Rudolf Henning. "Saxon Farm-House," 1882.

and clay construction materials, extension bays (*cumba*), platforms at the periphery of rooms (*sedir*s) that could be used as beds and couches, built-in closets, double-height windows, and ornamented ceilings.[48]

Egli's lecture notes in German indicate that he frequently referred to a space called *sofa* while speaking about the old Turkish houses. However, he was quite imprecise in using this term, at times defining *sofa* as the "core of the house,"[49] at other times using it to indicate a courtyard, a main room, or even an ordinary room. At one point, he translated *sofa* as *Wohndiele*—a common term in Germany that usually designated the main central space in farmhouses.[50] Tellingly, it was Egli's translator, Cemal Köprülü, who changed these terms for the Turkish version.[51] The translation of the word *sofa* had indeed created considerable confusion in historical studies. Wilde also was perplexed about what would be an appropriate German translation, using *Wohnraum* in some examples that would come to be known as *sofa* to the Republican readers, and *Vorraum* in others.⁵² Eldem translated *sofa* as *antichambre* in French (as opposed to *chambre* [*oda*] in Turkish), and as *hall* in English.⁵³ Egli left the term *sofa* untranslated, even though he usually misused it.

This difficulty in translation was indicative. According to Eldem, the *sofa* indeed distinguished the Turkish house from any other house. He might have thus been satisfied with its seeming untranslatability in other languages. Just two years after the foundation of the National Architecture Seminar, Eldem published "Anciennes Maisons d'Ankara" (Ancient houses of Ankara), in which he started formulating a taxonomy of the old Turkish house and making a series of distinctions. The first was the differentiation between the urban house (*maison citadine*) and the country house (*maison de campagne*): he defined the former as one with a private courtyard separated from the street by a high wall, and the latter as a free-standing building in the middle of nature (fig. 4.7).⁵⁴ The second was the separation of the service and served spaces, the former almost always located on the semi-open ground floor, and the latter on the upper floors.⁵⁵ More important, Eldem made a distinction between the spaces reserved for reception and the life of the family. He would soon name this as the *sofa-oda* duality and theorize it as the main characteristic organization that made the Turkish house unique.

Eldem did not have the opportunity to publish the findings of the National Architecture Seminar until 1954, but he declared that the research was completed in 1940.⁵⁶ *Türk Evi Plan Tipleri* (Basic plan types of the Turkish house) concentrated exclusively on the typological study of the old Turkish houses, illustrating 267 floor plans without a single photograph or elevation that gave information about what these houses actually looked like. (There was only one rough section that did not communicate much other than the number of floors.) First, the book claimed a new theory on the origin and dissemination of these houses. Unlike Arseven's thesis that traced the original Turkish house to the ancient tribes of Central Asia, Eldem suggested that the type must have emerged in Anatolia during the reign of the Ottomans, and once the Ottoman Empire colonized new lands, it must have been gradually integrated into Bulgaria, Yugoslavia, and parts of Greece. On the East and South, Eldem drew the border at Iran and Syria, which, he claimed, were under the influence of the Arabic and Iranian house. In differentiating the Turkish house from that of the Arabic and the Iranian, and in claiming the impact of the Turkish house on the Balkans, Eldem's theory conformed readily to the contemporary ideologies of nationalist historiography.

İstanbul, 1933–1948

4.7. Sedad Eldem. Sketch of urban house and country house, 1935.

Second, he was unmistakably clear about the urgent need to raise consciousness about the obliteration of these houses due to modernization: "Old houses are being pulled down continually and replaced by new products of a totally foreign conception. Fires, wars, and disasters of all kinds have altered old towns beyond recognition."[57] In a sentence omitted from the English translation also published in the book, he continued: "The allegedly European lifestyle [*Avrupai olduğu zannedilen bir yaşama tarzı*], the fascination with the cubic house, and alienation from garden and nature, have deteriorated our residential culture like a deadly disease."[58]

Third, Eldem offered a typological assessment. Despite their geographical expansion, these houses shared the "same conception in plan"[59] — an argument that he sought to prove in the rest of the book. Unlike Arseven's descriptive analyses or Egli's hypothesis about the original Turkish house, Eldem was interested in finding the common aspects in the floor plans of the existing examples, which, he asserted, were all composed of *oda* (room), *sofa* (common room, translated in the book as *hall*) and transition areas (stairs and corridors). The service spaces, such as kitchens

4.8. Sedad Eldem. Drawing of an outdoor *sofa*.

and baths, were often placed outside. The rooms in the old Turkish house were different from their European counterparts because they were the "equivalent of a house," used by one nuclear family for multiple functions. *Hane* (dwelling) was another common name for *oda*. This also gave a unique meaning to the *sofa*—which received by far the largest share of Eldem's attention and was the indispensable key to his theory: "It is in this that the Turkish house differs most greatly from the West European house.... Apart from being a circulation space, the *sofa* is where the whole household gets together."[60] The *sofa* was the public realm, the street, the square inside the house, Eldem continued (fig. 4.8).

Based on this definition, Eldem identified four types of the old Turkish house, which were also conceived as stages of a historical evolution.[61] The one without a *sofa* (*sofasız tip*), what he calls the most primitive type, was used in the hot southern regions, where the functions of the *sofa* took place in the courtyard. The one with an outer *sofa* (*dış sofalı tip*), used in moderate climates, had an agreeable open but covered gallery (also called *hayat*) that overlooked the garden or the courtyard. The one with an inner *sofa* (*iç sofalı tip*) must have evolved from the previous type by adding a second row of rooms to the open *sofa*. And finally, the one with a central *sofa* (*orta sofalı tip*) was what he deemed the most advanced type of house found in İstanbul, the *telos* in Eldem's theory. It had an orderly, oval main hall—shaped like a cross, a *T*, or an *L*—surrounded on all sides

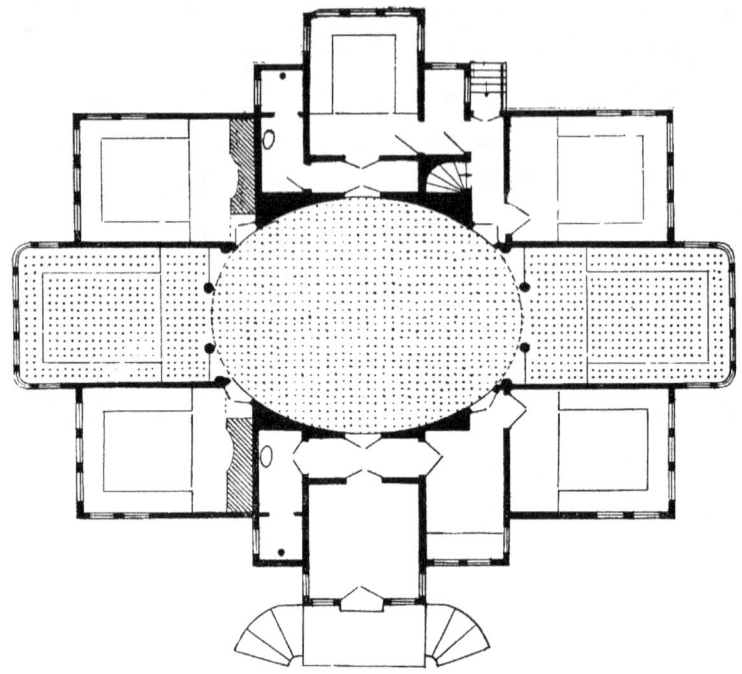

4.9. Sedad Eldem. Turkish house with a central *sofa* (Nispetiye waterfront house in Bebek).

with rooms (fig. 4.9; also see fig. 2.23).[62] Even though some regions still remained faithful to the previous stages, the evolution must have culminated in İstanbul, Eldem suggested; progress must have moved from the provincial to the metropolitan. If Egli extended his methodological tools and notions of the Saxon house to the Turkish house, Eldem behaved similarly by extending his observations on İstanbul houses to define the Turkish house as a whole. This evolutionary theory opposed two contemporary arguments: first, that the houses in İstanbul were distorted examples of the original Turkish house because they were allegedly diluted by foreign influences; and second, that they were a variation of the Greco-Roman houses.[63]

Eldem continued his research and publications on the Turkish house until the end of his life. The research was finally documented not only with plans but also with comprehensive section, elevation, and detail drawings as well as photographs, in the two-volume *İstanbul Yalıları* (Waterfront houses of İstanbul) and the five-volume *Türk Evi* (Turkish house) — whose final two volumes remain unpublished due to his death.[64]

The decision to document the old Turkish houses systematically meant to define them in texts, with photographs and drawings; it meant to represent them with objective drawings that could be preserved in archives, published, and shared with other professionals. This was ultimately a decision to translate the old Turkish house into a modern language. Unlike the makers of these houses, the architects of the National Architecture Seminar represented these buildings with their modern professional tools, such as floor plans, sections, and elevations, which had been the results of prior translations of the European educational system. The floor plans produced in the National Architecture Seminar were published in 1944,[65] the floor plans in *Türk Evi Plan Tipleri* were redrawn with a unified representative style. The carpenters and masons who built these old Turkish houses, especially the ones in villages, hardly ever designed them by using these representational modes. It was only after a professional architectural education that the architects and students could notate these houses in Cartesian ground plans and sections, and Eldem could prepare a typological matrix of these houses. His theory on the old Turkish house, which in turn influenced the architectural practice of his generation and after, was hence possible only after this translation. In other words, the particular translation from building to drawing was predicated on a prior cross-cultural translation in architectural representation. Ironically, it was with this translation that the architects claimed to have discovered the allegedly untranslatable core of a culture: the origin of the Turkish house.

Contemporary writers and architects of the National Architecture Seminar often drew attention to the fires that demolished these wooden houses. Little did they know that another fire at the Academy of Fine Arts would wipe out the recorded history of these houses as well. Between 1,000 and 1,500 examples were said to have been measured, recorded, and translated into modern drawings in the seminar before a fire at the school burned them on April 1, 1948.[66] The recorded history of the houses, some of which had already been demolished by then due to fires and neglect thus disappeared in another fire.

AGAINST TRANSLATION?
THE NATIONAL HOUSE AND *SIEDLUNG*

By the end of the 1920s, the productivity of the social housing programs such as Berlin's GEHAG (to which Martin Wagner, Bruno Taut and others had contributed) and Das Neue Frankfurt (led by Ernst May), as well as

Stuttgart, 1927–1943

the success of what was commonly named as *Neues Bauen* (new buildings or new architecture) were well recognized.[67] The works associated with both were shown in major exhibitions and published in influential periodicals. Meanwhile, the dispute between the aesthetically conservative and innovative architects took on ever more strident tones, which will only be briefly summarized here due to the existing scholarship. One of the main topics in this opposition was the controversy over the flat roof, whose beginnings predated the Weimar period.[68] Richard Linneke, associated with Berlin's GEHAG, wrote in favor of the flat roof, especially for the multifamily urban blocks in a *Siedlung* due to its economical and practical advantages. However, he also stated that single-family row houses had other criteria. In this case, the GEHAG was "unprejudiced" in its use of pitched roofs because of the agreeable street scale and proportionate façades they generated on the outside, as well as the pleasant atmosphere and additional attic space they provided in the inside.[69] The mouthpiece of the Frankfurt housing program, *Das Neue Frankfurt*, devoted a special issue to the flat roof (parts reprinted in GEHAG's mouthpiece *Wohnungswirtschaft*), with support from May, Le Corbusier, Adolf Behne, Josef Frank, Andre Lurçat, J. J. P. Oud, and others.[70] The flat roof was discussed in relation to technical matters, including new potentials of reinforced concrete, insulation, water proofing, drainage, maintenance, and cost, but commentators did not fail to conclude that these technical parameters led to the establishment of the flat roof as the new unifying expression of the age.[71]

Meanwhile the circles advocating *Heimatstil* criticized flat roofs for having no national character, for copying oriental forms, and for being inappropriate to the German climate and culture. Paul Schultze-Naumburg's increasingly racist statements after 1925 deemed "exotic foreign influences" to be causes of the German culture's degeneration and associated the flat roof with the "Oriental"—that is, Jewish—people.[72] The flat and pitched roofs were soon loaded with reified political meanings, respectively symbolizing internationalism versus nationalism. The controversy caused its first biggest practical consequence when local officials prevented Walter Gropius from building a housing neighborhood in the city of Weimar, probably because of the proposed flat roofs.

The second round ended with the victory of the flat roofers, when Mies van der Rohe required that participating architects use flat roofs and white walls as one of the unifying features of the *Siedlung* Weissenhof in Stuttgart in 1927.[73] This *Siedlung* was conceived of as a building exhibition associated with the new architecture, with the participation

4.10. Propaganda against *Siedlung* Weissenhof as an Oriental village, Stuttgart, 1927. Postcard.

of international architects including Mies, Le Corbusier, Bruno Taut, Hans Scharoun, J. J. P. Oud, and Hans Poelzig, who were asked to demonstrate the transformation of the residential sphere due to industrialization. Mies designed the site plan and the only multifamily building with steel-frame construction that eliminated load-bearing walls as inner separators. Despite the emphasis on industrialization, and despite the launch of the dwellings as prototypes of mass housing, *Siedlung* Weissenhof was hardly collective housing. In the exhibition catalogue, Mies declared that he intentionally kept away from "typification and rationalization" to give creative freedom to the participants. Consequently, the project did not explore the possibilities of repetition, dwelling types, and standardization in mass-produced units. Most of the architects designed single-family free-standing houses for wealthy families with generous spaces, terraces, garages, and maids' rooms. Its limits for mass production and lower-income housing notwithstanding, the building exhibition became a cornerstone for the launch of new architecture to a wider audience, while its success sparked strident opposition from the established Stuttgart architects Schmitthenner and Bonatz, who launched a campaign denouncing it for its Oriental or Jewish character (fig. 4.10).

The third round in the flat roof controversy took place in 1929 over Bruno Taut's *Siedlung* Onkel Toms Hütte in Berlin. Taut was criticized in popular newspapers and architectural magazines for putting "ugly modern boxes with flat roofs into our beautiful forest" (see fig. 3.13).[74] His building blocks were contrasted with the pitched roofs and freestanding houses that Schmitthenner, Heinrich Tessenow, and Alexander Klein built for another cooperative, Gemeinnützige Aktien-Gesellschaft für Angestellten-Heimstätten (GAGFAG), just across the street. In Taut's own words, "what was played out in the forest suburb of Zehlendorf in Berlin in 1929 was the precursor of that which the whole Germany would experience in 1933."[75]

The controversy that surfaced as a difference of aesthetic and professional choice between the flat and pitched roof of these particular *Siedlung* architects was indeed an ethical split. In some respects, it was a mirror of the rising controversy between Berlin and the countryside during the Weimar period. Some writers condemned Berlin as a source of "demonic life," whose cosmopolitan culture, they believed, threatened the allegedly authentic and pure culture of the German countryside, especially of the south. Already in 1919, Ludwig Finckh stated:

> A small minority in Berlin keeps German people in suspense. What do they want? At bottom, nothing other than what the pacifists and the cosmopolitans want: the worldwide brotherhood of peoples.... *But Berlin is not Germany*.... We in southern Germany will no longer go along with it. We want to have a nation.... To the spirit of Berlin another must be opposed, *the spirit of Germany*.[76]

There was but one step from the attack on cosmopolitanism to the advent of nationalism and racism. In 1930, Finckh's attitude resonated in Wilhelm Stapel's words, so clearly indicative of what was to be expected in the following decade:

> All opposition of this sort concerns itself not only with the struggle against the metropolitan as such, against *deracination*; but in particular with the struggle against the spirit of *this* metropolis.... All too many Slavs and all too many altogether uninhibited East European Jews have been mixed into the population of Berlin. It is an embarrassing mixture.... The spirit of the German people rises against the spirit of Berlin. The demand of the day can be summarized like this: the rebellion of the countryside against Berlin.[77]

The established architects of the Stuttgart circle had been unambiguously vocal in this controversy. In *Baukunst im neuen Reich* (Building art in the new reich), Schmitthenner denounced the social housing programs during the Weimar period as "ugly international buildings of *Neue Sachlichkeit* with a Bolshevik spirit."[78] Wagner replied to this by defending his group's program with the technological shifts of the age, rather than responding to the political implications of such an accusation:

> If you just want to remain being an artist—which nobody would contest—you may live in your old world of old forms with your entire heart. If you also want to perform as a social politician and a life reformer, and if you want to make promises to the masses, then you must also think about the means and methods to fulfill these purposes. You will not be able to build your village houses—and I say this with total empathy—without the sharpest immersion of your whole work in the modern technical zeitgeist.[79]

Paul Bonatz (1877–1956) had become one of the foremost architects associated with Stuttgart, working with his partner Friedrich August Scholer.[80] They were especially well known for the design of the Stuttgart Railway Station.[81] Bonatz was an influential professor at the Stuttgart Technical University and an architect much in demand by the upper-income families in the city for designing houses for them.[82] Bonatz joined Schultze-Naumburg and Schmitthenner in the group called Block, which opposed the architects of the *Neues Bauen*. Yet he was a close follower of the technological advances in architectural construction, rather than a faithful supporter of traditional methods. Bonatz's seemingly ambiguous position in regard to the established architectural camps challenged easy categorization, and this must have led to the architectural historian Hartmut Frank's words: "Bonatz was fighting on two fronts. He wanted a modern architecture different from that of the *Neues Bauen* and a traditionalism different from Speer's neoclassicism."[83]

However, Bonatz's position in the campaign against *Siedlung* Weissenhof in Stuttgart was evident when he denounced it as a "suburb of Jerusalem" in the local newspaper.[84] Bonatz was not an architect of *Siedlungen*, yet he did participate in the collective housing project for the German Wooden House Exhibition (*Ausstellung Deutsches Holz für Hausbau und Wohnung*) in Stuttgart in 1933. Organized by Schmitthenner, the *Siedlung* was envisioned as an anti-Weissenhof project, where the architects were asked to design for wooden construction that resulted in pitched roofs. It brought together twenty-five single and double houses designed by Bonatz, Paul Heim, and Hans Volkart, among others. Bonatz designed the only multifamily building (fig. 4.11).[85]

When the National Socialist party came to power in 1933, the values of collective housing in Germany became significantly less popular, and conservative views became more widespread. In addition to the residential aesthetics with pitched roofs and traditionalist aesthetics, the Nazi

4.11. Paul Bonatz. Multifamily house in the German Wooden House Exhibition, Stuttgart, 1933.

housing program promoted single-family houses with private gardens. Due to the regime change, Wagner moved to Turkey in 1935. Taut had already escaped from Germany in 1933, entering Switzerland via Stuttgart with only a few books. From there he had gone to Russia and then to Japan for three years, eventually reaching Turkey, where he stayed until his untimely death (chapter 5).

Bonatz built several autobahns, gas stations, and bridges for Hitler's Germany (fig. 4.12). Although he did not get any satisfying commissions for the Third Reich's institutional buildings, his participation in the Nazi environmental program was incontestable given the emphasis on autobahns and bridges in the making of a controlled society.[86] As a matter of fact, these structures were meant to be the keystones in the process of combining the antimetropolitan settlements in the countryside and creating a unified spirit among the nation, since they connected small towns with fast communication systems.[87] Bonatz took the National Socialist propaganda exhibition *Neue deutsche Baukunst* (New German architecture) to Turkey in 1943, and he moved there the following year. If we are to believe his memoirs, written after the war, Bonatz was not hostile to his colleagues who were exiled from Germany, despite their different political and professional affiliations. He helped Taut escape from Germany via Stuttgart just after the National Socialists came to power.[88]

4.12. Caricature of Paul Bonatz leaving the office to show his projects to Hitler.

Bonatz was also one of the most influential teachers at the Stuttgart Technical University, where he had started working as an assistant to Theodor Fischer in 1902.[89] This school had many Turkish graduates, including Arif Hikmet Holtay, Kemali Söylemezoğlu, and the Bulgarian immigrant Ahmet Sabri Ozan, who all had important practices in Turkey later.[90] With his students, Bonatz continued his search for modern monumentality and nationalist expression. Söylemezoğlu, who was Bonatz's student in 1936 and worked in his office after graduation from 1939 to 1940, recalled that his professor asked students to explore German architecture but segregated him from this task, requesting Turkish examples instead. Bonatz also assigned his students to design the Railway Station in Ankara in 1930, for which Fritz Schumacher, Robert Hussendörfer, and Walter Hertkorn produced quite outstanding visions. Ozan designed a mosque in İstanbul in Bonatz's studio at the university (fig. 4.13).

Ankara, 1942–1946

The controversy between the flat and the pitched roof resonated for one more time in Turkey. Franz Hillinger, a colleague of Taut, informed the Turkish audience about the flat roof debate in Germany in an article published in 1941.[91] Nevertheless, the debate in Turkey was less about the flat roof than about international architecture as opposed to the national Turkish house. Nowhere was the paradoxes of a strident nationalism in collective housing as openly exposed as in *Siedlung* Saraçoğlu, designed

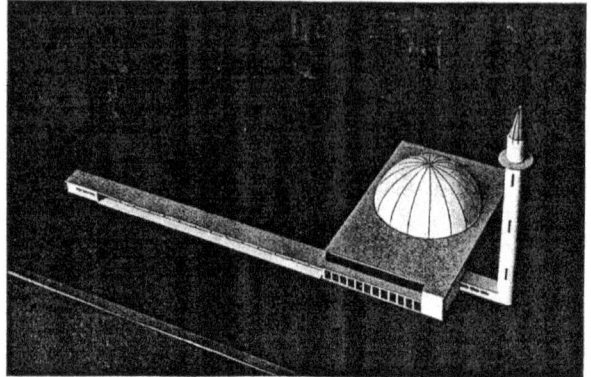

Modell 1 : 500

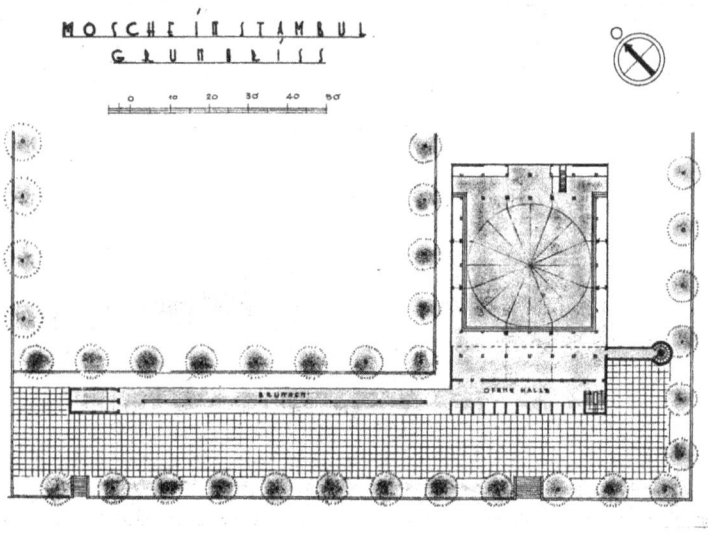

Grundriß 1 : 100

4.13. Ahmet Sabri Ozan. Student project for a mosque in İstanbul in Paul Bonatz's studio at Stuttgart Technical University.

by Bonatz, a collective housing project with 435 dwelling units built for government officials at the center of Ankara, close to the National Assembly. The project was on the agenda as early as the 1930s. Ernst Egli had already designed an initial proposal for the site, which was canceled after the implementation of the main streets in accordance with Jansen's master plan.[92] Jansen had tried to secure the commission for himself in 1935.[93] In 1937, Taut guided an architectural design studio at the Academy of Fine

Arts in preparing a plan for this site; the students proposed parallel building blocks and efficient dwelling units for families in various sizes (see fig. 3.24). Yet it was Bonatz who eventually received the commission, in 1944. Bonatz's design for Saraçoğlu was the most obvious hybrid of the German *Siedlung* and the Turkish house trajectories, but one that was not directed toward a cosmopolitan ethics.

Previously a jury member in the architectural competition for Atatürk's mausoleum in Ankara in 1942, Bonatz became an unmistakable defender of nationalism in Turkey, as his opening speech for the National Socialist propaganda exhibition *Neue deutsche Baukunst* already foreshadowed.[94] Starting with Hitler's statement that "no People lives longer than the documents of its Culture,"[95] Albert Speer's introduction to the catalogue of this exhibition—which was published both in German and Turkish—stressed the importance of architecture for National Socialism and the inadequacy of bourgeois culture to create a great civilization. Speer claimed that the National Socialist program had achieved a new German architecture within a very short period of time. In his speeches, Bonatz made similar statements. After a glorification of classical architecture, he complained about the decline of this tradition due to "industrialization," "liberalism," and "individualism." He accused modern architecture, especially Expressionism and Romanticism, for obliterating classical architecture and creating "ugly buildings of technique" and fashionable individual styles for the sake of originality. Not surprisingly, Bonatz defended the revival of cultural roots and the search for nationalist architecture: "Erasing [cultural values] means impoverishment. Seizing one's own culture consciously means building national strength. This brings us to tradition. . . . We can sense the strength springing out of the essential land of every place and feel the pain of rootlessness."[96] The days of the Neues Bauen had passed, in favor of a new phase in monumental architecture. "The time is not the time of tender feelings," Bonatz wrote. "What needs to be expressed and represented is a solid and merciless destiny [*sert ve insafsız bir talih*]."[97] Although he had scorned industrialization and technical progress in modernist aesthetics, he did not hesitate to put all advanced technical possibilities in the service of this monumentality.[98] Needless to say, for Bonatz, monumentality was the true expression of a strong state and revolution, which he claimed to be the only possible impetus for a "new style."[99] Moreover, Bonatz quite explicitly pointed out some similarities between Hitler's Germany and Atatürk's Turkey: "Ankara is an example of what a nation can construct under the direction of a strong statesman in less than twenty years. Great movements in architecture do not always appear with great movements in politics. However, if these two take place together, as in the rise of Turkey and today's Germany, if all the forces are directed to great ambitions, one can witness wonderful accomplishments."[100]

The rise of fascist architecture in Germany and Italy through the late 1930s and early 1940s was closely observed in *Arkitekt*'s circles. B. O. Celal, who wrote frequent articles on ancient Anatolian and Ottoman monuments, criticized amnesiac and dismissive attitudes toward historical architecture, comparing "art nouveau, cubism, and modern" art to the fashionable taste of "spoiled children."[101] He praised the rise of national architecture in Germany and Italy, criticized the "rude, foreign, and dull imitations" of Western forms in current architecture, and called on artists to take national architecture seriously as a "national duty." Maintaining the "Turkish history thesis" that claimed archaic origins for Turkish architecture, he asked architects to continue this "glory."[102] Abdullah Ziya [Kozanoğlu] praised the fifth architectural exhibition for Mussolini, as well as the fascist program for building an architectural expression of the new Italian regime.[103] Many Turkish architects referred to Germany and Italy to justify their demand for state support for the rise of a national architecture.[104] In this milieu, Eldem himself adopted more nationalist tones, as demonstrated in his article "Yerli Mimariye Doğru" (Toward a regional architecture), among others, where he shifted rather randomly between the categories of the regional and the national, and proposed to limit foreign architects' influence on Turkish architecture.[105] Nobody criticized the ideology of the National Socialist exhibition in professional journals (although some criticized it on a stylistic basis).[106] Behçet Ünsal described it as the unmistakable move toward another era in world architecture.[107]

With or without the influence of the *Neue deutsche Baukunst* exhibition, but certainly related to the move toward nationalism in fascist countries, a stylistic shift took place in Turkey in the mid-1940s in favor of neoclassical architecture and a traditionalist approach to the Turkish house. The old Turkish house could now be used as an inspiration not only for residential architecture, but also for monumental buildings. Bonatz was one of the main promoters of nationalism in Turkey, through his architectural and educational practice throughout the 1940s as well as his role as a senior juror in almost every competition.[108] Bonatz regarded himself as the first foreigner who did not import a European style to Turkey but instead searched for a national one. In a letter to a friend in Germany, he wrote: "I am very much in agreement with the professors at the Academy and the T[echnical] U[niversity], working with them in friendly terms.

And here I have authority.... In total harmony with the students, we all search together for a healthy Turkish contemporary style that could be developed out of the Turkish tradition."[109] In this search for a national expression, Bonatz too looked for the origins of the old Turkish house and did not hide his appreciation for Sedad Eldem:

> Sedad is the *Führer* of the Turkish architectural school — that is, he is the young architect who has set himself free from the guardianship of foreign fashions [*Vormundschaft von Mode-Fremden*].... After two decades of lame European imitations [*Nachahmung*] — one might say fashionable journalism — Sedad showed that one could awaken the roots of his own new life right out of the reasonable traditions, not from the Arabic ornament, but from the eternal values of climate, material, customs [*Lebensgewohnheit*], elaborate Turkish proportion, rhythm, and crafts.... [I] argue that the youth must be brave and should not imitate Europe. I emphasize this search in the examples that I build.[110]

In the *Siedlung* Saraçoğlu in Ankara, Bonatz put these ideas into practice. The project was sponsored by the Turkish Emlak Bank for government officials, and it received extensive media coverage from the day that construction began in 1944 until the opening ceremony of its first phase, during the annual celebration of the republic's foundation in 1945.[111] The second phase was finished a year later, although the construction of common services such as the casino, school, and lieutenant's building was delayed.[112] The *Siedlung* covered an area of 300 by 500 meters and contained eight different dwelling types. As an alternative to the single-family freestanding houses of the Bahçelievler Housing Cooperative, apartments were placed in three- or four-story multifamily buildings that ran parallel in the site. Rather than relying on the *Zeilenbau* principle, Bonatz preferred that the entrances of the buildings face each other, defining city streets and shared backyards. The common park offered a spectacular view of the Ankara Castle, something Bonatz carefully designed by drawing numerous perspectives (fig. 4.14). The dwelling units were composed of two, three, or five rooms, with a spacious space named *hol* in between — which Bonatz might have considered as a version of a *sofa*. This was rather an unusual choice in a unit priding itself on efficiency and the maximum use of space. Service spaces were also atypically organized for a collective housing project of this kind: the bathrooms were as big as the kitchens, they were sometimes placed at opposite sides of a unit, and they thus made extra infrastructure pipes necessary. Bonatz's attention was directed instead toward the symbolism of the neighborhood. As he underlined in

4.14. Paul Bonatz. *Siedlung* Saraçoğlu, perspective of the common garden, Ankara, 1944–46.

his explanation report, he provided balconies with wooden balustrades of tightly woven patterns and lots of extension bays (*Erker*) in "accordance with the Turkish style" (fig. 4.15).[113] In providing these Turkish elements, Bonatz did not pay the same attention, however, to their use.[114]

Among the enthusiastic accolades in the Turkish media, a journalist who went by the initials T. I. reported on public acclamations at the opening ceremony: "For the first time in my life, I feel I am in a modern neighborhood suitable for Ankara."[115] The newspaper *Ulus* devoted a whole page to the article "Toward a National Architecture" (which, so the rumor went, was written by Bonatz himself, but was signed by Fatih Metigil).[116] Here, the Saraçoğlu neighborhood was characterized as a perfect example of nationalist architecture still complying with the requirements of modern life: "In short, Turkish spirit [*Türk ruhu*] rules in these houses, and the Saraçoğlu neighborhood is a beautiful example of modern national Turkish architecture that we wish every architect in this country would reflect upon."[117]

What was once a hesitant response to the foreignizing translations of the Kemalist regime now became the voice of the victor. The old Turkish house was now regarded as the inspiration for the new architecture of the regime. Unlike in Bahçelievler, where the government officials had prided themselves in 1935 for living in a European residential settlement that they made sure would be untouched by the old Turkish style, the government officials in *Siedlung* Saraçoğlu a decade later appreciated a neighborhood that allegedly originated from the old Turkish house. In less than two decades, a movement that had started as a melancholic attachment to İstanbul's wooden houses had turned into an exclusive nationalism.

4.15. Paul Bonatz. *Siedlung* Saraçoğlu, Ankara, 1944–46. The drawings of trees on the photograph have been added by Bonatz himself.

Turkish architects involved with professional journals were not equally satisfied with *Siedlung* Saraçoğlu.[118] Yet they seem to have been particularly provoked by the media applause, as if Bonatz was the only architect who was searching for a national architectural expression. The editors of *Arkitekt* often attacked Bonatz for having opportunistic relations with the state and for "behaving like a politician rather than an artist."[119] Critics opposed the project based on functionalist criteria, disapproving the long corridors, lack of privacy in some rooms, and inappropriate circulation—such as the long distance between the kitchen and dining room, and the access to the maid's room from the bathroom.[120] Yet it was still the project's symbolism that aroused the biggest discontent. In Orhan Alsaç's words:

> However, it is clear that these houses are designed by a foreigner who has been dazzled by the enchanting effect of the old Turkish houses [*eski Türk evlerinin büyüleyici tesiri*], and has sacrificed a lot of things for the sake of imitating them. . . . The interiors of the buildings have always been sacrificed to the desire to imitate the exteriors of the old Turkish houses. . . . These may be interesting for a foreign architect. Or travelers [*seyyahlar*] sightseeing the neighborhood may like it. Yet this sacrifice is not correct at the expense of the dweller's comfort. . . . All of us find beautiful features that we admire in our old clothes. But still, no Turk would attend a

ball with a *zeybek* clothing, unless it is a costume ball; and this would not make him lose any of his Turkishness. Foreigners always pity us for throwing away our old clothes, but they never ever think of wearing these clothes themselves.[121]

This passage alone reveals multiple tensions in the contact zone of translation, as well as the inconsistencies of the ideology of untranslatable national culture. If the Saraçoğlu neighborhood was the expression of a purely Turkish architecture, as Bonatz, newspaper columnists, and government officials liked to argue, why was it translating values from *Siedlungen* in Germany, such as collectivity in housing, functionalist orientation, rationalization of dwelling types, repetition, and standardization? How could Bonatz, a foreigner believing in the essentiality of cultures, practice a pure and original Turkish architecture, even if such a thing existed? Or, if the project was just a stage set, a costume ball for sentimental nostalgia, as the critics said, how was it possible that it nevertheless complied with many of the contemporary requirements in the city? The old Turkish house had been a source of inspiration for Turkish architects well before Bonatz moved to Turkey, so why did they suddenly become anxious when a foreigner engaged in this effort as well? Did not this mean that their ideas, too, were predicated on the premise of an original and untranslatable Turkish culture, which could only be revitalized by a pure Turkish designer? *Siedlung* Saraçoğlu was an obvious hybrid of the trajectories of the Turkish house and *Siedlung*, whose emergences were analyzed in previous chapters — but it was promoted as an example of pure nationalism. Moreover, the fact that the old Turkish house itself had come into being as a collective production of various ethnic groups of the Ottoman Empire was conveniently forgotten.

Both in Germany and Turkey, the design of a *Siedlung* was a matter of constant struggle between standardization and flexibility, mass and aura, sameness and difference. In the case of the Saraçoğlu neighborhood, the individual dwelling units were identical, but their ensemble was designed to build up a collective identity, a national expression that would differentiate this neighborhood from any other one in the world. The struggle for individual difference in generic housing in Germany resonated in Turkey as the search for cultural difference. However, within the nationalist climate of Turkey, as well as the fascist context growing throughout Europe before and during World War II, this request for cultural identity was now attached to the myth of the pure essential culture, which was allegedly radically different and, in most cases, superior to others.

The stronger the belief that East and West belong together, the stronger the energy to get to know the foreignness in one's nature. With the growth of this energy, the melancholy will sink down to the grave it deserves.

BRUNO TAUT, "Japans Kunst"

FIVE | Toward a Cosmopolitan Architecture

Throughout this book, I illustrated convictions about translatability in a paternalistic fashion and convictions about untranslatability in a chauvinistic fashion. I would now like to turn my attention to an exception that emerged to these two. If a building that is an obvious hybrid of multiple geographical influences can be claimed to symbolize pure nationalism, as illustrated in the previous chapter, we might as well ask what makes a hybrid distinctive. In a century that was shaped by ceaseless series of translations, hybrids were ubiquitous. Why would hybrid artifacts or multicultural populations matter if they could not accomplish the promises of modernity? For modernity, as indefinable as it may be, promises egalitarian, peaceful societies with sovereign citizens. Why would a hybrid residential culture matter if it imposed from above a way of living on some, created melancholic responses in others, maintained gender hierarchies against women, failed to sustain decent housing for the global poor, or erased the contribution of minorities? This chapter differentiates a hybrid artifact from cosmopolitan ethics and argues that the promises of translation would be fulfilled if the resulting hybrid were also motivated by a cosmopolitan ethics. I will make this argument by focusing on a specific aspect of Bruno Taut's career. Chapter 3 explored Taut's contribution to collective housing both in Germany and in Turkey, accentuating his primary role in the transformation of the German prewar garden city ideal into the interwar conception of *Siedlung*. This chapter focuses on the architect's theoretical writings at the end of his career and analyzes his own house in İstanbul through the lens of these theories. I suggest that Taut was one of the few modern architects who was consciously engaged in understanding the tensions and potentials inherent in cross-cultural translations, and in genuinely confronting the problems of modernization outside Europe. Exiled from Germany in 1933, he spent three years in Japan and two years in Turkey before his untimely death in 1938. Taut had taken an interest in non-Western architecture long before he moved to Japan and Turkey. Curiosity about the East is obviously not a value in itself, since it hardly qualifies anything unless its distinction from the Orientalist interest (in Edward Said's sense) of numerous painters, poets, or writers can be specified. Taut considered his architectural engagements in Japan and Turkey as continuous experiences.[1] Therefore, his career after leaving Germany and his last theoretical statements can hardly be understood without discussing their gradual development in all three countries. By tracing Taut's letters, diaries, and manuscripts written in Japan and Turkey, this chapter suggests the reconstruction of a theory that might be called a cosmopolitan ethics in architecture.

During the opening talk at his exhibition at the İstanbul Academy of Fine Arts, Taut linked his own intellectual growth to Immanuel Kant's humanism.[2] Perhaps it is only fitting, then, that Taut, who shared his hometown with Kant, was striving to establish a cosmopolitan ethics in architecture. In his essay "Perpetual Peace," Kant defined cosmopolitan law as the legal order that will establish what he called "perpetual peace," a peace that is not attained because both sides have temporarily consumed their material and human resources or because they have decided to provisionally suspend hostility, but a peace that annihilates the possibility of any future war.[3] This cosmopolitan ideal depended on the confidence that enlightened reason would bring peace—because, it must follow, human reason was universal, and because every human being could act in relation to universal maxims. Rather than an epilogue to his *oeuvre*, perpetual peace should be considered a guarantee, a bearer of Kant's moral theory, as formulated in *Groundwork for a Metaphysics of Morals*. For Kant, ethics is possible because human beings ought to be capable of acting with unconditional goodwill, a goodwill that motivates actions that are done out of pure duty,[4] and one that shapes categorical imperatives — that is, the maxims that can be willed to become universal laws.[5] This would construct the world as a kingdom of ends, where every human being is treated by the others as an end, rather than a means to another end; and where every human being is understood to possess equal reason, capable of acting in relation to universalizable maxims.[6]

Kant suggested a global federation of lawful states — not a single world state that he defined as "soulless despotism" — where each state, just like each individual in a society, preserves its own autonomy and treats the others with the understanding that they exist in a world of ends (not means).[7] Kant apparently uses a partial analogy to enlightened individuals who use their reasoning in order to realize their own freedom without diminishing the freedom of others in his definition of the global federation that will secure the cosmopolitan law and grant each state its own autonomy without jeopardizing that of others.[8] Perpetual peace must be an inherent requirement for the Kantian ethics because war cannot generate moral human beings. In a context where one's duty is to kill someone else or sacrifice oneself, one cannot treat all human beings as ends in themselves or act in a way that is beneficial for humanity as a whole. Therefore, placed in the context of his other writings, Kant's pursuit in "Perpetual Peace" cannot be reduced merely to a legal formula for a global federation of lawful states, which one might falsely deem accomplished in the failed institutions such as the League of Nations or the United Nations (which was not yet established in Taut's time). Rather, Kant's aspiration must have also been toward a system of ethics that identifies an individual's response to the idea of an inclusive universal community. However, as I will discuss in more detail in this chapter, the tension between the legal and ethical aspects of cosmopolitanism remained unresolved in Kant's theory, which also had Eurocentric resonances.

EX ORIENTE LUX

Taut's early texts (the ones usually attributed to his Expressionist period) were full of references to Asia.[9] Rosemarie Bletter has demonstrated that the glass utopias of Paul Scheerbart and Taut or the latter's Glass Pavilion for the Werkbund Exhibition in 1914 were more than technocratic impulses to explore the potentials of a new material. On the contrary, as Taut and Scheerbart were also aware, glass had a long history as the metaphor of sacred, spiritual, and romantic sources, including Asian ones.[10]

Germany, 1919–1933

In *Die Stadtkrone* (written during the war and published in 1919), Taut illustrated examples of cities with a "city crown" from all over the world to show how an "organic unity" could be achieved in urban settlements, in contrast to the "chaos" of the modern European cities. Taut's examples included medieval European, Indian, Chinese, and Ottoman cities, as well as a comparison between Ebenezer Howard's garden city and the Chinese city of Küfu. For Taut, this comparison proved that "all rational men end up with similar principles," although he ranked the garden city slightly higher for its potential to guide modern settlements.[11] This emphasis on rational human beings as bearers of universal values was likely a reflection of the Enlightenment ideals formulated by Kant. Through this comparison Taut was not just adding one more example from the East to his list. The assertion that the garden city's principles could be observed in a Chinese city claimed a universal truth for the model he was promoting, without any evidence of communication between the two or any in-depth analysis of the Chinese example. Here an example from the East became a vehicle to prove the alleged universality of the architect's own principles, rather than being evaluated in its own right.

In "*Ex oriente lux*" (The sun rises from the East, 1919), Taut's ideas about the East as the "savior of Europe" were most radically asserted:

> Kill the European, kill him, kill him, kill him off! Sings St. Paulus [Scheerbart]....
>
> Each tiny part of the great culture from the fourth to the sixteenth century in upper India, Ceylon, Cambodia, Amman, Siam, and on Indulines—what melting of form, what fruitful maturity, what restraint and strength and what unbelievable fusion with plastic art! ... Bow down in humility, you Europeans![12]

The forcefulness of Taut's prose needs to be understood within the bellicose context of World War I. By offering dozens of architectural examples from non-European countries as a proof of redemption, Taut not only continued his social utopian position in assigning a sanctifying value to architecture, but he also turned his gaze eastward for this purpose. Taut's antiwar ideas must have motivated his search for a model of peace and harmony in the Orient that he could not find in modern European cities at the dawn of the war.[13] This is not a type of common Orientalism that claims the superiority of the West, nor does it claim any desire to control, manipulate, or dominate the Orient. However, another sort of Orientalist undertone is still present here. The idea of the Orient's saving power in times of crisis is one of the basic symptoms of Orientalism — still in Said's sense — in its seemingly affirmative face. This type of Orientalism not only distances the Orient as the ready-at-hand solution to be taken out of the medicine chest whenever Western progress is under suspicion, but it also treats the Orient as an exotic, unchanging, and harmonious dream land deprived of progress, modernity, and the idea of history.

Taut's approach to these questions became much more refined in Japan and Turkey. The transformation may have started before he was exiled from Germany, as indicated in his book *Die Neue Wohnung: Die Frau als Schöpferin* (The new house: woman as creator).[14] The book's historical examples of anonymous Japanese and Ottoman houses held a specific place in Taut's formulation of modern dwellings. For instance, rooms without walls in Japan fascinated Taut. The movable partitions that continuously changed the division of space, and the sliding exterior walls that created different levels of continuity with the outside, inspired him to make flexibility an important principle of the modern dwelling. Taut also admired the built-in wall closets of Ottoman vernacular houses (*Wandschränke*) that functioned as minimized service spaces, freeing the rest of the room. In his own modern dwellings during the Weimar period, the service spaces such as the kitchen, bath, and closets were inspired by the Ottoman closets and similarly handled as minimum boxes to be opened up or closed down, leaving the maximum space for the living sections (fig. 5.1).[15]

To summarize, first Taut claimed — before he had left Germany — to have found the true law of land settlement simply by declaring that a Chinese city had the same principles as Howard's garden city. In doing so, he not only effortlessly assimilated the non-Western example into his own frames of reference, but he also used it to claim the universality of his own approach. A few years later, Taut treated the Orient as a region where one could search for an alternative to solve what he perceived as the Western crisis that culminated in World War I. He did not claim that Oriental architecture was inferior — quite the contrary — yet he still separated and stereotyped it almost as a nonhistorical style that was opposed to the historical progress of Western civilization. During the Weimar period, Taut continued exploring the building practices in Japan and Turkey in ways that integrated them into his own designs. Nevertheless, the occasional references to the historical examples from these regions rarely came to terms with their actual problems of modernization. This changed once Taut immigrated to these countries, when he was forced into exile after the National Socialists seized power in Germany in 1933.

5.1. Bruno Taut. Illustration of a modern room, 1924. Photo: Jan Wils.

MELANCHOLY OF THE EAST

Japan, 1933–1936

The Japanese International Association of Architects invited Taut to Japan, where he was mainly occupied with designing craft objects and researching the country's anonymous houses. As opposed to his heavy professional responsibilities in Germany and later in Turkey, Taut had fewer opportunities to build in Japan and spent his time writing books on Japanese architecture.[16] A new theory of architecture emerged from this research, which culminated in *Mimari Bilgisi* (Lectures on architecture), a book written and published in Turkey just before Taut's death.

For most of his projects in exile, Taut did more than simply transport his German practice to new locations. His designs appeared so transformed that many scholars and colleagues interpreted them as a radical change. For instance, in Germany, Taut had been highly critical of promoting the revival of values embodied in traditional German farmhouses. In Japan, however, after spending most of his time researching the country's anonymous houses, he promoted what was named as the Japanese houses and the Katsura Palace as a guide to the properties of an appropriate modern architecture in this country. Taut's texts from the period, I suggest, had two main intentions: to criticize the Western Orientalist perceptions of these regions, and to criticize the current modernization in Japan and Turkey.

Houses and People of Japan (the title was originally intended to be *The Japanese House and Its Homelife*, 1937)[17] where Taut presented the results of his research, was written in the form of a diary chronicling a one-year sojourn in Japan. Envisioned as a "contribution to international friendship,"[18] the book is a lively, detailed, interrogative representation of Taut's research on traditional Japanese houses, living habits, crafts, and clothes, as well as the Japanese confrontation with the demands of modern living. Determined not to "go back as ignorant as [he] came,"[19] Taut aspired to disclose and challenge the Western Orientalist views of Japan, which eventually led him to develop deeper thoughts on the notion of non-Western modernization: "I failed to see how the Japanese could possibly claim that their house is their castle.... But after all, these houses are nothing more than tents, though provided with roofs and structural refinements."[20] This was how Taut expressed his astonishment at his first visit to his house in Japan. Using deliberately ironic words, Taut described how he bumped his head against the low door frames during his first day, had a hard time finding door handles and other such things, desperately looked for familiar furniture, and tried to get used to the "oddities" of his new habitat—such as taking off his shoes before entering the house, surviving the hot water in the bathroom and the freezing temperature of the house, sleeping on mats, eating with chopsticks, and so on. About the houses and ways of living that he passionately researched during the rest of his stay in Japan, Taut continued:

> But could it be called a room? It was really nothing more than an open hall, raised above the level of the ground.... The problem was where to

eat, sleep, and work.... [F]urniture could hardly be used on the soft straw mats.... Where was I to work, and how was I to dispose my books and papers?... My wife was not less perturbed when she came to inspect the kitchen ... there was neither stove, nor gas, nor even a kitchen table.... [T]here was nothing else to see.... But how on earth were we to make ourselves at home?[21]

These words at the beginning of *Houses and People of Japan* are deliberately misleading. By repeating some of the Orientalist stereotypes, Taut was actually preparing the ground for criticizing European perceptions of Japan. His real intentions were disclosed in the following pages of the book:

What is still today the image of Japan, which — apart from a few connoisseurs — generally prevails among the masses of the West? Is it not that of a strange island whose singular inhabitants, contrary to the custom everywhere else, have introduced into art an affected elegance, faintness, dwarfish diminutiveness, irregularity, abnormality, oddity — in a word, whim (*Marotte*)?... The West only saw what it understood, and relished it the more as it appeared to be an exotic, piquant curiosity.[22]

And further:

The intention [of this book] has been to show that strange and unaccustomed ways have very natural and simple reasons. Whosoever looks at these ways as something exotic, behaves like a child in the zoo gaping in front of the glass cage of the boa-constrictor. But such a sentimental and romantic approach to the unfamiliar is as unjust as it is unreasonable, since human beings all over the world are endowed with an equal amount of reason.[23]

The West "only saw what it understood" and deemed the East to be nothing more than an "exotic" fairyland, distant and strange, abnormal and odd. During his life in Japan, Taut became conscious of the risks of Orientalism. It is significant that he also affirmed the Kantian principle of the universality of human reason as a remedy for Orientalism, as well as a guarantee of justice. In order to criticize the exotic and sentimental reception of unfamiliar non-Western customs as "unjust" and "unreasonable," Taut showed how such a claim would contradict one of the basic postulates of modernist ethics: that all human beings should be treated with the unbreakable imperative that they are "endowed with equal amount of reason."

Furthermore, Taut also intuitively realized some of the basic problems that non-European countries undergo in westernization. For instance, based on the increasing number of suicides and the dark depictions in movies, Taut asserted—in a chapter titled "Melancholie," in his manuscript "Japans Kunst" (Japan's art)—that a depressive mood and melancholy governed the Japanese artistic scene, about which he freely speculated throughout the manuscript.[24] Taut mainly talked about a fundamental dichotomy or conflict (*Zwiespalt*) that caused some sort of "depression" and "resignation." The recent indications of this dichotomy, he argued, were largely due to the perceived gap between the East and Europe, the declining state of the Japanese tradition as a mere "exotic museum piece," and the perceived opposition between the traditional ways of living and European modernism.[25] Taut's choice of the word *melancholy* is more theoretically suggestive than it appears at first. It implies his intuitive recognition of one of the most pertinent cultural reactions to modernization in some non-Western countries. Melancholy is the tension that stems from the perceived inequality between West and non-West at the moment of a cross-cultural interaction—a condition that I have explained in chapter 2 as the melancholy in translation.

Taut's observations in "Melancholie" can be additionally supported by analyzing his manuscripts and published pieces for Japanese journals, in which he delivered his criticism of and suggestions for the practices of modern architecture.[26] In *Houses and People of Japan*, for instance, he discussed his confrontation with the contemporary modern problems of Japan in the chapter entitled "What Now?" This chapter was written as an imaginary discussion with Mr. Suzuki, but it was actually a collage of real conversations between Taut and his Japanese colleagues.[27] It contained some phrases that may suggest Taut's relapse into the Orientalist hopes of his early career. Yet this dream about the redemptive power of the Orient took place only momentarily in this conversation, since Taut's imaginary friend Mr. Suzuki warned him not to idealize the "glorious days of the past" and not to ignore the modern developments of Japan.[28] Besides, the fact that Taut was now in Japan obliged him to notice the country's expanding modernization. Unlike his earlier accounts, in which he treated the Orient as nonhistorical and redemptive, Taut was now much more attentive to the development of modern architecture in Japan, as well as the actual problems emerging during this process. He assessed the main conflict as the dilemma between copying Western forms and searching for an alternative modernism. In "What Now?" Taut questioned both the enthusiasm for and reaction to Westernization:

> TAUT: What I do mean is the admirable way in which the Japanese house has adapted itself to the special *climate of Japan* and is

in harmony with local customs and daily occupations.... And then, why is there nowhere that splendidly conceived veranda adapted to modern style building? Where are the broad gables, in Japan a most necessary thing to keep the large window openings shaded from sun and rain, since you must leave everything open during the heat. Terraces and balconies are *Western imitations*!

SUZUKI: Ah, well, you may be right. But then, you see, for modern life the old style of building is not suitable at all.

TAUT: Nobody said you were to imitate the old style completely! That would be as terrible a mistake as *slavish imitation of foreign styles*. But it does seem as if some of your countrymen *feel ashamed*, if their houses don't look exactly like every house in Paris or Berlin. This seems to lead others into reaction, causing them to construct their homes entirely in the old classical way, which is wrong too. After all, it can't be terribly difficult to find an arrangement for simultaneously shading roofs and providing light for the rooms inside.[29]

A feeling of insecurity, Taut observed, unsettled his Japanese colleagues. In a previous part of the text, Taut had already criticized the "European reception rooms" that were placed in modern houses, despite the disfavor of their owners, just because they were "consider[ed] necessary ... to please the Europeans."[30] The theme of inferiority was also repeated when Taut and Suzuki talked about the Japanese people's desire to be taller, since they took the European height as the human standard and considered the "Western way of living" "much more healthy" (fig. 5.2).[31] Thus ideologies of Eurocentrism traveling to the Orient constructed the Western body (that varies in any case and should not be standardized) as the ideal human norm. The Oriental himself—Suzuki—believed in the superiority myth of this Western norm. If the ideal European masculine body was considered a universal norm, then we can assert that a regional and particular truth had been universalized during modernization. Therefore, we should be able to speak of a feeling of insecurity in non-Western individuals caused by the lost natural right of belonging to this universality.

The ideology of ergonomics influenced world architecture more than it might be imagined. From graphic standard books such as Neufert,[32] generations of architects worldwide learned and applied several physical standards to their modern furniture, kitchens, bathrooms, and stairs. These modern norms were based on the dimensions and proportions of

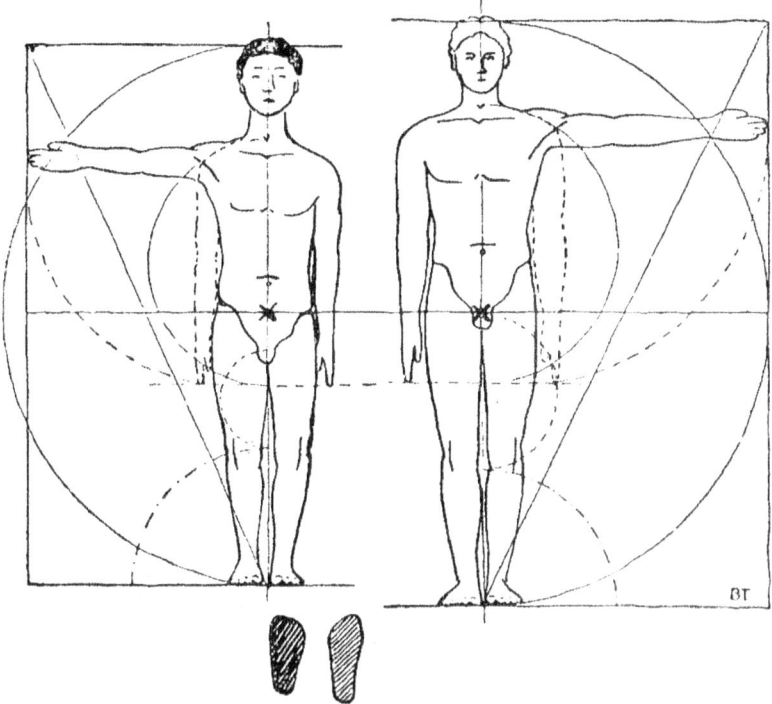

5.2. Bruno Taut. Comparative body diagram.

the idealized white masculine body à la Vitruvius and ignored racial or gender differences. In this sense, Taut's diagram comparing the idealized European and Japanese bodies can be assessed as a groundbreaking, yet overlooked, comment on the politics of ergonomics. With this diagram, which appeared in both *Houses and People of Japan* and *Mimari Bilgisi*, the architect admitted that his initial uneasiness in moving about his house in Japan, because of the low door frames, "uncomfortable" heights of the door handles and the like, was not caused by a lack of refinement in ergonomic design but was a matter of difference. Today, this diagram must be considered an unheard warning against the ideology of standardization based on European and North American norms. Rather than take the Western man's body as the human standard, this diagram challenges the notion of a universal norm by representing two norms. Unlike the white man's body, the Japanese man's body does not fit into a geometric square when his arms are wide open. While the white man's legs are half of his whole body, the Japanese man's legs are proportionately not the same. Even though Taut's comparative diagram ignores gender or other ethnic differences, it must be considered as a step toward de-universalizing the Western masculine body as the standard of ergonomic design. Hence, already by the mid-1930s, Taut's intuitive realization of the non-Western individual's perceived distance from the ego ideal led him to one of the most critical contributions to the state of architectural standardization.

Houses and People of Japan was a study of the anonymous architecture in Japan and its implications for the modern period. Apart from the research on Japanese architecture, the book opened multiple perspectives for Taut's thinking about architecture. For instance, it led him to reflect on the definition of architecture as an institutionalized profession. In various passages, Taut commented on the distinction between the mason and the architect, which still remains one of the main criteria where the professionalization of architecture or the distinction between architecture and vernacular building is in dispute.[33] Rather than suggest a hierarchical difference between a craftsman and an architect, or vernacular and modern architecture, Taut was interested in improving the standardization of architectural materials in relation to the legacy of Japanese mats, which he considered an example of preindustrial standardization.[34] At another point, Taut started to formulate a typological matrix of the Japanese house according to its historical development.[35] Even more important, he increasingly commented on the importance of climate for shaping architecture after his research on the Japanese vernacular.[36]

For our purposes, the most relevant point is Taut's definition of the Japanese farmhouses (*Bauernhaus*) as cosmopolitan buildings. In "The Japanese Village," Taut claimed that the Japanese farmhouse was both "national" and "international."[37] In *Houses and People of Japan*, he collected an impressive number of comparative images of farmhouses from Japan and Europe that looked strikingly identical. Putting a picture of a house in Japan next to a curiously similar one from Austria, Germany, Italy, Serbia, Sweden, or Switzerland, the architect drew the reader's attention to a provocative body of evidence (fig. 5.3). Although he admitted that the reasons for these striking similarities had to be explained after some research, he did not retreat from claiming that the "cosmopolitanism" of the Japanese farmhouse, as well as the "universality" of peasant life, could well have created this resemblance:

> The Japanese farmer, who does not speak to the world with words, speaks through his houses. He is the Japanese nation and his tongue is a *cosmopolitan* one. And being *cosmopolitan* it has *universal power*.... The cosmopolitan mind of the peasants shows itself in its sociability and in their tol-

5.3. Bruno Taut. Comparison of Japanese and European farmhouses.

erance of different kinds of wishes or inclinations. Nevertheless, there is ever the same spirit, which unites all the many variations and produces an aesthetic whole.[38]

The organism of the Japanese house very naturally originates from the life and work of the country folk. However much climate and types of agriculture differ, the peasants all over the world are fundamentally alike. . . . Farmhouses all over the world once had the same open fireplace as is found nowadays in Japan. . . . A kettle hung or stood over the fire at which the people gathered together to warm themselves, and dry their wet clothes, the fireplace being the central point for the family and the household.[39]

The validity of these assertions is naturally suspect, yet my point is not about the historical evolution or geographical expansion of these houses themselves, but about Taut's aspirations in interpreting them. The architect's choice of the word *cosmopolitanism* here, as opposed to, say, *nationalism*, is crucial. During the same period, the anticosmopolitan sentiments and the revival of the German farmhouse were abruptly becoming a tool for the cultural politics of National Socialism, as the previous chapter illustrated. A similar danger was also becoming more and more evident in other countries, including Turkey, because of the rise of chauvinistic nationalism. In contrast, Taut was promoting the study of farmhouses to disclose the architectural principles not of nationalism but of cosmopolitanism. What could have motivated Taut to see a cosmopolitan chord in anonymous Japanese houses? If he was trying to differentiate his own interest in these houses from that of the architects of the German *Heimatstil*, and if he was trying to prove the similarity between farmhouses of different nations, why did he refrain from using the word *international*? The implicit answers to these questions can be found in Taut's next book, *Mimari Bilgisi*.

Turkey, 1936–1938

On September 30, 1936, Martin Wagner, Taut's colleague from the Weimar housing reform who was in Turkey at the time, sent a telegram to Japan, directing Taut to depart "immediately" for Turkey. After Hans Poelzig's sudden death just before reaching Turkey, Wagner had convinced the authorities to invite Taut instead.[40] Taut's work in Turkey would later disappoint his friends and a number of architectural historians. For instance, Wagner himself complained in a letter to Walter Gropius about Taut's steps back from modern architecture: "As everyone who gets old, Taut is stuck with Renaissance principles and he can't find a way towards the New! I am very disappointed. . . . It is a shame for such an avant-gardist."[41] To give another example, Paul Bonatz relied on Taut's allusions to the traditional Almaşık constructional system on the walls of the Faculty of Languages, History, and Geography building in Ankara as support for his own position advocating nationalism in architecture.[42] Were these judgments correct? Did Taut start promoting a nationalist *Heimatstil* in Turkey after criticizing such a development in Germany during the 1920s? What was the visionary architect of the German Expressionist utopias; the designer of 10,000 workers' and middle-class houses in over twenty *Siedlungen* and urban housing blocks; the promoter of colorful, functional, flexible, and efficient houses for modern Germans really up to in Turkey?[43]

As soon as he arrived, Taut was given serious responsibilities. He became the head of both the Department of Architecture at the Academy of Fine Arts and the Department of Construction in the Ministry of Education. In letters to his fellow architects Ernst May and Hans Scharoun, Wagner claimed that Taut's career in Turkey was not a bright one, because he was able to get commissions for "only" a few buildings,[44] and because he "turned all teachers and patrons against him" by committing lots of "faux pas" at the academy.[45] Although Taut's relations with his Turkish colleagues at the academy were not always smooth,[46] the architect's own diary and letters indicate that he was often intensely busy yet content with his work,[47] and that he had a fulfilling life in finding his "homeland" and "happiness" in architecture, not necessarily in a specific country.[48] Taut was also one of the first German architects whose work was extensively covered in the Turkish professional journal *Arkitekt*, in which young architects had been attacking their foreign colleagues for lacking the necessary background to create a new Turkish architecture. Taut nevertheless soon won their appreciation, as his correspondence with the journal's editor Zeki Sayar suggests.[49]

Taut designed numerous schools in Ankara, İstanbul, İzmir, and Trabzon. These built projects are usually considered to be his only designs in Turkey, yet his diary and a report to the Ministry of Education indicate that he worked on over twenty buildings, most of which remained pending at his death.[50] Taut collaborated with several assistants and colleagues from Germany, including Grimm (who had worked in Taut and Hoffmann's office), Mundt, Franz Hillinger (who had worked with Taut for GEHAG), and Margarete Schütte-Lihotzky and Wilhelm Schütte (whom Taut himself invited to Turkey; they collaborated on a couple of projects at the Turkish Ministry of Education).[51] He organized a large and well-received exhibition of his lifetime work at the academy in 1938.[52]

Taut was also extremely influential as a teacher and prepared a reformed pedagogical program for the academy.[53] As his diary suggests, he was in touch with many of the young and established architects of Turkey, working closely with them either at the academy or in the design and drawings of his own projects. From his diaries and letters, we understand that Taut spoke German and French with his Turkish colleagues, and German, French, and English with his Japanese friends, yet he also learned some Turkish as well as Japanese. Shortly after designing the catafalque of Atatürk, Taut died suddenly, on December 24, 1938, in Turkey. He had been suffering from asthma. The last words in his diary, written eleven days before his death, were about his students, seeking permission for them to work at the academy until 9:00 P.M.[54]

When Taut came to Turkey he found himself under the same kind of pressures that he had observed in Japan. Here, too, he reacted against blindly copying forms from both Western modernism and an anachronistic past.[55] In *Houses and People of Japan, Fundamentals of Japanese Architecture*, and "New Japan: What Its Architecture Should Be," Taut had already disparaged examples of imported European modernism in Japan. Strolling down the road between Yokohama and Tokyo was "a cold shower of disillusionment" for him because of the "many ugly things, many 'modern' things and much trash" that were the legacy of a "frantic importation of Western civilization."[56] Instead of improving the structural conditions, the modern works had augmented the risk of earthquake and fire in big cities.[57] The modern houses had none of the traditional sensitivity to climate.[58] The statistics showed that one-third of the school-age children in Tokyo were sick, because of the "falsely built houses."[59] In his publications in Turkey, Taut did not hide his hostility toward similar architectural practices. He openly criticized the "house as a machine,"[60] imported cubic architecture that "put boxes on needles,"[61] skyscrapers in United States that paid no tribute to the idea of proportion,[62] and "degenerated" modernism.[63] Yet this does not mean that he advocated a traditionalist vision, because he was equally against a blind "imitation of old styles" as a reaction to the "slavish imitation of foreign styles."[64] In Japan, Taut had concluded:

> For more than seventy years now Japan had been importing Western civilization with all her might. But what had happened during those seventy years could not be compared to a natural growth. . . . One would have to give the Japanese time. Perhaps they have to make even more mistakes yet before they finally solve their problem of cultural synthesis. The day will come when [the] foreign plant will have taken root in the new soil. But for the time being, *enthusiasm for foreign taste* will be followed by corresponding reactions in the direction of an *uninspired "Nipponism."*[65]

Taut's stance in Turkey was similar. In letters to friends in Japan, he wrote that he "remains faithful fighting against" the architectural approach "named as *cubic*" in Turkey.[66] Taut's observations of modernism's basic dilemmas outside Europe should not be swiftly dismissed as easy generalizations. On the contrary, these remarks can be suggestive in disclosing typical conditions. As long as modernism was perceived as a universal form of expression, then, we should be able to speak about the reaction of an individual that was gauged by his or her ability to catch up with this modernism as a style. The "slavish imitation of foreign styles" and "uninspired" nativism that Taut observed as two dead-end paradigms of modern architecture in Japan and Turkey can rightly be interpreted as nothing but the two faces of this reaction. Here the subject oscillates between fascination with and resistance toward the West. In the phase of "slavish imitation of foreign styles," there was an attachment to the West as a substitute for the deprived right of sharing this notion of universality. In the phase of "uninspired" nativism, there was a resistance against the West or the universality that it supposedly embodied, and an attachment to traditional forms as a substitute for lost days of glory. It was these days of the past that were perceived not to have been ruined by the feeling of insecurity. Three decades earlier, Taut had observed a similar dilemma, which Frantz Fanon outlined as the two basic but unproductive responses of the colonized Algerian individual to the perceived "inferiority of his culture." The individual either "unfavorably criticizes his own national culture" or "takes refuge" in passionately defending it.[67]

Rather than perceive this dilemma as a struggle between two groups with opposite positions, it is usually more helpful to conceive of it as a tension that exists simultaneously in one person or a group. In other words, "slavish imitation of foreign styles" and "uninspired" nativism, or fascination with and resistance toward the West, are two faces of the same condition—a condition that I call the melancholy of the non-Western during the moment of translation. On the one hand, accusing all regionalist tendencies of chauvinism and anachronism would have failed to suggest an alternative to the hegemonic westernization of non-Western contexts. These accusations would have ignored the strategic and emancipatory potential in the provisional promotion of regional or national expressions in these regions. On the other hand, underlining some supposedly fixed identities with increasing inflexibility would have fallen into essentialist definitions and myths of origins and would have maintained the segregation of the non-West from the West. Taut's suggestion for resolving this fundamental dilemma was nothing less than the aspiration to construct a cosmopolitan ethics in architecture.

WELTARCHITEKTUR—TRANSLATION OF A TREATISE

In 1937, Taut noted in his diary that he was working on the manuscript of a book that he described as his "great work." He had started writing a similar book under the title *Arkitalürüberlegungen* in Japan, which testifies to the continuity of his position in the two countries.[68] This book first appeared in Turkish as *Mimari Bilgisi* (fig. 5.4)—usually translated as "Lectures on Architecture," the title actually means "Architectural Knowledge"—in Adnan Kolatan's translation, published shortly before Taut's death.[69] The first German version, *Architekturlehre*,[70] did not appear until 1977, and it was published without figures; the full German version with illustrations was republished in a magazine issue only at the end of 2009.[71] Kolatan's translation of Taut's manuscript was careful and creative, often using appropriating translation. No expressions were omitted and no terminology was confused, yet at times Kolatan dramatized the content. He frequently split sentences in two or three for easier reading, added relevant idioms, and in a few instances quite intentionally picked words that suggested slightly different meanings. Kolatan frequently translated

Turkey, 1937–1938

5.4. Bruno Taut. *Mimari Bilgisi*, cover.

the German exiles' works for *Arkitekt*, including pieces by Ernst Reuter, Wilhelm Schütte, and Gustav Oelsner. Considering that the life of Taut's book was significantly longer in Turkey than in Germany, and that Taut oversaw only the publication of the Turkish version, I venture to treat both the German and the Turkish texts as originals, rather than prioritizing one over the other or putting the translation to a test of fidelity.

While putting Taut's words into Turkish, Kolatan simultaneously developed an architectural terminology, especially for the new terms of urban housing: *Siedlung* was translated as *ikametgah*, *Type* as *tip*, *Sauberkeit* as *temizlik* (cleanliness), *bessere Hygiene* as *iyi bir hıfzıssıhha* (better hygiene), *Zweckmäßigkeit* as *maksada elverişli* (appropriate for its use), *Nützlichkeit* as *faidelik* (usefulness), *Städtebau* as *şehircilik* (city planning), *Hochhaus* as *yüksek evler* (tall houses), *Zeilenbau* as *sıra evler* (usually used for row houses [*Reihenhaus*]), *Bandstadt* as *şerid halinde binalar* (buildings in a row), *Radiale Anlage* as *radyal tarzda tesis edilmiş binalar* (radial placement), *Trabantenstadt* as *trabant şehirler* (city of satellites), and *Laubenganghaus* as *müşterek geçitli evler* (houses or apartments on a common circulation axis).[72] For Taut's four principles (*Grundlage*, *esas*) that structured the argument, Kolatan chose to use the German terms in French phonetics, as was commonly done during the late Ottoman Empire. Accordingly, *Technik* became *teknik*, *Konstruktion* became *konstrüksiyon* (not the now common word *inşaat*), *Funktion* became *fonksiyon* (not *işlev*). For Taut's highest principle, *Die Proportion*, Kolatan used both the Western and Ottoman terms divided with the conjunction "or": *proporsiyon yani tenasüb* (the more common Turkish word today is *orantı*).[73] Kolatan similarly multiplied synonyms in a number of occasions: for *Raum* (space) he used as many as three words (*raum yani mahal yahut hacim*); for *Kontinuität* he combined the French and Turkish words with the algorithmic sign of equivalence, *Continuité=süreklilik*; and for *Spielraum* he used the Ottoman term but put the French one in parentheses, *imhiraf payı* (*marge*). He translated *gut funktioniert* with two words as *iyi işleyen yani iyi fonksiyonlu* (well-functioning); for *Wolkenkratzer* he used only the French term *gratte-ciel* (skyscraper); and he left some of the architectural terminology of historical buildings untranslated, such as *Cella, Peristyl,* and *Filigran*.[74] During the writing of the two originals, the terminology was not only translated from German to Turkish, but also in the opposite direction: when discussing the tiles in the Ottoman mosques, Taut translated the word *çini* as *Fayence*.[75] Kolatan's choices may at first appear to indicate linguistic indecisiveness, but in fact they seem to have been guided by a decisive appropriation tendency in an attempt to make the text available and comprehensible to Turkish readers at the time. The eclecticism of his terminology testifies to the creolization of language with multiple sources.

Although Taut warned against treating the Western man's body as a global norm, he was still immersed in the belief that architecture could embody universality. *Mimari Bilgisi* was an attempt to define the four universal principles of architecture in a way that would integrate geographical and cultural differences. Taut's first step in his argument was linguistic, which made the translation even more challenging. In explaining what gave a building its character as architecture, as opposed to a piece of technical equipment, a pure construction, or merely a useful space, Taut relied on a few German idioms, many of which could be replaced by appropriate substitutes in Turkish. In a few difficult cases, however, such as the translation of the common term *Weltgebäude* (world building), Kolatan's literal translation (*dünya denilen bu bina*) had a foreignizing effect and brought his readers face to face with the fact that they were reading a translation. By showing several idiomatic uses in the German language, Taut concluded that it was a sense of proportion that gave architecture its distinctive character and produced the architectural metaphors in language. "Accordingly, there is no doubt [*Zweifel, şüphe*] that humans have a distinct sense of proportion. This is what generates [*erzeugt, yaratan*] architecture."[76] Although the sense of proportion was indefinable in concrete terms, Taut referred to evenness [*Ebenmaß, ölçülülük*] and ratio [*Verhältnis, nisbet*] as its indicators.[77]

The three "supplementary" principles of architecture — technique, construction, and function — would turn a building into something less than architecture unless they served the sense of proportion. Unambiguously maintaining the common distinction between the engineer and the architect, and attacking those who blurred it, Taut differentiated technique as architecture's "ruler" [*Herrscherin, mimariye hakim*] and its "servant" [*Dienerin, hizmetkar*].[78] Only when the most advanced technique served proportion could an architect reach the heights of the Greek temple and the Japanese house, the two examples he discussed in detail. In the case of construction, he illustrated the Gothic cathedral and the Turkish mosque as examples of advanced construction emerging as architecture itself due to the commitment to proportion. Function was not the essential aspect of architecture either, because time could render a building's use anachronistic but the building itself a landmark — an argument that would be rephrased by Aldo Rossi three decades later.[79] The sense of proportion had admittedly guided Taut's *Siedlung* designs, despite the emphasis on function and technique: while searching for the most efficient way to use space, Taut declared that he had discovered the "relativity of function" (*Relativität der Funktion, fonksiyonun izafiliği*).[80] Truly economic and affordable houses were proportionate because they neither encouraged useless luxury, nor minimized the floor plans unnecessarily. Having a proportionate sense of technique in designing a house meant avoiding enslavement to technical amenities.

Throughout his book, Taut criticized contemporary architectural values.[81] Old houses were irresponsibly perceived as inferior to the new hygienic, functional, and technical houses.[82] The modern world was "the age of technique and distastefulness" [*Zeitalter der Technik und der Geschmacklosigkeit, teknik ve zevksizlik devresi*];[83] "the age of limitless opportunities" in construction [*Zeitalter der unbegrenzten Möglichkeiten, hudutsuz imkanlar devri*], which were pointless due to the loss of the sense of proportion.[84] In modern times, "construction was named as the dictator" [*Die Konstruktion wurde zum Diktator ernannt*], much more dramatized in the Turkish version as "the sole sovereign, the dictator"

5.5. Bruno Taut. Hiding the façade.

of architecture [*Konstrüksiyon mutlak bir hakim, bir diktatör ilan edilmişti*].[85] Accordingly, one of Taut's main concerns was the generalization of modern architecture as a style across the globe (fig. 5.5):

> The world is increasingly getting uniform [added to Turkish] and homogeneous [*uniformiert sich*; *üniformalaşıyor, birörnekleşiyor*]. . . . Soldiers' uniforms show the cultural weakness of the modern world. The same goes for architecture.[86]
>
> When technique is the *ruler* of architecture, the house is conquered by/occupied with [*versehen*, *techiz edilmek*] machines, equipment, mechanical utilities, and the like that can be used anywhere in the world. . . . This brings a situation where buildings all around the world look like machines that can be utilized without changing their form. This outcome is commonplace architecture [*Allerweltsarchitektur, cihan mimarisi*], that is, the many modern buildings whose pictures we see in all magazines. . . . Architecture is thus confronted with such devastation that it will take it too long to recover. If this was just an aesthetical error, it would not be too wrong. However, nature, in our case climate, will soon take its revenge on this criminal negligence [*sträflich vernachlässigt, cezaya layık bir ihmal*]: it will soon be understood that a building that is correct in one country is unusable [*unbrauchbar, işe yaramayan*] in another.[87]

In *Modern Architecture*, written in 1929 in Germany, Taut had already made it clear that he was worried about homogenization through modernization.[88] He was concerned that European modernism was spreading over the whole world by claiming a smoothly translatable character for a form of expression that originated from a limited region. Yet he was also wary of the reactionary nationalism taking control in countries such as his native one. *Mimari Bilgisi* was full of passages that severely criticized advocates of nationalism, whether they expressed themselves in modern or historical forms: "Whether the architects are forced to create national architecture through modern expressions" as in "fascist Italy" or "they are forced to use historical styles … [b]oth of the results are a disaster [*Fiasko, hüsran*]."[89]

How did Taut think, then, he could reconcile the two forces at the very heart of the dilemma he had unveiled with his works in Japan and Turkey? "If the artist is tormented [*quälen, üzüyorsa*] by his doubt, he too can find his universal basis [*üniversale Basis, üniversal esas*] like the artists of the past."[90] The doubt of modern architecture could be lifted by searching for universality. Revising his theory on type, Taut differentiated between machine and architecture types and asserted that all temples of the world shared the same architecture type [*gleichartigen Typ, aynı tarzda bir tip*]; they were the "variations of the identical archetype" [*Grundtyps, esas tip*], "the classical highpoints of different and totally original cultures."[91] Yet even the most successful building would melt or freeze in a different climate. The deadly mistake of modernism was indeed the ignorance of this fact, an argument that Taut illustrated with the drawing of a Zeppelin touring around the world.[92] The sketch was slightly transformed due to the erasure of a couple of lines when Taut's handwriting in German was replaced with Turkish terms (fig. 5.6). Taut seems to have suggested the category of climate as something that would guarantee geographical differences in architecture: "The types of architecture regenerate [*erhalten dadurch Leben, canlanmak*] when each building receives another form in relation to the country [in which] it is situated."[93] Almost all external conditions of architecture were a function of climate, the only basis for all the other real factors.[94] Climate not only gave "a specificity, a tonality, a musical color to the building," but it also, Taut asserted, mirrored the ethnic differences in body proportions and human expressions (*Temperamente, mizac*).[95]

Here, Taut came dangerously close to the racial theory in which climatic differences around the world were used to make an argument about racial difference and, subsequently, the superiority of one race over an-

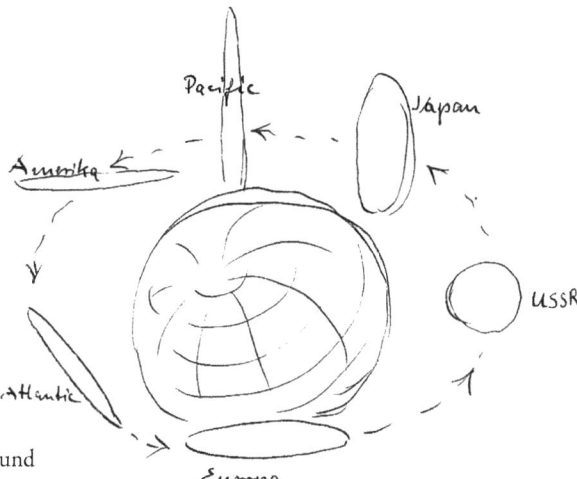

5.6. Bruno Taut. Zeppelin touring around the world.

other. This was after all one of the charges against Kant's theory of cosmopolitanism. In his books *Geography* and *Observations on the Feeling of the Beautiful and the Sublime*, Kant seems to have felt no duty to rethink his race theory, whose perils were exposed as he commented on the populations of distant lands, including Native Americans, Africans, and East Asians. David Harvey, for one, has written on the paradoxes of Kant's cosmopolitan ideal when it is juxtaposed with his geographical prejudices. In Kant's formula, the "smelly and ugly" peoples of the distant lands either need to shape themselves up to be "qualified for consideration under universal ethical code," or "the universal laws will have to operate as a discriminatory code."[96]

Although Kant had not freed himself from the racial conceptions of his time, at least not in some of his writings, one might nevertheless work toward a more affirmative interpretation of Taut's theory on climate, given his own critical remarks on Orientalism and the unjust perceptions in Europe of its other. What distinguishes Taut's notion of climate is that he conceived of it as a category to help attain universality, rather than geographical difference:

> It [technique under the rule of proportion] builds the forms in which architecture receives its universal character, namely makes it appropriate to climate, weather [*Wetters, hava*], and nature [*Natur, tabiat*]. The more architectural forms correspond [*entsprechen, uygun olmak*] to the nature where the building is located, to the light and air [*Licht und Luft, ışığına ve havasına*], the more they are universal.[97]

In making this statement, Taut must have been suggesting that climate specificity forged a universal architecture that was non-European, an architecture that captured what might be called a non-Eurocentric universality. The idea of nature was universal; it could be applied worldwide; it was the earth itself. Climate, on the other hand, was both a fact of nature, something of the earth, and also place specific. Thus climate, it followed for Taut, could be the foundation for a non-Eurocentric universal architecture. Taut's time in Japan and Turkey led him to test the geographical limits of Western European modernism and to propound a theory of modern architecture that would challenge the universalizing claims of modernization (in the sense of the importation of Western modernism) but nevertheless safeguard a notion of universality. In this way, Taut was able to maintain the importance he had assigned to nature as a guide for architecture during his early career in Germany.[98] Although he had not elaborated a category of difference in nature then, he was now interpreting climate as that which came to terms with geographical diversity.

Clearly, Taut had the Turkish audience in mind while writing several parts of *Mimari Bilgisi*. He used the term *cubic* to criticize contemporary architecture, a term quite uncommon in Germany but used as a synonym of modernism in Turkey.[99] Many of Taut's ideas must have sounded pleasant to Turkish nationalist ears. His sharp distinction between architecture and engineering had its resonances in the culture-civilization debate in Turkey formulated through Ziya Gökalp, and his ideas about the inadequateness of technical know-how for achieving proportionate architecture might have sounded similar to the consensus on the translatability of civilization and untranslatability of culture's essence (chapter 4). Taut's lengthy chapter on the Ottoman mosque and his appreciative comments that the architect Sinan had eliminated the "rigidity [*Starrheit, donukluk*] of pure rational construction" in the Pantheon and Hagia Sophia, and thereby redeemed their "imperialist intentions" (*imperialistische Absicht, emperyalist gaye*) and "pedantic expressions" (*Pedanterie, bilgiçlik*), must have pleased the nationalist historians in Turkey.[100] Most significantly, Taut's assertion that "all good architecture will be a national architecture" (*Her iyi mimari, milli bir mimari olacaktır*) became one of the most cited phrases in the book.[101] However, Taut was ultimately giving an antinationalist message in this work and in his *oeuvre* as a whole. For instance, the German manuscript of this sentence read differently: "All good architecture will be national" (*Jede gut Architektur wird national sein*).[102] In the sentence's context in the book, Taut was warning against subjugating architecture under political agendas and architects under state control; he had already cited Hansen's words: "all good architecture is national, all national architecture is bad."[103] A few other translation gestures nationalized the Turkish original more than Taut might have intended. For instance, in a sentence where the German means "one *does not* build for a Berliner in İstanbul" (*man baut weder*), the Turkish version means "one *cannot* do so" (*ne ... yapılabilir*).[104] Taut criticized the homogenization of architecture in Turkey, Germany, France, and other countries, but Turkey was conveniently omitted from the phrase in the Turkish publication.[105] It is hard to interpret these as unintentional mistakes given the otherwise careful (and creative) nature of Kolatan's translation. The original Turkish version of the book might have had a slightly more regionalist effect, but it is Taut's cosmopolitan message that I would like to bring forth here.

Taut criticized those who rejected foreign influences in rejuvenating domestic norms.[106] Artists had to lead a nomadic life (*Nomadenleben, göçebe hayatı*) because all nations were nurtured by foreign influences (*fremden Einflüsse, yabancı tesir*).[107] Yet Taut advocated a foreign influence that would be, he said, "no false internationalism, no uniformalization of the world [*Weltuniformierung*], no dullification [*Langweiligmachen*] of the whole earth," but a hybridization that would "make both sides richer."[108] In *Mimari Bilgisi*, he used the word *Allerweltsarchitektur* to criticize the homogenizing tendencies of contemporary architecture, and he predicted that sensitive foreign architects would be attracted to the differences of their new locations.[109]

If Taut was against uniformalization of the world, which word did actually capture his intentions? What would be a construct that could open a country to foreign influences, without totally assimilating its local norms within the norms of the foreign? Can it be that the cosmopolitan farmhouse that Taut so willingly defended in *Houses and People of Japan* was a bearer of an ideal that he aspired to see rejuvenated through contemporary architecture?

The word *cosmopolitan* not only assures openness to the foreign, but it also defies the Orientalist segregations between East and West. The possibility that a cosmopolitan farmhouse exists must have been the very evidence Taut sought against the persistence of the geographical divide. The epigraph of this chapter anticipates a theory that Taut did not live to pursue: "The stronger the belief that East and West belong together, the stronger the energy to get to know the foreignness in one's nature. With the growth of this energy, the melancholy will sink down to the grave it deserves." Only when a culture opens itself to the foreign with "the belief that East and West belong together" can it challenge melancholy.[110]

Several anti-American ideas infiltrated parts of *Mimari Bilgisi*, which stood out as contradictions in the context of Taut's cosmopolitan views. For the most part he held the stereotypical opinion of the United States as the land of technological progress, whose rule, it followed in his theory, would obliterate architecture.[111] That said, Taut's frank confrontation with and eventual denunciation of the Orientalist perceptions about non-Western countries, as well as the consequences of the spread of Western modernism, led him to his search for a cosmopolitan ethics. Although he genuinely criticized the dissemination of stylistic modernism to countries such as Japan and Turkey, he was equally critical of the rising nationalist discourses. In an attempt to reconcile his aspiration for a universally valid set of architectural principles with his admiration of the vitality of differences, Taut emphasized the cosmopolitan value of a climate-based architecture. In this, his theory in progress sought ways to differentiate *Allerweltsarchitektur*—defined as the exportation of European modern architecture to the rest of the world—from his aspiration for what might be called a cosmopolitan *Weltarchitektur*.

İstanbul, 1938

In *Houses and People of Japan*, Taut wrote:

> Would a European ever want to build in Europe a Japanese house with European workmen? If one would work upon the bridge of cultures, this is only possible by an awakened understanding of foreign singularities and by showing how the human spirit works logically and reasonably although its conceptions may vary completely from place to place. . . . In this way we become aware of the same spirit whose various products are merely the consequence of different premises.[112]

Visitors are usually caught off guard when they first see the house Taut designed for himself in Ortaköy, İstanbul (fig. 5.7). Like his own house in Dahlewitz, Taut's house in İstanbul strikes one as slightly off. The building stands out like a floating lighthouse over a dense sea of trees on the slopes overlooking the Bosphorus. Taut's house often provokes surprise for its symbolic gestures. Local people commonly refer to it as the "Japanese house." If the multiple layers of eaves are meant to be references to pagodas or temples in China, what exactly do they mean in Turkey? Why Japan in Turkey? Why a reference to any symbol from any country, whatsoever? The Dahlewitz house was built to embody the principles of rational houses advocated during the Weimar period in Germany; the İstanbul house seems to assert the Enlightenment ideal of the universality of human reason.

TOWARD A COSMOPOLITAN ARCHITECTURE   273

5.7. Bruno Taut. Own house, İstanbul, 1938. Photo: Esra Akcan.

Based on the previous discussion, one may view Taut's house (and other projects by him in Turkey and Japan) from a different angle, despite the initial sense of shock at its out of placeness. Taut himself recognized this building as an important realization of his later thought. In his letters from Turkey to Walter Segal and Kurata, he wrote about his eagerness to "show how to apply theory into practice" and to design buildings that would stand as "samples of my architectural understanding today."[113]

One enters Taut's house from the back and moves forward to the main octagonal living room with high ceilings (fig. 5.8). The panorama and light of the Bosphorus stream through the windows, which are situated at two different heights across the space. A narrow, built-in wooden stair in one corner of the living room leads up to the study. This smaller octagonal room looks like the tower of the house from the exterior and has an inclined ceiling in the interior as in a Seljuk tomb. It is also surrounded on

5.8. Bruno Taut. Own house, interior of the living room, İstanbul, 1938.
Photo: Esra Akcan.

almost all sides with windows at table height overlooking the Bosphorus. A mirror is placed at the door at the same height as the windows, so that when one closes the door and lets the mirror reflect the view of the Bosphorus, one finds oneself in a room with a full-circle Bosphorus panorama. The room becomes a microcosmos made out of glass, where the East and the West have disappeared in the circle of the panorama.[114]

Rather than cover over the foreign, totally domesticate an imported idea, or assimilate and contain it as if it had no foreignness, Taut was explicit in expressing the legacy of Japan in his house. This house had an estranging, foreignizing effect, but a totally different one from the other foreign buildings that had become commonplace in Turkey by the time of his arrival. In a country wide open to foreign influences from its west, but equally closed to those from its east, building a Japanese house was definitely a critical and innovative gesture. The house integrated elements from Germany and Turkey as well. In two houses in Germany (his own house in Dahlewitz and Haus K, 1925) and in Turkey, Taut differentiated the service spaces from the main living halls, whose circular plans were meant to capture the maximum opening to the outside. The organization of the plan and the tripartite massing of Haus K is especially similar to the house in Ortaköy. In the latter, sun-shading devices replace the terraces. As a matter of fact, the more one looks at Taut's Ortaköy house from different angles, the more complicated the building becomes. From some viewpoints, the multilevel hanging eaves of this house may look like pagodas, may be a direct reference to Temple of Heaven in Beijing, a photograph of which Taut published in *Mimari Bilgisi*, or may refer even to Mu ta (Timber pagoda) in Yingxian Shanxi.[115] But seen from other perspectives, they resemble the anonymous houses of İstanbul (fig. 5.9). One realizes that the eaves in Taut's house were designed as sun-shading devices for the double-height windows of the interior. This use of such devices was actually very common in the anonymous houses of the region. In an interview for a Turkish magazine, Taut was asked to comment on the modern Turkish house. His answer was concerned with a residential modernism that explicitly condemned both the copying of modern European houses, and the "kitsch" imitation of traditional ones. He suggested instead the filtering of the principles of both through the category of climate. Taut's definition for the "modern Turkish house" was in reality a description of his own house in İstanbul:

> [The modern Turkish house will be born] whenever the architects free themselves from the fashion of cubic style that has become an ordinary practice here. Only then will the principles of modern architecture be applied with a freedom of thought. Both for houses and for some other buildings, *climate* will be given priority, and thus some characteristics of the traditional Turkish house will be applied automatically, such as *shading eaves*, *pavilion*-like structures, and *double-height windows* in rooms with high ceilings.... To be sure, one should avoid direct copies. Otherwise, this attempt will turn into a sentimental romanticism, namely a misunderstood nationalism. The result will be the ugly pretension called *kitsch*.[116]

From what he noted in his diary, we understand that Taut had just studied a typical wooden house during his trip to Edirne with Celal Esat Arseven. Long before he left Germany, Taut had already included a lengthy description of an "Oriental *oda*" (room) in his book *Die Neue Wohnung*.[117] At the academy, he had already become familiar with Sedad Eldem's National Architecture Seminar. In his diary, Taut also referred briefly to Eldem's idea of national architecture (*milli mimari*), based on the modernized interpretation of anonymous houses.[118] The double-height windows of the old Turkish house were a topic of interest for Taut during the writing of *Mimari Bilgisi*, where he claimed that the proportions of these windows were taken from nature.[119]

Taut had several opportunities to communicate his work and ideas to the Turkish audience, through his teaching, publications, and retro-

5.9. Bruno Taut. Own house, İstanbul, seen from different perspectives, 1938. Photos: Bülent Özer, 1980.

5.10. Bruno Taut. Exhibition opening at the İstanbul Academy of Fine Arts, 1938. Taut stands in front of Köster's photographs of his own *Siedlungen*, which have also been used in this book.

spective exhibition at the Academy (fig. 5.10). He was one of the first architects to engage with the tough problems of a world characterized by increased connections and negotiations between different geographies. What stands out in Taut's late career is his openness to hybrid influences from a variety of regions and his willingness to translate those influences. But hybridity in itself is not enough to make his theoretical suggestion unique, nor does it sufficiently show its continuing relevance. Therefore, I suggest that his contribution needs to be understood in terms of a cosmopolitan aspiration.

TOWARD ANOTHER COSMOPOLITAN ETHICS IN ARCHITECTURE

The last two chapters in this book differentiated the concept of a hybrid artifact from one that embodies cosmopolitan ethics. I define *hybrid* as a de facto product of modern times, where there are no pure national or pure Western and pure Eastern artifacts, due to the constant translations between countries. Although this hybridization has been amplified under globalization, it is definitely not a recent phenomenon; indeed, we can trace it back as far as our historiographical tools allow us. The architects of the modern period translated the foreign into the local and the local into the foreign on so many occasions that after a while there were only hybrids, making a much more nuanced understanding of translation necessary. The opinions of most architects have been shaped by regional or international associations assigned to forms, rather than by the existence of pure local or pure international forms themselves. Hybrid artifacts are testimonies to the paradigmatic existence of translations between countries. There are many of them. Hybrid artifacts are prerequisites of cosmopolitan ethics, but they alone are not capable of achieving it. Having a mixed palette of influences from numerous parts of the world is hardly a value in itself in the modern world. The hybrid escapes its potential risk of maintaining separatist ideologies only when it is coupled with a cosmopolitan ethics.

It is not possible, however, to conclude that this cosmopolitan ethics was accomplished in Kant's theory that inspired Taut. There were two major unresolved points in Kantian cosmopolitanism, which makes the comparison to Taut even more revealing. Both might be characterized as Kant's arguably Eurocentric conditions to be able to participate in the cosmopolitan legal order (even if his theory need not be inherently Eurocentric); and both are exposed when one analyzes the three definitive articles of perpetual peace.[120] A global federation that functioned in relation to the cosmopolitan law was suggested in Kant's proposal (definitive article 2), but only states that were constituted as republics were eligible to participate fully in this federation (definitive article 1). If perpetual peace was to be possible, Kant asserted, all states had to be republics, both because only republics could embody rational civic constitution, and because only republican constitutions could secure the freedom and equality of all citizens under law.[121] The "other" nations that were not yet republics either had to reshape themselves and "enter a common lawful state" or "move away from [the] vicinity."[122] Given the fact that when Kant wrote only a few territorial states defined as republics existed in the world—and moreover they existed only in the West—the implication must be that the global federation to secure perpetual peace would start as a small pact among Western states and expand around the world as more and more non-Western nations reconstituted themselves. At worst, this was a Eurocentric ambition to extend European legal structures to the rest of the world; at best, it was an expected result of Kant's cosmopolitanism predicated on the universality of human reason, and subsequently his confidence that all humans would reach the same conclusion about the need for a republican constitution and would join the federation of lawful states.

Taut owed his formation in no small part to Kant's humanism, as he declared himself in the opening speech of his İstanbul exhibition. Nevertheless, Taut's criticism of the extension of European modernism to the rest of the world might imply that his real aspiration was in the name of a non-Eurocentric cosmopolitan architecture. The history of the twentieth century must have given Taut a more informed perspective about social constructions of race and geography. On the one hand, the cosmopolitan ethics that Taut must have discovered through Kant was the ultimate task of modernism as the heir of Enlightenment. On the other hand, many of Taut's writings and projects aimed to construct an alternative to the homogenizing tendencies of what he called *Allerweltsarchitektur*. Nevertheless, Taut shared Kant's initial and fundamental premise on the universality of human reason. Taut's starting point, that all human beings all over the world used the same type of rationality to construct their houses in relation to climate, was not too different from Kant's. Taut's cosmopolitanism was hence also predicated on the universality of human reason, and subsequently the confidence that the same architectural principles would be reasonable across the world, while cultural differences would naturally emerge from a rational engagement with climate.

The second unresolved issue in Kant's cosmopolitanism presents a bigger challenge. The third definitive article of perpetual peace, that "all states and individuals must have cosmopolitan right limited by conditions of hospitality," raises questions about the conditional nature of Kant's cosmopolitanism. Kant then defines hospitality, which sets the limits of this cosmopolitanism, as the "right of a stranger not to be treated with hostility when he arrives on someone else's territory," even though the newcomer can be "turned away."[123] This has indeed set historical limits to Kant's theory because such a limited definition of hospitality cannot effectively respond to any of the issues raised by the refugees, exiles, and immigrants of the twentieth and twenty-first centuries. Nevertheless, in Kant's defense, one might argue that the philosopher's historical context makes this limit more reasonable. By refusing to grant foreigners the right to reside in a country, Kant simultaneously urged the protection of the rights of the colonized to have the possession of their own land, certainly a consistent, albeit ignored, right in Kant's time of extensive European colonialist expansion.[124]

Nevertheless, the conditional hospitality that defines the limits of cosmopolitan rights raises further questions about its consistency with Kant's theory of ethics. A conditional hospitality—that is, a hospitality that comes with an "if" clause, a hospitality that grants individuals cosmopolitan rights if they behave according to predefined norms—may indeed be a contradiction in terms. It is definitely not a hospitality in the highest order in Kant's own theory, where it is the unconditional goodwill, the imperative without the "if" clause, the unconditional categorical imperative that makes modern ethics possible. "Perpetual Peace" shifts back and forth between defining a cosmopolitan ethics and a cosmopolitan political or legal order. One cannot exist without the other, as Kant did not fail to declare,[125] but the two have totally different processes where conditionality is concerned. Jacques Derrida scrutinized the tension between the political and ethical notions of Kantian cosmopolitanism.[126] For cosmopolitan politics, on the one hand, conditional hospitality is necessary, because otherwise hospitality would be just a naive and "irresponsible desire."[127] That is why, throughout his text, Kant's biggest concern was to define regulations, limitations, and conditions of a cosmopolitan legal order. For cosmopolitan ethics, on the other hand, unconditional hospitality is necessary, because otherwise hospitality would not be true hospitality. Welcoming the guest only on the condition that the guest behaves does not go too far from preserving the authority of the host. Here the guest's norms must either be assumed to be the same as the host's, providing another evidence of universality, or they must be considered a possible threat from which the host needs to be protected. For Derrida, in either case, such hospitality violently covers over the differences of the radical other, and bestows on the guest the right to inclusion only on the condition that she or he is assimilated. Unconditional political hospitality is a contradiction in terms because it annihilates the very notion of the nation-state on which it is predicated. However, conditional ethical hospitality is also a contradiction in terms because hospitality is not then in its highest order. Unconditional hospitality is necessary for cosmopolitan ethics, but it is impossible for a cosmopolitan political order.

Kant's ethical notion of hospitality is one in which individuals welcome the foreign because they consider it their duty. In defining why human beings need to be hospitable, Kant declares: "Since the earth is a globe, they cannot disperse over an infinite area, but must necessarily tolerate one another's company."[128] It is thus the enlightened reason's duty to tolerate the foreign. In Kant's mind, the foreign person must be a stranger who is different in a quite uncharming way, a stranger to be tolerated for the sake of reason and peace, but not someone to open oneself up to, not someone to translate from, and hence nobody whom one could expect to be enriched by. Although Kant's essay may define the political rules and regulations for perpetual peace, it does not annihilate the perception of the other as a possible threat. Kantian hospitality is not an intrinsic, but an obligatory way to peace. It is definitely not unconditional, unlike the categorical imperatives of the highest goodwill, without which ethics in the modern world, according to Kant himself, would not be possible.[129]

In this context, Taut's words reiterated at the beginning of this chapter acquire additional value. A dedication to the "belief that East and West belong together," and a commitment to "get to know the foreignness in one's nature" will send "melancholy to the grave it deserves." Taut's statement rephrases the Kantian assumption that it is possible for humans to share common aspirations. Moreover, Taut—unlike Kant—seems to suggest that humans open themselves up to the foreign for the sake of being enriched, not only for the sake of protecting their peaceful boundaries. Taut's theory on what might be called *Weltarchitektur* was neither complete nor an ahistorical ready-at-hand solution. Needless to say, today it would be questionable to glorify Taut's position as the therapy for melancholy, as he might have liked to see it. The overemphasis on the redemptive value of climate as a critical position against Eurocentrism is not totally irrelevant, but it is an exaggeration, as well as a limited notion that disavows the potentials of non-climate-specific buildings. Still, although Kant's text has been legitimately challenged on numerous grounds, especially for its hidden Eurocentrism, it was admittedly the Kantian ideal that inspired Taut to propose a non-Eurocentric cosmopolitan ethics.

In this chapter, I reformulated the unresolved issues of cosmopolitanism as questions of translation. The theoretical possibility or impossibility of translation as discussed in the introduction also reveals an open question about cosmopolitan ethics. Which prepare the way for a better cosmopolitan future, translation practices that are committed to the untranslatability of cultures, their radical otherness, and their irreducible particularities that should not be assimilated into each other's norms; or translation practices that are committed to the mutual translatability of cultures, their opening out toward each other, one translation at a time? In any event, let us hope that truly cosmopolitan translations will make history.

EPILOGUE

This book has illustrated two distinct but connected histories of modern residential architecture. First, it traced the translation of the garden city ideal in Germany from the late nineteenth century until World War I, and then its transformation into the Weimar *Siedlungen* during the interwar period in Germany, by observing the differences between Berlin, Frankfurt, and Stuttgart. And second, it traced the translation of the garden city and then the Weimar *Siedlung* theories in Turkey, as well as their different hybridizations with the Turkish house discourse during the early republican period. Most of the architects discussed in the book aspired to find better solutions in the context of industrialization and rapid urbanization in Germany, and of westernization in Turkey, than the uncontrolled or colonizing approaches that these might have caused if left to their own devices. While discussing visions of innovative, alternative, or paradigmatic house and housing in the first half of the twentieth century, I simultaneously demonstrated how these visions shaped and were shaped by the urban culture beyond residential architecture. In that regard, this book was an attempt to write an intertwined history of the modern city and architecture, told through its visions of house and housing.

Writing this book, I often found myself trying to differentiate my position from three influential and often competing ideologies of the twentieth century, and to avoid the misunderstanding that a critique of one implies that I endorse another. That is, I attempted to develop an alternative voice through translation, which does not perpetuate the colonial terms of cultural criticism, such as *civilized* and *backward*, or *international style* and *regionalism*; continue the myth of problem-free modernization, nationalization, and westernization; or see a solution in a return to a traditional "origin." To put it in simplified terms for summarizing purposes, I tried to accomplish the first by disclosing the colonial imagination of the architects involved, the second by criticizing top-down modernization programs, and the third by warning against noncosmopolitan positions based on the superiority myth of a nation. The antidote for the first was the nonsupremacist notion of translation as it has been developed in this book via postcolonial theory; for the second, the criticism of the assumption that culture is smoothly translatable between places when geopolitical hierarchies are operating; and for the third, the demystification of origins by welcoming the very act of translation in the sense of a society opening itself up to the foreign. It is this inverted value invested in the foreign—a term that has abundant connotations in translation studies—as a rejuvenating contribution in a society rather than as a threat that sharply differentiates this book from hidden or explicit nationalist positions. Like all cases involving violence, however, when the foreign is imposed through force, it creates an aggressive reaction. One of the underlying arguments in the book was that while cultural interactions, hybrid artifacts, or cities with multinational populations are regular qualities of modern times, due to constant and copious translations across physical and cultural boundaries, they are not politically or psychologically neutral, and they do not necessarily fulfill their potential unless they are directed toward a cosmopolitan ethics. Given the continuing geopolitical hierarchies in a world whose institutions in power seem to perceive a benefit in perpetual war, today between the West and Islam, it seems ever more necessary to demonstrate the intertwined histories.

In unfolding the plot, I preferred intertwined histories over chronological linearity and fixed geographical separations. Translation studies broaden the established norms of art and architectural historiography that perpetuate either narrow national or broad but fixed geographical categories ("Western," "Islamic"). By discussing Germany and Turkey together, which are usually reserved for European and Islamic art historical fields, and by tracing the paths of German- and Turkish-speaking architects who had also lived in Austria, France, Japan, Switzerland, and Russia that added further levels of complexity to their translations, I hope to have shown the limits of these fixed categorizations that continue to frame the discipline.

The effects of the translations recorded in this book continued to unfold.

Seyfi Arkan's later career never matched his achievements of the 1930s after Atatürk's death. He died in 1966.

Celal Esad Arseven maintained his position as one of the foremost art historians in Turkey and was elected as a deputy in 1942 and 1946. He died in 1971.

Kemal Ahmet Aru continued as the assistant of Gustav Oelsner after studying with Bruno Taut, and directed his attention to social housing and city planning. He died in 2005.

Paul Bonatz received major state commissions and worked as a professor at İstanbul Technical University until he left Turkey for Stuttgart in 1954. He died in 1956.

Ernst Egli continued working on the effects of climate on the built environment and city design as a professor at the Eidgenössische Technische Hochschule (ETH). He died in 1974.

Sedad Eldem continued his productive pursuit of modernized versions of the old Turkish houses throughout his career. He received the Aga Khan Prize shortly before passing away in 1988.

Martin Elsaesser never moved to Turkey. In the postwar period, he taught architecture at Munich Technical University. He died in 1957.

Franz Hillinger finished the working drawings of Taut's buildings in Turkey after the latter's untimely death. Hillinger then moved to Canada.

Arif Hikmet Holtay continued working as an architect and teacher in Turkey, designing the observatory of İstanbul University, among other projects. He died in 1971.

Clemens Holzmeister became a permanent resident of Turkey in 1938 and stayed until 1954, working as an architect on official commissions as well as a professor at İstanbul Technical University (1940–47). He returned to Austria and died in Salzburg in 1983.

Hermann Jansen never moved to Turkey. He continued working on his projects in Germany until he died in 1945.

Reşat Ekrem Koçu started the second edition of the *Encyclopedia of Istanbul* in 1958 and continued working on it until 1973. He had reached the letter *G* when he died in 1975.

Abdullah Ziya Kozanoğlu continued working on village houses and writing novels. He died in 1966.

Abidin Mortaş edited *Arkitekt* with Zeki Sayar until 1942 and continued working on cooperative housing projects. He died in 1963.

Gustav Oelsner immigrated to Turkey in 1939 and stayed there permanently until 1949, when he chose to pursue his career in Hamburg. He died in 1956.

Burhan Arif Ongun continued working as a city planner in Turkey. He died in 1986.

Ernst Reuter stayed in Turkey until 1946 and became the mayor of West Berlin soon after returning to Germany. He died in 1953.

Zeki Sayar continued working as the legendary editor of *Arkitekt* until 1980, when the journal was forced to cease publication at the time of the military coup. It never resumed publishing under the same team. He died in 2001.

Wilhelm Schütte spent World War II in Turkey, moved to Vienna with his wife, Margarete Schütte-Lihotzky, in 1947, and continued designing school buildings. He died in 1968.

Margarete Schütte-Lihotzky, after being liberated from Nazi captivity in 1945, continued working on school buildings and feminist issues in Austria, Bulgaria, China, and Cuba. She died in 2000.

Kemali Söylemezoğlu worked first as Bonatz's assistant and later as an influential architect and professor at İstanbul Technical University. He died in 1995.

Bruno Taut died on Christmas Eve in 1938 in Turkey. He is buried in Edirnekapı Şehitliği Graveyard in İstanbul.

Behçet Ünsal became one of the foremost architectural historians of Turkey. He died in 2006.

Martin Wagner moved from Turkey to Boston in 1938 and worked with Walter Gropius at Harvard University. He was planning to move back to Germany when he died in 1957.

The translated idea of collective housing as a form of modern urban living shaped Turkish cities particularly in the years that immediately followed the period covered in this book. Many milestones of urban housing were designed during this period, building on the legacy of the German-Turkish encounters of the early twentieth century. However, the number of subsidized mass housing units remained well below the need, as it was

E.1. *Gecekondu* settlements in Ankara, 2011. Photo: Esra Akcan.

most clearly revealed in the growth of the illegal *gecekondu* (built overnight) houses, where more than half of the urban Turks resided throughout the second half of the twentieth century (fig. E.1). İstanbul ranks at the top of the lists of cities with informal, slum, and squatter housing. This is a form of urban living that has become so widespread, shaped so many global cities even if in slightly different forms, and has perpetuated an environment with no convenient transportation, proper infrastructure, formal electricity or waste collection—and hence keeps the urban poor living outside the social contract on an unimaginable scale—that our world in the early twenty-first century is indeed a "planet of slums," to use a term coined by Mike Davis.[1] Although this development might have saved urban residents from top-down regulations of state housing, whose postwar examples have been rightly criticized for their gigantic scale, monotony, and nonindividualized spaces, it would be hard to consider illegal slums as a superior alternative to mass housing. The historical contributions and limits of urban housing projects during the first half of the twentieth century hence gain additional value in hindsight. The discourse of the Turkish house periodically emerged on the scene and gained paradigmatic status during the rise of postmodern architecture. The melancholy of the non-Western individual also continued to set the tone of cultural production in Turkey well into the age of globalization, and it was coupled with the economic and political hardships of the Cold War years. Needless to say, translation is continuing to make history in the age of globalization, when cultural flows and transnational architectural practices have become more effortless than ever before.

German-Turkish relations entered a new phase when so-called Turkish guest workers met West Germany's labor shortage after the first recruitment contract was signed between the two governments in 1961, the same year that the Berlin Wall was constructed. By 1973, Turks made up the biggest portion (23 percent) of the noncitizen population in Germany. The housing laws and regulations for the immigrant population took numerous turns in conjunction with the integration debates, anti-immigration policies, and naturalization and asylum norms. The ban on entry and settlement in Berlin in 1975, for example, prohibited noncitizen families from moving into specified neighborhoods; regulations limited the number of foreign families permitted to live in each housing block. Some of the most innovative collective housing projects continued to take place in Germany during the Cold War over the legacy of the garden city and Weimar *Siedlung*. Today, German citizens of Turkish descent live in many of the *Siedlungen* that were discussed in this book. As of August 2010, there were no Turkish families residing in Bruno Taut's *Siedlungen* Britz, Schillerpark, Freie Scholle, Carl Legien, or other blocks in Prenzlauer Berg, but many lived in *Siedlung* Siemensstadt and Taut's urban blocks in Neukölln, including the one in Ossastrasse, where almost 50 percent of the apartments are rented out to Turkish families (see fig. 3.12).

A Turkish immigrant whom I will call Ş. K., for one, has been living since 1977 in a corner unit with three and a half rooms in Der Bruno Taut Block in Berlin, a *Siedlung* that gets its name from its architect (fig. E.2). She unhesitatingly welcomes me, a stranger at her door doing architectural research. Over a cup of tea, we appreciate the proper size and landscaping of the *Siedlung*'s pleasant courtyard garden, the organization of rooms, the big entrance, and two balconies of the apartment. As we discuss how it would have been better if the corner windows were much bigger and a bit lower, she says: "Even after I got a German passport, my verdict was given once they saw my black hair." Soon after she tells me of the long-lasting bonds and community feeling in this block, the daughter of her neighbor, who now lives in Kreuzberg but who grew up here with Ş. K.'s children, comes in and starts recounting her own fond memories of playing in the *Siedlung*'s courtyard garden with Turkish and German kids. A generation younger than Ş. K., the neighbor's daughter does not complain as much about discrimination and seems to have completely forgotten about the

E.2. Antenna for watching Turkish television, Der Bruno Taut Block, Berlin, 2010. Photo: Esra Akcan.

"foreigner's class" at the district school in which Ş. K. had to fight long and hard to avoid the placement of her kids. Soon, she tells us a secret that she had not told anyone else before. As I look astonished and flattered over such an undeserved confidence, she declares that she is pregnant and that she is looking for a new apartment, hopefully in this *Siedlung*, for which she uses the now common but slightly different Turkish term *site*.

NOTES

INTRODUCTION

1 "Ankara'nın beş yıllık planı," *Ulus*, January 15, 1935.
2 One of the earliest books that theorized the cultural impacts of globalization by tracing the different types of flows between places was Appadurai's *Modernity at Large*. I come to terms with similar types of flows through a theory of translation. One might justifiably ask why translation, rather than another term? Although words such as *transportation*, *transfer*, *import*, *export*, and *flow* connote the act of carrying from one place to the other, they do not necessarily involve the act of changing during this process. Although the word *transformation* embodies the idea of change, this change does not necessarily involve transportation but can take place in time without changing the place of the transforming object. The word *translation* is used here to explore the transformation during the act of transportation. Other terms such as *assimilation*, *adaptation*, *integration*, and *appropriation* refer to only one type of translation, in which a foreign object is reformed according to the determining rules of local conditions. Although such practices are certainly part of the historical process explored in this book, they leave out other types of translation in which some foreignness of the object is deliberately or accidentally maintained, and in which challenging the conditions in either location is preferred over assimilation.

3   Schleiermacher, "On the Different Methods of Translating," 42.
4   Eco, *Baudolino*.
5   The words *denoted* and *connoted* refer to Barthes, "Rhetoric of the Image."
6   Two influential works in architectural discipline on translating between drawing and building, and philosophy and architecture, are Evans, *Translations from Drawing to Building*, and Wigley, *The Architecture of Deconstruction*. Recently, a special issue of *Journal of Visual Culture* brought together articles that mostly analyzed translations between visual art mediums. Bal and Moora, "Acts of Translation."
7   Bassnett and Trivedi, "Introduction."
8   After reviewing two thousand years of translation theories, George Steiner concluded: "It can be argued that all theories of translation — formal, pragmatic, chronological — are only variants of a single, inescapable question. In what ways can or ought fidelity to be achieved?" (*After Babel*, 275).
9   Wittgenstein, *Tractatus-Logico Philosophicus*, 5.6.
10 I use the term *theoretical possibility* here because the practices of translation have shown plenty of times that a sort of conversion between languages is evidently possible. Yet no translator has ever conceived of this conversion as being trouble free, and translation's possibility has opened up significant discussions on language and philosophy.
11 The introduction of "translation theory" into the *Modern Language Association International Bibliography* as a separate entry in 1983 is usually credited as the date that made it an official field of study. However, the production of translation theories is part of a much older intellectual activity.
12 For basic historical surveys and anthologies on translation in English, see Brower, *On Translation*; Schulte and Biguenet, *Theories of Translation*; Lefevere, *Translation, History, Culture*; Robinson, *Western Translation Theory*; Venuti, *The Translation Studies Reader*; Gentzler, *Contemporary Translation Theories*; Munday, *Introducing Translation Studies*.
13 O'Brien, "From French to English," 81.
14 Paz, "Translation, Literature and Letters."
15 Ibid., 154. He also writes: "The world is presented to us as . . . translations of translations of translations. . . . No text can be completely original because language itself, in its very essence, is already a translation — first from the nonverbal world and then . . . from another sign, another phrase" (ibid.).
16 Ibid., 152.
17 See especially Chomsky, *Syntactic Structures* and *Aspects of the Theory of Syntax*.
18 The linguistic theorists of the late 1950s and 1960s aspired to establish translation as a universal "science." Also see Nida, "Principles of Correspondence" and "Principles of Translation as Exemplified in Bible Translating." For a discussion of the similarities and differences between Chomsky's ideas and Nida's translation theories, see Gentzler, *Contemporary Translation Theories*.
19 Derrida, "Des Tours de Babel," and "Roundtable on Translation."
20 Derrida, "Des Tours de Babel," 218.
21 Derrida, *Of Grammatology*.

22 Derrida, "What Is 'Relevant' Translation?" 176.
23 Ibid.
24 In "Letter to a Japanese Friend," Derrida comments on the problems of translating the word "deconstruction": "To be very schematic, I would say that the difficulty of *defining* and therefore also *translating* the word 'deconstruction' stems from the fact that all the predicates, all the defining concepts, all the lexical significations, and even the syntactic articulations, which seem at one moment to lend themselves to this definition or to that translation, are also deconstructed or deconstructible" (274).
25 Derrida, "Roundtable on Translation," 120.
26 Benjamin expressed this with the following words: "Translatability is an essential quality of certain works, which is not to say that it is essential that they be translated; it means rather that a specific significance inherent in the original manifests itself in its translatability. . . . [B]y virtue of its translatability the original is closely connected with the translation" ("The Task of the Translator," in *Illuminations*, 71).
27 Benjamin, "The Concept of Criticism in German Romanticism," trans. David Lachterman, in *Walter Benjamin: Selected Writings*. For more discussion of German Romantic's translation theories, see Huyssen, *Die frühromantische Konzeption von Übersetzung und Aneignung*; Berman, *The Experience of the Foreign*. For an annotated anthology, see Lefevere, *Translating Literature*.
28 Written works need translations because it is the translated version that brings any text to life for future generations and in other places. The metaphor "medical injection" comes from the Turkish writer Yunus Kazım Köni.
29 Benjamin, "The Concept of Criticism in German Romanticism," in *Walter Benjamin: Selected Writings*. 72.
30 The task of a translator is to "make . . . both the original and the translation recognizable as fragments of a greater language" (ibid., 78).
31 The "basic error of translators," according to Benjamin, is that "they want to turn Hindi, Greek, English into German instead of turning German into Hindi, Greek, English" (ibid., 81).
32 Ibid.
33 Benjamin's "pure language" has usually been assessed as an already existing but hidden metaphysical bond between languages, or a prewritten echo existing in all languages to be revealed through translation. Many writers have thus seen his theory of translation as a messianic gesture, with all different languages expected to return to their source at the end of history. For more discussion, see Steiner, *After Babel*; Berman, *The Experience of the Foreign*, 7; Dharwadker, "Ramanujan's Theory and Practice." Also see Wolin, *Walter Benjamin*.
34 To put this in Lawrence Venuti's terms, "implicit in any translation is the hope for a consensus, . . . the hope that linguistic and cultural differences will not result in the exclusion of foreign constituencies from the domestic scene" ("Translation, Community, Utopia," 485, 488).
35 Derrida, "What Is 'Relevant' Translation?" 178.
36 Reşat Nuri Güntekin, "Türkçenin Eksikleri," *Ulus*, July 25, 1944. All transla-

tions from Turkish, German, and French are by the author, unless otherwise indicated.

37 Ataç, "Tercümeye Dair"; Ataç, "Tercüme Üzerine."
38 Ataç, "Tercümeye Dair." For instance, while deliberating on how to translate "*je ne mange jamais*" (I don't/never eat), Ataç finds the direct translation "*ben asla yemem*" (I never eat) inadequate. The author is probably making a deliberate reference to the French idiom "*je ne fume jamais*" (I don't smoke), as if the speaker treats eating as an unnecessary and addictive act like smoking, and so the translator needs to find an adequate idiom in Turkish, even if this changes the original words. Ataç, "Tercüme Üzerine," 155.
39 Venuti, *The Translator's Invisibility*.
40 Köni, "Tercümeye Dair Düşünceler."
41 Ibid., 159.
42 Ibid., 158.
43 Ibid., 159.
44 Ibid., 158.
45 Schleiermacher, "On the Different Methods of Translating," 42.
46 Pratt, *Imperial Eyes*; Clifford, "Museums as Contact Zones"; Simon, "Translating and Interlingual Creation in the Contact Zone."
47 Eldem, sketchbooks. This quotation is from several entries in Eldem's diary. A more detailed analysis appears in chapter 2.
48 This book partly engages with the transformed scholarship on Orientalism and the postcolonial theories after Edward Said's book *Orientalism* was published in 1978. While a comprehensive list of works on postcolonial discourse in architecture, which is still evolving, would distract the focus here, here are a few influential texts that also discussed the Ottoman Empire and Turkey's place in it: Said, *Orientalism*; Baydar (Nalbantoğlu) and Wong, *Postcolonial Spaces*; Bozdoğan, "Architectural History in Professional Education"; Crinson, *Empire Building*; Çelik, "Le Corbusier, Orientalism, Colonialism"; Alsayyad, *Forms of Dominance*; and Roberts, *Intimate Outsiders*. For my views on postcolonial theories in architecture, see Akcan, "Critical Practice in the Global Era."
49 Cheyfitz, *The Poetics of Imperialism*. For a half-heartedly appreciative overview of writers who demonstrated the relations between imperialism and translation, see Robinson, *Translation and Empire*.
50 Edward Fitzgerald, *Rubaiyat of Omer Khayyam*, 1859 (reprinted by Oxford Classics in 2009). The claim also arrived in Turkey through translation. See Weidle, "Tercüme Sanatı." For more examples, see Bassnett and Trivedi, "Introduction."
51 Venuti, *The Scandals of Translation*; Jacquemond, "Translation and Cultural Hegemony."
52 Spivak, "The Politics of Translation," 180. Also see Cronin, *Translation and Globalization*.
53 Spivak, "The Politics of Translation," 183.
54 Ibid., 181.
55 Niranjana, *Siting Translation*; Venuti, *The Translator's Invisibility*.

56 For instance, see Chamberlain, "Gender and the Metaphorics of Translation"; Simon, *Gender in Translation*; K. Harvey, "Translating Camp Talk."
57 Asad, "The Concept of Cultural Translation in British Social Anthropology."
58 Lévi-Strauss, *Myth and Meaning*, 12–13.
59 Mukherjee, *Translation*; Bassnett and Trivedi, *Post-Colonial Translation*. Of particular note is Haroldo de Campos, who subversively found a similarity between translation and cannibalism, seeing translation as a source of nourishment for the Brazilian languages (Vieira, "Liberating Calibans").
60 Bassnett and Lefevere, *Translation, History and Culture*; Bassnett, "The Translation Turn in Cultural Studies."
61 For essays that explore the explanatory power of Bourdieu's theories, see Inghilleri, "Bourdieu and the Sociology of Translation and Interpreting." Also see Wolf and Fukari, *Constructing a Sociology of Translation*.
62 Zantop, *Colonial Fantasies*. Also see Friedrichsmeyer, Lennox, and Zantop, *The Imperialist Imagination*; Ames, Klotz, and Wildenthal, *Germany's Colonial Pasts*.
63 The clash of civilizations has by now become a common phrase, but the two authors who coined and disseminated the term were Bernard Lewis ("The Roots of Muslim Rage," September 1990, http://www.theatlantic.com/issue/90sep/rage.htm, part 1, p. 16) and Samuel Huntington, *The Clash of Civilizations*.
64 Arendt's evocative analysis in *The Origins of Totalitarianism* raised questions that were as difficult as the ones it answered.
65 Kant, "Perpetual Peace."
66 Marcus Aurelius, *Meditations*.
67 Schlegel, "The Speaking Voice of the Civilized World," 221.
68 Pollock, Bhabha, Breckenridge, and Chakrabarty, *Cosmopolitanism*; Vertovec and Cohen, *Conceiving Cosmopolitanism*.
69 Zubaida, "Middle Eastern Experiences of Cosmopolitanism," 37.
70 P. Cheah and Robbins, *Cosmopolitics*; Pollock, Bhabha, Breckenridge, and Chakrabarty, *Cosmopolitanism*; Vertovec and Cohen, *Conceiving Cosmopolitanism*.
71 Habermas, "Kant's Idea of Perpetual Peace."
72 Nussbaum, "Patriotism and Cosmopolitanism," 14.
73 Pollock, "Cosmopolitan and Vernacular History," xx.
74 Robbins, "Introduction," 3.
75 Appiah, *Cosmopolitanism*.
76 Kaldor, "Cosmopolitanism versus Nationalism."
77 Kurasawa, "A Cosmopolitanism from Below."
78 Mercer, "Introduction."

ONE | MODERNISM FROM ABOVE

1 For past surveys of modern architecture in Turkey during the early republican era, see Alsaç, *Türkiye Mimarlık Düşüncesinin Cumhuriyet Dönemindeki Evrimi*; Aslanoğlu, *Erken Cumhuriyet Dönemi Mimarlığı*; Batur, "Cumhuri-

yet Döneminde Türk Mimarlığı"; Baydar, "The Professionalization of the Ottoman-Turkish Architect"; Bozdoğan, *Modernism and Nation Building*; Bozdoğan and Kasaba, *Rethinking Modernity and National Identity in Turkey*; Holod and Evin, *Modern Turkish Architecture*; Kuban, *Istanbul Yazıları*; Rona*, Bilanço 1923–1998*; Sey, *Yetmişbeş Yılda Değişen Kent ve Mimarlık*; Sözen, *Cumhuriyet Dönemi Türk Mimarlığı*; Sözen and Tapan, *Elli Yılın Türk Mimarisi*; and Tanyeli, *Mimarlığın Aktörleri*.

For German-Turkish relations in architecture during the early republican era, see Akcan, "Intertwined Histories"; Doğramacı, *Kulturtransfer und nationale Identität*; and Nicolai, *Moderne und Exil*. For the history of housing in Turkey, especially see Bilgin, "Modernleşmenin ve Toplumsal Hareketliliğin Yörüngesinde Cumhuriyet'in İmarı"; Bilgin, "Anadolu'da Modernleşme Sürecinde Konut ve Yerleşme"; and Tekeli, *Türkiye'de Yaşamda ve Yazında Konut Sorununun Gelişimi*. For a recent compilation of the Armenian architects of the later Ottoman Empire, see Kuruyazıcı, *Batılılaşan İstanbul'un Ermeni Mimarları*.

2 Ülken, *Uyanış Devirlerinde Tercümenin Rolü*.
3 Ibid., 15, 18.
4 After the foundation of the Translation Office and the launch of its journal, *Tercüme*, in 1940, the translation of world classics into Turkish accelerated rapidly. Between 1941 and 1945, 214 classics were translated under the Translation Office's program; by 1953 this number had reached 1,000. In 1947, the office was planning to translate immediately 336 German books. *Tercüme* 10, no. 55 (1944): 1; *Tercüme* 7, nos. 41–42 (1947): 476–88.
5 The Translation Office and *Tercüme* gathered important intellectuals and translators of the time, including Nurullah Ataç, Sabahattin Eyüboğlu, Azra Erhat, Lütfi Ay, Erol Güney, and Nusret Hızır. Also see Daldeniz and Tükel, "Çeviri ve Felsefe"; Paker, "A Historical Perspective."
6 Between 1729 and 1929, out of 24,367 books published in the Ottoman Empire, 3,534 were translations (Anamur, "Önsöz," iv). For a list of translated books after the Tanzimat reform, see Hulisi, "Tanzimattan Sonraki Tercüme Faaliyeti." Also see Besen, Diriker, and Tahir, "Tanzimat'tan Önce Türk Edebiyatı Tarihinde Çeviri."
7 Öner, *Çeviri Bir Süreçtir . . . Ya Çeviribilim?*
8 Yücel, "Giriş."
9 Luxemburg, "Die Krise der Sozialdemokratie." Also see Earle, "The Baghdad Railway"; Baykal, *Das Bagdad-Bahn-Problem*; R. Hüber, *Die Bagdadbahn*; Lothar, *Berlin-Bagdad*; Önsoy, *Türk-Alman İktisadi Münasebetleri*; Karabekir, *Tarih Boyunca Türk-Alman İlişkileri*.
10 Luxemburg, "Die Krise der Sozialdemokratie."
11 Turan, *Türk-Alman Eğitim İlişkilerinin Tarihi Gelişimi*; Ortaylı, *Osmanlı İmparatorluğunda Alman Nüfusu*.
12 Trumpener, *Germany and the Ottoman Empire*; Yılmaz, *Birinci Dünya Harbi'nde Türk-Alman İttifakı ve Askeri Yardımlar*; Önsoy, *Türkiye'deki Almanya*.
13 The widespread French-Ottoman relations are discussed comprehensively in Çelik, *Empire, Architecture, and the City*.

14 There were only 27 German schools in the Ottoman Empire, compared to 560 French, 410 British, 67 Italian, and 56 Russian schools (Schaefer, *Deutsch-Türkische Freundschaft*; Ortaylı, *Osmanlı İmparatorluğunda Alman Nüfusu*, 62–64; Haydaroğlu, *Osmanlı İmparatorluğu'nda Yabancı Okullar*, 159–61).
15 Dietrich, *Deutschsein in İstanbul*; Haydaroğlu, *Osmanlı İmparatorluğu'nda Yabancı Okullar*.
16 For *Osmanischer Lloyd*, see Farah, *Die Deutsche Pressepolitik und Propagandatätigkeit im Osmanischen Reich von 1908–1918*.
17 Quoted in Önsoy, *Türkiye'deki Almanya*, 85.
18 The twelve invited German architects by Werkbund were German Bestelmeyer (first prize), Peter Behrens (second prize), Paul Bonatz, August Endell, Theodor Fischer, Hugo Eberhardt, Martin Elsaesser, Bruno Paul, Richard Riemerschmid, Walter Gropius, Hans Poelzig, and Bruno Taut. Walter Gropius could not enter; Eric Mendelsohn proposed a project independently. The construction of the building and the association's goals were disrupted by the outbreak of the First World War. See Deutsches Werkbund, Deutsch-Türkische Vereinigung, *Das Haus der Freundschaft in Konstantinopel*; Özkan, "Türk-Alman Dostluk Yurdu Öneri Yarışması." Only a few architectural historians have included this episode in comprehensive histories of modernism in Germany. See dal Co, *Figures of Architecture and Thought*. For a recent comprehensive book on Werkbund, see Schwartz, *The Werkbund*.
19 Koçak, *Türk-Alman İlişkileri*; Özgüldür, *Türk-Alman İlişkileri*.
20 Texier, *Asie Mineure*, 940.
21 Yavuz, "19. Yüzyıl Ankarasında Ekonomik Hayatın Örgütlenmesi ve Kent-İçi Sosyal Yapı"; Ortaylı, "19. yüzyılda Ankara."
22 As Ilber Ortaylı argued, even though there is no question that drastic changes were executed in Ankara after the founding of the republic, the city of the nineteenth century was not as poor and underdeveloped as the official historiography liked to claim ("19. yüzyılda Ankara"). Whereas official publications continuously promoted the contrast between Ankara and İstanbul. See, for instance, "Ankara İstanbul."
23 "İstanbul had turned into a prison under the occupational forces of the enemy; the word Ankara, the ideal of Ankara, whispered in every ear as a parole of liberation and redemption, sparkled every eye with the light of hope, acquired a mysterious charm by its own secrecy" (Karaosmanoğlu, *Ankara*, 12).
24 Refik Halid [Karay], "Hülya Bu Ya."
25 Ibid., 426.
26 Lörcher, "Der Neue Bebauungsplan für Angora"; Lörcher, "Stadtbaufragen in der Türkei"; Lörcher, "Das Neue Regierungsviertel der Stadt Angora"; letter by "Der Reichsminister des Innern," Nr. III 14129/26, Berlin, January 4, 1927, Bernd Nicolai archive. For more discussion of Lörcher's plan, see Vardar, "Başkentin İlk Planları"; Cengizkan, "Ankara 1924–25 Lörcher Planı."
27 Lörcher, "Stadtbaufragen in der Türkei," 8.
28 A Turkish committee from the Ankara municipality organized a trip to Berlin in order to offer the job to Ludwig Hoffman, who declined because of his age and suggested Jansen and Brix. The committee decided to add Jaussely to the list and hold a competition among the three. See Jaussely, "Izahname," 3.

29 For more information about Ankara's planning, see Tankut, *Bir Başkentin İmarı*, 26–40, and "Ankara'nın Başkent Olma Süreci"; F. Yavuz, *Ankara'nın İmarı ve Şehirciliğimiz*; Kezer, "The Making of a National Capital"; Şenyapılı, "Cumhuriyet'in Dokuduğu Kent Ankara"; Altaban, "Ulusal Yönetimin ve Toplumsallığın Kurgulandığı Başkent"; Bademli, "1920–40 Döneminde Eski Ankara'nın Yazgısını Etkileyen Tutumlar"; Nasır, "Ankara'nın imarı ve Almanca konuşulan ülkelerden gelen mimarlar"; Tekeli, "Türkiye'de Cumhuriyet Döneminde Kentsel Gelişme ve Kent Planlaması"; *50 Yılda İmar ve Yerleşme*.
30 Jaussely, "Izahname," 50, 63, 99, 109.
31 Ibid., 11.
32 Ibid., 12–13, 36.
33 Ibid., 23–31.
34 Later historians interpreted Jaussely's plan as the Hausmannization of Ankara. For Jaussely's coverage in contemporary newspapers, see Tankut, *Bir Başkentin İmarı*, 54–55.
35 Jansen, "Izahname," 137. The manuscript is in a document issued by Dahiliye Vekaleti Umuru Mahalliye, March 9, 1929, No. 030 10 122 867 2, Turkish Republican State Archives, Ankara.
36 Jaussely, "Izahname," 60–63, 99–102.
37 Jansen, "Izahname," 137.
38 Modernism in Turkey has not been included in the surveys of modern architecture, but the architectural movements in England and Germany, including the garden city movement, and major architects around Werkbund, Bauhaus, Expressionism and Das Neue Frankfurt have usually been acknowledged as important agents of architectural modernism. Surprisingly, social housing has received noticeably little attention in literature in English in comparison to its treatment in scholarship in German. For surveys on modern architecture, see Pevsner, *Pioneers of the Modern Movement*; Giedion, *Space Time and Architecture*; Banham, *Theory and Design in the First Machine Age*; Collins, *Changing Ideals in Modern Architecture*; Frampton, *Modern Architecture*; Tafuri and dal Co, *Modern Architecture*; Curtis, *Modern Architecture since 1900*; Colquhoun, *Modern Architecture*; Cohen, *Modern Architecture*.
39 See the articles on the British, French, Japanese, German, Australian, and American versions of the garden city in Ward, *The Garden City*. For those who interpret the results as a distortion of the original idea, see, for instance, Mumford, "The Garden City and Modern Planning"; Hall, *Cities of Tomorrow*; Ward, "The Garden City Introduced," 24; Watanabe, "The Japanese Garden City," 69–87.
40 Howard, *Garden Cities of Tomorrow*.
41 Moss-Eccardt, *Ebenezer Howard*; Beveers, *Garden City Utopia*; Hall and Ward, *Sociable Cities*.
42 Williams, *The Country and the City*.
43 Howard, *Garden Cities of Tomorrow*, 45–47.
44 Ibid., 114, 131.
45 Hall and Ward, *Sociable Cities*, 28.

46 Ibid., 17–40.
47 Howard, *Gartenstädte in Sicht*.
48 The DGG's journal, *Gartenstadt*, started publication in Karlsruhe as a small pamphlet distributed with *Hohewarte* in 1907 and then became a separate journal. Edited by Hans Kampffmeyer, *Gartenstadt* continued publication till 1917 and was relaunched in 1925. Numerous articles were on English garden cities and possible translations in Germany: H. Kampffmeyer, "Die Gartenstadt in ihrer kulturellen und wirtschaftlichen Bedeutung," "Zur Erweiterung unseres Programms"; B. Kampffmeyer, "Aus der Englischen Gartenstadtbewegung" and "Die Englische Genossenschaftsbewegung und die Gartenstadt"; Migge, "Die Entwicklung der englischen Gartenstadtbewegung" and "Die industrielle Entwicklung von Letchworth"; Katscher, "Ebenezer Howard"; Behnisch, "Was wir von der englischen Gartenstadtbewegung lernen können?"; Otto, "Das Wohnungswesen in England"; Berlepsch-Valendas, "Zum Thema 'Das englische Kleinhaus'"; Fuchs, "Nochmals zum Thema, Das englische Kleinhaus."

The editors promoted garden cities in other publications, too: H. Kampffmeyer, "Ebenezer Howard und die englische Gartenstadt-Bewegung," "Von der Kleinstadt zur Gartenstadt," *Wohnungen, Siedlungen und Gartenstädte in Holland und England, Wohnstätte und Arbeitsstätte, Die deutsche Gartenstadtbewegung*, and *Grünflächenpolitik und Gartenstadtbewegung*. Also see *Aus Englischen Gartenstädten*.
49 For instance, see Baum, "Mutter, Kind und Wohnung" and "Die Bedeutung der genossenschaftlichen Gartenstadtbewegung für die Frauen und Kinder der Industrie-Arbeiterschaft"; Altmann, "Frau und Gartenstadt"; Kassowitz, "Die Frau und die Gartenstadt."
50 Gruber, "Kolonisation in der Heimat"; Howard, *Garden Cities of Tomorrow*, 102–3.
51 For instance, see B. Kampffmeyer, "Zu den Baukosten des Kleinhauses"; Behnisch, "Vom billig Bauen."
52 The distinction between community and society refers to the influential thinker Ferdinand Tönnies's *Community and Society*. For literature on the history of German Garden City, see Hartmann, *Deutsche Gartenstadtbewegung*; Wiedenhoeft, *Berlin's Housing Revolution*; Posener, *Berlin auf dem Wege zu einer neuen Architektur*; Bullock and Read, *The Movement for Housing Reform in Germany and France*; Schollmeier, *Gartenstädte in Deutschland*; Bollerey, Fehl, and Hartmann, *Im Grünen wohnen*; *Geschichte des Wohnens*; Lane, *National Romanticism and Modern Architecture*; Rodriguez-Lores, *Sozialer Wohnungsbau in Europa*; Lejeune, "From Hellerau to the Bauhaus"; Lampugnani, "Moderne, Lebensreform, Stadt und Grün Urbanistische Experimente in Berlin 1900 bis 1914"; Ciré, "'Hinter der Weltstadt' Städtebau und Architektur der Landhauskolonien und Gartenstädte in den Berliner Vororten vor 1914."
53 Gruber, "Kolonisation in der Heimat," 17; Thoma, "Kultur und Gartenstadt," 98.
54 The program read: "A garden city is a planned and unified settlement that is

built on inexpensive land and obtained through the collective ownership of a community so that any kind of land speculation is permanently prevented. It is a new type of city that makes far-reaching housing reforms possible, ensures advantageous conditions of production for industries and trades, and secures a great portion of its land for agriculture and gardening. The ultimate purpose of a progressive garden city development is an inner colonization that decentralizes industries through the planned establishment of garden cities, and thereby strives for an even distribution of business life throughout the country" (quoted in Kampffmeyer, *Die deutsche Gartenstadtbewegung*, 7).

55 Contemporary writers argued that Howard's garden city had many "parallel" intentions with inner colonization since it "secured country life in the city" and "put a special emphasis on agriculture" by emphasizing private gardens for everybody (B. Kampffmeyer, "Innenkolonisation und Gartenstadt"). See also "Die innere Kolonisation"; Gruber, "Kolonisation in der Heimat." The term "inner colonization" was discussed in Turkey, too, by the editor of the foremost professional journal *Arkitekt*: Sayar, "İç kolonizasyon," parts 1–2.

56 On Huber, see Bullock and Read, *The Movement for Housing Reform in Germany and France*, 25–28, 31–36; Rauchbach, "Der Gedanke einer inneren Kolonisation."

57 Fritsch, *Die Stadt der Zukunft*.

58 As early as 1906, A. Abendroth claimed that Fritsch's book was the origin of the garden city ("Die Großstadt als Städtegründerin"). Gustav Simons mentioned Fritsch's book as a work as important and pioneering as Howard's work (*Die Deutsche Gartenstadt*). Also see H. Kampffmeyer, "Die Gartenstadt in ihrer kulturellen und wirtschaftlichen Bedeutung," 115; Otto, "Gartenstadtbewegung," 110.

59 B. Kampffmeyer, "Gartenstadt — Gartenvorstadt — Gemeinschaftsbesitz" and "Gartenstadt, Gartenvorstadt, Gartendorf"; H. Kampffmeyer, "Gartenstadt und Gartenvorstadt"; Behnisch, "Was wir von der englischen Gartenstadtbewegung lernen können?" 44.

60 "Die Gartenstadt Hellerau"; Wolf-Dohrn, "Gartenstadt Hellerau"; "Die Gartenvorstadt Falkenberg bei Berlin"; Behne, "Die Bedeutung der Farbe in Falkenberg"; Weiß, "Die Garten-Wohnstadt Margaretenhöhe bei Essen."

61 Hans Kampffmeyer explained that the revision was necessary to include garden suburbs and housing neighborhoods ("Zur Erweiterung unseres Programms").

62 Quoted in Kampffmeyer, *Die deutsche Gartenstadtbewegung*, 7.

63 "Zum 70. Geburtstag von Hermann Jansen"; "Zum Gedenken an Hermann Jansen"; Luben, "Hermann Jansen Zum Gedächtnis."

64 Muthesius, *Das englische Hau*, "Das sogenannte Moderne in der Architektur der Neuzeit," "Das englische Haus der Gegenwart," and "Die Lage des Landhauses zur Sonne und zum Garten"; "Neuere Bauten von Arch. Dr. Ing. Hermann Muthesius." For Muthesius's books on single houses, see Muthesius, *Landhäuser*, *Wie baue ich mein Haus*, *Kleinhaus und Kleinsiedlung*, and *Kann ich auch jetzt noch mein Haus bauen*.

65 Jansen, "Landhaus und Garten."

66 Jansen, "Die Architektur auf der Kunstausstellung Berlin 1904," "Gedanken

über Architekturausstellungen spez. die Berliner von 1908," "Die Allgemeine Stadtbau-Ausstellung Berlin 1910," "Der Wettbewerb von Gross-Berlin," "Wettbewerb Gross-Zürich," "Die Siedlung Berlin-Treptow," "Berliner Grossmarkthalle," and "Bauten Otto Schulzes."

67 Jansen, "Das Einzelwohnhaus der Neuzeit," "Landhaus und Garten," "Ausbildung des Daches beim städtischen Mietshause," "Das Mietshaus," and "Wohnhaustypen der Großstadt."

68 Jansen, "Die Allgemeine Stadtbau-Ausstellung Berlin 1910."

69 Fehl, *Kleinstadt, Steildach, Volksgemeinschaft*.

70 Jansen and Müller, "Bebauungsplan der Beamten- und Arbeiterkolonieen Streiffeld und Kellersberg bei Aachen" and "Hermann Jansen und seine Schule"; Jansen, "Bebauungsplan für das Johannistal zu Eisenach," "Wettbewerbsentwürfe zur Ausgestaltung der Frankfurter Wiesen in Leipzig," "Die preisgekrönten Wettbewerbsentwürfe für die Kleinhaussiedlung Friesland in Emden," and "Erschliessung des Rayons der Stadt Köln"; Säume, "Hermann Jansens neue Platzgestaltungen" and "Arbeiten aus der Schule Hermann Jansen"; Hegemann, "Hermann Jansen zu seinem sechzigsten Geburstag."

71 Jansen, "Wohnhaustypen der Großstadt."

72 Jansen, *Vorschlag zu einem Grundplan für Groß-Berlin*, "Der Wettbewerb von Gross Berlin," "Vorschlag zu einem Grundplan von Groß-Berlin," and "Der Meister des Bebauungsplanes," *Die Volkswohnung*; "Wettbewerb Gross-Berlin 1. Prize: Hermann Jansen," "Wettbewerb Gross-Berlin 1. Prize: Hermann Jansen."

73 Hegemann, "Hermann Jansen zu seinem sechzigsten Geburstag"; Jansen, "Erschliessung des Rayons der Stadt Köln"; the competition plan of Trier was published in *Der Städtebau* (1927): 102, 104.

74 Sonne, "Ideen für die Großstadt."

75 Jansen, *Vorschlag zu einem Grundplan für Groß-Berlin*, 76.

76 For reform housing, see Geisert, "Reformmodelle für das städtische Wohnen."

77 Jansen, *Vorschlag zu einem Grundplan für Groß-Berlin*, 53.

78 Ibid., 58.

79 Ibid., 53.

80 The information in this section comes from documents in Hermann Jansen, Nachlaß, ZR ABK 785, Germanisches Nationalmuseum, Nürnberg (hereinafter GN-Nürnberg); Hermann Jansen, Nachlaß, PSBTU; Ankara Municipality Archives.

81 *Deutsche Bauzeitung* 23 (1939): 496.

82 Alfred Cuda wrote his doctoral dissertation on Jansen's urban planning projects for Turkey (*Stadtaufbau in der Türkei*). Also see Cuda, Bangert, "Professor Jansens Arbeiten für die Türkei"; Cuda, "Deutscher Städtebau im Orient."

83 Jansen, *Ankara İmar Planı*, 46.

84 Jansen's report for Ankara's master plan was divided into four sections of "new/modern city planning" (*neuzeitlichen Städtebaues*; translated into Turkish as *Yeni Şehircilik*): transportation (*Verkehr*; *Seyrüsefer*), free areas (*Freiflächen*; *Serbest Sahalar*), areas for community buildings (*Gemeinschafts-*

lagen; *Teşekküller Kısmı*) and residential areas (*Wohngebiete*; *Oturma Mahalleleri*). The continuing influence of Sitte can be observed in Jansen's approach to community areas. Within this category, he listed a quarter of governmental buildings (*Regierungsviertel*; *Bakanlıklar Mahallesi*) and a quarter of higher education (*Hochschulviertel*; *Yüksek Mektepler Mahallesi*). Jansen went far beyond zoning specifications and studied these areas' architectural qualities with three-dimensional drawings. The drawings portrayed the governmental and higher education areas as unified and harmonious environments, single-handedly determined by the architect. See Jansen, "Der Generalbebauungsplan von Ankara," manuscript, September 17, 1936, Hermann Jansen, Nachlaß, ZR ABK 785, Folder: B7, GN-Nürnberg. The document was translated into Turkish as *Ankara İmar Planı*.
85 Jansen, "Der Generalbebauungsplan von Ankara," 32–42.
86 Ibid., 3.
87 Ibid., 10.
88 The density was fixed as 116 people per hectare, while Howard's was 75 per hectare. See Tankut, *Bir Başkentin İmarı*, 57.
89 Jansen, Plan for "Ankara: Südl. Erweiterung," 1937, Hermann Jansen, Nachlaß, No. 22735, PSBTU.
90 Jansen drew a plan at 1/2,000 scale for a residential neighborhood near Çankırı Avenue in 1934. He prepared the site plans and dwelling units for Bahçelievler (1935–38), the Agricultural School (1937–38), and the Emlak Bank Cooperative Housing neighborhoods (1937); collective housing in Atatürk Orman Çiftliği (Atatürk's Forest Farm) — a large recreational and agricultural region at the outskirts of Ankara and one of Atatürk's favorite escapes. The architectural projects for the housing neighborhood at Atatürk's Forest Farm was prepared by Ernst Egli. See Hermann Jansen, "Erläuterungsbericht für die Emlak Bankası Kooperatifi," manuscript, September 9, 1937, Hermann Jansen, Nachlaß, ZR ABK 785, Folder: B7, GN-Nürnberg.
91 Jansen, "Der Generalbebauungsplan von Ankara," 47–50.
92 For Leberecht Migge's ideas on the self-sufficient garden, see Haney, *When Modern was Green*.
93 "Die preisgekrönten Wettbewerbsentwürfe für die Kleinhaussiedlung Friesland in Emden."
94 Jansen, "Angora," manuscript, June 11, 1929, Hermann Jansen, Nachlaß, ZR ABK 785, Folder: B6a, GN-Nürnberg.
95 Ibid., 5.
96 Historians trace the first break away from the vernacular housing in Ankara to 1878, when a new neighborhood just outside the city walls of the Castle (in Sakarya) was built with wider streets on a grid plan. See Aktüre, *Ondokuzuncu Yüzyıl Sonunda Anadolu Kenti Mekansal Yapı Çözümlemesi*; Denel, "Ondokuzuncu Yüzyılda Ankara'nın Kentsel Formu ve Konut Dokusundaki Farklılaşmalar."
97 Holzmeister, *Clemens Holzmeister*, 30.
98 For more discussion on the government buildings built in Ankara by German-speaking architects, see Nicolai, *Moderne und Exil*.

99 The information in this section comes from documents on Holzmeister in the following archives: Clemens Holzmeister, Nachlaß, Universität für Angewandte Kunst Bibliothek, Vienna; Clemens Holzmeister, Nachlaß, Graphische Sammlung Albertina, Vienna; Turkish Republican State Archives, Ankara; Ankara Municipality Archives, Ankara. For Holzmeister's work, see Gregor, "Clemens Holzmeister" and *Clemens Holzmeister. Das architektonische Werk*; Holzmeister, *Bauten, Entwürfe und Handzeichnungen*, *Clemens Holzmeister*, *Clemens Holzmeister: Aussereuropäische Kirchen und Paläste*, and *Architekt in der Zeitenwende. Selbstbiographie*; Becker, *Clemens Holzmeister und Salzburg*; Rigele and Loewit, *Clemens Holzmeister*; Balamir, *Clemens Holzmeister*.

100 Gregor, "Clemens Holzmeister," 161.

101 Koschatzky, "Vorwort."

102 Blau, *The Architecture of Red Vienna*, 320.

103 "Werkbund *Siedlung*."

104 The information in this section comes from documents in Ernst Egli, Nachlaß, Special Collections, Eidgenössische Technische Hochschule (ETH) Library, Zurich (hereinafter Ernst Egli, Nachlaß). Also see Aebli, Meyer, and Winkler, *Stadt und Umwelt*. For more information on Egli's work in Turkey, see "Neue Bauten von Ernst Egli"; "Arbeiten von Prof. Dr. Ernst Egli, Ankara"; Nicolai, *Moderne und Exil*; Franck (Atalay), "Politik und Architektur."

105 In the manuscript of his memoirs, Egli wrote appreciatively about his experience with Atatürk and other Turkish statesmen, including Yakup Kadri, Falih Rıfkı, Yunus Nadi. Nonetheless, Egli's position toward the rapidly westernizing urbanization was ambivalent at times, as I will discuss in chapter 3. See Egli, "Im Dienst zwischen Heimat und Fremde, Einst und Dereinst: Erinnerungen," manuscript, 1969, HS 787-1, Ernst Egli, Nachlaß.

106 Tanpınar, *Beş Şehir*, 7.

107 Kasapoğlu Mansion was given as a gift to Mustafa Kemal by the Ankara *müftü*, Rıfat Börekçi. Some documents state that the house belonged to an Armenian merchant, while others state that the owner was a British merchant. The owners must have left during the War of Independence. See Y. Yavuz, "Ankara Çankaya'daki Birinci Cumhurbaşkanlığı Köşkü."

108 Ağaoğlu Ahmet recalled Atatürk saying these words at a dinner on January 4, 1923. See Belli, *Fikriye*, 93.

109 Cengizkan, "'Söz' ve Tarih: III Çankaya'da Cumhur Reisi İçin Köşk."

110 For instance, see Aslanoğlu, *Erken Cumhuriyet Dönemi Mimarlığı*; Özkan and Yavuz, "Finding a National Idiom"; Sözen, *Cumhuriyet Dönemi Türk Mimarlığı*.

111 Years later, Sedad Eldem, who was then an architectural intern, recalled his astonishment on learning that Atatürk had chosen the Viennese team over Mongeri (*Sedad Hakkı Eldem*, 49). The editor of *Arkitekt*, Zeki Sayar, noted that Mongeri could not secure any commissions after 1930 because of Atatürk's withdrawal of support for the revivalist style (Kumral, "Interview with Zeki Sayar," 104).

112 On Holzmeister's design, see Frischauer, "Das Haus Kemal Paschas in An-

gora"; "Das Präsidenten-Palais in Ankara"; Balamir, "Holzmeister'in Atatürk ve Kral Faysal İçin Saray Projeleri."
113 Von Bischoff, *Ankara*, 101–2.
114 Turkish Republican State Archives (Bakanlar Kurulu Kararları), December 10, 1932 (030.18.1.2. 32.74.10 Kat. 20); Holzmeister Archive in Universität für Angewandte Kunst, Vienna.
115 Cantek, *"Yaban"lar ve Yerliler*, 135–42.
116 Holzmeister's curriculum vitae lists the projects for these houses: apartment for Mehmet Galip Bey in İstanbul, 1930; house for Atatürk, Izmir, 1930; *Beamtenwohnhauser* (houses for officials), Ankara, 1932; house for Falih Rıfkı Bey, İstanbul, 1932; house for Tefik Rüştü Aras, Ankara, 1933; house for Director Hakkı Saffet, Ankara, 1933–34; house for Minister of Internal Affairs Şükrü Kaya, Ankara, 1933; house for Hasan Cevat Çobanlı, Ankara, 1935; house for General Kazım Özalp, Ankara, 1935; House Eckert, Emirgan 1943; Siedlung Surgagop, İstanbul, 1941; house for Sinosin Devrin, Ankara, 1944; house for Cemil Bey, Yeniköy, İstanbul, 1945; house for Sami Ozan, İstanbul, 1946; house for Professor Mürhen, İstanbul, 1946; Ali Sipali House, İstanbul, 1946.
117 For the discussion of the differences between Holzmeister's and Egli's governmental buildings, see Nicolai, "Ernst Egli and the Emergence of Modern Architecture in Kemalist Turkey."
118 Egli, "Im Dienst zwischen Heimat und Fremde, Einst und Dereinst," 57.
119 It is hard to determine the precise reasons why Arkan was chosen among other Turkish architects to undertake such representative tasks for Atatürk. See Tanyeli, "Seyfi Arkan. Bir Direnme Öyküsü."
120 Arkan's fellowship award was mentioned in the newspaper *Vakıf*, October 8, 1929.
121 Two letters of recommendation from Hans Poelzig and one from Erich Zimmerman confirm that Arkan (still using the name Nassih at the time) worked "intensely" with Poelzig, both at Charlottenburg Technical University (*Technische Hochschule*) and at the Prussian Academy of Arts (*Preussische Akademie der Künste*) in Berlin between 1930 and 1933. He presented work in the exhibition *Poelzig und seine Schüler* (Poelzig and his students) and worked in the architect's private office. Hans Poelzig, letters of recommendation for Seyfi Nassih [Arkan], March 9, 1931, and January 14, 1933; Erich Zimmerman, letter of recommendation for Seyfi Nassih [Arkan]; March 9, 1931, all Seyfi Arkan papers, Milli Saraylar Archive, İstanbul.
122 These projects were published in *Mimar/Arkitekt* just after Arkan returned to Turkey. The German titles on the drawings indicate that they were designed in Germany, probably in Poelzig's studio. See Arkan, "Deniz Kenarında bir Malikane" and "Ev Projesi." Also see "Hariciye Köşkü."
123 A comprehensive discussion of the pedagogic, architectural, and political implications of the split between Tessenow and Poelzig would distract from the purposes of this book. See Akcan, "Ambiguities of Transparency and Privacy in Seyfi Arkan's Houses for the New State." For Tessenow's letters about this split and students' accounts, see Heinrich Tessenow, Nachlaß, Briefwechsel, Kunstbibliothek, Berlin. IV.1.1; III.1.2.3; III.1.2.4; III. 1.2.5. For Tessenow's

architecture and its relation to German modernism, see Tessenow, *Hausbau und dergleichen*; *Gedenken eines Baumeisters*; de Michelis, *Heinrich Tessenow*; Anderson, "The Legacy of German Neoclassicism and Biedermeier."

124 Posener, "Hans Poelzig and Heinrich Tessenow at the Technische Hochschule, Berlin-Charlottenburg" and *Hans Poelzig*.

125 Hegemann, "Poelzig-Schüler." This article portrayed the work of Egon Eiermann, Max Cetto, Theo Kellner, and Hans Heinz Hinssen.

126 *Poelzig und seine Schule*, 3.

127 Frank, "Ein Bauhaus vor dem Bauhaus"; Schirren, "Eine Bauhütte für Berlin."

128 Posener, *Hans Poelzig*.

129 See especially Poelzig, "Vom Bauen unserer Zeit" and "The Architect."

130 After winning the first prize in İstanbul Opera Competition, Poelzig was invited to Turkey. He also designed two other unbuilt projects, the German-Turkish House of Friendship (1916) and the House of Diplomats in Ankara (1935, two versions). T. Heuss, *Hans Poelzig*, 79. For more on Poelzig's unbuilt projects in Turkey, see Nicolai, *Moderne und Exil*, 130–33.

131 In his will, Atatürk specified that Makbule Atadan could keep the house until her death, and afterward the residence became the Mansion for the Prime Minister and Guests (Misafir ve Başvekil Köşkü). Information on Arkan has been obtained from Seyfi Arkan, papers, Melih Şallı's collection, İstanbul (private); Seyfi Arkan, papers, Milli Saraylar Archive, İstanbul. For more information on the relation between Atatürk and his sister, see biographies of Atatürk such as Mango, *Atatürk*; Aydemir, *Tek Adam*.

132 Belli, *Makbule Atadan Anlatıyor*, 89–91.

133 In publications about the project, Arkan often made it clear that this house was designed for a woman. Arkan, "Villa Projesi" [1], "Villa Projesi" [II]; "Çankaya'da bir villa."

134 Robertson, "Two Villas for Kemal Atatürk and His Sister," 363 (my emphasis).

135 Pektaş, "Turkish Women," 10. Also see Baydar, "Tenuous Boundaries."

136 Here, I am not making any statement about whether women should veil or not, but simply pointing out the fact that we hardly heard from the woman herself in the making of these decisions. This was perhaps quite symptomatic, too: the voices of women themselves, which need not be unified in the first place, have usually been overpowered by the voices of competing men, whose political agenda depended on the visibility of women's hair.

137 Kandemir, "Florya Deniz Köşkü."

138 Banoğlu, *Atatürk'ün İstanbul'daki Hayatı*.

139 Banoğlu, *Atatürk'ün İstanbul'daki Hayatı*, 336. Also see 201. His visits were recorded in August 4, 1936, and September 24, 1937.

140 Quoted in Nicolai, *Moderne und Exil*, 127.

141 Karaosmanoğlu, *Ankara*, 11.

142 Ibid., 102.

143 Ibid., 106.

144 Ibid., 122.

145 Namık, "Yapı kooperatifleri"; Uzgören, "Ankara Bahçelievler Yapı Kooperatifi Nasıl Doğdu?" "Ankara'da Yeni Bir Mahalle Kuruluyor."

146 The Emlak and Eytam Bank had been established in 1926 to give credit for

housing construction. The Turkish Society for Cooperatives moved to Ankara in 1933 and started the publication of its journal, *Karınca*, in 1934. In its main convention of the same year, the society decided to begin building cooperatives. The general secretary of the society, Allaettin Cemil Topçubaşı, used every opportunity to promote the ideals of collective housing and to advocate close analysis of Western models. "In order to make fast progress without losing time, we must analyze the experience of Europe," he declared, and he idealized the West as countries where the majority of people owned their own homes and where governments spent billions for affordable houses (*ucuz ev*). See "Memurları Meskenleştirmek"; Topçubaşı, "Yapı Kooperatifleri ve Ucuz Ev," 33.

147 See also Tekeli and İlkin, *Bahçelievlerin Öyküsü*.
148 Gerhard Kessler, "Yapı Kooperatifleri," *Hakimiyet-i Milliye*, June 20, 1934.
149 "Yamaçlarda Yapılan Evlerde Mimarinin Örneğini Meydana Getiren bir Sanatkar Behrens," *Hakimiyet-i Milliye*, April 29, 1934; "Modern Şehir Mimarisi," *Hakimiyet-i Milliye*, September 18, 1930.
150 Nusret Uzgören, "Nusret Uzgören'den Gelen Cevap," *Karınca* (March 1936): 74.
151 Uzgören, "Ucuz Otru Kooperatifleri ve Şehircilik." Quoted in Tekeli and Ilkin, *Bahçelievlerin Öyküsü*, 33.
152 Uzgören, "Ankara Bahçelievler Yapı Kooperatifi Nasıl Doğdu?"
153 All of the answers were reprinted in a special issue on *Bahçelievler* (*Karınca* [March 1936]).
154 "Ulus'un Anketi. Ankara'da Mesken Meselesini Nasıl Halledebiliriz?" 17.
155 Promoting *Bahçelievler*, Affan Ataçeri said, "People are now giving up apartments even in the most populated and condensed cities of Europe. Instead, people build houses with gardens, and establish societies of *cite jardins* in all countries with the support of governments and municipalities.... Taking into account all these experiences that have sufficiently enlightened this issue, it would naturally be an error to attempt to construct apartments." Affan Ataçeri, "Affan Ataçeri tarafından gönderilen cevap," *Karınca* (March 1936): 109.
156 "We should be sorry for those who have to live in boxes on top of each other ... receiving sunlight from only one side of a light well. Their peace and quiet is bound to be destroyed, work and sleep to be disrupted.... Obviously, the houses surrounded with clean air and bright sun from all four sides have more to offer to a healthy and happy life than the boxlike apartments." E. F. Çobanoğlu, "E. F. Çobanoğlu tarafından gönderilen cevap," *Karınca* (March 1936): 93–94.
157 Baha Arkan, "Dr. Baha Arkan'ın gönderdiği cevap," *Karınca* (March 1936): 38.
158 Veli Atauz, "M. Veli Atauz'dan gelen cevap," *Karınca* (March 1936): 55–61; Turkan Baştuğ, "Saylav Turkan Baştuğ tarafından gönderilen cevap," *Karınca* (March 1936): 87–91.
159 "Saylav Turkan Baştuğ tarafından gönderilen cevap," 87–91.
160 Stress management, the healing power of nature, and the need of former farmers to see sunlight after moving to the city were some of the other rea-

sons to prefer garden city models. See Vietti Violi, "Ankete ilk cevap," *Karınca* (March 1936): 19–21; M. F., "M.F imzası ile gelen cevap," *Karınca* (March 1936): 33.

161 Vietti Violi, Sadi Reşid Dilek, and Vehbi Ergene expressed their hesitations about the expenses of dispersed settlements. They called for multifamily building blocks—still in gardens, but in common rather than private ones—with up to eight units per block (Ergene). Some found private gardens overrated, warned against the search for a single and standardized residential type, and advocated instead multiple forms of living for different types of people and families. There were Turkish architects and planners, including B. E. Asım and Burhan Arif, who advocated Weimar-style housing as much more efficient models than the prewar garden city. Vietti Violi, "Ankete ilk cevap," 19–21; S. Reşid Dilek, "Sadi Reşid Dilek'ten gelen cevap," *Karınca* (March 1936): 48–51; Vehbi Ergene, "Maden mühendisi Vehbi Ergene'den gelen cevap," *Karınca* (March 1936): 52–54; B. Laprad, "B. Laprad'ın konferansı," *Karınca* (March 1936): 77–82; Laprad, "Laprad'dan gelen cevap," *Karınca* (March 1936): 99–100; Kazalonga, "Fransız mühendislerinden M. Kazalonga tarafından gelen cevap," *Karınca* (March 1936): 101–6; B. E. Asım, "Berlin'den B.E. Asım imzası ile gelen cevap," *Karınca* (March 1936): 113–20; Burhan Arif, "Şehirci Mimar Burhan Arif tarafından gönderilen cevap," *Karınca* (March 1936): 121–26.

162 Vedat Nedim Tör, "Vedat Nedim Tör'den gelen cevap," *Karınca* (March 1936): 83.

163 Jansen, "Yapı Kooperatifleri," 46.

164 Atay, *Çankaya*, 417–28.

165 Atay, "Mesken Anketimiz Bitti," 138.

166 Fehl, "The Nazi Garden City."

167 Jansen and Müller, "Bebauungsplan der Beamten- und Arbeiterkolonien Streiffeld und Kellersberg bei Aachen."

168 De Fries, "Einige Siedlungspläne," 135; "Die preisgekrönten Wettbewerbsentwürfe für die Kleinhaussiedlung Friesland in Emden."

169 During the late 1910s, Jansen worked on the development plans of Berlin neighborhoods, including *Heimstätten-Gesellschaft* in Wittenau and another settlement in Charlottenburg. See Hane, "Hermann Jansen und seine Schule."

170 Jansen, *Bebauungsplan für Treptow* and "Die Unzulänglichkeit neuzeitlicher Platzanlagen."

171 Jansen, *Bebauungsplan für Treptow*, 3.

172 "The main objective is the unity of the masses, not a mass of units," he stated, summarizing his main goal for collective housing (Jansen, "Die Unzulänglichkeit neuzeitlicher Platzanlagen," 44).

173 This is confirmed in the class notes of one student. See Wolfgang Jungermann, "Notizen aus den Studiensemestern," Heinrich Tessenow, Nachlaß, III.1.2.5 Kunstbibliothek, Berlin.

174 "Arbeiten aus der Schule Hermann Jansen," 23. See also Hane, "Hermann Jansen und seine Schule," 7.

175 "Ulus'un Anketi," 23–32.
176 This was clear in the correspondence between Jansen and the cooperative. See Hermann Jansen, Nachlaß, ZR ABK 785, Folder: B7, Ankara from January 1, 1932, Folder: Ankara Kooperatif, GN-Nürnberg.
177 This is discussed in its abbreviated form here. For details, see Akcan, "Reciprocal Translations of Garden City Housing."
178 These requirements were formulated in a series of letters. See Mithat Dülge and Nusret Uzgören, letter to Hermann Jansen, January 3, 1936, and Mithat Dülge, letter to Hermann Jansen, February 5, 1936, Hermann Jansen, Nachlaß, ZR ABK 785, GN-Nürnberg.
179 Surface areas required for rooms were salon, twenty-two square meters; bedroom, twenty-five square meters; child's bedroom, twelve square meters; dining room, thirty square meters; and living room, twenty square meters.
180 These visions did not necessarily entail radical changes for many families in the cooperative. Many elite families of İstanbul had started using Western-style furniture after the Tanzimat reforms. See Duben and Behar, *Istanbul Households*.
181 Hermann Jansen, letter to Mithat Dülge, January 16, 1936, Hermann Jansen, Nachlaß, ZR ABK 785, GN-Nürnberg.
182 Ibid.; Jansen, Manuscript "Der Generalbebauungsplan von Ankara," 52–53, manuscript, September 17, 1936, Hermann Jansen, Nachlaß, ZR ABK 785, Folder: B7, GN-Nürnberg.
183 Instead, as Jansen rephrased the functionalist motto, "the exterior of a house should be a faithful mirror image of its interior functions" (Hermann Jansen, letter to Mithat Dülge, January 16, 1936, 7).
184 Mithat Dülge, letter to Hermann Jansen, February 5, 1936, 2, Hermann Jansen, Nachlaß, ZR ABK 785, GN-Nürnberg.
185 Hermann Jansen, letter to Mithat Dülge, February 14, 1936, 2, Hermann Jansen, Nachlaß, ZR ABK 785, GN-Nürnberg.
186 He got rid of the reminiscences of the old Turkish houses in the revisions. The extension bays in the single and row houses were removed; the loggias incorporated into the façade in the double houses were turned into balconies sticking out of the walls.
187 In April 1936, the cooperative informed Jansen that they wanted to continue the rest of the design themselves and supervise construction from a local office because time was tight and geographical distance was making on-site decisions impractical. Two years later, when the cooperative sent Jansen the modified plans to be built, the architect was disappointed by the changes. Another major cause of this shift was the departure from Bahçelievler of some members, who constructed a separate housing settlement designed by Martin Elsaesser (Güven housing). See Bahçelievler Cooperative, letter to Hermann Jansen, April 12, 1936, and Hermann Jansen, letter to Mithat Dülge, March 1, 1938, Hermann Jansen, Nachlaß, ZR ABK 785, GN-Nürnberg; "Ankara Bağçeli Evler Kooperatifi." For more information on Elsaesser's design, see Martin Elsaesser, Nachlaß, Architekturmuseum der Technischen Universität, Munich; "Ankara Güven Yapı Kooperatifi"; Akcan, *Çeviride Modern Olan* and "Modernity in Translation."

188 Hermann Jansen, "Erläuterungsbericht zum Generalbebauungsplan von Adana," manuscript, September 22, 1937, Folder: B6; "Erläuterungsbericht zum Generalbebauungsplan von der Stadt Ceyhan," manuscript, October 1, 1937, Folder: B6, "Erläuterungsbericht zum Generalbebauungsplan von der Stadt Tarsus," manuscript, October 14, 1937, Folder: B6; "Erläuterungsbericht zum Generalbebauungsplan von der Stadt Mersin," manuscript, January 4, 1938, Folder B6; "Erläuterungsbericht zum Generalbebauungsplan von Gazientep," manuscript, August 4, 1937, Folder B7a; and "Erläuterungsbericht zur Umarbeitung des Generalbebauungsplan der Stadt Izmit," manuscript, July 15, 1936, Folder: B10, Hermann Jansen, Nachlaß, ZR ABK 785, GN-Nürnberg.

189 Jansen's reports for these master plans followed a similar outline: an explanation of the existing conditions, problems, and unique characteristics of the city; and decisions for the new development plan categorized as transportation, free zones, industry and crafts, public buildings, and residential neighborhoods. As he had done for Ankara, Jansen submitted perspective and axonometric drawings of symbolic governmental institutions. Alfred Cuda, Jansen's assistant, prepared his dissertation on the master plans of these cities (*Stadtaufbau in der Türkei*).

190 Jansen indicated that six families could share a building block in workers' settlements, but the rest of the inhabitants would enjoy single-family houses with private gardens.

191 Kızıltoprak, Bostancı, and Erenköy were regarded to have developed as garden cities. See Menteşe, "İstanbul'un İmarı."

192 For example, for Tarsus, Jansen wrote: "It is the task of the future organizations and development plans to preserve and enhance these characters in order to make Tarsus a beautiful, healthy and tranquil *garden city*" ("Erläuterungsbericht zum Generalbebauungsplan von der Stadt Tarsus," 2).

193 Bozdoğan, *Modernism and Nation Building*.

194 Arseven, *Yeni Mimari*; Baltacıoğlu, "Yeni Adam İçin Yeni Mimarlık" and "Yeni Mimarlık."

195 One caption was "Those who are tired of gloomy darkness and heavy air find rest in these photographs" (*Yedigün*, no. 177 [1936]: 8).

196 "Ideal Küçük Bir Yuva," *Yedigün*, no. 140 (1935): 27.

197 "Orta Halli Bir Aile İçin," *Yedigün*, no. 451 (1940): 16.

198 "Türkiye'de ne kadar yapı kooperatifi var?"; Tekeli and İlkin, *Bahçelievlerin Öyküsü*, 106.

199 Mortaş, "Ankara tasarruf evleri kooperatifi," "Az Para ile Ev Yapmak ve Bizde Kooperatifçilik," and "Bir Memur Evi Tip Projesi."

200 Cengizkan, "Discursive Formations in Turkish Residential Architecture." Also see Aru, "4. Levent"; Kemal Ahmet Aru archives, İstanbul.

201 For an evaluation of population estimates and Jansen's plan, see Tankut, *Bir Başkentin İmarı*.

202 Jansen, *Ankara İmar Planı*, 46.

203 Tekeli and İlkin, *Bahçelievlerin Öyküsü*, 106–11.

204 Foucault, *Discipline and Punish*.

TWO | MELANCHOLY IN TRANSLATION

1. Khosla, "Crashing through Western Modernism into the Asian Reality," 58–60.
2. Fanon, *The Wretched of the Earth*, 257.
3. Banguoğlu, "Aşağılık Duygusu."
4. Çelik, *The Remaking of Istanbul*.
5. Tanpınar, *Mahur Beste*, 121–23.
6. See Radden, *The Nature of Melancholy*.
7. Aristotle, "Brilliance and Melancholy."
8. For instance, Al'Kindi's *Medical Formulary* shows that these writers shared a body of knowledge about natural ingredients that cured melancholy. When the Persian philosopher and scientist Ibn'Sina entered the service of the Sultan's court, he treated the prince of Rayy for melancholia. In *The Canon of Medicine*, Ibn'Sina used similar definitions for the signs of melancholy, such as bad judgment, fear without cause, quick anger, delight in solitude, and anxiety (this section of *The Canon of Medicine* appears also as "On the Signs of Melancholy's Appearance"). He also improved on the Aristotelian specifications of the relationship between melancholy and disorder in the black bile. Also see Goodman, *Avicenna*, 26.
9. Ficino, *Three Books of Life*, trans. Kaske, Clark.
10. Burton, *Anatomy of Melancholy*.
11. Freud, "Mourning and Melancholia," 176.
12. Ibid., 172.
13. Ibid., 168.
14. Considering that Freud's theory does not come to terms with the individuals with melancholia who are excluded from normalcy and deemed to be others, we need to use the term *melancholy* here (denoting an emotion) rather than *melancholia* (representing a pathological case). This also points to the ambiguous boundary between the "normal" melancholy and pathological melancholia. Also see Butler, *The Psychic Life of Power*; Crimp, "Mourning and Militancy."
15. Anne Anlin Cheng has discussed the melancholy of Asian and African Americans in the context of American assimilation politics. Working with Toni Morrison's *The Bluest Eye*, Cheng discusses the story of the black girl in segregated America in terms of the melancholy caused by the "imaginative loss of a never possible perfection" (*The Melancholy of Race*, 17). Also see Eng and Kazanjian, *Loss*.
16. Said, *Orientalism*, 72.
17. Karaosmanoğlu, *Kiralık Konak*.
18. A detailed historical analysis of the nineteenth-century and early twentieth-century (prior to 1923) apartment buildings in İstanbul cannot be given here, but it would have included buildings of Pera and Galata, the collectively built row houses of Beşiktaş Akaratler and Surp Agop, the row houses in Fener (on Külhani Street and Yıldırım Avenue), and the Vakıf and Harikzadegan [Fire victims] Apartments of Architect Kemalettin. See Y. Yavuz, "İkinci Meşru-

tiyet Döneminde Ulusal Mimari Üzerindeki Batı Etkileri"; Batur, Yücel, and Fersan, "İstanbul'da Ondokuzuncu Yüzyıl Sıra Evleri Koruma ve Kullanım için Bir Monografik Araştırma"; Çelik, *The Remaking of Istanbul*.
19 Karaosmanoğlu, *Kiralık Konak*, 88–89.
20 Ibid., 95–96.
21 It would exceed the scope of this short footnote to give a comprehensive list of the texts in which the term *melancholy* is used, so let a few influential examples suffice: the famous poem by Sabahattin Ali titled "Melancholy," which was turned into a popular song in the 1970s; Tanpınar, *Beş Şehir*; Gök, "Rene'nin Melankolisi."
22 Pamuk, *İstanbul*.
23 Sırrı, "Kanlıcanın Bir Yalısında."
24 Hisar, "Madalyonlar"; "Büyükadada'ki Ev"; "Kanlıca'daki Yalı"; "Havuzlu Oda"; "Yıkılan Yalı"; "Çamlıca'daki Köşk"; "Çamlıca'da Bir Mevsim."
25 Hisar, "Ankara'nın Güzellikleri" and "Ankara'nın Kıymeti ve Güzelliği İçin."
26 Hisar, "Çamlıca'da Bir Mevsim," 277.
27 Hisar, "Madalyonlar," part 1, 826.
28 A big room with a water fountain had a long monologue about life (Hisar, "Havuzlu Oda," part 2, 166).
29 Hisar, "Yıkılan Yalı," 245.
30 Hisar, "Havuzlu Oda," part 1, 151.
31 Hisar, *Boğaziçi Mehtapları*.
32 Most of the photographs referred to in this book are obtained from the Getty Research Institute, Gigord and Jacobson Collections, Los Angeles; and the Canadian Center for Architecture, Photography Collections, Montreal. For photography in the Ottoman Empire, see Ölçer, Beaugé et al., *Images d'Empire*. Also see Çizgen, *Photography in the Ottoman Empire*; Perez, *Focus East*; Tekin and Tekin, "Imperial Self-Portrait."
33 Oettermann, *The Panorama*, trans. Schneider, 22, 30.
34 Hisar, "Madalyonlar," part 2, 344–45.
35 Baudelaire, *Journaux Intimes*, 84. I have followed the translation of Max Pensky (Baudelaire, *Melancholy Dialectics*, 151) with slight modifications.
36 Hisar, "Yıkılan Yalı," 245.
37 Tanpınar, "İstanbul." The text was revised in 1960 and was subsequently reprinted. See Tanpınar, *Beş Şehir*.
38 "İstanbul," part 1, 9.
39 Ibid.
40 Tanpınar, *Beş Şehir*, 257–58.
41 Ibid., 13.
42 Koçu, *İstanbul Ansiklopedisi* and "Ev, Ahşab Evler." Besides Koçu, the encyclopedia's writers included Sermet Muhtar Alus, Semavi Eyice, Reşid Haid Gönç, Ismail Ersevim, and Hakkı Göktürk; the illustrations were by artists such as Nezih Izmirlioğlu, Ferzan Baydar, Reşat Sevinçsoy, and Abdullah Tomruk. Also see Pamuk, *İstanbul*, 144–63.
43 Koçu, "Akbıyık caddesinde demiryolu köprüsü yanında bir ahşab ev," in *İstanbul Ansiklopedisi*, 322.

44 "Ahşab Yapı," in *İstanbul Ansiklopedisi*, 311–15.
45 "Ev, Ahşab Evler,'" in *İstanbul Ansiklopedisi*, 169.
46 For instance, "Ağa Sebili Street," in *İstanbul Ansiklopedisi*, 166.
47 "Köprülü Amcazade Hüseyin Paşa Yalısı," in *İstanbul Ansiklopedisi*, 503.
48 Eldem, *Sedad Hakkı Eldem*, 5–6.
49 Ibid., 8.
50 The architect mentions that he had prepared forty to fifty watercolors in this period, but I could locate only about a dozen of them remaining in Eldem's drawings and papers at Koç University (which is closed to the public and some of whose drawers were unreachable). Eldem, *Sedad Hakkı Eldem*, 13.
51 Ibid.
52 Bozdoğan, "Unutulmuş Bir Başka Sedad Eldem Çizgisi."
53 The twenty-year-old architect started his journey to the West in June 1928 from Athens, continued it in the southwestern regions of France and in Paris (August 1928–June 1929), visited some of the growing industrial towns of Great Britain such as Glasgow and London (July 1929), and eventually ended the journey with a long stay in Munich and Berlin (August 1929–1930), from where he returned to Turkey. Although these are the towns that Eldem mentions in his diary, his map of the journey implies that he also went to other cities and regions such as Vienna, Zurich, Geneva, Venice, southern Italy, and the Balkans. Based on the dates noted on the map, it is possible that Eldem listed all the European cities he visited during both this research trip and his childhood spent in Nice, Geneva, Zurich, and Munich. For other accounts on Eldem's formative years, including this trip, see Edhem Eldem, "Mimar Sedad Eldem'in Gençlik Yazıları (1928-1929)" and "Sedad Hakkı Eldem. Düşünceler, Hayaller, Tespitler"; Tanyeli and Tanju, *Sedad Eldem*, vol. 1.
54 Sedad Eldem, manuscript, Font-Romeu, August 1928, sketchbooks, Edhem Eldem's collection, İstanbul (hereinafter sketchbooks).
55 Eldem, manuscript, Paris, January 29, 1929, sketchbooks.
56 Eldem, Book 7, 1929-30, sketchbooks.
57 Eldem, Book 6, Berlin, 1929?, sketchbooks.
58 Eldem, manuscript, Font-Romeu, August 1928, sketchbooks.
59 Eldem, manuscript, Paris, February 2, 1929, sketchbooks.
60 Eldem, manuscript, Paris, March 22, 1929, sketchbooks.
61 Eldem, manuscript, Paris, April 27, 1929, sketchbooks.
62 Le Corbusier, *Vers Une Architecture* (*Toward an Architecture*). It is hard to know whether Eldem was aware of Le Corbusier's *Voyage d'Orient* (*Journey to the Orient*) where he, too, had been attracted to the wooden houses in Turkey. Le Corbusier's journey to the East had not been published in book form yet, but some of the sketches of İstanbul's houses had appeared in his 1930 *Ouevre Complet*.
63 Eldem, "Toward a Local Idiom," 91.
64 Eldem, Book 5, London, July 1929, sketchbooks.
65 Eldem, Book 5, Chester, July 1929, sketchbooks.
66 Eldem, Book 5, near Glasgow, July 1929, sketchbooks.
67 Ibid.

68 Eldem, manuscript, Munich, August 1929, sketchbooks.
69 Ibid.
70 Eldem, Book 6, Berlin, 1929, sketchbooks. See also Hays, *Modernism and the Posthumanist Subject*.
71 Eldem, manuscript, Munich, August 1929, sketchbooks.
72 This topic had become widespread in Germany especially following the exhibition "Das Wochenendhaus" (The weekend house) in Berlin in 1927. See "Sparbaumethoden beim Wochenendhaus"; Rühle, "Das Wochenendhaus"; Stein, "Wochendhäuser auf der Ausstellung"; "Wochenendhäuser," *Neubau*; "Wochenendhäuser," *Wasmuths*.
73 Eldem wrote four possible endings to this story, in which he portrayed the achievements of European modernism either as "unserious," "Middle-Age like," "silly" (*bêtise*), or "pleasant" (*gemütlich*). These alternative endings demonstrate his own undecided position in the face of contemporary developments.
74 "Erich Mendelsohn: Bauten und Skizzen."
75 Eldem, "Toward a Local Idiom," 91.
76 Eldem, *İstanbul Anıları*, xxix.
77 Eldem, "Anciennes Maisons d'Ankara," 11.
78 Ibid.
79 Eldem, "Maçkada Prof. A. A. Evi" and "Beylerbeyinde bir Yalı."
80 Eldem, "Ev Projesi" (1931), "Ev Projesi" (1932), "Bir Villa Projesi," and "Villa Projeleri."
81 Safa, "Bizde ve Avrupa'da Kübik," 7.
82 Ibid., 8.
83 Ünsal, "Kübik Yapı ve Konfor," 60, 62.
84 Sermet Muhtar Alus, "Eski Konaklar Bize Neler Anlatıyor." The series began on October 22, 1936, and ended on December 8 of the same year.
85 Some of these essays have been collected in Alus, *İstanbul Yazıları*, *İstanbul Kazan Ben Kepçe*, and *Masal Olanlar*.
86 "Eski Türk Evi Bugünün Türk Evine Örnek Olmalıdır," *Tan*, November 27, 1936.
87 Mortaş, "Müstakil Evler."
88 In Sayar's words, Mortaş proposed the idea of having a journal because "nobody, neither the people nor the state, knew" them and they were "left in the cold." Mortaş, Sayar, Eldem, Abdülhak Ziya Kozanoğlu, and Samih Akkaynak started the journal. See Kumral, "Interview with Zeki Sayar," 100.
89 Mortaş, "Müstakil Evler," "H. Ziya B. Evi—Samatya," and "Tek katlı evler."
90 Mortaş, "Tek katlı evler," 310.
91 Arif Hikmet [Holtay], "Çiftlik Evi ve Han." The house was called a farmhouse but designed as a summer house for an architect.
92 Rüstem, "Bir Mimar İkametgahı" and "Şevket Bey Evi."
93 Celal, "Villa Projesi"; Arif Hikmet [Holtay], "Dr. Celal B. Evi"; Abdullah Ziya [Kozanoğlu], "Bir Kira Evi"; Hüsnü, "Hasan B. Apartmanı."
94 Emre, "Karantinada bir Villa—İzmir"; Baysal, "Ankara'da Ev"; Selim Zeki [Sayar], "Ev Projesi"; Gorbon, "B. Yusuf Evi."

95 Arif Hikmet [Holtay], "Köşk Projesi" and "Bir Ev Projesi"; Sayar, "Kalamış'ta Bir Villa" (1936), "Kalamış'ta Bir Villa" (1937), and "Suadiye'de bir Villa."
96 Eldem, "Evlerimizin Içi," "Ev Projesi" (1931), "Ev Projesi" (1932), and "Bir Villa Projesi."
97 Eldem, "Beylerbeyinde bir Yalı," 213.
98 Eldem, "Villa Projeleri."
99 Vogt, *Le Corbusier, the Noble Savage*.
100 Banguoğlu, "Aşağılık Duygusu," part 1, p. 1.
101 Ibid., part 3, p. 2.
102 Fanon, *The Wretched of the Earth*, 237.
103 Aristotle, "Brilliance and Melancholy," 55. For a recent account on the positive influence of melancholy on art and literature, see Kristeva, *Black Sun*.
104 Benjamin, "Theses on the Philosophy of History," in *Illuminations*, 256.

THREE | *SIEDLUNG* IN SUBALTERN EXILE

1 Widmann, *Exil und Bildungshilfe*; Erichsen, "Die Emigration deutschsprachiger Naturwissenschaftler von 1933 bis 1945 in die Türkei in ihrem sozial- und wissenschaftshistorischen Wirkungszusammenhang"; Shaw, *Turkey and the Holocaust*; Hillebrecht, *Haymatloz*; Bozay, *Exil Türkei*.
2 Turan, *Türk-Alman Eğitim İlişkilerinin Tarihi Gelişimi*.
3 Widmann, *Exil und Bildungshilfe*, 5.
4 Schwartz, *Notgemeinschaft* (the Turkish translation is Schwartz, *Kader Birliği*).
5 Widmann, *Exil und Bildungshilfe*, 131.
6 Glasneck, *Türkiye'de Faşist Alman Propagandası*; Dietrich, *Deutschsein in Istanbul*.
7 Glasneck argues that the periodicals *Beyoğlu*, *İstanbul*, *Yeni Dünya*, and *Signal* were controlled by the Nazis. See Glasneck, *Türkiye'de Faşist Alman Propagandası*, 19–26.
8 Schwartz, *Notgemeinschaft*, 95–98.
9 *Notgemeinschaft deutscher Wissenschaftler im Ausland* in Zurich was in cooperation with the Society for the Protection of Science and Learning in England and the Emergency Committee in Aid of Displaced Foreign Scholars in the United States. *Deutscher Freiheitsbund*, another anti-Hitler group, was led by Ernst Reuter, Gerhard Kessler, and Alexander Rustow, then in Turkey. Dietrich, *Deutschsein in Istanbul*, 257–324.
10 Halet Çambel, telephone conversation with the author, November 23, 2002.
11 Schütte-Lihotzky, *Erinnerungen aus dem Widerstand*, 38.
12 Official documents from the British Information Office have come to light proving that Wilhelm Schütte was "a member of a group engaged in anti-Nazi activities aiming at the liberation of Austria" between 1942 and 1945. Letter issued by British Information Office in İstanbul, January 15, 1945, Bernd Nicolai archive.
13 Apter, "Global Translatio."
14 Neumark, *Zuflucht am Bosporus*, 138–44. This work appeared in Turkish as *Boğaziçine Sığınanlar*.

15 Ernst Reuter, Nachlaß, REP 200 Nr 59, REP 200 Nr 163–168, Landesarchiv, Berlin; P. Schwartz, *Notgemeinschaft*; Neumark, *Zuflucht am Bosporus*.
16 Martin Wagner, letter to Ernst May, May 1, 1937, İstanbul, Martin Wagner, Nachlaß, Letters 26, Akademie der Künste, Berlin.
17 Auerbach, *Mimesis*; Said, "Secular Criticism"; Mufti, "Auerbach in Istanbul"; Konuk, *East West Mimesis*.
18 Quoted in Apter, "Global Translatio," 263.
19 For more information, see Bozay, *Exil Türkei*.
20 Letters between Thomas Mann and Ernst Reuter, 1943, Ernst Reuter, Nachlaß, REP 200 Nr 166, Landesarchiv, Berlin.
21 Neumark, *Zuflucht am Bosporus*, 124–25; Hillebrecht, "Emigrantenkinder in Ankara," in *Haymatloz*.
22 Edzard Reuter, *Schein und Wirklichkeit*; Ernst Reuter, letters to personal friends between 1935 and 1945, Ernst Reuter, Nachlaß, REP 200 Nr 59, 165, Landesarchiv, Berlin.
23 The word *Siedlung* is usually left untranslated in English. It refers to the residential estates that will be examined in this chapter. In Turkish, *Siedlung* was very often discussed by using the term *mahalle* (neighborhood) or *ikametgah bölgeleri* (residential areas). The translation of the term *mass housing* into Turkish would be *toplu konut*, a term that became common only after the 1950s.
24 For the most complete biography of and list of works by Bruno Taut, see Nerdinger, Hartmann, Schirren, and Speidel, *Bruno Taut*.
25 Nippa, *Bruno Taut in Magdeburg*. Also see Prinz, "Bruno Taut als Stadtbaurat in Magdeburg 1921 bis 1923."
26 Falkenberg was originally designed for 7,000 people with 1,500 houses, but only 127 houses could be constructed before the First World War. See Stimmann, *Gartenstadt am Falkenberg*.
27 Taut, "Siedlungsmemorien," 205. The newspaper *Berliner Tageblatt* named the project *Siedlung Tuchkasten* (paint box).
28 Taut, *Die Stadtkrone*, 55.
29 It is beyond the scope of this book to explain the crucial place of glass and crystal symbolism in Taut's career. For more on this point, see especially Bletter, "Bruno Taut and Paul Scheerbart's Vision," "The Interpretation of the Glass Dream," and "Expressionism and the New Objectivity"; Whyte, *Bruno Taut and the Architecture of Activism*; Thiekötter, *Kristallisationen, Splitterungen*; Speidel, *Natur und Fantasie 1880–1938*; Schirren, *Bruno Taut*. For more comparison between Taut's and Howard's diagrams, see Speidel, "Nachwort."
30 Taut, "Ein Architektur Programm" (translated into English as "A Program for Architecture"), "Die Erde eine gute Wohnung" (translated into English as "The Earth Is a Good Dwelling"), and *Die Auflösung der Städte*.
31 Taut, "A Program for Architecture," 433.
32 Taut, "The Earth Is a Good Dwelling," 456.
33 Bletter, "Bruno Taut and Paul Scheerbart's Vision," 223.
34 Taut, *Die Auflösung der Städte*, 458–59.
35 Until 1924, Taut continued to work on revolutionary architectural programs.

He founded *Arbeitsrat für Kunst* and the Glass Chain groups in order to exchange ideas and produce visionary manifestoes, projects, and exhibitions.
36 For the documentation of GEHAG housing settlements between 1924 and 1999, see Schäche, *75 Jahre GEHAG*.
37 Lane, *Architecture and Politics in Germany*.
38 One can see in the photographs of the exhibition that Köster's photographs of the Berlin *Siedlungen* as they were published in the journal *Wohnungswirtschaft* were used. The photographs in this book were collected at the Canadian Center for Architecture, Montreal.
39 Linneke, "Fünf Jahre DEGOG-Arbeit."
40 Wagner, "Englische Gartenstädte"; "Englische Gartenstädte II"; and "Das Problem der reinen Gartenstadt."
41 For a full bibliography of Wagner's publications, see *Martin Wagner*.
42 Ibid.
43 Wagner, "Englische Gartenstädte."
44 Wagner, "Das Problem der reinen Gartenstadt."
45 Ibid.
46 Ibid.
47 Lampugnani, "Modernism and the Metropolis."
48 Taut, "Was ist die Groß-Siedlung und welche Bedeutung hat sie für die Gartenstadtbewegung."
49 Taut, *Modern Architecture*, 205–6.
50 Bruno Taut, "Außenwohnraum," *Gehag—Nachrichten* II 1–2 (1931): 9.
51 Haney, *When Modern Was Green*, 179–90.
52 Taut, "Wohnstadt Carl Legien," 30.
53 Quoted in "Die Neue Gehag-Siedlung in Berlin."
54 Taut, "Forschung-Siedlung Berlin-Spandau-Haselhorst" and "Siedlungsmemorien."
55 Taut, "Gegen den Strom."
56 Even when Taut used the *Zeilenbau* principle, as in *Siedlung* Friedrich Ebert (1929–31), he articulated the corners of the blocks facing the street differently than the rest of the row in order to provide privacy to the shared garden behind.
57 Benjamin, "A Berlin Chronicle," in *Reflections*, and "One-Way Street," in *Selected Writings*; Kracauer, *Berliner Nebeneinander*; Nicolson, "The Charm of Berlin."
58 Akcan, "Manfredo Tafuri's Theory of the Architectural Avant-Garde."
59 Oelsner, "Şehircilik," 71.
60 Oelsner, "Modern İskan Semti ve Şehircilik," 168, 169, 170.
61 Bruno Taut, Manuscript "Siedlung für Japan," manuscript, 1933, Manfred Speidel archive, Sammlung Taut, Mappe II, No. 28, Akademie der Künste, Berlin; "Nippon mit europäischen Augen gesehen," manuscript, 1933, Bruno Taut, Nachlaß, BTS-01-80, Akademie der Künste; and "Tip ve Sıra Evler"; Gülsen, "Erinnerungen an Bruno Taut."
62 Behne, "Yeni mimaride milli ve beyneminel vasıflar"; Fischer, "Şehir İnşa Sanatı."

63 Sayar, "Müşterek İkametgahlar" and "İnşaatta Standard"; Akkaynak, "Berlin Mesken Kongresi"; "33 Mimar"; Arif, "Yeni Şehirlerin İnkişafı ve 'Siedlung'lar"; Şahabettin, "Şehir mimarisinde usuller."
64 Aru, "Levend Mahallesi." More information in Kemal Ahmet Aru Archives, İstanbul.
65 Aru, "4. Levent." More information in Kemal Ahmet Aru Archives, İstanbul.
66 Aru, interview with the author, December 2002, İstanbul.
67 For more discussion on postwar housing in Turkey, see Akcan and Bozdoğan, *Turkey*, chapter 5.
68 Wagner, "İstanbul'un Seyrisefer Meselesi," "İstanbul Havalisinin Planı," "İstanbul Nufusunun Yayılışı ve Münakele," and "İstanbul'un Münakele Tarihi." For a contemporary appreciation of Wagner in the Turkish press, see Oran, "Büyük Şehirci Mimar Martin Wagner'in Ölümü."
69 Wagner, "Büyük Şehirler Nasıl Tadil Edilir?" part 2, 71.
70 Wagner, "Türk Şehirleri ve Mevcut Sahalardan İstifade Ekonomisi."
71 For instance, Wagner wrote: "The new İstanbul has to be shaped with totally different financial standards and formal methods than the ones for the Western European cities.... Since İstanbul is a much poorer city, it cannot tolerate the irresponsible mistakes and false expenses of European cities" ("Şehir İnşasında Sermayenin Rolü," 140–41). But in making this statement, Wagner's implicit motivation could have been to criticize the master plan of İstanbul by Henri Prost, who had been invited to draw it up after the rejection of Wagner's proposals. Wagner perceived Prost's plan as a beautiful but naive project and criticized it for importing European city planning models without translating them in relation to the financial constraints in Turkey. However, this did not prompt Wagner himself to develop new models for Turkey. On the contrary, his own proposals repeated many of the norms he had helped establish in Germany. For more information on Prost's İstanbul plan, see Prost, *İstanbul'un Yeni Çehresi*; Kuban, *İstanbul: An Urban History*, 419–22; Tekeli, *The Development of the İstanbul Metropolitan Area*; "Cumhuriyetten Bu yana İstanbul Planlaması"; Akpınar, "From Secularization to Turkish Modernization"; Pinon and Bilsel, *From the Imperial Capital to the Republican Modern City*.
72 Wagner, "İstanbul'un Seyrisefer Meselesi" and "İstanbul'un Münakele Tarihi."
73 Wagner, "İstanbul Nüfusunun Yayılışı ve Münakele."
74 Wagner condensed his argument into four points: "1. At the moment, only a few sections of the wealthy population approve the modern houses. Nevertheless, the middle and working classes will also definitely accept them in the future. 2. A large part of the contemporary residences do not comply with even the basic needs of hygienic and civilized life. 3. It will definitely be necessary to cleanse the old and ruined parts of the city and redirect the population to the new sections. 4. And these new sections will definitely be placed in the direction of the Marmara Sea that has the most beautiful, most hygienic shores and residential areas with the brightest future" (ibid., 114).
75 Ibid., 113.
76 Wagner, "Städtebau als Wirtschaftsbau und Lebensbau."

77 Wagner, "Büyük Şehirler Nasıl Tadil Edilir?" part 2, p. 73.
78 Wagner, "Şehir İnşasında Sermayenin Rolü," "Şehircilikte Sermayenin Yanlış İdaresi," and "İstanbul Şehrinin Düzeltilmesi Meseleleri."
79 Wagner, "Şehircilikte Sermayenin Yanlış İdaresi," 188.
80 Wagner, "İstanbul Şehrinin Düzeltilmesi Meseleleri," 217.
81 "İstanbul Planı Etüdü."
82 Egli, "Şehir Planları," 196.
83 Egli, "Şehirlerde Mesken ve İskan Meselesi," 213.
84 Martin Elsaesser was invited to Turkey by the state, and is most well known for his Sümerbank building. On Das Neue Frankfurt, May, and Elsaesser, see especially Ernst May and Martin Elsaesser papers, Stadtarchiv, Frankfurt; Mohr and Müller, *Funktionalität und Moderne*; Mohr, "Martin Elsaesser and the New Frankfurt"; M. Elsaesser, *Bauten und Entwürfe*; T. Elsaesser et al., *Martin Elsaesser und das Neue Frankfurt*; Meyer, "Martin Elsaesser von 1925–1932."
85 Schütte, Curriculum Vitae, Universität Für Angewandte Kunst, Vienna, Oskar Kokoscka Sammlung.
86 Schütte, "Büyük Şehirlerin İnkişaf Meselesi," "Zelzele Sahalarının Yeniden İmarı Hakkında Düşünceler," "Th. Fischer ve Proporsiyonlar," "Adolf Loos," "Karl Friedrich Schinkel Bugün Bizlere Ne İfade Eder?" "Yer Depremleri Hakkında Yeni Araştırmalar," and "Mimar Yetiştirimi."
87 Schütte, "Sefalet Mahalleleri," 82.
88 Ibid., 80.
89 Schütte proposed that only buildings added afterward inside the courtyards should be pulled down; in other instances, only buildings on one side should be demolished in order to widen the street. As an example, he made specific suggestions for the Eminönü neighborhood, which looked like it needed a total cleanup at first sight, but which could actually be renewed by lowering its density and assigning appropriate functions to it.
90 Ibid., 87.
91 Schütte, "Bugünkü Kültür ve İkametgah."
92 Oelsner, "Şehircilik," 71.
93 Eldem, "İstanbul ve Şehircilik," 2.
94 Ernst Reuter wrote extensively on the organizational aspects of *Siedlungen*. See Ernst Reuter, *Mesken Meselesinin Hal Çareleri*; the German manuscript of this article can be found as "Wege zur Lösung der Wohnungsfrage," Ernst Reuter, Nachlaß, REP 200 Acc. 2326 Nr. 56, Landesarchiv, Berlin. Ernst Reuter "Şehirlerimizin Gelişme Problemleri"; the German manuscript of this article can be found as "Die Entwicklungsprobleme unserer Städte," Ernst Reuter, Nachlaß, REP 200 acc2326 Nr. 56, Landesarchiv, Berlin.
95 The information in this section comes from documents in Ernst Reuter, Nachlaß, Landesarchiv, Berlin. Also see F. Yavuz, *Prof. Ernst Reuter*.
96 Wagner, letter to the director of the School of Political Science, April 29, 1938, Ernst Reuter, Nachlaß, Landesarchiv, Berlin.
97 Reuter wrote his manuscripts in German, and they were translated into Turkish for publication.

98 Ernst Reuter, *Komün Bigisi*.
99 Neumark, *Komün Bilgisinin Esas Meseleleri*.
100 Egli, "Şehir Planları" and "Şehirlerde Mesken ve İskan Meselesi"; Ali, "Şehirlerde mesken ve sokaklar hijyeni, genel temizlik işleri"; İnan, "İstanbul Şehir Planı ve İstanbul'da Mesken Meselesi."
101 Gerhard Kessler mentioned in his review of Reuter's book that Turkish cities had long been under the influence of the French system, and that the book was an attempt to introduce German ideas of city planning to the Turkish audience ("Komün Bilgisi").
102 Ernst Reuter, "Teknik, Güzel Sanatlar ve Şehirlerin İdaresi."
103 Ernst Reuter, "Köylerimizde ne gibi şehircilik işleri yapılabilir?" and "Küçük Belediyeler Meselesi."
104 Ernst Reuter, "Şehirlerimizin Gelişme Problemleri"; the German manuscript of this article is "Die Entwicklungsprobleme unserer Städte."
105 Ernst Reuter, *Mesken Meselesinin Hal Çareleri*, 5, 7; the German manuscript of this article is "Wege zur Lösung der Wohnungsfrage," 2, 3.
106 "Wege zur," 6; *Mesken Meselesinin*, 11.
107 "Wege zur," 11; *Mesken Meselesinin*, 20.
108 Reuter's letters to Alaettin Cemil Topçuoğlu, who was the editor of *Belediyeler Mecmuası* ("Dergisi" is modern Turkish for "Mecmuası," attributed to Ottoman Turkish), reveal that he was closely involved in the foundation as well as the editorial side of the journal. See especially Ernst Reuter, letter to Alaettin Cemil Topçuoğlu. Ernst Reuter, letter to Alaettin Cemil Topçuoğlu, 10 May 1941, Ernst Reuter, Nachlaß, REP 200 ACC 2326, Nr. 53.54, Landesarchiv, Berlin.
109 Ernst Reuter, "Şehir planında iktisadi kaideler," "İçme sularının satışında esaslar," "Müstacel bir vazife," "Belediyeler Bankası Faaliyeti," "Köylerimizde ne gibi şehircilik işleri yapılabilir," "Belediyeler İstatistiği," "Vilayet hususi idarelerin istatistiği," and "Türk Dilinde Bibliografya."
110 Ernst Reuter, "Teknik, Güzel Sanatlar ve Şehirlerin İdaresi," "Belediyelerin Yapı İşletmeleri," "Belediye Meclisleri Azalarının Hak ve Selahiyetleri," "Kasabalarımız," "Belediye Reisliği," "Belediye Yapı İşlerine Luzumlu Paranın Temini," "Mesken Meselesinin Hal Çareleri," "Küçük Belediyeler Meselesi," "Gayri Menkullerin Üzerine Kredi Meselesi," and "Die Selbstverwaltung in der Turkei."
111 Ernst Reuter, "Komünlerin Kalkınması Usulleri," Conference in Manisa, 24.4.1939. Ernst Reuter, Nachlaß, REP 200-21, Nr. 56–57, Landesarchiv, Berlin, 57.
112 Ernst Reuter, "Beledi Vakıfların Modern Şehir İdaresindeki Ehemmiyetleri."
113 Ibid., 1.
114 Ernst Reuter, "Belediyelerin Yapı İşletmeleri."
115 Ibid., 30.
116 Sayar, "Mesken Davası." For more discussion, see Akcan and Bozdoğan, *Turkey*.
117 The long history of the different meanings of the term *rational architecture* will not be repeated here. For an article that juxtaposes these different mean-

ings, see Vidler, "The Third Typology." The idiom "dared to know" is from Kant's "What Is Enlightenment."
118 Scheffler, *Die Architektur der Großstadt*, 130. Also see Scheffler, *Berlin*.
119 Sonne, "Ideen für die Großstadt: Der Wettbewerb Groß Berlin 1910."
120 Benjamin, "The Work of Art in the Age of Mechanical Reproduction," in *Illuminations*.
121 Tafuri, *Architecture and Utopia*, and "Toward a Critique of Architectural Ideology." Also see Tafuri and dal Co, *Modern Architecture*, 158.
122 Wagner, "Gross-Siedlungen."
123 Taut, "Siedlungsmemorien," 208.
124 Hays, *Modernism and the Posthumanist Subject*.
125 Taut, "Von der architektonischen Schönheit des Serienbaues," 106. Also see "Erklärung zur Siedlung der 'GEHAG' in Zehlendorf."
126 Taut, "Neue und Alte Form im Bebauungsplan."
127 Taut, "Grundrißfrage."
128 Ibid.
129 Haney, *When Modern Was Green*, 210–13.
130 Taut, *Ein Wohnhaus*, 9–10.
131 Taut, "Grundrißfrage," 317. "There is no mathematical or constructional common denominator for the study of ground plans. No ideal type, no aesthetical auxiliary line [*Hilfslinie*] (for example, the theory of A[lexander] Klein) — on the contrary, this makes us go backward. From the piles of papers with countless and nameless 'types,' the social view will emerge, which shapes the intricateness of Being [*Dasein*] with its understanding of truth" (ibid.).
132 Goettel designed five different ways to subdivide and furnish the rooms in a house of fifty-four square meters. Possible occupants ranged from a couple with one to three children, or those who would prefer to use their kitchen and study differently. In the first variation, the big room (twenty-three square meters) was divided into a sitting place, an eating corner, and a bed niche. The midsize room (fourteen square meters) was used as a bedroom, and the kitchen was placed in the smallest space (eight square meters). In the second variation, the smallest space was turned into a *Kammer* (calculated as half a room in the assessment of the number of rooms in a unit) and the midsize room was furnished as a *Wohnküche*. In the third and fourth variations, two small rooms (*Kammer*) were used for two children. And in the last variation, the two small rooms of the third variation were turned into one big room (Jakobus Goettel, "Beitrag zur Erhöhung des Wohnwertes der Kleinwohnungen).
133 Taut, *Die Neue Wohnung*.
134 Ibid., 15–16.
135 Ibid., 64.
136 Ibid., 60.
137 Ibid., 40.
138 Ibid., 46.
139 Taut reproduced Frederick's circulation diagram (ibid., 66–67).
140 Sayar, "İnşaatta Standard," 10–11.

141 Ünsal, "Zamanımız mimarlığının morfolojik analizi," part 2, 222.
142 Arif, "Sıra Evler"; Egli, "Şehirlerde Mesken ve İskan Meselesi"; Schütte, "Bugünkü Kültür ve İkametgah."
143 Taut, "Tip ve Sıra Evler." Also see Gülsen, "Erinnerungen an Bruno Taut."
144 Mortaş, "Herkesin Kendi Evi," 128.
145 Mortaş, "Tek katlı evler," 310.
146 Eldem, "Küçük ev projeleri."
147 İhsan, "Ev Projeleri" and "Küçük ev projeleri." Nizamettin Hüsnü designed two similar projects for single-story, free-standing houses and also declared that the houses were designed with the principle of "maximum saving" (*azami tasarruf*). See Hüsnü, "Bir ev projesi," 176. Also see Hüsnü, "Bir katlı ev projesi."
148 Based on the area of a bed, Aru designated the minimum space needed for a bedroom as six and a half square meters. He explained how the old idea of the German *Wohnküche* had been discarded in favor of smaller, "laboratory-like" kitchens of around five or six square meters with maximum efficiency and sanitation. He suggested 3.23 square meters for a bathroom that would also be comparable to the "showering ways" in the old Turkish baths. See Aru, "Bugünün Evi Nasıl Olmalı? Evin İç Dekoru," 10, 11.
149 Ünsal, "Bahçe İçinde Küçük bir Ev," 10–11. Also see "Halk İçin Evler."
150 Kozanoğlu, "Müşterek Evler."
151 In addition to affordable collective housing, the architect defined metropolitan living in Ankara as follows: Commercial activities were placed on the ground level and provided with floor-to-ceiling windows on the street; large windows and balconies were granted to each family; and a large, common roof deck was available for the residents. See "Himayei Etfal Apartmanı Proje Müsabakası."
152 The information in this section comes from documents in Margarete Schütte-Lihotzky, Nachlaß, Universität Für Angewandte Kunst, Vienna. Also see Allmayer-Beck, Baumgartner, Linder-Gross, and Zwingl, *Margarete Schütte-Lihotzky*.
153 Heßler, "The Frankfurt Kitchen."
154 Lihotzky, "Einiges über die Einrichtung Östereichischer Häuser unter besonderer Berücksichtigung der Siedlungsbauten," "Die Siedlerhütte," "Die Siedlungs- Wohnungs- und Baugilde Österreichs auf der 4. Wiener Kleingartenausstellung," "Wiener Kleingarten- und Siedlerhütten-Aktion," "Das vorgebaute raumangepasste Möbel," and "Rationalisierung im Haushalt"; Schütte-Lihotzky, "Neue Frankfurter Schul- und Lehrküchen."
155 In the exhibition called *Die Wohnung für das Existenzminimum* (1930), May presented a studio apartment with a kitchen and a bath that was only 23 square meters. A unit with a small room was 26.1 square meters, another one with two rooms only 41.3 square meters, and a single-family house in row housing was 55.4 square meters. A bedroom in May's plans could be as small as 8.3 square meters, a half room only 4.2 square meters. In *Siedlung* Hellerhof in Frankfurt, a three-room house was 43 square meters. In Berlin, on the other hand, a house built by GEHAG with a living room, kitchen, and

one additional room was bigger, around 50 square meters. There, one with two additional rooms was 60 square meters, and one with two additional rooms and one half-room was 68 square meters; a single-family house was around 65–75 square meters. A bedroom in Taut's designs was usually around 12–15 square meters if not more; the smallest half-room was around 7 square meters. See Bourgeois, *Die Wohnung für das Existenzminimum*; Dreysse, *May—Siedlungen*; Linneke, "Zwei Jahre GEHAG-Arbeit."

156 Heynen, *Architecture and Modernity*, 49–50.
157 Schütte-Lihotzky, "Die Frankfurter Küche."
158 Heßler, "The Frankfurt Kitchen"; Akcan, "Civilizing Housewives versus Participatory Users."
159 Nolan, "Housework Made Easy"; Henderson, "A Revolution in the Woman's Sphere."
160 Schütte-Lihotzky complained in an interview in 1997 that the Frankfurt kitchen's reception overshadowed her other important works. See Heßler, "The Frankfurt Kitchen."
161 Henderson, "The Work of Ernst May (1919–1930)" and "A Revolution in the Woman's Sphere."
162 Nicolai, *Moderne und Exil*.
163 Akcan, "Modernity in Translation" (translated by the author with minor changes as *Çeviride Modern Olan*).
164 Bruno Taut, letter to the Schüttes, March 17, 1938, Manfred Speidel archive.
165 For more discussion, see Akcan, "Modernity in Translation" and *Çeviride Modern Olan*.
166 A drawing similar to the Frankfurt kitchen was published in the "Ev ve Eşya" (House and furniture) series in *Yedigün*, 1933, no. 1, 2. Incila Yar drew and discussed a modern rational kitchen that was very similar to Christine Frederick's ideal kitchen. See Yar, "Modern Ev Idaresi: Evimizde Taylorizm."
167 Navoro-Yaşın, "Evde Taylorizm."
168 Altunç, *Ev İdaresi*; Arel, *Taylorisme*.
169 Altunç, *Ev İdaresi*, 4.
170 In sewing classes, students combined rational and scientific, fast and efficient Western sewing methods with authentic Turkish motifs. See Navoro-Yaşın, "Evde Taylorizm."
171 Altunç, *Ev İdaresi*, 38, 88.
172 Navoro-Yaşın, "Evde Taylorizm," 70.
173 Altunç, *Ev İdaresi*, 101–3.
174 Ibid., 103.
175 Eser, "Modern Ev Mutfakları." Modern kitchens continued to be a subject of scholarly research in the second half of the century. See İzgi, "Konutta Yemek Hazırlama ve Pişirme Eylemi"; Ünügür, "Kültür Farklarının Mutfaklarda Mekan Gereksinmelerine Etkilerinin Saptanmasında Kullanılabilecek Ergonomik Metod"; Ağat, "Konut Tasarımında Mutfağın Etkisi."
176 Eser, "Modern Ev Mutfakları," 5.
177 Ibid., 4,5.
178 Spivak, "Can the Subaltern Speak?"; Guha and Spivak, *Selected Subaltern Studies*.

179 Tafuri, *Architecture and Utopia*.
180 Marx, "Alienated Labor," in *The Marx-Engels Reader*, 79. Also see Marx, "Private Property and Communism," *The Marx-Engels Reader*, 87.
181 Marx, excerpt from *Capital*, vol. 1, *The Marx-Engels Reader*, 329–36. Also see Marx, "Private Property and Communism," *The Marx-Engels Reader*, 84.
182 The following articles are all from *Wohnungswirtschaft*: "Wie soll der Kleinwohnungsbau der minderbemittelten Volksklassen finanziert werden?" "Vereinigte Selbsthilfe im Wohnungsbau"; Wagner, "Neusiedlungen — Ein Wirtschaftlicher Wahnsinn," "Neue Wege," "Industrie, Wohnungsbau und Baumarkt," "Gross-Siedlungen," and "Her mit den Wohnungsbauprogrammen"; "Das Alte System"; "Siedlungswirtschaft"; "Von Flandern bis Liegnit"; "Unsere Wohnungsfürsorgebewegung"; "Der Rest. Die Finanzgrundlagen für ein Wohnungsbauprogram"; "Wien-Berlin"; "Die Wohnungspolitik der Sowjetregierung"; Linneke, "Zwei Jahre GEHAG-Arbeit," and "Das Jahr *Wohnungswirtschaft*, fängt gut an"; "Richtlinien der Gewerkschaften für ein Wohnungsbauprogram."
183 Tafuri, "Toward a Critique of Architectural Ideology," 23.
184 Ibid., 23.
185 Ibid., 32.
186 Tafuri, "Sozialpolitik and the City in the Weimar Germany."
187 Wagner, "Die Organisation des Städtebau" and "Gross-Siedlungen."
188 Tafuri, "Sozialpolitik and the City in the Weimar Germany," 210.
189 Ibid., 214.
190 Tafuri and dal Co, *Modern Architecture*, 158.
191 Taut, "Gegen den Strom."
192 Also see Jameson, "Architecture and the Critique of Ideology."
193 Akcan, "Manfredo Tafuri's Theory of the Architectural Avant-Garde."
194 Ciucci, "The Formative Years"; Dunster, "Critique: Tafuri's Architecture and Utopia."
195 Tafuri, "Toward a Critique of Architectural Ideology."
196 Çelik, "Le Corbusier, Orientalism, Colonialism."
197 Ernst Reuter, "Mustacel bir vazife."
198 Naim, *Zonguldak Havzası*.
199 Sarıkoyuncu, *Milli Mücadele'de Zonguldak ve Havalisi*.
200 Quoted in Tuncer, *Tarihten Günümüze Zonguldak'ta İşçi Sınıfının Durumu*, 46–47.
201 Naim, *Zonguldak Havzası*, 117.
202 Çıladır, *Zonguldak Havzasında İşçi Hareketlerinin Tarihi*, 173.
203 Ibid.
204 Quoted in Tuncer, *Tarihten Günümüze Zonguldak'ta İşçi Sınıfının Durumu*, 72.
205 Quoted in ibid., 74.
206 Quoted in ibid.
207 Arkan, "Amele evleri, ilkokul, mutfak ve çamaşırlık binası" and "Kömür-iş İşçi Uramı." Also see Arkan, "Adana'da ucuz evler mahallesi."
208 Arkan, "Ankara için Ucuz Aile Evi Tipleri" and "Ankara'da Sıra Evler Tipi."
209 Arkan, "Kömür-iş İşçi Uramı," 9.

210 Ibid.
211 Ibid.
212 The following books discuss the Zonguldak issue from different political viewpoints, yet all use the word *imperialism* or *semicolonization*: Naim, *Zonguldak Havzası*; Çıladır, *Zonguldak Havzasında İşçi Hareketlerinin Tarihi*; Sarıkoyuncu, *Milli Mücadele'de Zonguldak ve Havalisi*; Tuncer, *Tarihten Günümüze Zonguldak'ta İşçi Sınıfının Durumu*. Semicolonization and capitulations were basic themes for Mustafa Kemal during the War of Independence, most notably in his opening speech at the Izmir Economy Conference in 1923.
213 Spivak, "Can the Subaltern Speak?"
214 Tuncer has argued that the workers' conditions during the republican period were hardly different from the period of semicolonization (*kumpanya dönemi*). Tuncer himself was a former miner who later became an important agent of unionization (*Tarihten Günümüze Zonguldak'ta İşçi Sınıfının Durumu*).
215 Schütte-Lihotzky, *Erinnerungen aus dem Widerstand*.
216 She quoted: "Sen yanmazsan, Ben yanmazsam, Biz yanmazsak, Nasıl çıkar karanlıklar aydınlığa?" (If you don't burn, If I don't burn, If we don't burn, How will darkness turn into light?) Ibid., 1.
217 "L'Immigration en Turquie."
218 "Köy Okulları Proje Müsabakası."
219 "İlk Öğretmen Evleri Proje Müsabakası."
220 Bayrak, *Köy Enstitüleri and Köy Edebiyatı*.
221 Nazım Hikmet, "Yalnayak," in *Bütün Eserleri*, 53–56. To a large extent, I followed Taner Baybars's translation in Hikmet, *Selected Poems*, 13–14.
222 Nazım Hikmet, "Şark-Garp (Piyer Loti'ye)," in *Bütün Eserleri*, 94–97. I followed Taner Baybars's translation in Hikmet, *Selected Poems*, 19–22.
223 Margarete Schütte-Lihotzky, "Über Zwei Jahre in Istanbul," manuscript, Margarete Schütte-Lihotzky, Nachlaß, Universität Für Angewandte Kunst, Vienna.
224 Margarete Schütte-Lihotzky, "Schulen auf dem Lande," manuscript, 1, Margarete Schütte-Lihotzky, Nachlaß, Universität Für Angewandte Kunst, Vienna. The report was translated by Hayrullah Örs into Turkish as a booklet: "Yeni Köy Okulları Bina Tipleri Üzerine Bir Deneme."
225 Ibid., 4.
226 Ibid., 1.
227 Ibid.
228 Ibid., 6–7.
229 Ibid., 5–6.
230 In the private houses designed as part of her own practice in Turkey, Schütte-Lihotzky continued to make hybrids of German modernist standards and local building knowledge. Unlike the icons of socialist modernism in Frankfurt, the houses designed in Turkey combined principles of rationalization and orientation with the Turkish vernacular she observed while working on Anatolian villages. She designed houses for Kemal Ozan, Nusret Evcen, and

Lütfi Tozan. She took countless photographs of anonymous houses in villages and cities in Turkey, focusing her attention both on the basic Ottoman and Seljuk monuments and the traditional vernacular houses. Her design for Lütfi Tozan intended to integrate the space-making principles of anonymous houses with a central *sofa*. For more discussion, see Akcan, "Modernity in Translation" and "Civilizing Housewives versus Participatory Users."

FOUR | CONVICTIONS ABOUT UNTRANSLATABILITY

1. Gökalp, *The Principles of Turkism*, trans. Devereux; Gökalp, *Turkish Nationalism and Western Civilization*, trans. Berkes.
2. Sayar. "Yabancı Mimar Problemi." Also see Tümer, *Cumhuriyet Döneminde Yabancı Mimar Sorunu*.
3. Akkaynak, "Güzel, Ucuz, Sıhhatli Ev," "Mösyö Jakın Asri Villası," and "Yeni Unsurlar."
4. Kozanoğlu, "Yeni Sanat," 98.
5. Kozanoğlu, "Binanın içinde mimar," 14.
6. "Cumhuriyetin on senelik san'at hayatı," 263.
7. Behçet Ünsal (1912–2006), a 1933 graduate of the İstanbul Academy, would become an influential historian. He joined the İstanbul Municipality in 1940, where he worked with the French city planner Henri Prost on the city's master plan and contributed to preservation projects. He also cofounded the journal *Yapı* (1941–43); and he wrote *Mimarlık Tarihi*, vols. 1 and 2 (History of architecture, 1949, 2001), *Turkish Islamic Architecture* (1959), and *Türk Sanatı İncelemeleri*, vols. 1 and 2 (Studies on Turkish art, 1963, 1969).
8. Ünsal and Hamdi, "Mimarlık ve Türklük."
9. Ibid., 18.
10. Ünsal and Hamdi, "Türk Inkılap Mimarisi," 265 (my emphasis).
11. The list of books defining the old Turkish house written after the 1950s are too extensive to list here. For comprehensive accounts and bibliography, see *Türk Evi ve Biz*. Kuban, *The Turkish Hayat House*; Küçükerman, *Turkish House*. For historical studies about the impact of the old Turkish house on modern architecture in Turkey, see (in addition to the surveys already listed in the first endnote of chapter 1) Bozdoğan, Özkan, and Yenal, *Sedad Eldem*; Baydar, "Between *Civilization* and *Culture*"; Bozdoğan, "Vernacular Architecture and Identity Politics"; Bertram, "The Turkish House, an Effort on Memory"; Özkan, Turan, and Üstünkök. "Institutionalised Architecture, Vernacular Architecture and Vernacularism in Historical Perspective"; and Tanyeli, "Türkiye'de Modernleşme ve Vernaküler Mimari Gelenek."
12. Bozdoğan, "Reading Ottoman Architecture through Modernist Lenses," 4.
13. Bertram, "The Turkish House, an Effort on Memory," 122–28. Also see Tanrıöver, "Eski Türk Evleri."
14. [Koyunoğlu?] Arif Hikmet, "Ankara Evleri."
15. Wilde, *Brussa*.
16. Ibid., 106–25.
17. Celal Esad [Arseven], *Constantinople* and *Eski İstanbul*.

18 Also see Arseven, *Sanat ve Siyaset Hatıralarım*.
19 Arseven, *L'art Turc*, 5. Also see Arseven, *Türk Sanatı*.
20 Arseven, *Constantinople*, 153.
21 Bozdoğan, "Reading Ottoman Architecture through Modernist Lenses," 4.
22 Arseven, *Türk Sanatı* and *L'art Turc*.
23 The architectural historians Doğan Kuban and Burcu Doğramacı have suggested similarities between Arseven's theory and the argument by the Austrian art historian Josef Strzygowski in *Altai-Iran und Völkerwanderung* (Altai-Iran and the migration of peoples). See Kuban, "Celal Esad Arseven ve Türk Sanatı Kavramı"; Doğramacı, *Kulturtransfer und nationale Identität*, 323–25; Strzygowski, *Altai-Iran und Völkerwanderung*.
24 Arseven, *Türk Sanatı*, 104.
25 Eldem, "Amca Hüseyin Paşa Yalısı."
26 Egli writes about Holtay's contribution in his diary. See Ernst Egli, "Im Dienst zwischen Heimat und Fremde, Einst und Dereinst: Erinnerungen," 58, 73, 1969, HS 787-1, Ernst Egli, Nachlaß.
27 The information in this section comes from documents in Ernst Egli, Nachlaß.
28 Also see chapter 1, notes 104, 105.
29 For Egli's reports on this trip, see HS 785 155–160, Ernst Egli, Nachlaß.
30 Egli, *Climate and Town Districts*, *Sinan*, *Şehirciliğin ve Memleket Planlamasının Esasları*, and *Geschichte des Städtebau*.
31 Arseven referred to him as the architect who introduced cubic architecture in Turkey, and illustrated his argument with Egli's buildings in Ankara (*Yeni Mimari*), 8–12.
32 Egli, "Mimari Muhit."
33 Ibid., 34.
34 Ibid., 35.
35 Ibid., 36.
36 Egli, "Im Dienst zwischen Heimat und Fremde, Einst und Dereinst," 47, 91–98.
37 Egli, "Das Türkische Wohnhaus."
38 Ibid., 15.
39 Ibid., 11–12, 18.
40 At the Eidgenössische Technische Hochschule (ETH), Egli gave the following courses: "Turkish Architecture: Past and Present," summer 1942; "Sinan: The Turkish Architect," winter 1942; "Constantinople-Istanbul: The Building History of a City between two Continents," summer 1943; and "National and Regional Basis of Urban Design," summer 1944. For lecture notes for these courses, see Egli, "Türkische Baukunst in Geschichte und Gegenwart," manuscript, 1942, HS 785-1; "Konstantinopel-Istanbul, Baugeschichte einer Stadt zwischen zwei Kontinenten," manuscript, 1943, HS 785-2; and "Nationale und Regionale Grundlagen im Städtebau," manuscript, 1944, HS 785-4, all Ernst Egli, Nachlaß.
41 Egli, "Landesplanung und Städtebau in der Türkei," manuscript, 1945, HS 785-64; "Erinnerungen an den Orient," manuscript for lecture on February 6, 1963, HS 785-68; "Reisen im Orient," manuscript, 1959, HS 785-65; and "Drei

Reisen in Anatolien," manuscript for lecture on October 7, 1963, HS 785-67, all Ernst Egli, Nachlaß.
42 Egli, untitled manuscripts HS 785-100, HS 785-101, and HS 785-102, Ernst Egli, Nachlaß.
43 Egli, "Ein Triptychon der Liebe, Venedig, Stambul, Wien," manuscript circa 1955, HS 785-88a, Ernst Egli, Nachlaß.
44 Egli, "Türk Evi."
45 Ibid., 205.
46 Henning, *Das deutsche Haus in seiner historischen Entwicklung*; von Huber, *Das deutsche Haus zur Zeit der Renaissance*; Meringer, *Das deutsche Haus und sein Hausrat*; Ranck, *Kulturgeschichte des deutschen Bauernhauses*; Schmidt, *Das sächsische Bauernhaus und seine Dorfgenossen*; Lauffer, *Das deutsche Haus in Dorf und Stadt*; Junge, *Das friesische Bauernhaus*; Walter, *Das westfälische Bauernhaus*; Wolfrom, *Das Bauernhaus im Magdeburger Land*.
47 Egli, "Türkische Baukunst in Geschichte und Gegenwart," manuscript, 1942, HS 785-1, Ernst Egli, Nachlaß.
48 Ibid., 133–36.
49 Ibid., 144.
50 Ibid., 290.
51 Egli referred both to the courtyard in the Aynalıkavak pavilion and the main room in the Mustafapaşa house as a *sofa* (ibid., 136–38). Describing a waterfront house in Bebek, he used the word *sofa* to refer to the everyday rooms (139). The translated version, published in *Ülkü* as "Türk Evi," used other terms (202–3).
52 Wilde, *Brussa*.
53 Sedad Eldem, "Anciennes Maisons d'Ankara" and *Türk Evi Plan Tipleri*.
54 Sedad Eldem, "Anciennes Maisons d'Ankara," 10.
55 Ibid., 11.
56 Sedad Eldem, *Türk Evi Plan Tipleri*, 7.
57 Ibid., 12. English translation, 216.
58 Ibid.
59 Ibid.
60 Ibid., 16. Translation modified, 218.
61 Sedad Eldem, "Türk Odası."
62 Sedad Eldem, *Türk Evi Plan Tipleri*, 24.
63 Ibid., 127–28.
64 Sedad Eldem, *İstanbul Yalıları* and *Türk Evi*.
65 Sedad Eldem, "Türk Odası."
66 For an incomplete list of the burned documents, see Serdengeçti, "Yanan 'Milli Mimari' Röleveleri Arşini'nde Neler Vardı?"; Sayar, "Güzel Sanatlar Akademisinin Yanışı Münasebetiyle."
67 Two books published at the time by two influential critics were the best testimonies to this success. Behne, *Neues Wohnen neues Bauen*; Behrendt, *The Victory of the New Building Style*. For accounts from the GEHAG circle itself, see Albert Jaeger, "Die Sache Gefühl"; Martin Wagner, "Zivilization, Kultur, Kunst." For scholarship on the topic, especially, see Lampugnani and

Schneider, *Moderne Architektur in Deutschland 1900 bis 1950*; Lane, *Architecture and Politics in Germany*; Willett, *The New Sobriety*. Bletter, "Expressionism and the New Objectivity."

68 Pommer, "The Flat Roof."
69 Linneke, "Zwei Jahre GEHAG Arbeit."
70 May, *Das Neue Frankfurt*.
71 "Das Flache Dach."
72 See especially Schultze-Naumburg, *Kunst und Rasse*.
73 The contemporary publication launching the project was *Bau und Wohnung*. The scholarship about *Siedlung* Weissenhof is extensive and hence will not be cited here. See especially Pommer and Otto, *Weisenhof 1927 and the Modern Movement in Architecture*; Kirsch, "Die Weissenhofsiedlung. Ein internationales Manifest." Similarly, Mies van der Rohe has been the German architect who has received the most attention in scholarship published in English, and a full bibliography would therefore exceed the scope here. For recent scholarship, see especially Bergdoll and Reiley, *Mies in Berlin*; Cohen, *Mies van der Rohe*; Mertins, *The Presence of Mies*; Neumeyer, *The Artless Word*; Schulze, *Mies van der Rohe*.
74 Taut, "Siedlungsmemorien," 206.
75 Ibid.
76 Finckh, "The Spirit of Berlin."
77 Stapel, "The Intellectual and His People," 424, 425.
78 Schmitthenner, *Baukunst im neuen Reich*.
79 Martin Wagner, letter to Paul Schmitthenner, June 10, 1934, Martin Wagner, Nachlaß, Akademie der Künste, Berlin.
80 The information in this section comes from documents about Paul Bonatz in Paul Bonatz, drawings and papers, Peter Dübers's personal collection, Stuttgart (hereinafter drawings and papers); Paul Bonatz, Nachlaß, Stuttgart Universität, Stuttgart; Municipality Archives, Ankara.
81 Tamms, *Paul Bonatz*; Werner, "The Myth of the Atemporal"; Worbs, "Paul Bonatz—ein konservativer Reformer?"
82 Roser, *Paul Bonatz*.
83 Frank, "Monuments in Arbeitsstil."
84 Paul Bonatz, "Noch einmal die Werkbund Siedlung," *Schwäbische Chronik*, May 5, 1926.
85 *Die 25 Einfamilienhäuser der Holzsiedlung am Kochenhof*.
86 Bonatz and Wehner, *Reichsautobahn–Tankanlagen*.
87 Taylor, *The Word in Stone*. Also see Zukowsky, *The Many Faces of Modern Architecture*.
88 Bonatz, *Leben und Bauen*.
89 Graubner, *Paul Bonatz und seine Schüler*; Bonatz, *Paul Bonatz*.
90 Both Söylemezoğlu and Ahmet Sabri maintained close relations with Bonatz. After coming to Turkey, Ahmet Sabri worked on the designs of people's houses all over the country and then joined Bonatz's office. Söylemezoğlu also worked under Bonatz, first in his office in Stuttgart (where Bonatz worked on alternative projects to Speer's designs for Hitler's regime), and then in

Bonatz's office in Turkey as well as at İstanbul Technical University. See Söylemezoğlu, *Anılarda Mimarlık*.
91. Hillinger, "Damın İnşa Şekli Hakkında."
92. Letter from Ministry of Finance to the Ankara Municipality, September 5, 1935, Ankara Municipality Archives.
93. Hermann Jansen, letter to Ankara Municipality, July 23, 1935, Ankara Municipality Archives.
94. Like many of his colleagues, Bonatz's first encounter with Turkey took place during the Turkish-German House of Friendship competition in 1916. The Turkish audience was familiar with Bonatz's work. His sports field in Stuttgart had been published in *Mimar*, as Bonatz, "Büyük idman sahası." Also see Çelik-Hinchliffe, "Rootedness Uprooted."
95. Quoted in Speer, Introduction.
96. Bonatz, "Yeni Alman Mimarisi," part 1, 73; part 2, 119.
97. Ibid., part 1, 74.
98. Ibid., 75.
99. Ibid., part 2, 119.
100. Ibid., part 1, 75.
101. Celal, "San'atta Snobism." Also see Celal, "Büyük Inkılap Önünde Milli Mimari Meselesi."
102. Celal, "Türk Sanatı," 219, 220.
103. Kozanoğlu, "Inkılap ve San'at."
104. *Mimarlık* held a survey on the definition of national architecture and how its creation could be achieved. Many architects responded by advocating state support ("Milli Mimari Anketimiz"). Nationalist demands and antiforeign sentiments infiltrated the pages of architecture magazines quite frequently, most significantly in the newly founded journals *Yapı* (1942–43) and *Mimarlık* (1944–53). See "Türk Mimarları Ne İstiyorlar?"; "Mimarlık ve Millicilik Davamız"; Çavdarlı, "Sanatkarlık, Mimarlık, Türklük" and "İlk Ressamlar, İlk Mimarlar: Türkler"; Çetintaş, "İnkılap Mimarisi İsteriz," and "Kendimizi Nasıl Bulalım"; Uçar, "Mimarlığımızı Yaşatalım, Mimarlığımızı Tanıtalım," and "Büyük Davamız." Even architects like Sedad Eldem and those around the *Arkitekt* circle who were open to foreign influences as discussed in chapter 2 did not put enough distance to the growing nationalism of the 1940s. See Sedad Eldem, "Milli Mimari Meselesi," and "Milli ve Yerli Davamız"; Mortaş, "Modern Türk Mimarisi"; Kömürcüoğlu, "Büyük Türk İnkılabının Mimari Cephesi."
105. Sedad Eldem, "Yerli Mimariye Doğru," 73.
106. Mortaş, "Yeni Alman Mimarisi Sergisi."
107. Ünsal, "Eminönü Halkevinde Açılan Alman Mimari Sergisi Dolayısıyla."
108. See Alsaç, "The Second Period of Turkish National Architecture."
109. Paul Bonatz, letter to [Karl?] Siegler, December 25, 1945, drawings and papers.
110. Paul Bonatz, letter to Professor [Ivar?] Tengbom, September 1946, drawings and papers.
111. The following articles appeared in "Saraçoğlu Mahallesi," *Ulus*: June, 10 1945;

October 31, 1944; and October 31, 1945. Also see *Cumhuriyet*, October 31, 1945; *Son Posta*, October 31, 1945.

112 Paul Bonatz, "Der Şükrü Saraçoğlu Stadtteil in Ankara," manuscript, October 6, 1947; and letter to Emlak Bank, February 7, 1947, both drawings and papers.

113 Paul Bonatz, "Şükrü Saraçoğlu Stadtteil in Ankara" (c. 1945), and "Der Şükrü Saraçoğlu Stadtteil in Ankara," October 6, 1947, drawings and papers.

114 The balcony in one type was built to revive the outdoor *sofa* and wooden balustrades of the traditional Turkish houses, but it was placed in front of the kitchens and bathrooms of two neighboring units.

115 Quoted in T. I., "Yankılar," *Ulus*, October 31, 1945.

116 Fatih Metigil, "Milli Mimariye Doğru," *Ulus*, November 20, 1945.

117 *Ulus*, October 31, 1945.

118 Alsaç, "Saraçoğlu Mahallesi"; Sayar, "Saraçoğlu Mahallesi."

119 For example, see Sayar, "Mimarlık ve Politikamız."

120 Mortaş, "Memleketimizde Yapı ve İmar İşleri."

121 Alsaç, "Saraçoğlu Mahallesi," 16, 17, 18.

FIVE | TOWARD A COSMOPOLITAN ARCHITECTURE

1 Bruno Taut, letters from İstanbul, manuscripts, Bruno Taut, Nachlaß, Akademie der Künste, Berlin.

2 Taut, "Ansprache zur Eröffnung der Taut." Rosemarie Bletter also suggests that Kant's humanism, particularly in "Perpetual Peace," had a strong influence on the young Taut. See Bletter, "Bruno Taut and Paul Scheerbart's Vision."

3 Kant, "Perpetual Peace." For informative essays on this work, see Bohman and Lutz-Bachmann, *Perpetual Peace*; Wood, "Kant's Project for Perpetual Peace."

4 "It is impossible to think of anything at all in the world, or indeed even beyond it, that could be considered good without limitation except a good will" (Kant, *Groundwork for a Metaphysics of Morals*, 393). Goodwill is a will that acts from duty (397).

5 One of the three formulas for the Kantian moral test to determine a categorical imperative was the formula of universal law: "Act as if the maxim of your action were to become by your will a universal law of nature" (ibid., 421).

6 The two other formulas were: "So act that you treat humanity, whether in your own person or in the person of any other, always at the same time as an end, never as a means. . . . Act in such a way that you treat every human being as a member in the kingdom of ends" (ibid., 429); and "Act under the idea of the will of every rational being as a will giving universal law" (431).

7 "But in the light of the idea of reason, this state is still to be preferred to an amalgamation of the separate nations under a single power which has overruled the rest and created a universal monarchy. For the laws progressively lose their impact as the government increases its range, and a soulless despotism, after crushing the germs of goodness, will finally lapse into anarchy" (ibid., 113).

8   For more on this analogy and its limits, see Lutz-Bachmann, "Kant's Idea of Peace and the Philosophical Conception of a World Republic."
9   Scheerbart, *Glass Architecture*; Taut, *Die Stadtkrone, Alpine Architektur*, and "*Ex Oriente Lux*: Call to Architects." Also see Hain, "Ex Oriente Lux."
10 Bletter, "Bruno Taut and Paul Scheerbart's Vision," "The Interpretation of the Glass Dream," and "Expressionism and the New Objectivity."
11 Taut, *Die Stadtkrone*, 82.
12 Taut, "*Ex Oriente Lux*," 81–82.
13 Ian Boyd Whyte has also argued that Taut's interest in Eastern sources was directly linked to his disappointment with the events in Europe after and during World War I. See Whyte, *Bruno Taut and the Architecture of Activism*.
14 Taut, *Die Neue Wohnung*.
15 Taut noted how the division between sleeping and living spaces does not exist in the rooms (*oda*) of Ottoman houses. This was an organization that, he later suggested, could be plausible for small, working-class houses in Germany (ibid., 21–23).
16 Bruno Taut,"Nippon mit europäischen Augen gesehen," manuscript, 1933, BTS-01-80; "Die Architektur des Westens mit ihrer Bedeutung für Japan," manuscript for a conference at the University of Tokyo, July 9–17, 1934, BTS-01-75; "Japans Kunst: Mit europäischen Augen gesehen," manuscript, 1936, Mappe 1. Nr. 14 BTS 323; "Japanese Village," manuscript in English, 1936, BT-SLG-01-85; "New Japan: What Its Architecture Should Be," manuscript in German, 1936, BT-SLG-01-86, all Akademie der Künste, Berlin; *Fundamentals of Japanese Architecture*; *Houses and People of Japan*.
17 Taut, *Houses and People of Japan*. "The Japanese House and Its Homelife" was the title Taut used for the prospectus for the book in 1935. The book was first published in English in 1937 under Taut's own guidance. The German version, *Das japanische Haus und sein Leben*, did not appear until 1997.
18 Taut, *Houses and People of Japan*, ii.
19 Ibid., 40.
20 Ibid., 21.
21 Ibid., 5–8.
22 Ibid., 175.
23 Ibid., 75.
24 Taut, "Japans Kunst."
25 Ibid., 12–13.
26 See, most notably, Taut, "New Japan."
27 This information comes from Manfred Speidel's editorial note in Taut, "Houses and People of Japan."
28 Taut, *Houses and People of Japan*, 259–60.
29 Ibid., 262–63 (my emphasis).
30 Ibid., 177–78.
31 The discussion is introduced when Mr. Suzuki adds to the "catalogue of our progress" that Japanese people are getting taller. Taut objects to this statement because "the stature has nothing to do with the genius," and neither the proportions of the Japanese body nor the traditional way of sitting or sleeping

had caused an unhealthier life (compared to the Europeans). Suzuki replies: "Well, this is amusing and interesting, I must say! . . . We generally think that the Western way of living is much more healthy. And there you come along, a European, telling us the contrary" (ibid., 261–62).

32 Neufert, *Bauentwurfslehre*. The work was brought to Turkey by Paul Bonatz.
33 Taut, *Houses and People of Japan*, 173, 193.
34 Ibid., 206–8.
35 Ibid., 121.
36 For instance, he wrote: "Thus it was the climate that built the Japanese house, more especially the summer. . . . Otherwise one would have to use expensive apparatus to give the same airing effect. But such ventilation is artificial and can only be used temporarily" (Taut, *Houses and People of Japan*, 72).
37 "Anyone who undertakes a closer study of the Japanese village, should not be struck by any impression of seemingly 'exotic' strangeness. Rather, except for some Japanese specialties such as floor-mats and paper-windows, he will feel that all species of farmhouse throughout the world reflect themselves in the Japanese farmhouse. . . . The Japanese farmhouse is thus an enigma in itself. It is remarkable indeed that here, in contrast to any machinery of war or peace, is a cultural phenomenon born of the very soil of Japan, and which is absolutely national, though the various forms of this same culture in all its details and variations happen to be quite international" (Taut, "Japanese Village").
38 Taut, *Houses and People of Japan*, 112–13 (my emphasis).
39 Ibid., 116–17.
40 After receiving the news, Taut wrote in his diary: "Bums!!! Schluss mit Japan" (Bum!!! end with Japan). He reported that he ate his last breakfast and lunch with friends and departed for Turkey, his third country of exile after a brief stay in Russia and three years in Japan. Ten days later, on October 10, Taut arrived in Turkey. See Bruno Taut, "Tagebuch–Japan," manuscript, July 16–November 2, 1936, BTS 01-75, P.20-21, Akademie der Künste, Berlin.
41 Quoted in Speidel, "Bruno Taut."
42 Bonatz, *Leben und Bauen*.
43 The following biographies include brief information about Taut's work in Turkey: Junghanns, *Bruno Taut*; Capaccioli, *Bruno Taut*; Zöller-Stock, *Bruno Taut*. The following articles comment on Taut's works in Turkey: Aslanoğlu, "Dışavurumcu ve Usçu Devirlerinde Bruno Taut (1880–1938)" and "Bruno Taut's Wirken als Lehrer und Architekt in der Türkei in den Jahren 1936-38"; Özer, "Casa del Anima/A House of the Soul"; Hartmann, "Bruno Taut im Türkishen Exil"; Manfred Speidel, "Natürlichkeit und Freiheit" and "Bruno Taut"; Bozdoğan, "Against Style"; Nicolai, "Bruno Taut's Akademiereform und sein Weg zu einer neuen Architektur für die Türkei" and *Moderne und Exil*; Tanju, "Türkiye'de Farklı bir Mimar"; Akcan, "Öteki' Dünyanın Melankolisi."
44 Martin Wagner, letter to Hans Scharoun, December 30, 1937, Hans Scharoun, Nachlaß, Mappe 6.3; and Martin Wagner, letter to Ernst May, March 12, 1937, Martin Wagner, Nachlaß, Doc. 26, both Baukunst Sammlung, Akademie der Künste, Berlin.

45 Martin Wagner, letter to Ernst May, February 10, 1939, Martin Wagner, Nachlaß, Doc. 26, Baukunst Sammlung, Akademie der Künste, Berlin.
46 Asım Mutlu, Sedad Eldem, Rebi Gorbon, Eyüp Kömürcüoğlu, and Zeki Sayar also mentioned how strong the Japanese influence was on Taut when he first arrived in Turkey. Yet they added that Taut was soon interested in learning about the Turkish (Ottoman) architectural heritage. See Mutlu, "Asım Mutlu"; Gülsen, "Erinnerungen an Bruno Taut."
47 Taut's diary in İstanbul shows that he spent almost all of his time working either on the designs of buildings or the revision of the architectural program at the academy. In his letters to Carl Krayl, Tokugen Mihara, and Isaburo Ueno, Taut also mentions his loaded but fulfilling program in Turkey. Bruno Taut, "Istanbul Journal," manuscript, Mappe III, 18, Akademie der Künste, Berlin; letter to Karl and Li Crayl, BTS-01-337; letter to Tokugen Mihara, undated, BT-SLG-01-141 and BT-SLG-01-145/2; and letter to Isaburo Ueno, August 9, 1938, BT-SLG-0-9 till 13, all Akademie der Künste, Berlin.
48 In a letter to Ueno, Taut wrote: "Where is homeland? Answer: Building [*Sheerbart*]. Where is happiness? Answer: Building." Bruno Taut, letter to Isaburo Ueno, August 9, 1938, BT-SLG-0-9 till 13, Akademie der Künste, Berlin.
49 At the opening of his own exhibition at the academy, Taut had a brief conversation with *Arkitekt*'s editor, Zeki Sayar, who had written a critical editorial about foreign architects using a sketch of Taut's Faculty of Language, History, and Geography. At the exhibition, Sayar thanked Taut and voiced his interest in publishing the architect's project for the Parliament Competition. Taut said playfully, "Enfin je suis aussi turque" (Finally, I am also Turkish), and the two had a better relationship thereafter. Apart from the exhibition project, Sayar also published chapters of Taut's *Mimari Bilgisi* in a series of issues of *Arkitekt*. Taut, "Istanbul Journal," entry for June 4, 1938, 125.
50 Bruno Taut, report to the Ministry of Education, Manfred Speidel archive.
51 Bruno Taut, letter to the Schüttes, March 17, 1938, Manfred Speidel archive.
52 Taut's public lecture at the opening of his Exhibition on June 4, 1938, was published (Taut, "Ansprache zur Eröffnung der Taut—Ausstellung in Istanbul am 4.6.1938").
53 Taut changed Egli's program at the academy and concentrated on social issues such as social housing projects. Bozdoğan, "Against Style"; Nicolai, "Bruno Taut's Akademiereform und sein Weg zu einer neuen Architektur für die Türkei"; Gülsen, "Erinnerungen an Bruno Taut."
54 Taut, "Istanbul Journal," entry for December 13, 1938, 144.
55 Taut, "Ansprache zur Eröffnung der Taut—Ausstellung in Istanbul am 4.6.1938," 260.
56 Ibid., 53–54.
57 Ibid., 239.
58 Ibid., 53.
59 Taut, "New Japan."
60 Taut, *Mimari Bilgisi*, 89.

61 Ibid., 166.
62 Ibid., 43.
63 Ibid., 166.
64 Taut, *Houses and People of Japan*, 263.
65 Ibid., 265 (my emphasis).
66 Taut, letter to Tokugen Mihara, undated, BT-SLG-01-141 and BT-SLG-01-145/2, Akademie der Künste, Berlin.
67 Fanon, *The Wretched of the Earth*, 237.
68 Speidel, "Was ist Architektur?"
69 Various parts of *Mimari Bilgisi* appeared in *Arkitekt* during the course of 1938.
70 Taut might have considered titling the book *Architekturgedanken* (Thoughts on architecture), as his wife, Erica Taut, suggested to Isaburo Ueno. Erica Taut, letters to Isaburo Ueno, February 1, 1939, and February 10, 1939, BTS-01-16, BTS-01-17, Akademie der Künste, Berlin.
71 Taut, "Architekturlehre."
72 Taut, *Mimari Bilgisi*, 25, 27, 124, 202, 204, 236, 241, 247; "Architekturlehre," 46, 36, 77, 110, 119, 120, 122.
73 Taut, *Mimari Bilgisi*, 8, 12.
74 Ibid., 22, 69, 32, 204, 55, 228, 142; Taut, "Architekturlehre," 42, 57, 47, 110, 53, 117, 86.
75 Taut, *Mimari Bilgisi*, 152; "Architekturlehre," 91.
76 Taut, *Mimari Bilgisi*, 24; "Architekturlehre," 42.
77 Taut, *Mimari Bilgisi*, 25; "Architekturlehre," 46.
78 Taut, *Mimari Bilgisi*, 85; "Architekturlehre," 66.
79 Taut, *Mimari Bilgisi*, 211. Also see Rossi, *L'architettura della città*.
80 Taut, *Mimari Bilgisi*, 247; "Architekturlehre," 122.
81 Taut, *Mimari Bilgisi*, 205; "Architekturlehre," 111.
82 Taut, *Mimari Bilgisi*, 255; "Architekturlehre," 117.
83 Taut, *Mimari Bilgisi*, 131; "Architekturlehre," 78.
84 Taut, *Mimari Bilgisi*, 199; "Architekturlehre," 106.
85 Taut, *Mimari Bilgisi*, 164; "Architekturlehre," 95.
86 Taut, *Mimari Bilgisi*, 45–46; "Architekturlehre," 51.
87 Taut, *Mimari Bilgisi*, 85–86; "Architekturlehre," 66.
88 Taut, *Modern Architecture*.
89 Taut, *Mimari Bilgisi*, 334; "Architekturlehre," 150.
90 Taut, *Mimari Bilgisi*, 322; "Architekturlehre," 145.
91 Taut, *Mimari Bilgisi*, 55–56; "Architekturlehre," 53.
92 Taut, *Mimari Bilgisi*, 56; "Architekturlehre," 53.
93 Taut, *Mimari Bilgisi*, 59–60; "Architekturlehre," 54.
94 Taut, *Mimari Bilgisi*, 62; "Architekturlehre," 55.
95 Taut, *Mimari Bilgisi*, 65; "Architekturlehre," 56.
96 D. Harvey, "Cosmopolitanism and the Banality of Geographical Evils," 535.
97 Taut, *Mimari Bilgisi*, 92; "Architekturlehre," 67.
98 Taut, "The Earth Is a Good Dwelling." This emphasis on climate is similar to what Kenneth Frampton would advocate forty-five years later in his highly regarded essay in the Third World countries (as they were commonly

called then), where he also pointed out that climate specificity could be one of the ways to resist homogenization of architecture through modernization. Frampton, "Critical Regionalism."
99 Taut, *Mimari Bilgisi*, 185; "Architekturlehre," 101.
100 Taut, *Mimari Bilgisi*, 147; "Architekturlehre," 91.
101 Taut, *Mimari Bilgisi*, 336.
102 Taut, "Architekturlehre," 152.
103 Taut, *Mimari Bilgisi*, 333; "Architekturlehre," 150.
104 Taut, *Mimari Bilgisi*, 74; "Architekturlehre," 58.
105 Taut, *Mimari Bilgisi*, 86; "Architekturlehre," 66.
106 In *Japans Kunst*, Taut had argued that a fruitful modern architecture in Japan would be the result of a synthesis with European influences (206).
107 Taut, *Mimari Bilgisi*, 64; "Architekturlehre," 55.
108 Taut, "Architekturlehre," 206.
109 Taut, *Mimari Bilgisi*, 64, "Architekturlehre," 55.
110 Taut, "Japans Kunst," 24.
111 Taut, *Mimari Bilgisi*, 228–32; "Architekturlehre," 117–19.
112 Taut, *Houses and People of Japan*, 40.
113 Quoted in Speidel, "Bruno Taut," 57.
114 During renovations, the house has been radically changed. Therefore, these descriptions do not hold true for its present state.
115 I would like to thank Rob Linrothe for this reference.
116 Taut, "Türk Evi, Sinan, Ankara" (my emphasis).
117 Taut, *Die Neue Wohnung*, 21.
118 For instance, see Taut, "Istanbul Journal," entries for May 10 and June 30, 1938.
119 Taut, *Mimari Bilgisi*, 92–93. Also see 151–52.
120 These definitive articles in order were (1) "The Civil Constitution of Every State shall be Republican"; (2) "The rights of nations shall be based on a Federation of Free States"; and (3) "Cosmopolitan Right shall be limited to Conditions of Universal Hospitality." Kant, "Perpetual Peace."
121 Kant defined republican constitution with three principles: freedom, legal equality of all citizens, and all citizens being bound by legislation. Ibid., 100.
122 Kant uses these words in a footnote, when he is constructing an analogy between individuals giving up the state of nature to enter a peaceful social contract with each other, and nations entering a global federation. Ibid., 98.
123 Ibid., 106.
124 In defining hospitality, Kant criticizes the discoverers of America for not considering the natives as owners of their own land. Therefore, by excluding the stranger's right to reside, Kant was actually making a statement about preserving the rights of the colonized. Ibid.
125 "A true system of politics cannot therefore take a single step without first paying tribute to morality." Ibid., 125.
126 Derrida, *On Cosmopolitanism and Forgiveness* and *Of Hospitality*.
127 Derrida, *On Cosmopolitanism and Forgiveness*, 23.
128 Kant, "Perpetual Peace," 106.
129 This was also Derrida's objection to a Kantian definition of hospitality, which

he contrasted to that of Levinas. In Kant, hospitality is a forced way to peace; in Levinas, everything begins with hospitality, and a natural desire to open oneself up to the other. Derrida, *Adieu to Emanuel Levinas*.

EPILOGUE

1 Davis, *Planet of Slums*.

BIBLIOGRAPHY

ARCHIVES AND PRIVATE DOCUMENT COLLECTIONS

Ankara Municipality Archives (Ankara Belediyesi Arşivi), Ankara
Arkan, Seyfi, papers, Melih Şallı's collection, İstanbul (private)
Arkan, Seyfi, papers, Milli Saraylar Archive, İstanbul
Aru, Kemal Ahmet, archives, İstanbul (private)
Bonatz, Paul, drawings and papers, Peter Dübers's collection, Stuttgart (private)
Bonatz, Paul, Nachlaß, Stuttgart Universität, Stuttgart
Canadian Center for Architecture, Photography Collections, Montreal
Egli, Ernst, Nachlaß, Special Collections, Eidgenössische Technische Hochschule Library, Zurich
Eldem, Sedad Hakkı, drawings and papers, Koç University, İstanbul (private)
Eldem, Sedad Hakkı, drawings, sketchbooks, and papers, Edhem Eldem's collection, İstanbul (private)
Elsaesser, Martin, Nachlaß, Architekturmuseum der Technischen Universität, Munich
Getty Research Institute, Gigord and Jacobson Collections, Los Angeles
Gropius, Walter, Nachlaß, Bauhausarchiv, Berlin
Holzmeister, Clemens, Nachlaß, Graphische Sammlung Albertina, Vienna

Holzmeister, Clemens, Nachlaß, Universität für Angewandte Kunst Bibliothek, Vienna
Jansen, Hermann, Nachlaß, Germanisches Nationalmuseum, Nürnberg (GN-Nürnberg)
Jansen, Hermann, Nachlaß, Plansammlung of Berlin Technical University (PSBTU), Berlin
May, Ernst, and Martin Elsaesser papers, Stadtarchiv, Frankfurt
Nicolai, Bernd, archive (private)
Reuter, Ernst, Nachlaß, Landesarchiv, Berlin
Schütte-Lihotzky, Margarete, Nachlaß, Universität für Angewandte Kunst Sammlung, Vienna
Speidel, Manfred, archive, Aachen (private)
Taut, Bruno, Nachlaß, Akademie der Künste, Berlin
Tessenow, Heinrich, Nachlaß, Kunstbibliothek, Berlin
Turkish Republican State Archives (T. C. Başbakanlık Cumhuriyet Arşivleri), Ankara
Wagner, Martin, Nachlaß, Akademie der Künste, Berlin

PUBLISHED MATERIAL

Die 25 Einfamilienhäuser der Holzsiedlung am Kochenhof. Stuttgart: Julius Hoffmann, 1933.
"33 Mimar." *Mimar*, no. 10 (1931): 343.
50 Yılda İmar ve Yerleşme. Ankara: İmar ve İskan Bakanlığı, 1973.
Abendroth, A. "Die Großstadt als Städtegründerin," parts 1–3. *Der Städtebau* 2, no. 1 (1905): 24–27; no. 2 (1905): 32–38; no. 3 (1905): 49–51.
Aebli, Werner, Rolf Meyer, and Ernst Winkler, eds. *Stadt und Umwelt: Festschrift zum siebzigsten Geburtstag von Ernst Egli*. Zurich: Eugen Rentsch, 1964.
Ağat, Nilüfer. "Konut Tasarımında Mutfağın Etkisi." PhD diss., İstanbul Technical University, İstanbul, 1983.
Akcan, Esra. "Ambiguities of Transparency and Privacy in Seyfi Arkan's Houses for the New State." *METU Journal of Architecture* (Spring 2006): 25–49.
———. *Çeviride Modern Olan: Şehir ve Konutta Türk-Alman İlişkileri*. İstanbul: YKY, 2009.
———. "Civilizing Housewives versus Participatory Users: Margarete Schütte Lihotzky in the Employ of the Turkish Nation State." In *Cold War Kitchen: Americanization, Technology and European Users*, edited by Ruth Oldenziel and Karin Zachman, 185–207. Cambridge: MIT Press, 2009.
———. "Critical Practice in the Global Era. Question Concerning 'Other' Geographies." *Architectural Theory Review* 7, no. 1 (2002): 37–58.
———, ed. "Intertwined Histories. Turkey and Central Europe." Special Issue, *Centropa* 7, no. 2 (May 2007).
———. "Manfredo Tafuri's Theory of the Architectural Avant-Garde." *Journal of Architecture* 7, no. 2 (Summer 2002): 135–70.
———. "Modernity in Translation: Early Twentieth Century German-Turkish Exchanges in Land Settlement and Residential Culture." PhD diss., Columbia University, 2005.

———. "Öteki' Dünyanın Melankolisi: Bruno Taut'un Doğu Deneyimi." *Domus m* (February–March 2001): 36–41.
———. "Reciprocal Translations of Garden City Housing." In *Intertwined Histories: Turkey and Central Europe*, edited by Esra Akcan, "Intertwined Histories. Turkey and Central Europe." Special Issue, *Centropa* 7, no. 2 (May 2007): 163–79.
Akcan, Esra, and Sibel Bozdoğan. *Turkey*. "Modern Architectures in History" series. London: Reaktion, 2012.
Akkaynak, Samih Saim. "Berlin Mesken Kongresi." *Mimar*, no. 3 (1931): 102–3.
———. "Güzel, Ucuz, Sıhhatli Ev." *Muhit* 1, no. 7 (1929): 498–501.
———. "Mösyö Jakın Asri Villası." *Muhit* 1, no. 11 (1929): 766–67.
———. "Yeni Unsurlar." *Mimar*, no. 4 (1931): 133–40.
Akpınar, İpek. "From Secularization to Turkish Modernization: the rebuilding of Istanbul after the plan of Henri Prost, 1937–1960." PhD diss., Bartlett School, University of London, 2003.
Aktüre, Sevgi. *Ondokuzuncu Yüzyıl Sonunda Anadolu Kenti Mekansal Yapı Çözümlemesi*. Ankara: ODTU Mimarlık Fakültesi, 1978.
Ali, Süreyya. "Şehirlerde mesken ve sokaklar ijyeni, genel temizlik işleri." In *Komün Bilgisinin Esas Meseleleri*, edited by Fritz Neumark, 156–73. İstanbul: Cumhuriyet Matbaası, 1936.
Al'Kindi. *Medical Formulary*. Translated by Martin Levy. Madison: University of Wisconsin Press, 1966.
Allmayer-Beck, Renate, Haindl Baumgartner, Susanne Linder-Gross, and Marion Christine Zwingl, eds. *Margarete Schütte-Lihotzky: Soziale Architektur Zeitzeugin eines Jahrhunderts*. 2nd ed. Vienna: Böhlau, 1996.
Alsaç, Orhan. "Saraçoğlu Mahallesi." *Mimarlık*, no. 6 (1945): 16–21, 30.
Alsaç, Üstün. "The Second Period of Turkish National Architecture." In *Modern Turkish Architecture*, edited by Renata Holod and Ahmet Evin, 94–104. Philadelphia: University of Pennsylvania Press, 1984.
———. *Türkiye Mimarlık Düşüncesinin Cumhuriyet Dönemindeki Evrimi*. Trabzon: KTÜ Baskı Atölyesi, 1976.
Alsayyad, Nezar, ed. *Forms of Dominance. On the Architecture and Urbanism of the Colonial Enterprise*. Aldershot, England: Avebury, 1992.
Altaban, Özcan. "Ulusal Yönetimin ve Toplumsallığın Kurgulandığı Başkent." *Arredamento Dekorasyon* 90, no. 3 (1997): 89–94.
"Das Alte System." *Wohnungswirtschaft* 1 (July 1, 1924): 65–67.
Altmann, Elisabeth. "Frau und Gartenstadt." In *Die Deutsche Gartenstadtbewegung*, 95–96. Berlin: Deutschen Gartenstadt-Gesellschaft, 1911.
Altunç, Süheyla. *Ev İdaresi*. İstanbul: Devlet Basımevi, 1936.
Alus, Sermet Muhtar. *İstanbul Kazan Ben Kepçe*. İstanbul: Iletişim, 1995.
———. *İstanbul Yazıları*. İstanbul: İstanbul Büyükşehir Belediyesi, 1994.
———. *Masal Olanlar*. İstanbul: İletişim, 1995.
Ames, Eric, Marcia Klotz and Lara Wildenthal, eds. *Germany's Colonial Pasts*. Lincoln: University of Nebraska Press, 2005.
Anamur, Hasan. "Önsöz." In *Hommage to Hasan Ali Yücel Anma Kitabı*, edited by Hasan Anamur, iv. İstanbul: Yıldız Teknik Üniversitesi, 1997.

Anderson, Stanford. "The Legacy of German Neoclassicism and Biedermeier: Behrens, Tessenow, Loos and Mies." *Assemblage* 15 (August 1991): 63–89.

"Ankara Bağçeli Evler Kooperatifi." *Karınca* 5 (July–August 1938): 39–47.

"Ankara Güven Yapı Kooperatifi." *Karınca* 3 (July 1936): 30–32.

"Ankara İstanbul." *La Turquie Kemaliste* 48 (December 1947): 38–43.

Ankara Posta Kartları ve Belge Fotoğrafları Arşivi Kataloğu. Ankara: Belko, 1994.

Ankara Şehrinin Profesör M. Jausseley, Jansen ve Brix tarafларından yapılan plan ve projelerine ait izahnameler. Ankara: Hakimiyeti Milliye Matbaası, 1929.

"Ankara'da Yeni Bir Mahalle Kuruluyor." *Karınca* 3 (November 1936): 44–46.

Appadurai, Arjun. *Modernity at Large: Cultural Dimensions of Globalization*. Minneapolis: University of Minnesota Press, 1996.

Appiah, Kwame Anthony. *Cosmopolitanism: Ethics in a World of Strangers*. New York: W. W. Norton, 2006.

Apter, Emily. "Global Translatio: The 'Invention' of Comparative Literature, İstanbul, 1933." *Critical Inquiry* 29, no. 2 (2003): 253–81.

"Arbeiten aus der Schule Hermann Jansen." *Der Städtebau* 22, no. 1 (1925): 23–25.

"Arbeiten von Prof. Dr. Ernst Egli, Ankara." *Das Werk* 25, no. 9 (1938): 275–78.

Arel, Süheyla. *Taylorisme*. İstanbul: Devlet Basımevi, 1936.

Arendt, Hannah. *The Origins of Totalitarianism*. 1951. New York: Schocken, 1994.

Arif, Burhan. "Sıra Evler." *Arkitekt*, no. 6 (1935): 179–80.

———. "Yeni Şehirlerin İnkişafı ve 'Siedlung'lar." *Mimar*, no. 7–8 (1932): 213–16.

Aristotle. "Brilliance and Melancholy." Translated by W. S. Hett. In *The Nature of Melancholy*, edited by Jennifer Radden, 55–61. New York: Oxford University Press, 2000.

Arkan, Seyfi. "Adana'da Ucuz Evler Mahallesi." *Arkitekt*, no. 1–2 (1939): 33–36.

———. "Amele Evleri, İlkokul, Mutfak ve Çamaşırlık Binası." *Arkıtekt*, no. 9 (1935): 253–58.

———. "Ankara için Ucuz Aile Evi Tipleri." *Mimar*, no. 6 (1933): 174.

———. "Ankara'da Sıra Evler Tipi." *Mimar*, no. 12 (1933): 383.

———. "Çankaya'da bir villa." *Arkitekt*, no. 7 (1936): 179–86.

———. [Seyfettin Nasih]. "Deniz Kenarında bir Malikane." *Mimar*, no. 4 (1933): 111–10.

———. [Seyfettin Nasih]. "Ev Projesi." *Mimar*, no. 1 (1934): 6–8.

———. "Hariciye Köşkü." *Arkitekt*, no. 11–12 (1935): 311.

———. "Kömür-iş İşçi Uramı: Zonguldak Kozlu." *Arkitekt*, no. 1 (1936): 9–10.

———. "Villa Projesi" [I]. *Arkitekt*, no. 4 (1935): 114–15.

———. "Villa Projesi" [II]. *Arkitekt*, no. 6 (1935): 167–69.

Arseven, Celal Esad. *L'art Turc: depuis son origine jusqu'a nos jours*. İstanbul: Devlet Basimevi, 1939.

———. *Constantinople: De Byzance à Stamboul*. Paris: Renouard H. Laurens, 1909.

———. *Eski İstanbul*. 1912. Edited by Dilek Yelkenci. İstanbul: Çelik Gülersoy Yayınları, 1989.

———. *Sanat ve Siyaset Hatıralarım*. Edited by Ekrem Işın. İstanbul: İletişim, 1993.

———. *Türk Sanatı*. 1928. Reprint, İstanbul: Cem Yayınevi, 1984.

———. *Yeni Mimari*. İstanbul: Agah—Sabri Kitaphanesi, 1931.
Aru, Kemal Ahmet. "4. Levent." *Arkitekt* 285 (1956): 140-53.
———. "Bugünün Evi Nasıl Olmalı? Evin İç Dekoru." *Yapı* 1 (January 15, 1942): 10-11.
———. "Levend Mahallesi." *Arkitekt*, no. 9-10 (1952): 174-81.
Asad, Talal. "The Concept of Cultural Translation in British Social Anthropology." In *Writing Culture: The Poetics and Politics of Ethnography*, edited by James Clifford and George Marcus, 141-65. Berkeley: University of California Press, 1986.
Aslanoğlu, İnci. "Bruno Taut's Wirken als Lehrer und Architekt in der Türkei in den Jahren 1936-38." In *Bruno Taut 1880-1938*, edited by Barbara Volkmann, 143-50. Berlin: Akademie der Künste, 1980.
———. "Dışavurumcu ve Usçu Devirlerinde Bruno Taut (1880-1938)." *METU Journal of Architecture* 2, no. 1 (1976): 35-47.
———. *Erken Cumhuriyet Dönemi Mimarlığı*. Ankara: ODTU Yayınları, 1980.
Ataç, Nurullah. "Tercümeye Dair." *Tercüme* 1, no. 6 (1941): 505-7.
———. "Tercüme Üzerine." *Tercüme* 5, no. 26 (1944): 155-57. Reprinted from *Ulus*, August 14, 1944.
Atay, Falih Rıfkı. *Çankaya: Mustafa Kemal'in Çankaya'sı*. İstanbul: Bateş Atatürk Dizisi, 1998.
———. "Mesken Anketimiz Bitti." *Karınca* 3 (March 1936): 138.
Auerbach, Erich. *Mimesis: The Representation of Reality in Western Literature*. Translated by Willard R. Trask. Princeton: Princeton University Press, 1953.
Aus Englischen Gartenstädten. Berlin: Deutsche Gartenstadt-Gesellschaft, 1910.
Aydemir, Şevket Süreyya. *Tek Adam: Mustafa Kemal*. İstanbul: Remzi Kitabevi, 1966.
Bademli, Raci. "1920-40 Döneminde Eski Ankara'nın Yazgısını Etkileyen Tutumlar." *Mimarlık*, no. 2-3 (1985): 10-16.
Bal, Mieke, and Joanne Moora, eds. "Acts of Translation." Special Issue. *Journal of Visual Culture* 6, no. 1 (2007).
Balamir, Aydan. "Holzmeister'in Atatürk ve Kral Faysal İçin Saray Projeleri." *Arredamento Mimarlık* 161, no. 9 (2003): 88-95.
———, ed. *Clemens Holzmeister: An Architect at the Turn of an Era*. Ankara: Boyut, 2010.
Baltacıoğlu, İsmail Hakkı. "Yeni Adam İçin Yeni Mimarlık." *Yeni Adam* (April 9, 1934): 7.
———. "Yeni Mimarlık." *Yeni Adam* (January 15, 1934): 7.
Banguoğlu, Tahsin. "Aşağılık Duygusu," parts 1-3. *Ülkü* 5, no. 49 (1943): 1; no. 50 (1943): 1; no. 53 (1943): 2.
Banham, Reyner. *Theory and Design in the First Machine Age*. 2nd ed. Oxford: Butterworth Architecture, 1962.
Banoğlu, Niyazi Ahmet. *Atatürk'ün İstanbul'daki Hayatı*. İstanbul: Itımat Matbaası, 1974.
Barthes, Roland. "Rhetoric of the Image." In Roland Barthes, *Image, Music, Text*, 32-51. Translated by Stephen Heath. New York: Hill and Wang, 1977.
Bassnett, Susan. "The Translation Turn in Cultural Studies." In *Constructing Cul-*

tures: Essays on Literary Translation, edited by Susan Bassnett and André Lefevere, 123–40. Clevedon, England: Multilingual Matters, 1998.
Bassnett, Susan, and André Lefevere, eds. *Translation, History and Culture*. London: Routledge, 1990.
Bassnett, Susan, and Harish Trivedi. "Introduction: Of Colonies, Cannibals and Vernaculars." In *Post-Colonial Translation: Theory and Practice*, edited by Susan Bassnett and Harish Trivedi, 1–18. London: Routledge, 1999.
———, eds. *Post-Colonial Translation: Theory and Practice*. London: Routledge, 1999.
Batur, Afife. "Cumhuriyet Döneminde Türk Mimarlığı." In *Cumhuriyet Dönemi Türkiye Ansiklopedisi*. İstanbul: İletişim Yayınları, 1984.
Batur, Afife, Atilla Yücel, and Nur Fersan. "İstanbul'da Ondokuzuncu Yüzyıl Sıra Evleri Koruma ve Kullanım için Bir Monografik Araştırma." *ODTÜ Mimarlık Fakültesi Dergisi* 5, no. 2 (1979): 185–205.
Bau und Wohnung. Stuttgart: Fr. Wedekind, 1927.
Baudelaire, Charles. *Journaux Intimes*, 1887, edited by A. Van Bever. Paris: Cres, 1920.
Baum, Maria. "Die Bedeutung der genossenschaftlichen Gartenstadtbewegung für die Frauen und Kinder der Industrie-Arbeiterschaft." In *Die deutsche Gartenstadtbewegung*, 94–95. Berlin: Deutschen Gartenstadt-Gesellschaft, 1911.
———. "Mutter, Kind und Wohnung." *Gartenstadt*, no. 5 (1908): 33–34.
Baydar (Nalbantoğlu), Gülsüm. "Between *Civilization* and *Culture*: Appropriation of Traditional Dwelling Forms in Early Republican Turkey." *JAE* 47, no. 2 (1993): 66–74.
———. "The Professionalization of the Ottoman-Turkish Architect." PhD diss., University of California, Berkeley, 1989.
———. "Tenuous Boundaries: Women, Domesticity and Nationhood in 1930s Turkey." *Journal of Architecture* 7, no. 3 (Autumn 2002): 229–44, 245–47.
Baydar (Nalbantoğlu), Gülsüm, and Wong, Chong Thai, eds. *Postcolonial Spaces*, New York: Princeton Architectural Press, 1997.
Baykal, Bekir Sıtkı. *Das Bagdad-Bahn-Problem: 1890–1903*. Freiburg, Germany: Druck von Rudolf Goldschagg, 1935.
Bayrak, Mehmet. *Köy Enstitüleri and Köy Edebiyatı*. Ankara: Özge Yayınları, 2000.
Baysal, İzzet. "Ankara'da Ev." *Arkitekt*, no. 7–8 (1935): 199–200.
Becker, Paul. *Clemens Holzmeister und Salzburg*. Salzburg: Residenz, 1966.
Behne, Adolf. "Die Bedeutung der Farbe in Falkenberg." *Gartenstadt* 7, no. 12 (1913): 248–50.
———. *Neues Wohnen neues Bauen*. Leipzig: Hesse & Becker, 1927.
———. "Yeni mimaride milli ve beyneminel vasıflar." *Mimar*, no. 10 (1931): 331–35.
Behnisch, E. "Vom billig Bauen." *Gartenstadt* 6, no. 2 (1912): 25–29.
———. "Was wir von der englischen Gartenstadtbewegung lernen können?" *Gartenstadt* 7, no. 3 (1913): 41–44.
Behrendt, Walter Curt. *The Victory of the New Building Style*. Translated by Harry Francis Mallgrave. Los Angeles: Getty Research Institute, 2000.

Belli, Şemsi. *Fikriye*. Ankara: Bilgi Yayınevi, 1995.

———. *Makbule Atadan Anlatıyor: Ağabeyim Mustafa Kemal*. Ankara: Ayyıldız Matbaası 1959.

Benjamin, Walter. *Illuminations*. Edited by Hannah Arendt, translated by Harry Zohn. New York: Schocken, 1968.

———. *Reflections: Essays, Aphorisms, Autobiographical Writing*. Edited by Peter Demetz, translated by Edmund Jephcott. New York: Schocken, 1986.

———. *Walter Benjamin: Selected Writings*. Edited by Marcus Bullock and Michael W. Jennings. 3 vols. Cambridge: Harvard University Press, 1996.

Bergdoll, Barry, and Terence Riley. *Mies in Berlin*. New York: Museum of Modern Art, 2001.

Berlepsch, Valendas. "Zum Thema 'Das englische Kleinhaus.'" *Gartenstadt* 7, no. 6 (1913): 102–7.

Berman, Antoine. *The Experience of the Foreign: Culture and Translation in Romantic Germany*. Translated by Stefan Heyvaert. Albany: State University of New York Press, 1992.

Bertram, Carel. "The Turkish House, an Effort on Memory." PhD diss., University of California, Los Angeles, 1998.

Besen, Pınar, Ebru Diriker, and Şehnaz Tahir. "Tanzimat'tan Önce Türk Edebiyatı Tarihinde Çeviri." In *Hommage to Hasan Ali Yücel Anma Kitabı*, edited by Hasan Anamur. İstanbul: Yıldız Teknik Üniversitesi, 1997.

Beveers, Robert. *Garden City Utopia: A Critical Biography of Ebenezer Howard*. London: Macmillan, 1988.

Bilgin, İhsan. "Modernleşmenin ve Toplumsal Hareketliliğin Yörüngesinde Cumhuriyet'in İmarı." In *75 Yılda Değişen Kent ve Mimarlık*, edited by Yıldız Sey, 255–72. İstanbul: Tarih Vakfı, 1998.

———. "Anadolu'da Modernleşme Sürecinde Konut ve Yerleşme." In *Tarihten Günümüze Anadolu'da Konut ve Yerleşme*, edited by Yıldız Sey, 472–90. İstanbul: Türk Tarih Vakfı, 1996.

Blau, Eve. *The Architecture of Red Vienna*. Cambridge: MIT Press, 1999.

Bletter, Rosemarie. "Bruno Taut and Paul Scheerbart's Vision: Utopian Aspects of German Expressionist Architecture." PhD diss., Columbia University, 1973.

———. "Expressionism and the New Objectivity." *Art Journal* 43, no. 2 (1983): 108–20.

———. "The Interpretation of the Glass Dream: Expressionist Architecture and the History of the Crystal Metaphor." *JSAH* 40 (March 1981): 20–43.

Bohman, James, and Matthias Lutz-Bachmann, eds. *Perpetual Peace: Essays on Kant's Cosmopolitan Ideal*. Cambridge: MIT Press, 1997.

Bollerey, Franziska, Gerhard Fehl, and Kristina Hartmann, eds. *Im Grünen wohnen—im Blauen planen*. Hamburg: Hans Christians, 1990.

Bonatz, Paul. "Büyük idman sahası." *Mimar*, no. 8 (1933): 259.

———. *Leben und Bauen*. Stuttgart: Engelhornverlag Adolf Spiemann, 1950.

———. *Paul Bonatz: Ein Gedenkbuch der Technischen Hochschule Stuttgart*. Stuttgart: Deutsche Verlagsanstalt, 1937.

———. "Yeni Alman Mimarisi," parts 1–2. *Arkitekt*, no. 3–4 (1943): 71–75, no. 5–6 (1943): 119–20.

Bonatz, Paul, and Bruno Wehner. *Reichsautobahn — Tankanlagen*. Berlin: Volk und Reich, 1942.

Bourgeois, Victor, ed. *Die Wohnung für das Existenzminimum*. Frankfurt: Englert and Schlosser, 1930.

Bozay, Kemal. *Exil Türkei: Ein Forschungsbeitrag zur deutschsprachigen Emigration in die Türkei (1933–1945)*. Münster: LIT, 2001.

Bozdoğan, Sibel. "Against Style: Bruno Taut's Pedagogical Program in Turkey, 1936–1938." In *The Education of the Architect: Historiography, Urbanism and the Growth of Architectural Knowledge*, edited by Martha Pollak, 163–92. Cambridge: MIT Press, 1997.

———. "Architectural History in Professional Education: Reflections on Postcolonial Challenges to the Modern Survey." *JAE* 52, no. 4 (May 1999): 207–15.

———. *Modernism and Nation Building: Turkish Architectural Culture in the Early Republic*. Seattle: University of Washington Press, 2001.

———. "Reading Ottoman Architecture through Modernist Lenses: Nationalist Historiography and the 'New Architecture' in the Early Republic." *Muqarnas* 24 (2008): 1–26.

———. "Unutulmuş Bir Başka Sedad Eldem Çizgisi: Makina Çağına Karşı Lirik Bir Anadolu/Akdeniz Modernizmi." In *Sedad Eldem II*, edited by Uğur Tanyeli, and Bülent Tanju, 14–23. İstanbul: Osmanlı Bankası Arşiv ve Araştırma Merkezi, 2009.

———. "Vernacular Architecture and Identity Politics. The Case of the 'Turkish House.'" *Traditional Dwellings and Settlements Review* 7, no. 2 (1996): 7–18.

Bozdoğan, Sibel, and Reşat Kasaba, ed. *Rethinking Modernity and National Identity in Turkey*. Seattle: University of Washington Press, 1997.

Bozdoğan, Sibel, Süha Özkan, and Engin Yenal. *Sedad Eldem: Architect in Turkey*. Singapore: Concept Media, 1987.

Brower, Reuben A. *On Translation*. New York: Oxford University Press, 1959.

Bullock, Nicholas, and James Read. *The Movement for Housing Reform in Germany and France 1849–1914*. Cambridge: Cambridge University Press, 1985.

Burton, Robert. *Anatomy of Melancholy*. 1621, 3 vols. Reprinted with the editions of Thomas Faulkner, Nicolas Kiessling, and Rhonda L. Blair. Oxford: Clarendon Press of Oxford University Press, 1989.

Butler, Judith. *The Psychic Life of Power*. Stanford: Stanford University Press, 1997.

Cantek, Funda Şenol. *"Yaban"lar ve Yerliler: Başkent Olma Sürecinde Ankara*. İstanbul: İletişim, 2003.

Capaccioli, Luciana. *Bruno Taut: Visione e Progetto*. N.p.: Delado Libri, 1981.

Çavdarlı, Rıza. "Sanatkarlık, Mimarlık, Türklük." *Yapı* 1, no. 13 (1942): 7–8.

———. "İlk Ressamlar, İlk Mimarlar: Türkler." *Yapı* 1, no. 14 (1942): 4.

Celal, B. O. "Büyük Inkılap Önünde Milli Mimari Meselesi." *Mimar*, no. 5 (1933): 163–64.

———. "San'atta Snobism." *Mimar*, no. 7–8 (1932): 193–94.

———. "Türk Sanatı." *Mimar*, no. 7 (1933): 219–20.

———. "Villa Projesi." *Mimar* (1932): 87–88.

Çelik, Zeynep. *The Remaking of Istanbul: The Portrait of an Ottoman City in the Nineteenth Century*. Berkeley: University of California Press, 1986.

———. *Empire, Architecture, and the City: French-Ottoman Encounters, 1830–1914*. Seattle: University of Washington Press, 2008.

———. "Le Corbusier, Orientalism, Colonialism." *Assemblage* 17 (April 1992): 59–77.

Çelik-Hinchliffe, Zeynep. "Rootedness Uprooted: Paul Bonatz in Turkey 1933–1954." Edited by Esra Akcan, "Intertwined Histories: Turkey and Central Europe." Special Issue, *Centropa* 7, no. 2 (May 2007): 180–96.

Cengizkan, Ali. "Ankara 1924–25 Lörcher Planı: Bir Başkenti Tasarlamak ve Sonrası." In *Modernin Saati*, 37–59. İstanbul: Boyut Yayın Grubu, 2002.

———. "Discursive Formations in Turkish Residential Architecture: Ankara 1948–1962." PhD diss., Middle East Technical University, 2000.

———. "'Söz' ve Tarih: III Çankaya'da Cumhur Reisi İçin Köşk; Fritz Hermann, 1927." *Arredamento Mimarlık* 153, no. 12 (2002): 40–4.

Çetintaş, Sedad. "İnkılap Mimarisi İsteriz!" parts 1–3. *Yapı* 1, no. 5 (1942): 9, 19; no. 6 (1942): 15, 19; no. 7 (1942): 12–13.

———. "Kendimizi Nasıl Bulalım?" *Yapı* 2, no. 39 (1943): 15–16.

Chamberlain, Lori. "Gender and the Metaphorics of Translation." 1988. In *The Translation Studies Reader*, edited by Lawrence Venuti, 314–29. New York: Routledge, 2000.

Cheah, Pheng, and Bruce Robbins, eds. *Cosmopolitics: Thinking and Feeling beyond the Nation*. Minneapolis: University of Minnesota Press, 1998.

Cheng, Anne Anlin. *The Melancholy of Race*. Oxford: Oxford University Press, 2001.

Cheyfitz, Eric. *The Poetics of Imperialism: Translation and Colonization from the Tempest to Tarzan*. New York: Oxford University Press, 1991.

Chomsky, Noam. *Aspects of the Theory of Syntax*. Cambridge: MIT Press, 1965.

———. *Syntactic Structures*. The Hague: Mouton, 1957.

Çıladır, Sina. *Zonguldak Havzasında İşçi Hareketlerinin Tarihi 1848–1940*. Ankara: Yeraltı Maden/İş Yayınları, 1977.

Ciré, Annette. "'Hinter der Weltstadt' Städtebau und Architektur der Landhauskolonien und Gartenstädte in den Berliner Vororten vor 1914." In *Architektur der Stadt*, edited by Thorsten Scheer, Josef Paul Kleihues, and Paul Kahlfeldt, 53–65. Berlin: Nicolai, 2000.

Ciucci, Giorgio. "The Formative Years." *Casabella* 59, no. 619–620 (January–February 1995): 13–25.

Çizgen, Engin. *Photography in the Ottoman Empire*. İstanbul: Haşet Kitabevi, 1987.

Clifford, James. *Routes: Travel and Translation in the Late Twentieth Century*. Cambridge: Harvard University Press, 1997.

dal Co, Francesco. *Figures of Architecture and Thought. German Architecture Culture 1880–1920*. New York: Rizzoli, 1982.

Cohen, Jean-Louis. *Mies van der Rohe*. Translated by Maggie Rosengarten. New York: E&FN Spon, 1996.

———. *Modern Architecture*. Tachen, forthcoming.

Collins, Peter. *Changing Ideals in Modern Architecture*. London: Faber and Faber, 1965.

Colquhoun, Alan. *Modern Architecture*. Oxford: Oxford University Press, 2002.

Le Corbusier. *Vers une Architecture*. 2nd ed. Paris: Les Editions G. Crès, 1924.
———. *Oeuvre Complet (1910-1929)*. 2nd ed. Zurich: Les Editions d'Architecture, 1964.
———. *Voyage d'Orient*. N.p.: Les Editions Forces Vives, 1966.
Crimp, Douglas. "Mourning and Militancy." *October* 51 (Winter 1989): 3-18.
Crinson, Mark. *Empire Building. Orientalism and Victorian Architecture*. London: Routledge, 1996.
Cronin, Michael. *Translation and Globalization*. New York: Routledge, 2003.
Cuda, Alfred. "Deutscher Städtebau im Orient." *Westermanns Monatshefte* 161, no. 963 (November 1936): 253-60.
———. *Stadtaufbau in der Türkei: Arbeit zur Erlangung des Grades eines Doktor Ingenieurs der Technischen Hochschule Berlin*. Berlin: Druck von Hopfer, 1939.
Cuda, Alfred, and Walther Bangert. "Professor Jansens Arbeiten für die Türkei." *Deutsche Bauzeitung* 4 (1936): 65-79.
Cumhuriyet'in Devraldığı İstanbul'dan Bugüne. İstanbul: TSKB, 1999.
"Cumhuriyet'ten Bu Yana İstanbul Planlaması." *Mimarlık* 105, no. 7 (1972): 37-110.
"Cumhuriyetin on senelik san'at hayatı." *Mimar*, no. 9-10 (1933): 263-64.
Curtis, William. *Modern Architecture since 1900*. 3rd ed. London: Phaidon, 1996.
Daldeniz, Elif, and Yeşim Tükel. "Çeviri ve Felsefe." Paper presented at a conference in the series Çeviriye Kuramsal Bakış (A Conceptual Perspective on Translation), organized by Yapı Kredi Yayınları (Yapı Kredi Publishing), İstanbul, April 9, 2004.
Davis, Mike. *Planet of Slums*. New York: Verso, 2006.
De Fries, H. "Einige Siedlungspläne." *Wasmuths Monatshefte für Baukunst* 4 (1919-20): 135-41.
de Michelis, Marco. *Heinrich Tessenow (1876-1950)*. Milano: Electa, 1991.
Denel, Serim. "Ondokuzuncu Yüzyılda Ankara'nın Kentsel Formu ve Konut Dokusundaki Farklılaşmalar." In *Tarih İçinde Ankara*, edited by Ayşıl Yavuz, 129-52. Ankara: ODTU Mimarlık Fakültesi, 2000.
Derrida, Jacques. *Adieu to Emanuel Levinas*. Translated by Pascale-Anne Brault and Michael Naas. Stanford: Stanford University Press, 1999.
———. "Des Tours de Babel." Translated by Joseph F. Graham. In *Theories of Translation: An Anthology of Essays from Dryden to Derrida*, edited by Rainer Schulte, and John Biguenet, 218-27. Chicago: University of Chicago Press, 1992.
———. "Letter to a Japanese Friend." In *A Derrida Reader: Between the Blinds*, edited by Peggy Kamuf, translated by David Wood and Andrew Benjamin, 270-76. New York: Columbia University Press, 1991.
———. *Of Grammatology*. Translated by Gayatri Spivak. Baltimore: Johns Hopkins University Press, 1976.
———. *Of Hospitality*. Translated by Rachel Bowlby. Stanford: Stanford University Press, 2000.
———. *On Cosmopolitanism and Forgiveness*. Translated by Mark Dooley and Michael Hughes. London: Routledge, 2001.
———. "Roundtable on Translation." In *The Ear of the Other*, translated by Peggy Kamuf, 91-161. Lincoln: University of Nebraska Press, 1985.

———. "What Is 'Relevant' Translation?" Translated by Lawrence Venuti. *Critical Inquiry* 27, no. 2 (2001): 174–200.
Dharwadker, Vinay. "Ramanujan's Theory and Practice," In *Post-Colonial Translation: Theory and Practice*, edited by Susan Bassnett and Harish Trivedi, 114–40. London: Routledge, 1999.
Dietrich, Anne. *Deutschsein in Istanbul: Nationalisierung und Orientierung in der deutschsprachigen Community von 1843 bis 1956*. Opladen, Germany: Leske und Budrich, 1998.
Doğramacı, Burcu. *Kulturtransfer und nationale Identität*. Berlin: Gebr. Mann, 2008.
Dreysse, D. W. *May-Siedlungen*. Cologne: Walther König, 2001.
Duben, Alan, and Cem Behar. *Istanbul Households: Marriage, Family, and Fertility*. Cambridge: Cambridge University Press, 1991.
Dunster, David. "Critique: Tafuri's Architecture and Utopia." *AD* 47, no. 3 (1977): 73–77.
Earle, Edward Mead. "The Baghdad Railway: A Study in Capitalistic Imperialism." Master's thesis, Columbia University, 1918.
Eco, Umberto. *Baudolino*. Translated by William Weaver. New York: Harcourt, 2002.
Egli, Ernst. *Die Neue Stadt in Landschaft und Klima. Climate and Town Districts: Consequences and Demands*. Zurich: Verlag für Architektur, 1951.
———. *Geschichte des Städtebau*. 2 vols. Zurich: Eugen Rentsch, 1959, 1962.
———. "Mimari Muhit." *Türk Yurdu* 4-24, no. 30-224 (1930): 32–36.
———. "Şehir Planları." In *Komün Bilgisinin Esas Meseleleri*, edited by Fritz Neumark, 185–200. İstanbul: Cumhuriyet Matbaası, 1936.
———. *Şehirciliğin ve Memleket Planlamasının Esasları*. Ankara: Yazar Matbaası, 1957.
———. "Şehirlerde Mesken ve İskan Meselesi." In *Komün Bilgisinin Esas Meseleleri*, edited by Fritz Neumark, 200–214. İstanbul: Cumhuriyet Matbaası, 1936.
———. *Sinan: Der Baumeister osmanischer Glanzzeit*. Zurich: Verlag für Architektur, 1954.
———. "Türk Evi." Translated by Cemal Köprülü. *Ülkü* 9, no. 99 (May 1941): 195–209.
———. "Das Türkische Wohnhaus." *La Turquie Kemaliste* 14 (August 1936): 11–19.
———. "Elastische Wohnung." *Wohnungswirtschaft* 2 (August 15, 1925): 127–28.
Eldem, Edhem. "Mimar Sedad Eldem'in Gençlik Yazıları (1928-1929)." In *Aptullah Kuran icin Yazılar. Essays in Honour of Aptullah Kuran*, ed. Çiğdem Kafesçioğlu and Lucienne Thys-Şenocak, 519–42. İstanbul: Yapı Kredi Yayınları, 1999.
———. "Sedad Hakkı Eldem. Düşünceler, Hayaller, Tespitler." *İstanbul* 28 (January 1999): 28–47.
Eldem, Sedad Hakkı. "Amca Hüseyin Paşa Yalısı." *Mimar*, no. 12 (1933): 377.
———. "Anciennes Maisons d'Ankara." *La Turquie Kemaliste* 7 (June 1935): 10–12.
———. "Beylerbeyinde bir Yalı." *Arkitekt*, no. 8 (1938): 213–16.
———. "Bir Villa Projesi." *Mimar*, no. 2 (1933): 50–52.

———. "Ev projesi." *Mimar*, no. 8 (1931): 264–67.
———. "Ev projesi." *Mimar*, no. 1 (1932): 17–18.
———. "Evlerimizin İçi." *Mimar*, no. 7 (1931): 233–36.
———. *İstanbul Anıları: Reminiscences of İstanbul*. İstanbul: Çelçüt Matbaacılık Kollektif, 1979.
———. "İstanbul ve Şehircilik." *Mimar*, no. 1 (1931): 1–4.
———. *İstanbul Yalıları*. 2 vols. İstanbul: Vehbi Koç Vakfı, 1993–94.
———. "Küçük ev projeleri." *Mimar*, no. 5 (1931): 156–59.
———. "Maçkada Prof. A. A. Evi." *Arkitekt*, no. 10–11 (1938): 277–85.
———. "Milli Mimari Meselesi." *Arkitekt*, no. 9–10 (1939): 220–23.
———. "Milli ve Yerli Davamız." *Mimarlık*, no. 4 (1944): 2–5, 8.
———. *Sedad Hakkı Eldem: 50 Yıllık Meslek Jübilesi*. İstanbul: Mimar Sinan Üniversitesi, 1983.
———. "Toward a Local Idiom: A Summary. History of Contemporary Architecture in Turkey." In Aga Khan Foundation, ed., *Conservation as Cultural Survival: Proceedings of Seminar Two in the Series Architectural Transformations in the Islamic World*, 89–99. Singapore: Aga Khan Publishing, 1980.
———. *Türk Evi*. 3 vols. İstanbul: Güzel Sanatlar Matbaası, 1984, 1986, and 1987.
———. *Türk Evi Plan Tipleri*. İstanbul: ITÜ Mimarlık Fakültesi Atölyesi, 1955.
———. "Türk Odası." *Güzel Sanatlar Dergisi*, no. 5 (1944): 1–27.
———. "Villa Projeleri." *Mimar*, no. 9 (1931): 302–5.
———. "Yerli Mimariye Doğru." *Arkitekt*, no. 3–4 (1940): 69–74.
Elsaesser, Martin. *Bauten und Entwürfe aus den Jahren 1924–1932*. Berlin: Bauwelt-Verlag, 1933.
Elsaesser, Thomas, Christina Gräwe, Jörg Schilling, and Peter Cachola Schmal, eds. *Martin Elsaesser und das Neue Frankfurt*. Berlin: Ernst Wasmuth, 2009.
Emre, Necmettin. "Karantinada bir Villa: Izmir." *Arkitekt*, no. 4 (1937): 100–3.
Eng, David, and David Kazanjian, eds. *Loss: The Politics of Mourning*. Berkeley: University of California Press, 2003.
"Erich Mendelsohn: Bauten und Skizzen." *Wasmuths Monatshefte für Baukunst* 8 (1924): 1–66.
Erichsen, Regine. "Die Emigration deutschsprachiger Naturwissenschaftler von 1933 bis 1945 in die Türkei in ihrem sozial- und wissenschaftshistorischen Wirkungszusammenhang." In *Die Emigration der Wissenschaften nach 1933*, edited by Herbert Strauss, Klaus Fischer, Christhard Hoffmann, and Alons Söllner, 73–104. Munich: K. G. Saur, 1991.
Eser, Lami. "Modern Ev Mutfakları." MPhil diss., İstanbul Technical University. İstanbul: Pulhan Matbaası, 1952.
Evans, Robin. *Translations from Drawing to Building*. Cambridge: MIT Press, 1997.
Fanon, Frantz. *The Wretched of the Earth*. Translated by Constance Farrington. New York: Grove, 1963.
Farah, Irmgard. *Die Deutsche Pressepolitik und Propagandatätigkeit im Osmanischen Reich von 1908–1918*. Stuttgart: Franz Steiner, 1993.
Fehl, Gerhard. *Kleinstadt, Steildach, Volksgemeinschaft: Zum "reaktionären Modernismus" in Bau- und Stadtbaukunst*. Wiesbaden, Germany: Vieweg, 1995.

———. "The Nazi Garden City." In *The Garden City: Past, Present, and Future*, edited by Stephen Ward, 88–106. London: E. and F. N. Spon, 1992.
Ficino, Marcillo. *Three Books of Life*. 1482. Translated by Carol Kaske and John Clark. Binghamton, N.Y.: Center of Medieval and Renaissance Studies, 1991.
Finckh, Ludwig. "The Spirit of Berlin." Translated by Don Reneau. In *The Weimar Republic Sourcebook*, edited by Anton Kaes, Martin Jay, and Edward Dimendberg, 414–15. Berkeley: University of California Press, 1994.
Fischer, Theodor. "Şehir İnşa Sanatı," parts 1–4. Translated by Kemali Söylemezoğlu. *Arkitekt*, no. 1-2 (1941): 24–27; no. 3-4 (1941): 69–71; no. 7-8 (1941): 175–78; no. 11-12 (1945): 276–80.
"Das Flache Dach." *Wohnungswirtschaft* 5 (January 15, 1928): 16–18.
Foucault, Michel. *Discipline and Punish*. Translated by Alan Sheridan. New York: Vintage, 1995.
Frampton, Kenneth. *Modern Architecture: A Critical History*. 3rd ed. London: Thames and Hudson, 1992.
———. "Towards a Critical Regionalism: Six Points for an Architecture of Resistance." In *Anti-Aesthetic: Essays on Postmodern Culture*, edited by Hal Foster, 16–30. Seattle: Bay Press, 1983.
Franck, Oya Atalay. "Politik und Architektur. Ernst Egli und die Suche nach einer Moderne in der Türkei." PhD diss., ETH, Zurich, 2004.
Frank, Hartmut. "Ein Bauhaus vor dem Bauhaus." *Bauwelt* 74, no. 41 (1983): 1640–58.
———. "Monuments in Arbeitsstil: Paul Bonatz's Public Works." *Lotus* 47, no. 3 (1985): 75–90.
Freud, Sigmund. "Mourning and Melancholia." Translated by Joan Riviere. In Sigmund Freud, *General Psychology Theory*, 164–80. New York: Touchstone, 1991.
Friedrichsmeyer, Sara, Sara Lennox, and Susanne Zantop, eds. *The Imperialist Imagination. German Colonialism and Its Legacy*. Ann Arbor: University of Michigan Press, 1998.
Frischauer, Stefanie. "Das Haus Kemal Paschas in Angora." *Wasmuths Monatshefte für Baukunst* 15 (November–December 1931): 534–35.
Fritsch, Theodor. *Die Stadt der Zukunft*. Leipzig: Verlag von Theodor Fritsch, 1896.
Fuchs, Carl Johannes. "Nochmals zum Thema, Das englische Kleinhaus." *Gartenstadt* 7, no. 8 (1913): 154–57.
"Die GAGFAG-Mustersiedlung. 'Bauen und Wohnen' in Berlin-Zehlendorf." *Wohnungswirtschaft* 5 (October 1, 1928): 276–87.
"Die Gartenstadt Hellerau." *Hohewarte* 3, no. 6 (1907): 313–28.
"Die Gartenvorstadt Falkenberg bei Berlin," parts 1–2. *Gartenstadt* 7, no. 5 (1913): 80–84; no. 6 (1913): 111–17.
Geisert, Helmut. "Reformmodelle für das städtlische Wohnen." In *Architektur der Stadt*, edited by Thorsten Scheer, Josef Paul Kleihues, and Paul Kahlfeldt, 41–51. Berlin: Nicolai, 2000.
Gentzler, Edwin. *Contemporary Translation Theories*. 2nd ed. Clevedon, England: Multilingual Matters, 2001.
Geschichte des Wohnens. 5 vols. Stuttgart: Deutsche Verlags-Anstalt, 1996–99.

Giedion, Sigfried. *Space, Time and Architecture: The Growth of a New Tradition*. Cambridge: Harvard University Press, 1941.

Glasneck, Johannes. *Türkiye'de Faşist Alman Propagandası*. Translated by Arif Gelen. İstanbul: Onur Yayınları, 1978.

Goettel, Jakobus. "Beitrag zur Erhöhung des Wohnwertes der Kleinwohnungen." *Wohnungswirtschaft* 7 (February 1, 1930): 34–39.

Gök, Nihad. "Rene'nin Melankolisi." *Varlık* 83 (December 15, 1936): 171.

Gökalp, Ziya. *The Principles of Turkism*. Translated by Robert Devereux. Leiden: E. J. Brill, 1968.

———. *Turkish Nationalism and Western Civilization*. Translated by Niyazi Berkes. New York: Columbia University Press, 1959.

Goodman, Lenn Evan. *Avicenna*. New York: Routledge, 1992.

Gorbon, Rebi. "B. Yusuf Evi." *Arkitekt*, no. 4 (1937): 68–70.

Graubner, Gerhard. *Paul Bonatz und seine Schüler*. Stuttgart: Deutsche Bauten, 1931.

Gregor, Joseph. "Clemens Holzmeister." *Profil: Österreichische Monatsschrift für bildende Kunst* 4, no. 4 (1936): 154–63.

———. *Clemens Holzmeister: Das architektonische Werk*. Vienna: Druck und Verlag der Österreichischen Staatsdrückerei, 1953.

Gropius, Walter. "Der Architekt als Organisator." *Wohnungswirtschaft* 5 (March 15, 1928): 47–48.

Gruber, Max. "Kolonisation in der Heimat." *Gartenstadt* 2, no. 3 (1908): 17–19.

Guha, Ranajit, and Gayatri Chakravorty Spivak, eds. *Selected Subaltern Studies*. New York: Oxford University Press, 1988.

Gülsen, Ömer. "Erinnerungen an Bruno Taut." *Bauwelt* 75, no. 39 (1984): 1675–84.

Habermas, Jürgen. "Kant's Idea of Perpetual Peace: At Two Hundred Years' Historical Remove." Translated by Ciaran Cronin and James Bohman. In *The Inclusion of the Other: Studies in Political Theory*, edited by Ciaran Cronin and Pablo de Greiff, 165–201. Cambridge: MIT Press, 1998.

Hain, Simone. "Ex Oriente Lux." In *Moderne Architektur in Deutschland 1900 bis 1950: Expressionismus und Neue Sachlichkeit*, edited by Vittorio Magnago Lampugnani and Romana Schneider, 133–60. Stuttgart: Gerd Hatje, 1994.

Hall, Peter. *Cities of Tomorrow: An Intellectual History of Urban Planning and Design in the Twentieth Century*. Oxford: Blackwell, 1988.

Hall, Peter, and Colin Ward. *Sociable Cities: The Legacy of Howard*. Chichester, England: John Wiley and Sons, 1998.

Haney, David. *When Modern Was Green: Life and Work of Landscape Architect Leberecht Migge*. London: Routledge, 2010.

Hartmann, Kristina. "Bruno Taut im Türkishen Exil." *Architekt* 2 (January 1992): 111–17.

———. *Deutsche Gartenstadtbewegung*. Munich: Heinz Moos, 1976.

Harvey, David. "Cosmopolitanism and the Banality of Geographical Evils." *Public Culture* 12 (2000–2): 529–64.

Harvey, Keith. "Translating Camp Talk: Gay Identities and Cultural Transfer." 1998. In *The Translation Studies Reader*, edited by Lawrence Venuti, 446–67. New York: Routledge, 2000.

Das Haus der Freundschaft in Konstantinopel. Compiled by Deutsches Werkbund, Deutsch-Türkische Vereinigung. Munich: F. Bruckmann, 1918.

Haydaroğlu, Polat. *Osmanlı İmparatorluğu'nda Yabancı Okullar*. Ankara: Kültür Bakanlığı Yayınları, 1990.

Hays, Michael. *Modernism and the Posthumanist Subject: The Architecture of Hannes Meyer and Ludwig Hilberseimer*. Cambridge: MIT Press, 1992.

Hegemann, Werner. "Hermann Jansen zu seinem sechzigsten Geburstag." *Städtebau* 26, no. 10 (1929): 269–85.

———. "Poelzig-Schüler." *Wasmuths Monatshefter für Baukunst* 15 (1931): 100–103.

Henderson, Susan. "A Revolution in the Woman's Sphere." In *Architecture and Feminism*, edited by Debra Coleman, Elizabeth Danze, and Carol Henderson, 221–53. New York: Princeton Architectural Press, 1996.

———. "The Work of Ernst May (1919–1930)." PhD diss., Columbia University, 1990.

Henning, Rudolf. *Das deutsche Haus in seiner historischen Entwicklung*. Strassburg: Karl J. Trübner, 1882.

"Hermann Jansen und seine Schule." *Der Städtebau* 19, no. 1–2 (1922): 7–9, Pl. 5–8.

Heßler, Martina. "The Frankfurt Kitchen: The Model of Modernity and the 'Madness' of Traditional Users, 1926 to 1933." In *Cold War Kitchen: Americanization, Technology and European Users*, edited by Ruth Oldenziel and Karin Zachman, 163–84. Cambridge: MIT Press, 2009.

Heuss, Theodor. *Hans Poelzig: Das Lebensbild eines deutschen Baumeisters; Bauten und Entwürfe*. Berlin: E. Wasmuth, 1939.

Heynen, Hilde. *Architecture and Modernity: A Critique*. Cambridge: MIT Press, 1999.

Hikmet, Nazım. *Bütün Eserleri*. Ankara: Dost Yayınları, 1968.

———. *Selected Poems*. Translated by Taner Aybars. London: Jonathan Cape, 1967.

Hillebrecht, Sabine. *Haymatloz: Exil in der Türkei*. Berlin: Verein Aktives Museum, 2000.

Hillinger, Franz. "Damın İnşa Şekli Hakkında." Translated by Adnan Kolatan. *Arkitekt*, no. 9–10 (1941): 221.

Hillinger, Franz, and Paul Schmidt. "Schuster bleib' bei deinem Leisten!" *Wohnungswirtschaft* 6 (December 1–15, 1929): 372–80.

"Himayei Etfal Apartmanı Proje Müsabakası." *Mimar*, no. 3 (1934): 71–76.

Hisar, Abdülhak Şinasi. "Ankara'nın Güzellikleri." *Varlık* 3 (August 15, 1933): 37–38.

———. "Ankara'nın Kıymeti ve Güzelliği İçin." *Varlık* 4 (September 1, 1933): 52–54.

———. *Boğaziçi Mehtapları*. 1943. Reprint, İstanbul: Bağlam, 1997.

———. "Büyükadada'ki Ev," parts 1–3. *Varlık* 51 (August 15, 1935): 34–36; 52 (September 1, 1935): 52–54; 53 (September 15, 1935): 66–68.

———. "Çamlıca'da Bir Mevsim." *Varlık* 66 (April 1, 1936): 277–78.

———. "Çamlıca'daki Köşk." *Varlık* 65 (March 15, 1936): 261–62.

———. "Havuzlu Oda," parts 1–2. *Varlık* 58 (December 1, 1935): 150–52; 59 (December 15, 1935): 165–67.
———. "Kanlıca'daki Yalı." *Varlık* 55 (October 15, 1935): 99–101.
———. "Madalyonlar," parts 1–2. *Varlık* 21 (May 15, 1934): 825–27; 22 (June 1, 1934): 844–45.
———. "Yıkılan Yalı." *Varlık* 64 (March 1, 1936): 245–46.
Holod, Renata, and Ahmet Evin, eds. *Modern Turkish Architecture*. Philadelphia: University of Pennsylvania Press, 1984.
Holtay, Arif Hikmet. "Bir Ev Projesi." *Mimar*, no. 2 (1934): 41–42.
———. "Çiftlik Evi ve Han." *Mimar*, no. 8 (1934): 235–37.
———. "Dr. Celal B. Evi." *Mimar*, no. 10 (1932): 286–87.
———. "Köşk Projesi." *Mimar*, no. 4 (1933): 109–10.
Holzmeister, Clemens. *Architekt in der Zeitenwende: Selbstbiographie*. Salzburg: Bergland, 1976.
———. *Bauten, Entwürfe und Handzeichnungen*. Salzburg: Anton Pustet, 1937.
———. *Clemens Holzmeister*. Vienna: Akademie der bildenden Künste, 1982.
———. *Clemens Holzmeister: Aussereuropäische Kirchen und Paläste*. Vienna: Graphische Sammlung Albertina, 1970.
———. *Neue Werkkunst Clemens Holzmeister*. Berlin: F. E. Hubsch, 1927.
Howard, Ebenezer. *Garden Cities of Tomorrow*. 1902. Reprint, Cambridge: MIT Press, 1965.
———. *Gartenstädte in Sicht*. Translated by Maria Wallroth-Unterilp. Jena, Germany: Diederichs, 1907.
Hüber, Reinhard. *Die Bagdadbahn*. Berlin: Junker und Dünnhaupt, 1943.
Hulısi, Şerif. "Tanzimattan Sonraki Tercüme Faaliyeti." *Tercüme* 1, no. 2 (1940): 286–96.
Huntington, Samuel P. *The Clash of Civilizations and the Remaking of World Order*. New York: Simon & Schuster, 1996.
Hüsnü, Nizamettin. "Bir ev projesi." *Mimar*, no. 5 (1933): 176.
———. "Bir katlı ev projesi." *Mimar*, no. 5 (1933): 177.
———. "Hasan B. Apartmanı." *Mimar*, no. 11–12 (1932): 322–23.
Huyssen, Andreas. *Die frühromantische Konzeption von Übersetzung und Aneignung: Studien zur frühromantischen Utopie einer deutschen Weltliteratur*. Zurich: Atlantis, 1969.
Ibn'Sina [Avicenna]. *Canon of Medicine*. Translated by O. Cameron Gruner. London: Luzac, 1930.
———. "On the Signs of Melancholy's Appearance." Translated by Martin Eisner. In *The Nature of Melancholy*, edited by Jennifer Radden, 77–78. New York: Oxford University Press, 2000.
İhsan, Bekir. "Ev Projeleri." *Mimar*, no. 1 (1933): 17–18.
———. "Küçük ev projeleri." *Mimar*, no. 2 (1933): 53–54.
"İlk Öğretmen Evleri Proje Müsabakası." *Arkitekt*, no. 1–2 (1944): 14–16.
"L'Immigration en Turquie." *La Turquie Kemaliste* 23–24 (April 1938): 15–18.
İnan, Ziya Koca. "İstanbul Şehir Planı ve İstanbulda Mesken Meselesi." In *Komün Bilgisinin Esas Meseleleri*, edited by Fritz Neumark, 215–26. İstanbul: Cumhuriyet Matbaasi, 1936.

Inghilleri, Moria, ed. "Bourdieu and the Sociology of Translation and Interpreting." Special issue, *Translator* 11, no. 2 (2005).
"Die innere Kolonisation," *Gartenstadt* 4, no. 3 (1910): 25–30.
"İstanbul Planı Etüdü." *Mimar*, no. 8 (1932): 258–59.
İzgi, Utarit. "Konutta Yemek Hazırlama ve Pişirme Eylemi." In *Konut Paneli: Şehir Konutları ve Standardların Tespiti*. İstanbul: ITU, 1963.
Jacquemond, Richard. "Translation and Cultural Hegemony: The Case of French-Arabic Translation." In *Rethinking Translation: Discourse, Subjectivity, Ideology*, edited by Lawrence Venuti, 139–58. London: Routledge, 1992.
Jaeger, Albert. "Die Sache Gefühl." *Wohnungswirtschaft* 7 (May 15, 1930): 198–99.
Jameson, Fredric. "Architecture and the Critique of Ideology." In *Architecture Criticism Ideology*, edited by Joan Ockman, 51–87. New York: Princeton Architectural Press, 1985.
Jansen, Hermann. "Die Allgemeine Stadtbau-Ausstellung Berlin 1910," parts 1–2. *Baumeister* 8 (August 1910): 121–27; (September 1910): 133–44.
———. *Ankara İmar Planı*. İstanbul: Alaeddin Kıral Basımevi, 1937.
———. "Die Architektur auf der Kunstausstellung Berlin 1904." *Baumeister* 2 (August 1904): 124–29.
———. "Ausbildung des Daches beim städtischen Mietshause." *Baumeister* 5 (September 1907): 133–36.
———. "Bauten Otto Schulzes." *Baumeister* 14 (March 1916): 17–24.
———. "Bebauungsplan für das Johannistal zu Eisenach." *Der Städtebau* 6, no. 9 (1909): 67.
———. *Bebauungsplan für Treptow: Siedlung Berlin Treptow*. Berlin: Ernst Wasmuth, 1914.
———. "Berliner Grossmarkthalle." *Baumeister* 13 (May 1915): 64–65.
———. "Das Einzelwohnhaus der Neuzeit." *Baumeister* 5 (January 1907): 45–48.
———. "Erschliessung des Rayons der Stadt Köln." *Städtebau* 17, no. 11–12 (1920): 101–5.
———. "Gedanken über Architekturausstellungen spez. die Berliner von 1908." *Baumeister* 6 (October 1908): 121–28.
———. "Izahname." In *Ankara Şehrinin Profesör M. Jausseley, Jansen ve Brix taraflarından yapılan plan ve projelerine ait izahnameler*. Ankara: Hakimiyeti Milliye Matbaası, 1929.
———. "Landhaus und Garten." *Baumeister* 5 (May 1907): 94–95.
———. "Der Meister des Bebauungsplanes." *Die Volkswohnung* (May 24, 1919): 132–34.
———. "Das Mietshaus." *Baumeister* 8 (November 1909): 13–22.
———. "Die Siedlung Berlin-Treptow." *Baumeister* 12 (May 1914): 77–80.
———. "Die Unzulänglichkeit neuzeitlicher Platzanlagen." *Wasmuths Monatshefte für Baukunst* 1, no. 15 (1914): 41–47.
———. *Vorschlag zu einem Grundplan für Gross-Berlin*. Munich: Georg D. W. Callwey, 1910.
———. "Vorschlag zu einem Grundplan von Groß-Berlin." *Gartenstadt* 4, no. 7 (1910): 76–81.

———. "Wettbewerb Gross-Zürich." *Baumeister* 14 (May 1916): B41–42.

———. "Der Wettbewerb von Gross Berlin." *Baumeister* 7 (November 1908): 13–23.

———. "Wohnhaustypen der Großstadt." *Baumeister* 9 (June 1911): 102–12.

———. "Yapı Kooperatifleri." *Karınca* 3 (March 1936): 46.

Jansen, Hermann, and William Müller. "Bebauungsplan der Beamten- und Arbeiterkolonien Streiffeld und Kellersberg bei Aachen." *Städtebau* 2, no. 7 (1905): 87–89.

Jaussely, Leon. "Izahname." In *Ankara Şehrinin Profesör M. Jaussely, Jansen ve Brix taraflarından yapılan plan ve projelerine ait izahnameler*. Ankara: Hakimiyeti Milliye Matbaası, 1929.

Junge, Kurt. *Das friesische Bauernhaus*. Oldenburg, Germany: Gerhard Stalling, 1936.

Junghanns, Kurt. *Bruno Taut, 1880–1938*. Berlin: Henschelverl, 1970.

Kaldor, Mary. "Cosmopolitanism versus Nationalism: The New Divide?" In *Europe's New Nationalism*, edited by Richard Kaplan and John Feffer, 42–58. Oxford: Oxford University Press, 1996.

Kampffmeyer, Bernhard. "Aus der Englischen Gartenstadtbewegung." *Gartenstadt* 3, no. 1 (1909): 16–18.

———. "Die englische Genossenschaftsbewegung und die Gartenstadt." *Gartenstadt* 3, no. 3 (1909): 23–25.

———. "Gartenstadt, Gartenvorstadt, Gartendorf." In *Aus Englischen Gartenstädten*, 96–101. Berlin: Deutsche Gartenstadt-Gesellschaft, 1910.

———. "Gartenstadt – Gartenvorstadt – Gemeinschaftsbesitz." *Gartenstadt* 1, no. 5 (1906–7): 33–35.

———. *Grünflächenpolitik und Gartenstadtbewegung*. Berlin: Deutscher Kommunal Verlag, 1926.

———. "Innenkolonisation und Gartenstadt." *Gartenstadt* 4, no. 3 (1910): 25–30.

———. "Zu den Baukosten des Kleinhauses." *Gartenstadt* 6, no. 2 (1912): 20–25.

Kampffmeyer, Hans. *Die deutsche Gartenstadtbewegung*. Berlin: Deutschen Gartenstadt-Gesellschaft, 1911.

———. "Ebenezer Howard und die englische Gartenstadt-Bewegung." 1908. In *Im Grünen wohnen-im Blauen planen*, edited by Franziska Bollerey, Gerhard Fehl, and Kristina Hartmann, 99–102. Hamburg: Hans Christians, 1990.

———. "Die Gartenstadt in ihrer kulturellen und wirtschaftlichen Bedeutung." *Hohewarte* 3, no. 7 (1906–7): 105–20.

———. "Gartenstadt und Gartenvorstadt." *Gartenstadt* 1, no. 5 (1906–7): 35–36.

———. "Von der Kleinstadt zur Gartenstadt." *Der Städtebau* 3, no. 10 (1906): 134–37.

———. *Wohnstätte und Arbeitsstätte*. Stuttgart: Julius Hofmann, n.d.

———. *Wohnungen, Siedlungen und Gartenstädte in Holland und England*. Berlin: Deutscher Kommunal Verlag, 1926.

———. "Zur Erweiterung unseres Programms." *Gartenstadt* 1, no. 4 (1906–7): 36–37.

Kandemir. "Florya Deniz Köşkü." *Ayda Bir* (1952): 35–37.

Kant, Immanuel. *Groundwork for a Metaphysics of Morals*. Translated by Mary Gregor. Cambridge: Cambridge University Press, 1997.

———. "Perpetual Peace: A Philosophical Sketch." 1795. Translated by H. B. Nisbet. In *Political Writings*, edited by Hans Reiss, 83–130. Cambridge: Cambridge University Press, 1991.

Karabekir, Kazım. *Tarih Boyunca Türk-Alman İlişkileri*. Edited by Orhan Hülagü and Ömer Hakan Özalp. İstanbul: Emre Yayınları, 2001.

Karaosmanoğlu, Yakup Kadri. *Ankara*. 1934. 4th ed. İstanbul: Remzi Kitapevi, 1972.

———. *Kiralık Konak*. 1922. Reprint, İstanbul: Remzi Kitapevi, 1947.

Karay, Refik Halid. "Hülya Bu Ya." 1921. In *Ankara Ankara*, edited by Enis Batur, 425–26. İstanbul: Yapı Kredi Yayınları, 1994.

Karınca (March 1936).

Kassowitz, Julie. "Die Frau und die Gartenstadt." In *Aus englischen Gartenstädten*. Berlin: Deutsche Gartenstadt-Gesellschaft, 1910.

Katscher, Leopold. "Ebenezer Howard." *Gartenstadt* 6, no. 3 (1912): 38–40.

Kessler, Gerhard. "Komün Bilgisi." *İstanbul Üniversitesi İktisat Fakültesi Mecmuası* (January 1941): 334–39.

Kezer, Zeynep. "The Making of a National Capital: Ideology and Socio-Spatial Practices in Early Republican Ankara." PhD diss., University of California at Berkeley, 1999.

Khosla, Romi. "Crashing through Western Modernism into the Asian Reality." In *Regionalism in Architecture. Proceedings of Regional Seminar Organized by Aga Khan Award for Architecture*, 58–60. Singapore: Concept Media, 1985.

Kirsch, Karin. "Die Weissenhofsiedlung. Ein internationales Manifest." In *Moderne Architektur in Deutschland 1900 bis 1950: Expressionismus und Neue Sachlichkeit*, edited by Vittorio Magnago Lampugnani and Romana Schneider, 205–24. Stuttgart: Gerd Hatje, 1994.

Koçak, Cemil. *Türk-Alman İlişkileri (1923–1939)*. Ankara: Türk Tarih Kurumu, 1991.

Koçu, Reşad Ekrem. "Ev, Ahşab Evler." In *İstanbul Ansiklopedisi*, edited by Reşad Ekrem Koçu. 2nd ed. Vol. 10, no. 143. İstanbul: Koçu Yayınları, 1968–71.

———, ed. *İstanbul Ansiklopedisi*. İstanbul: İstanbul Yayınevi, 1944–51.

Kömürcüoğlu, Eyüb. "Büyük Türk İnkılabının Mimari Cephesi." *Yapı* 2, no. 26 (1942): 16–18.

Köni, Yunus Kazım. "Tercümeye Dair Düşünceler." *Tercüme* 5, no. 26 (1944): 157–59.

Konuk, Kader. *East West Mimesis. Auerbach in Turkey*. Translated by Victoria Holbrook. Stanford: Stanford University Press, 2010.

Koschatzky, Walter. "Vorwort." In Clemens Holzmeister, *Clemens Holzmeister: Aussereuropäische Kirchen und Paläste*. 1–5. Vienna: Graphische Sammlung Albertina, 1970.

"Köy Okulları Proje Müsabakası." *Arkitekt*, no. 1–2 (1941): 12–23.

[Koyunoğlu?], Arif Hikmet. "Ankara Evleri." *Türk Yurdu* 211–12, no. 17–18 (1929): 45–47.

Kozanoğlu, Abdüllah Ziya. "Binanın içinde mimar." *Mimar*, no. 1 (1931): 14–19.

———. "Bir Kira Evi." *Mimar*, no. 2 (1933): 41–43.
———. "Inkılap ve San'at." *Mimar*, no. 9-10 (1933): 317–18.
———. "İnkılap ve Sanat." *Varlık* 5 (September 15, 1933): 69–70; 11 (December 15, 1933): 168.
———. "Müşterek Evler." *Mimar*, no. 6 (1932): 179–80.
———. "Yeni Sanat." *Mimar*, no. 4 (1932): 97–98.
Kracauer, Siegfried. *Berliner Nebeneinander: Ausgewählte Feuilletons 1930-33*. Edited by Andreas Volk. Zurich: Epoca, 1996.
Kristeva, Julia. *Black Sun: Depression and Melancholia*. New York: Columbia University Press, 1989.
Kuban, Doğan. "Celal Esad Arseven ve Türk Sanatı Kavramı." *Mimarlık*, no. 10 (1969): 18–20.
———. *İstanbul: An Urban History*. İstanbul: Tarih Vakfı, 1996.
———. *İstanbul Yazıları*. İstanbul: Yapı Endüstri Merkezi, 1998.
———. *The Turkish Hayat House*. İstanbul: Eren Yayıncılık, 1995.
Küçükerman, Önder. *Turkish House*. İstanbul: Türkiye Turing ve Otomobil Kurumu, 1988.
Kumral, Bülent. "Interview with Zeki Sayar." In *Anılarda Mimarlık*, 100–113. İstanbul: YEM, 1995.
Kurasawa, Fuyuki. "A Cosmopolitanism from Below: Alternative Globalization and the Creation of Solidarity without Bounds." *European Journal of Sociology* 45, no. 2 (2004): 233–55.
Kuruyazıcı, Hasan, ed. *Batılılaşan İstanbul'un Ermeni Mimarları*. İstanbul: Uluslararası Hrant Dink Vakfı Yayınları, 2010.
Lampugnani, Vittorio Magnago. "Moderne, Lebensreform, Stadt und Grün Urbanistische Experimente in Berlin 1900 bis 1914." In *Architektur der Stadt*, edited by Thorsten Scheer, Josef Paul Kleihues, and Paul Kahlfeldt, 19–38. Berlin: Nicolai, 2000.
———. "Modernism and the Metropolis: Plans for Central Berlin 1910-1941." In *Berlin/New York: Like and Unlike; Essays on Architecture and Art from 1870 to the Present*, edited by Josef Paul Kleihues and Christina Rathgeber, 249–63. New York: Rizzoli, 1993.
Lampugnani, Vittorio Magnago, and Romana Schneider, eds. *Moderne Architektur in Deutschland 1900 bis 1950: Expressionismus und Neue Sachlichkeit*. Stuttgart: Gerd Hatje, 1994.
Lane, Barbara Miller. *Architecture and Politics in Germany, 1918–1945*. Cambridge: Harvard University Press, 1968.
———. *National Romanticism and Modern Architecture in Germany and the Scandinavian Countries*. Cambridge, N.Y.: Cambridge University Press, 2000.
Lauffer, Otto. *Das deutsche Haus in Dorf und Stadt*. Leipzig: von Quelle and Mener, 1919.
Lefevere, André. *Translating Literature: The German Tradition from Luther to Rosenweig*. Assen, Netherlands: Van Gorcum, 1977.
———. *Translation, History, Culture: A Sourcebook*. London: Routledge, 1992.
Lejeune, Jean-François. "From Hellerau to the Bauhaus. Memory and Modernity of the German Garden City." *New City* 3 (Fall 1996): 51–68.

Lévi-Strauss, Claude. *Myth and Meaning.* New York: Schocken, 1979.
Lihotzky, Margarete. See entries under Schütte-Lihotzky, Margarete.
Linneke, Richard. "Das Jahr fängt gut an." *Wohnungswirtschaft* 4 (March 1, 1927): 33–35.
———. "Fünf Jahre DEWOG-Arbeit." *Wohnungswirtschaft* 6 (March 20, 1929): 78–80.
———. "Zwei Jahre GEHAG-Arbeit." *Wohnungswirtschaft* 3 (April 15, 1926): 53–60.
Loos, Adolf. "The Poor Little Rich Man." In Adolf Loos, *Spoken into the Void: Collected Essays 1897–1900*, 124–30. Translated by Jane O'Newman and John Smith. Cambridge: MIT Press, 1982.
Lörcher, Carl. "Der Neue Bebauungsplan für Angora." *Wasmuths Monatshefte für Baukunst* 9, no. 9 (1925): 25–26.
———. "Das Neue Regierungsviertel der Stadt Angora." *Städtebau* 22 (1925): 144–45.
———. "Stadtbaufragen in der Türkei." *Bauwelt* (1925): 6–8.
Lothar, Rathmann. *Berlin-Bagdad.* Berlin: Dietz, 1962.
Loy, Horst. "Zum Gedenken an Hermann Jansen," *Baumeister* 45, no. 8 (1948): 299.
Luben. "Hermann Jansen Zum Gedächtnis." *Bauhelfer* 4, no. 10 (1949): 253–54.
Lutz-Bachmann, Matthias. "Kant's Idea of Peace and the Philosophical Conception of a World Republic." In *Perpetual Peace. Essays on Kant's Cosmopolitan Ideal*, edited by James Bohman and Matthias Lutz-Bachmann, 59–77. Cambridge: MIT Press, 1997.
Luxemburg, Rosa. "Die Krise der Sozialdemokratie." In Rosa Luxemburg, *Ausgewählte Reden und Schriften* 1:294–300. Berlin: Dietz, 1951.
Mango, Andrew. *Atatürk.* London: John Murray, 1999.
Marcus Aurelius. *Meditations.* Translated by A. S. L. Farquharson. 1944. Reprint, Oxford: Oxford University Press, 2008.
Martin Wagner (1885–1957): Wohnungsbau und Weltstadtplanung. Berlin: Akademie der Künste, 1985.
Marx, Karl, and Friedrich Engels. *The Marx-Engels Reader*, edited by Robert Tucker. New York: W. W. Norton, 1978.
May, Ernst. *Das Neue Frankfurt.* Special Issue on Flat Roof, no. 7 (1926–27).
———. "Fünf Jahre Wohnungsbautätigkeit in Frankfurt am Main," parts 1 and 2, *Das Neue Frankfurt* (February–March 1930): 21–76; (April–May 1930): 77–132.
"Memurları Meskenleştirmek." *Karınca* (June 1936): 135.
Menteşe, Ertuğrul. "İstanbul'un İmarı." *Arkitekt*, no. 1–2 (1955): 27–38.
Mercer, Kobena. "Introduction." In *Cosmopolitan Modernisms*, edited by Kobena Mercer, 6–23. Cambridge: MIT Press, 2005.
Meringer, Rudolf. *Das deutsche Haus und sein Hausrat.* Leipzig: B. G. Teubner, 1906.
Mertins, Detlef, ed. *The Presence of Mies.* New York: Princeton Architectural Press, 1994.
Meyer, Rainer. "Martin Elsaesser von 1925–1932. Zum Werk eines avantgardistischen Baukünstlers." PhD diss., Universität zu Bremen, 1988.

Migge, Leberecht. "Die Entwicklung der englischen Gartenstadtbewegung." *Gartenstadt* 5, no. 11 (1911): 149–52.

———. "Die industrielle Entwicklung von Letchworth." *Gartenstadt* 5, no. 12 (1911): 165–69.

"Milli Mimari Anketimiz," parts 1–7. *Mimarlık*, no. 2 (1944): 2–4; no. 3 (1944): 11–12; no. 4 (1944): 6–8; no. 5 (1944): 7–8; no. 1 (1945): 22; no. 2–3 (1945): 16–18; no. 4–5 (1945): 20.

"Mimarlık ve Millicilik Davamız." *Yapı* 1, no. 13 (1943): 3.

Mohr, Christoph. "Martin Elsaesser and the New Frankfurt." *Archigrad*, no. 1 (1994): 49–51.

Mohr, Christoph, and Michael Müller. *Funktionalität und Moderne. Das Neue Frankfurt (1925–1933)*. Köln: Fricke im Rudolf Müller, 1984.

Mortaş, Abidin. "Ankara tasarruf evleri kooperatifi." *Arkitekt*, no. 3–4 (1943): 76–79.

———. "Az Para ile Ev Yapmak ve Bizde Kooperatifçilik." *Arkitekt*, no. 3–4 (1944): 90–92.

———. "Bir Memur Evi Tip Projesi." *Arkitekt*, no. 1–2 (1944): 45–46.

———. "H. Ziya B. Evi — Samatya." *Mimar*, no. 9 (1931): 255–60.

———. "Herkesin Kendi Evi." *Mimar*, no. 4 (1931): 128–32.

———. "Memleketimizde Yapı ve İmar İşleri." *Arkitekt*, no. 1–2 (1948): 41.

———. "Modern Türk Mimarisi." *Yapı* 1, no. 10 (1942): 13–14.

———. "Müstakil Evler." *Mimar*, no. 1 (1931): 42–3.

———. "Tek katlı evler." *Mimar*, no. 9 (1931): 310–11.

———. "Yeni Alman Mimarisi Sergisi." *Arkitekt*, no. 3–4 (1943): 67–70.

Moss-Eccardt, John. *Ebenezer Howard*. Aylesbury, England: Shire, 1973.

Mufti, Aamir. "Auerbach in Istanbul: Edward Said, Secular Criticism and the Question of Minority Culture." *Critical Inquiry* 25 (Autumn 1988): 85–125.

Mukherjee, Tutun, ed. *Translation: From Periphery to Centerstage*. New Delhi: Prestige, 1998.

Mumford, Lewis. "The Garden City Idea and Modern Planning." In *Garden Cities of Tomorrow* by Ebenezer Howard, 1902. Reprint, Cambridge: MIT Press, 1965.

Munday, Jeremy. *Introducing Translation Studies: Theories and Applications*. 2nd ed. London: Routledge, 2008.

Muthesius, Hermann. *Das englische Haus*, 3 vols. 2nd ed. 1904–5. Reprint, Berlin: Verlag Von Ernst Wasmuth, 1908–10.

———. "Das englische Haus der Gegenwart." *Baumeister* 2 (October 1904): 6–9.

———. *Kann ich auch jetzt noch mein Haus bauen*. Munich: Bruckmann, 1920.

———. *Kleinhaus und Kleinsiedlung*. Munich: Bruckmann, 1920.

———. "Die Lage des Landhauses zur Sonne und zum Garten," parts 1–2. *Baumeister* 6 (January 1907): 1–13; (February 1907): 19–23.

———. *Landhäuser*. Munich: Bruckmann, 1912.

———. "Das sogenannte Moderne in der Architektur der Neuzeit." *Baumeister* 1 (April 1903): 79–81.

———. *Wie baue ich mein Haus*. 4th ed. Munich: Bruckmann, 1925.

Mutlu, Asım. "Asım Mutlu." In *Anılarda Mimarlık*, 48–61. İstanbul: YEM, 1995.

Naim, Ahmet. *Zonguldak Havzası (Uzun Mehmet'ten Bugüne)*. İstanbul: Hüsnü Tabiat Matbaası, 1934.
Namık, Nusret. "Yapı kooperatifleri." *Karınca* (March 1936): 140–48.
Nasır, Ayşe. "Ankara'nın imarı ve Almanca konuşulan ülkelerden gelen mimarlar." *Arredamento Dekorasyon*, no. 7–8 (1997): 73–78.
Navoro-Yaşın, Yael. "Evde Taylorizm: Türkiye Cumhuriyeti'nin ilk yıllarında evişinin rasyonelleşmesi (1928–1940)." *Toplum Bilim* 84 (Spring 2000): 51–74.
Nerdinger, Winfried, Kristina Hartmann, Matthias Schirren, and Manfred Speidel, eds. *Bruno Taut: Architekt zwischen Tradition und Avantgarde*. Stuttgart: Deutsche Verlags-Anstalt, 2001.
"Neue Bauten von Ernst Egli." *Baumeister* 1, no. 2 (February 1936): 68–71.
"Neuere Bauten von Arch. Dr. Ing. Hermann Muthesius." *Baumeister* (April–May 1920): 13–20.
"Die Neue Gehag-Siedlung in Berlin." *Wohnungswirtschaft* 7 (August 1, 1930): 269–71.
Neufert, Ernst. *Bauentwurfslehre*. Berlin: Bauwelt, 1936.
Neumark, Fritz. *Boğaziçine Sığınanlar: Türkiye'ye İltica Eden Alman İlim Siyaset ve Sanat Adamları 1933–1953*. Translated by Şefik Alp Bahadır. İstanbul: İstanbul Üniversitesi İktisat Fakültesi Maliye Enstitüsü Yayını, 1982.
———, ed. *Komün Bilgisinin Esas Meseleleri*. İstanbul: Cumhuriyet Matbaasi, 1936.
———. *Zuflucht am Bosporus: Deutsche Gelehrte, Politiker und Künstler in der Emigration 1933–1953*. Frankfurt: Josef Knecht, 1980.
Neumeyer, Fritz. *The Artless Word: Mies van der Rohe on the Building Art*. Cambridge: MIT Press, 1991.
Nicolai, Bernd. "Bruno Taut's Akademiereform und sein Weg zu einer neuen Architektur für die Türkei." In *Atatürk için Düşünmek. İki Eser: Katafalk ve Anıtkabir. İki Mimar: Bruno Taut and Emin Onat*, 37–43. İstanbul: Milli Reasürans T.A.Ş., 1997.
———. "Ernst Egli and the Emergence of Modern Architecture in Kemalist Turkey," edited by Esra Akcan, "Intertwined Histories: Turkey and Central Europe." Special Issue, *Centropa* 7, no. 2 (May 2007): 153–62.
———. *Moderne und Exil: Deutschsprachige Architekten in der Türkei 1925–1955*. Berlin: Bauwesen, 1998.
Nicolson, Harold. "The Charm of Berlin." 1932. Reprinted in *The Weimar Republic Sourcebook*, edited by Anton Kaes, Martin Jay, and Edward Dimendberg, 425–26. Berkeley: University of California Press, 1994.
Nida, Eugene. "Principles of Correspondence." In *The Translation Studies Reader*, edited by Lawrence Venuti, 126–40. New York: Routledge, 2000.
———. "Principles of Translation as Exemplified in Bible Translating." In *On Translation*, edited by Reuben A. Brower, 11–32. New York: Oxford University Press, 1959.
Nippa, Annegret, ed. *Bruno Taut in Magdeburg: Eine Dokumentation*. Magdeburg, Germany: Landeshauptstadt Magdeburg, 1995.
Niranjana, Tejaswini. *Siting Translation: History, Post-Structuralism and the Colonial Context*. Berkeley: University of California Press, 1992.
Nolan, Mary. "Housework Made Easy: The Taylorized Housewife in Weimar

Germany's Rationalized Economy." *Feminist Studies* 16, no. 3 (Autumn 1990): 549–77.
Nussbaum, Martha. "Patriotism and Cosmopolitanism." In *For Love of Country*, edited by Joshua Cohen, 3–17. Boston: Beacon, 1996.
O'Brien, Justin. "From French to English." In *On Translation*, edited by Reuben Brower, 78–92. Cambridge: Harvard University Press, 1959.
Oelsner, Gustav. "Modern İskan Semti ve Şehircilik." Translated by Adnan Kolatan. *Arkitekt*, no. 7–8 (1946): 168–70.
———. "Şehircilik." *Arkitekt*, no. 3–4 (1945): 71–74.
Oettermann, Stephan. *The Panorama: History of a Mass Medium*. Translated by Deborah Lucas Schneider. New York: Zone, 1997.
Ölçer, Nazan, Gilbert Beaugé, Engin Çizgen, and François Neuville. *Images d'Empire*. Translated by Yiğit Bener. İstanbul: İstanbul Fransız Kültür Merkezi, 1993.
Öner, Işın Bengi. *Çeviri Bir Süreçtir . . . Ya Çeviribilim?* İstanbul: Sel Yayıncılık, 1999.
Önsoy, Rıfat. *Türk-Alman İktisadi Münasebetleri (1871–1914)*. İstanbul: Enderun Kitabevi, 1982.
———. *Türkiye'deki Almanya*. İstanbul: Atlas Yayınları, 2004.
Oran, Sabri. "Büyük Şehirci Mimar Martin Wagner'in Ölümü." *Arkitekt*, no. 287 (1957): 82–83.
Ortaylı, İlber. "19. yüzyılda Ankara." In *Ankara Ankara*, edited by Enis Batur, 109–19. İstanbul: Yapı Kredi Yayınları, 1994.
———. *Osmanlı İmparatorluğunda Alman Nüfusu*. İstanbul: Kaynak Yayınları, 1983.
Otto, Adolf. "Gartenstadtbewegung." *Tat* (1914–15): 110.
———. "Das Wohnungswesen in England." *Gartenstadt* 7, no. 3 (1913): 49–53.
Özer, Bülent. "Casa del Anima/A House of the Soul." *Domus*, no. 611 (1980): 28.
Özgüldür, Yavuz. *Türk-Alman İlişkileri*. Ankara: Genelkurmay Basımevi, 1993.
Özkan, Süha. "Türk-Alman Dostluk Yurdu Öneri Yarışması, 1916." *ODTÜ Mimarlık Fakültesi Dergisi* 1, no. 2 (1975): 177–210.
Özkan, Süha, Mete Turan, and Okan Üstünkök. "Institutionalised Architecture, Vernacular Architecture and Vernacularism in Historical Perspective." *METU Journal of the Faculty of Architecture* 5, no. 2 (Fall 1979): 127–55.
Özkan, Süha, and Yıldırım Yavuz. "Finding a National Idiom: The First National Style." In *Modern Turkish Architecture*, edited by Renata Holod and Ahmet Evin, 51–67. Philadelphia: University of Pennsylvania Press, 1984.
Paker, Saliha. "A Historical Perspective on the Diversity of Discourses in Turkish as a Target Language." In *Hommage to Hasan Ali Yücel Anma Kitabı*, edited by Hasan Anamur, 47–55. İstanbul: Yıldız Teknik Üniversitesi, 1997.
Pamuk, Orhan. *İstanbul: Hatıralar ve Şehir*. İstanbul: Yapı Kredi Yayınları, 2003.
Paz, Octavio. "Translation, Literature and Letters." Translated by Irene del Corral. In *Theories of Translation: An Anthology of Essays from Dryden to Derrida*, edited by Rainer Schulte and John Biguenet. Chicago: University of Chicago Press, 1992.
Pektaş, Mihri. "Turkish Women." *La Turquie Kemaliste* 32–40 (August 1939–December 1940): 10–14.

Pensky, Max. *Melancholy Dialectics: Walter Benjamin and the Play of Mourning.* Amherst: University of Massachusetts Press, 1993.

Perez, Nissan N. *Focus East: Early Photography in the Near East 1839–1885.* New York: Harry N. Abrams, 1988.

Pevsner, Nikolaus. *Pioneers of the Modern Movement from William Morris to Walter Gropius.* New York: F. A. Stokes, 1937.

Pinon, Pierre, and Cana Bilsel, eds. *From the Imperial Capital to the Republican Modern City: Henri Prost's Planning of Istanbul 1936–1951.* İstanbul: İstanbul Araştırmaları Enstitüsü, 2010.

Poelzig, Hans. "The Architect." 1931. Reprinted in Julius Posener, *Hans Poelzig: Reflections on His Life and Work*, edited by Kristin Feireiss, 188–96. Cambridge: MIT Press, 1992.

———. "Vom Bauen unserer Zeit." *Form*, no. 1 (1922): 16–29.

Poelzig und seine Schule. Ausstellung Veranstaltet von der Preussischen Akademie der Künste zu Berlin. Berlin: Ernst Wasmuth Verlag, 1931.

Pollock, Sheldon. "Cosmopolitan and Vernacular History." In *Cosmopolitanism*, edited by Sheldon Pollock, Homi Bhabha, Carol Breckenridge, Dipesh Chakrabarty, 15–53. Durham: Duke University Press, 2002.

Pollock, Sheldon, Homi Bhabha, Carol Breckenridge, and Dipesh Chakrabarty, eds. *Cosmopolitanism.* Durham: Duke University Press, 2002.

Pommer, Richard. "The Flat Roof: A Modernist Controversy in Germany." *Art Journal* 43, no. 2 (Summer 1983): 158–69.

Pommer, Richard, and Christian Otto. *Weisenhof 1927 and the Modern Movement in Architecture.* Chicago: University of Chicago Press, 1991.

Posener, Julius. *Berlin auf dem Wege zu einer neuen Architektur.* Munich: Prestel, 1979.

———. "Hans Poelzig and Heinrich Tessenow at the Technische Hochschule, Berlin-Charlottenburg." *Lotus* 16 (September 1977): 20–25.

———. *Hans Poelzig: Reflections on His Life and Work*, edited by Kristin Feireiss. Cambridge: MIT Press, 1992.

"Das Präsidenten-Palais in Ankara." *Innendekoration* 43 (1932): 409–25.

Pratt, Mary Louise. *Imperial Eyes: Travel Writing and Transculturation.* New York: Routledge, 1992.

"Die preisgekrönten Wettbewerbsentwürfe für die Kleinhaussiedlung Friesland in Emden." *Der Städtebau* 14, no. 1 (1917): 4–7, Pl. 1–3.

Prinz, Regina. "Bruno Taut als Stadtbaurat in Magdeburg 1921 bis 1923." In *Bruno Taut: Architekt zwischen Tradition und Avantgarde*, edited by Winfried Nerdinger, Kristina Hartmann, Matthias Schirren, and Manfred Speidel, 114–36. Stuttgart: Deutsche Verlags-Anstalt, 2001.

Prost, Henri. *Istanbul'un Yeni Çehresi.* İstanbul: n.p., 1950.

Radden, Jennifer, ed. *The Nature of Melancholy.* New York: Oxford University Press, 2000.

Ranck, Christoph. *Kulturgeschichte des deutschen Bauernhauses.* Leipzig: B. G. Teubner, 1907.

Rauchbach, Wolfgang. "Der Gedanke einer inneren Kolonisation: Betrachtungen zum 100; Todestag von Victor Aime Huber." *Bauwelt* 60, no. 38–39 (September 1969): 212–15.

Read, James, and Nicholas Bullock. *The Movement for Housing Reform in Germany and France, 1840–1914*. Cambridge: Cambridge University Press, 1985.

"Der Rest. Die Finanzgrundlagen für ein Wohnungsbauprogram." *Wohnungswirtschaft* 2 (March 15, 1925): 41–44.

Reuter, Edzard. *Schein und Wirklichkeit: Erinnerungen*. Berlin: Wolf Jobst Siedler, 1998.

Reuter, Ernst. "Beledi Vakıfların Modern Şehir İdaresindeki Ehemmiyetleri." Translated by Coşkun Üçok. *İktisat Fakültesi Mecmuası* 3, no. 3–4 (1942): 1–15.

———. "Belediye Meclisleri Azalarının Hak ve Selahiyetleri." *Arkitekt*, no. 3–4 (1943): 86–90.

———. "Belediye Reisliği." Translated by Adnan Kolatan. *Arkitekt*, no. 7–8 (1943): 174–78.

———. "Belediye Yapı İşlerine Luzumlu Paranın Temini." Translated by Adnan Kolatan. *Arkitekt*, no. 9–10 (1943): 216–19.

———. "Belediyeler Bankası Faaliyeti." *Belediyeler Dergisi* 6, no. 69 (1941): 7–10.

———. "Belediyeler İstatistiği." *Belediyeler Dergisi* 6, no. 69 (1941): 31–35.

———. "Belediyelerin Yapı İşletmeleri." Translated by Adnan Kolatan. *Arkitekt*, no. 1–2 (1943): 27–32.

———. "Gayri Menkullerin Üzerine Kredi Meselesi." *Arkitekt*, no. 7–8 (1945): 179–82.

———. "İçme Sularının Satışında Esaslar." *Belediyeler Dergisi* 6, no. 63 (1941): 16–19.

———. "Kasabalarımız." Translated by Adnan Kolatan. *Arkitekt*, no. 5–6 (1943): 121–26.

———. *Komün Bigisi: Şehirciliğe Giriş*. Translated by Niyazi Çıtakoğlu. Ankara: Bekir Sıtkı Baykal, 1940.

———. "Köylerimizde ne gibi Şehircilik İşleri Yapılabilir?" *Belediyeler Dergisi* 6, no. 66 (1941): 9–13.

———. "Küçük Belediyeler Meselesi," parts 1–2. Translated by Adnan Kolatan. *Arkitekt*, no. 9–10 (1944): 233–36; no. 3–4 (1945): 75–78, 90.

———. *Mesken Meselesinin Hal Çareleri*. Ankara: Klişecilik ve Matbaacılık, 1946.

———. "Mustacel bir vazife: Endüstri amelesinin meskenlere yerleştirilmesi." *Belediyeler Dergisi* 6, no. 65 (1941): 8–12.

———. "Şehir Planında İktisadi Kaideler." *Belediyeler Dergisi* 6, no. 64 (1941): 19–27.

———. "Şehirlerimizin Gelişme Problemleri." Translated by Bekir Sıtkı Baykal. *Ankara Üniversitesi Dil Tarih Coğrafya Fakültesi Dergisi*, no. 5 (1943): 149–63.

———. "Die Selbstverwaltung in der Türkei." *La Turquie Kemaliste* 47 (1947): 7–18.

———. "Teknik, Güzel Sanatlar ve Şehirlerin İdaresi." *Arkitekt*, no. 11–12 (1941–42): 265–67.

———. "Türk Dilinde Bibliografya." *Belediyeler Dergisi* 6, no. 70 (August 1941): 14–29.

———. "Vilayet Hususi İdarelerin İstatistiği." *Belediyeler Dergisi* 6, no. 70 (1941): 10–14.

"Richtlinien der Gewerkschaften für ein Wohnungsbauprogram." *Wohnungswirtschaft* 3 (November 15, 1926): 181–85.

Rigele, Georg, and Georg Loewit. *Clemens Holzmeister*. Innsbruck, Austria: Haymon, 2000.

Robbins, Bruce. "Introduction: Part I: Actually Existing Cosmopolitanism." In *Cosmopolitics: Thinking and Feeling beyond the Nation*, edited by Pheng Cheah and Bruce Robbins, 1–19. Minneapolis: University of Minnesota Press, 1998.

Roberts, Mary. *Intimate Outsiders: The Harem in Ottoman and Orientalist Art and Travel Literature*. Durham: Duke University Press, 2007.

Robertson, Howard. "Two Villas for Kemal Atatürk and His Sister." *Architect and Building News* 133 (March 1938): 362–64.

Robinson, Douglas. *Translation and Empire: Postcolonial Theories Explained*. Manchester, England: St. Jerome, 1997.

———, ed. *Western Translation Theory: From Herodotus to Nietzsche*. Manchester, England: St. Jerome, 1997.

Rodriguez-Lores, Juan. *Sozialer Wohnungsbau in Europa. Die Ursprünge bis 1918*. Basel: Birkhäuser, 1994.

Rona, Zeynep, ed., *Bilanço 1923–1998*. İstanbul: Tarih Vakfı, 1999.

Roser, Matthias. *Paul Bonatz: Wohnhäuser*. Stuttgart: G. Hatje, 1992.

Rossi, Aldo. *L'architettura della città*. Padova: Marsilio, 1966.

Rühle, H. "Das Wochenendhaus," parts 1–2. *Der Neubau* 9, no. 2 (1927): 4–12; no. 7 (1927): 73–87.

Rüstem, Semih. "Bir Mimar İkametgahı." *Mimar*, no. 4 (1932): 108–11.

———. "Şevket Bey Evi." *Mimar*, no. 4 (1933): 99–103.

Safa, Peyami. "Bizde ve Avrupa'da Kübik." *Yedigün*, no. 188 (1936): 7–8.

Şahabettin, Ş. "Şehir Mimarisinde Usuller." *Mimar*, no. 3 (1933): 65–70.

Said, Edward. *Orientalism*. New York: Vintage, 1978.

———. "Secular Criticism." In Edward Said, *The World, the Text, and the Critic*, 1–30. Cambridge: Harvard University Press, 1983.

Sarıkoyuncu, Ali. *Milli Mücadele'de Zonguldak ve Havalisi*. Ankara: Başbakanlık Basımevi, 1992.

Säume, Max. "Hermann Jansens neue Platzgestaltungen." *Städtebau* 22 (May–August 1925): 114–15.

Sayar, Zeki. "Ev Projesi." *Mimar*, no. 2 (1932): 78–79.

———. "Güzel Sanatlar Akademisinin Yanışı Münasebetiyle." *Arkitekt*, no. 3–4 (1948): 53–54, 58.

———. "İç kolonizasyon," parts 1–2. *Arkitekt*, no. 2 (1936): 46–51; no. 8 (1936): 231–35.

———. "İnşaatta Standard." *Mimar*, no. 1 (1931): 10–11.

———. "Kalamış'ta Bir Villa." *Arkitekt*, no. 2 (1937): 33–41.

———. "Kalamış'ta Bir Villa." *Arkitekt*, no. 5–6 (1936): 129–32.

———. "Mesken Davası," parts 1–2. *Arkitekt*, no. 3–4 (1946): 49–51; no. 7–8 (1946): 149–50.

———. "Mimarlık ve Politikamız." *Arkitekt*, no. 1–2 (1946): 3–4.

———. "Müşterek İkametgahlar." *Mimar*, no. 3 (1931): 97–99.

———. "Saraçoğlu Mahallesi." *Arkitekt*, no. 3–4 (1946): 56–59, 86.

———. "Suadiye'de bir Villa." *Arkitekt*, no. 10-11 (1937): 269-74.
———. "Yabancı Mimar Problemi." *Arkitekt*, no. 9-10 (1946): 201-2.
Schäche, Wolfgang. *75 Jahre GEHAG*. Berlin: Gebr. Mann, 1999.
Schaefer, Carl Anton. *Deutsch-Türkische Freundschaft*. Stuttgart: Austalt, 1914.
Scheerbart, Paul. *Glass Architecture*. 1914. Translated by James Palmes. New York: Praeger, 1972.
Scheffler, Karl. *Die Architektur der Großstadt*. Berlin: B. Cassirer, 1913.
———. *Berlin. Ein Stadtschicksal*. Berlin: E. Reiss, 1910.
Schirren, Matthias. "Eine Bauhütte für Berlin: Hans Poelzig und sein Meisteratelier an der Preußischen Akademie der Künste." In *Hans Poelzig*, edited by Matthias Schirren, 21-24. Berlin: Ernst and Sohn, 1989.
———, ed. *Bruno Taut: alpine Architektur: eine Utopie = a utopia*. Munich: Prestel, 2004.
Schlegel, August Wilhelm. "The Speaking Voice of the Civilized World: From *History of Romantic Literature*." Translated by Douglas Robinson. In *Western Translation Theory: From Herodotus to Nietzsche*, edited by Douglas Robinson, 200-221. Manchester, England: St. Jerome, 1997.
Schleiermacher, Friedrich. "On the Different Methods of Translating." Translated by Waltraud Bartscht. In *Theories of Translation: An Anthology of Essays from Dryden to Derrida*, edited by Rainer Schulte and John Biguenet, 36-54. Chicago: University of Chicago Press, 1992.
Schmidt, Bruno. *Das sächsische Bauernhaus und seine Dorfgenossen*. Dresden: Holze and Pahl, 1916.
Schmitthenner, Paul. *Baukunst im neuen Reich*. Munich: Georg D. W. Callmen, 1934.
Schollmeier, Axel. *Gartenstädte in Deutschland*. Hamburg: Lit, 1988.
Schulte, Rainer, and John Biguenet, eds. *Theories of Translation: An Anthology of Essays from Dryden to Derrida*. Chicago: Chicago University Press, 1992.
Schulze, Franz. *Mies van der Rohe: A Critical Biography*. Chicago: University of Chicago Press, 1985.
Schultze-Naumburg, Paul. *Kunst und Rasse*. Munich: J. F. Lehmanns, 1928.
Schütte, Wilhelm. "Adolf Loos." Translated by Halet Çambel. *Arkitekt*, no. 1-2 (1941): 41-45.
———. "Bugünkü Kültür ve İkametgah," parts 1-2. *Arkitekt*, no. 1-2 (1944): 28-31; no. 3-4 (1944): 66-70.
———. "Büyük Şehirlerin İnkişaf Meselesi." *Arkitekt*, no. 9-10 (1940): 211-13.
———. "Karl Friedrich Schinkel Bugün Bizlere Ne İfade Eder?" Translated by Adnan Kolatan. *Arkitekt*, no. 3-4 (1943): 131-35.
———. "Mimar Yetiştirimi." Translated by Halet Çambel. *Arkitekt*, no. 11-12 (1943): 258-60.
———. "Sefalet Mahalleleri." Translated by Adnan Kolatan. *Arkitekt*, no. 3-4 (1941-42): 78-86.
———. "Th. Fischer ve Proporsiyonlar." *Arkitekt*, no. 9-10 (1940): 224-25.
———. "Yer Depremleri Hakkında Yeni Araştırmalar." Translated by Adnan Kolatan. *Arkitekt*, no. 9-10 (1943): 211-15.
———. "Zelzele Sahalarının Yeniden İmarı Hakkında Düşünceler." *Arkitekt*, no. 3-4 (1940): 75-87.

Schütte-Lihotzky, Margarete. "Einiges über die Einrichtung östereichischer Häuser unter besonderer Berücksichtigung der Siedlungsbauten." *Schlesisches Heim*, no. 8 (1921): 217.

———. *Erinnerungen aus dem Widerstand*. Vienna: Promedia Druck, 1994.

———. "Die Frankfurter Küche." In *Die Frankfurter Küche von Margarete Schütte-Lihotzky*, edited by Peter Noever, 7–15. Berlin: Ernst and Sohn, 1992.

———. "Neue Frankfurter Schul- und Lehrkuchen." *Das Neue Frankfurt*, no. 1 (1929):18–21.

———. "Rationalisierung im Haushalt." *Das Neue Frankfurt*, no. 5 (1926–27): 120–23.

———. "Die Siedlerhütte." *Schlesisches Heim*, no. 2 (1922): 33–35.

———. "Die Siedlungs- Wohnungs- und Baugilde Österreichs auf der 4. Wiener Kleingartenaustellung." *Schlesisches Heim*, no. 10 (1922): 245–47.

———. "Das vorgebaute raumangepasste Möbel." *Schlesisches Heim*, no. 6 (1926): 294–97.

———. "Wiener Kleingarten- und Siedlerhütten-Aktion." *Schlesisches Heim*, no. 4 (1923): 83–85.

Schwartz, Frederic J. *The Werkbund*. New Haven: Yale University Press, 1996.

Schwartz, Philipp. *Kader Birliği: 1933 Sonrası Göç Eden Alman Bilim Adamları*. Translated by Nagehan Alçı. İstanbul: Belge Yayıncılık, 2003.

———. *Notgemeinschaft: Zur Emigration deutscher Wissenschaftler nach 1933 in die Türkei*, edited by Helge Peukert. Marburg, Germany: Metropolis, 1995.

Şenyapılı, Tansı. "Cumhuriyet'in Dokuduğu Kent Ankara." *Arredamento Dekorasyon* 90, no. 3 (1997): 83–88.

Serdengeçti, Ali Suat. "Yanan 'Milli Mimari' Röleveleri Arşini'nde Neler Vardı?" *Mimarlık*, no. 4 (1948): 14–16.

Sey, Yıldız. *Yetmişbeş Yılda Değişen Kent ve Mimarlık*. İstanbul: Tarih Vakfı, 1998.

Shaw, Stanford J. *Turkey and the Holocaust: Turkey's Role in Rescuing Turkish and European Jewry from Nazi Persecution*. London: Macmillan, 1993.

"Siedlungswirtschaft." *Wohnungswirtschaft* 1 (August 1, 1924): 85–88.

Simon, Sherry. *Gender in Translation: Cultural Identity and the Politics of Transmission*. New York: Routledge, 1996.

———. "Translating and Interlingual Creation in the Contact Zone." In *Post-Colonial Translation: Theory and Practice*, edited by Susan Bassnett and Harish Trivedi, 58–74. London: Routledge, 1999.

Simons, Gustav. *Die Deutsche Gartenstadt*. Wittenberg: Ziemfen, 1912.

Sırrı, Nahit. "Kanlıcanın Bir Yalısında," parts 1–3. *Varlık* 1 (July 15, 1933): 11–12; 2 (August 1, 1933): 29; 7 (October 15, 1933): 111–12.

Sonne, Wolfgang. "Ideen für die Großstadt: Der Wettbewerb Groß Berlin 1910." In *Architektur der Stadt*, edited by Thorsten Scheer, Josef Paul Kleihues, and Paul Kahlfeldt, 67–77. Berlin: Nicolai, 2000.

Söylemezoğlu, Kemali. "Kemali Söylemezoğlu." In *Anılarda Mimarlık*, 114–42. İstanbul: YEM, 1995.

Sözen, Metin. *Cumhuriyet Dönemi Türk Mimarlığı*. Ankara: Türkiye İş Bankası Yayınları, 1973.

Sözen, Metin, and Mete Tapan. *Elli Yılın Türk Mimarisi*. İstanbul: Türkiye İş Bankası Yayınları, 1973.

"Sparbaumethoden beim Wochenendhaus," parts 1–3. *Die Baugilde*, no. 10 (1927): 540–48; no. 11 (1927): 598–608; no. 13 (1927): 720–28.

Speer, Albert. Introduction to *Neue deutsche Baukunst—Yeni Alman Mimarisi*. Berlin: Volk und Reich, 1942.

Speidel, Manfred. "Bruno Taut: Wirken und Wirkung." In *Atatürk için Düşünmek. İki Eser: Katafalk ve Anıtkabir. İki Mimar: Bruno Taut and Emin Onat*, 54–62. İstanbul: Milli Reasürans T.A.Ş., 1997.

———. "Nachwort." In *Die Stadtkrone* by Bruno Taut with Paul Scheerbart, Erich Baron, and Adolf Behne, 1919, 1–42. Berlin: Gebrag Mann, 2002.

———. "Natürlichkeit und Freiheit: Bruno Tauts Bauten in der Türkei." In *Ankara 1923–50: Bir Başkentin Oluşumu*, 52–65. Ankara: TMMOB Mimarlar Odası, 1994.

———. *Natur und Fantasie 1880–1938*. Berlin: Ernst & Sohn, 1995.

———. "Was ist Architektur? Bruno Tauts 'Architekturlehre.'" *Arch + 194* (October 2009): 160–65.

Spivak, Gayatri Chakravorty. "Can the Subaltern Speak?" In *Marxism and the Interpretation of Culture*, edited by Cary Nelson and Lawrence Grossberg, 271–313. Urbana: University of Illinois Press, 1988.

———. "The Politics of Translation." In Gayatri Chakravorty Spivak, *Outside in the Teaching Machine*, 179–200. New York: Routledge, 1993.

Stapel, Wilhelm. "The Intellectual and His People." Translated by Don Reneau. In *The Weimar Republic Sourcebook*, edited by Anton Kaes, Martin Jay, and Edward Dimendberg, 423–25. Berkeley: University of California Press, 1994.

Stein, Georg. "Wochendhäuser auf der Ausstellung 'Das Wochenende,' Berlin." *Der Neubau*, no. 9 (1927): 101–3.

Steiner, George. *After Babel: Aspects of Language and Translation*. 3rd ed. Oxford: Oxford University Press, 1998.

Stimmann, Hans, ed. *Gartenstadt am Falkenberg*. Berlin: Senatsverwaltung für Bau und Wohnungswesen, 1993.

Strzygowski, Josef. *Altai-Iran und Völkerwanderung*. Leipzig: J. C. Hinrich, 1917.

Tafuri, Manfredo. *Architecture and Utopia: Design and Capitalist Development*. Translated by Barbara Luigia La Penta. Cambridge: MIT Press, 1976.

———. "Sozialpolitik and City in Weimar Germany." 1971. In Manfredo Tafuri, *The Sphere and the Labyrinth*. Translated by Pellegrino d'Acierno and Robert Connolly, 197–233. Cambridge: MIT Press, 1987.

———. "Toward a Critique of Architectural Ideology." 1969. Translated by Stephen Sartarelli. In *Architecture Theory since 1968*, edited by Michael Hays, 6–35. Cambridge: MIT Press, 1998.

Tafuri, Manfredo, and Francesco dal Co. *Modern Architecture*. Translated by Robert Erich Wolf. New York: Electa/Rizzoli, 1986.

Tamms, Friedrich. *Paul Bonatz: Arbeiten aud den Jahren 1907 bis 1937*. Stuttgart: Julius Hoffmann, 1937.

Tanju, Bülent. "Türkiye'de Farklı bir Mimar: Bruno Taut." In *Atatürk için Düşünmek. İki Eser: Katafalk ve Anıtkabir. İki Mimar: Bruno Taut and Emin Onat*, 22–26. İstanbul: Milli Reasürans T.A.Ş., 1997.

Tankut, Gönül. "Ankara'nın Başkent Olma Süreci." *METU Faculty of Architecture Journal* 8, no. 2 (1988): 93–104.

———. *Bir Başkentin İmarı: Ankara (1929-1939)*. Ankara: Orta Doğu Teknik Üniversitesi, 1990.
Tanpınar, Ahmet Hamdi. *Beş Şehir*. 1945. Reprint, İstanbul: MEB Yayınları, 1992.
———. "İstanbul," parts 1-3. *Ülkü* 13, no. 92 (July 1945): 9-13; no. 93 (August 1, 1945): 10-16; no. 94 (August 15, 1945): 10-13.
———. *Mahur Beste*. 1944. Reprint, İstanbul: Nurettin Uycan Baskı Evi, 1975.
Tanrıöver, Hamdullah Suphi. "Eski Türk Evleri." *Türk Yurdu*, no. 5 (1912): 1216-21.
Tanyeli, Uğur. *Mimarlığın Aktörleri. Türkiye 1900-2000*. İstanbul: Garanti Galeri, 2007.
———."Seyfi Arkan: Bir Direnme Öyküsü." *Arredamento Dekorasyon* 35, no. 3 (1992): 88-95.
———. "Türkiye'de Modernleşme ve Vernaküler Mimari Gelenek." In *Bilanço 1923-1998*, edited by Zeynep Rona, 283-90. İstanbul: Tarih Vakfı Yayınları, 1999.
Tanyeli, Uğur, and Bülent Tanju, eds. *Sedad Eldem*, vols. I-II. İstanbul: Osmanlı Bankası Arşiv ve Araştırma Merkezi, 2009.
Taut, Bruno. *Alpine Architektur*. Hagen, Germany: Folkwang, 1919.
———. "Ansprache zur Eröffnung der Taut—Ausstellung in Istanbul am 4.6.1938." In *Bruno Taut 1880-1938*, edited by Barbara Volkmann, 260. Berlin: Akademie der Künste, 1980.
———. "Ein Architektur Programm." *Mitteilungen des Deutschen Werkbund*, no. 4 (1918): 16-18.
———. *Architekturlehre*. Edited by Tilmann Heinisch and Goerd Peschken. Hamburg: VSA, 1977.
———. "Architekturlehre." *Arch + 194* (October 2009): 36-157.
———. *Die Auflösung der Städte, oder Die Erde eine gute Wohnung, oder auch Der Weg zur Alpinen Architektur*. Hagen, Germany: Folkwang Verlag, 1920.
———. "The Earth Is a Good Dwelling." 1919. Translated by Don Reneau. In *The Weimar Republic Sourcebook*, edited by Anton Kaes, Martin Jay, and Edward Dimendberg, 456-59. Berkeley: University of California Press, 1994.
———. "Die Erde eine gute Wohnung." *Volkswohnung* 1, no. 4 (February 24, 1919): 43-48.
———. "Erklärung zur Siedlung der 'GEHAG' in Zehlendorf." *Baugilde*, no. 8 (1926): 1017.
———. "*Ex Oriente Lux*: Call to Architects." 1919. Reprinted in *Form and Function*, edited by Tim and Charlotte Benton, 81-82. London: Crosby Lockwood Staples, 1975.
———. "Forschung-Siedlung Berlin-Spandau-Haselhorst." *Wohnungswirtschaft* 7 (August 1, 1930): 275-77.
———. *Fundamentals of Japanese Architecture*. Tokyo: Kokusai Bunka Shinkokai, 1935.
———. "Gegen den Strom." *Wohnungswirschaft* 7 (September 1, 1930): 315-24.
———. "Genossenschaftsarchitektur." *Wohnungswirtschaft* 3 (January 15, 1926): 12-14.
———."Grundrißfrage." *Wohnungswirtschaft* 5 (November 15, 1928): 311-17.

———. *Houses and People of Japan*. Translated by Estille Balk. 2nd ed. Tokyo: Sanseido, 1958.

———. "Houses and People of Japan." Reprint of the chapter "What Now?" from *Houses and People of Japan*. *Daidalos* 54 (December 1994): 62–73.

———. *Das japanische Haus und sein Leben*. 1937. Edited by Manfred Speidel. Berlin: Gebr. Mann, 1997.

———. *Japans Kunst*. Tokyo: Meiji Shobo, 1936.

———. *Mimari Bilgisi*. Translated by Adnan Kolatan. İstanbul: Güzel Sanatlar Akademisi, 1938.

———. *Modern Architecture*. London: Studio Limited, 1929.

———. "Neue und Alte Form im Bebauungsplan." *Wohnungswirtschaft* 3 (December 15, 1926): 199.

———. *Die Neue Wohnung: Die Frau als Schöpferin*. 2nd ed. Leipzig: Klinkhardt and Biermann, 1928.

———. "A Program for Architecture." 1918. Translated by Michael Bullock. In *The Weimar Republic Sourcebook*, edited by Anton Kaes, Martin Jay, and Edward Dimendberg, 432–34. Berkeley: University of California Press, 1994.

———. "Siedlungsmemorien." In *Bruno Taut 1880–1938*, edited by Barbara Volkmann, 204–11. 1936. Berlin: Akademie der Künste, 1980.

———. *Die Stadtkrone*. With Paul Scheerbart, Erich Baron, and Adolf Behne. Jena, Germany: Eugen Diederichs, 1919.

———. "Tip ve Sıra Evler." *Arkitekt*, no. 7 (1937): 211–18.

———. "Türk Evi, Sinan, Ankara." *Her Ay*, no. 2 (1938): 93–94.

———. "Über Arbeitsgemeinschaften bei Berliner Wohnungsbauten." *Wohnungswirtschaft* 7 (January 3, 1930): 3–4.

———. "Von der architektonischen Schönheit des Serienbaues." *Aufbau* 1, no. 7 (August 1926): 106.

———. "Was ist die Groß-Siedlung und welche Bedeutung hat sie für die Gartenstadtbewegung." *Gartenstadt*, no. 1–2 (1931): 7–11.

———. *Ein Wohnhaus*. Berlin: Gebr. Mann, 1929.

———. "Wohnstadt Carl Legien." EINFA *Nachrichtenblatt*, no. 2 (1930): 30.

Taylor, Robert R. *The Word in Stone: The Role of Architecture in the National Socialist Ideology*. Berkeley: University of California Press, 1974.

Tekeli, İlhan. *The Development of the Istanbul Metropolitan Area: Urban Administration and Planning*. İstanbul: International Union of Local Authorities, 1994.

———. *Türkiye'de Yaşamda ve Yazında Konut Sorununun Gelişimi*. Ankara: Toplu Konut İdaresi Başkanlığı, 1996.

———. "Türkiye'de Cumhuriyet Döneminde Kentsel Gelişme ve Kent Planlaması." In *75 Yılda Değişen Kent ve Mimarlık*, edited by Yıldız Sey, 1–24. İstanbul: Tarih Vakfı, 1998.

Tekeli, İlhan, and Selim İlkin. *Bahçelievlerin Öyküsü*. Ankara: Kent Koop, 1984.

Tekin, Şinasi and Gönül Alpay Tekin, eds. "Imperial Self-Portrait. The Ottoman Empire as Revealed in the Sultan Abdulhamid II's Photographic Albums." Special Issue, *Journal of Turkish Studies* 12 (1988).

Tessenow, Heinrich. *Hausbau und dergleichen* 1916. Baden: Woldemar Klein, 1953.

———. *Gedenken eines Baumeisters*, edited by Otto Kindt. Braunschweig/Wiesbaden: Friedr. Vieweg&Sohn, 1982.
Texier, Charles. *Asie Mineure*. Paris: Firmin Didot, 1882.
Thiekötter, Angelika. *Kristallisationen, Splitterungen: Bruno Tauts Glashaus*. Basel: Birkhäuser, 1993.
Thoma, Hans. "Kultur und Gartenstadt." In *Die Deutsche Gartenstadtbewegung*, 97-99. Berlin: Deutschen Gartenstadt-Gesellschaft, 1911.
Tönnies, Ferdinand. *Community and Society*. Translated by Charles Loomis. East Lansing: Michigan State University, 1957.
Topçubaşı, Alaettin Cemil. "Yapı Kooperatifleri ve Ucuz Ev," parts 1-2. *Karınca* 3 (March 1936): 4-5; (June 1936): 33.
Trumpener, Ulrich. *Germany and the Ottoman Empire*. Princeton: Princeton University Press, 1968.
Tümer, Gürhan. *Cumhuriyet Döneminde Yabancı Mimar Sorunu*. İzmir: Mimarlar Odası Yayınları, 1998.
Tuncer, Kadir. *Tarihten Günümüze Zonguldak'ta İşçi Sınıfının Durumu*. İstanbul: Göçebe Yayınları, 1998.
Turan, Kemal. *Türk-Alman Eğitim İlişkilerinin Tarihi Gelişimi*. İstanbul: Ayışığı Kitapları, 2000.
Türk Evi ve Biz. İstanbul: Türkiye Tarihi Evleri Koruma Derneği, 1993.
"Türk Mimarları Ne İstiyorlar?" *Yapı*, no. 21 (1942): 3.
"Türkiye'de ne kadar yapı kooperatifi var?" *Arkitekt*, no. 9-10 (1952): 181.
Uçar, Bedri. "Büyük Davamız." *Mimarlık*, no. 2 (1944): 1, 4.
———. "Mimarlığımızı Yaşatalım, Mimarlığımızı Tanıtalım." *Mimarlık*, no. 1 (1944): 2.
Ülken, Hilmi Ziya. *Uyanış Devirlerinde Tercümenin Rolü*. İstanbul: Vakit Gazete ve Matbaa, 1935.
"Ulus'un Anketi. Ankara'da Mesken Meselesini Nasil Halledebiliriz?" *Karınca* (March 1936): 4-163.
Ünsal, Behçet. "Bahçe İçinde Küçük bir Ev." *Yapı* (February 1, 1942): 10-11.
———. "Eminönü Halkevinde Açılan Alman Mimari Sergisi Dolayısıyla: Yeni Bir Mimariye Doğru," parts 1-3. *Yapı* 2, no. 43-44 (1943); 4, no. 45 (1943); 4, no. 48-49 (1943): 4-5.
———. "Halk İçin Evler." *Yapı* 1, no. 19 (1942): 7.
———. "Kübik Yapı ve Konfor." *Arkitekt*, no. 3-4 (1939): 60-62.
———. "Zamanımız mimarlığının morfolojik analizi," parts 1-2. *Arkitekt*, no. 7 (1937): 201-4; no. 8 (1937): 219-22.
Ünsal, Behçet, and Bedrettin Hamdi. "Mimarlıkta Inkılap." *Mimar*, no. 8 (1933): 245-47.
———. "Mimarlık ve Türklük." *Mimar*, no. 1 (1934): 18-20.
———. "Türk Inkılap Mimarisi." *Mimar*, no. 9-10 (1933): 265.
"Unsere Wohnungsfürsorgebewegung." *Wohnungswirtschaft* 2 (January 15, 1925): 9-11.
Ünügür, Mete. "Kültür Farklarının Mutfaklarda Mekan Gereksinmelerine Etkilerinin Saptanmasında Kullanılabilecek Ergonomik Metod." PhD diss., İstanbul Technical University, 1973.

Uzgören, Nusret. "Ankara Bahçelievler Yapı Kooperatifi Nasıl Doğdu?" *Karınca* (November 1936): 39–43.

———. "Ucuz Otru Kooperatifleri ve Şehircilik." *Belediyeler Dergisi*, no. 21 (1935): 33.

Vardar, A. "Başkentin İlk Planları." *Planlama*, no. 2–4 (1989): 38.

Venuti, Lawrence. *The Scandals of Translation: Towards an Ethics of Difference*. New York: Routledge, 1998.

———. "Translation, Community, Utopia." In *The Translation Studies Reader*, edited by Lawrence Venuti, 468–88. New York: Routledge, 2000.

———, ed. *The Translation Studies Reader*. New York: Routledge, 2000.

———. *The Translator's Invisibility: A History of Translation*. New York: Routledge, 1995.

"Vereinigte Selbsthilfe im Wohnungsbau." *Wohnungswirtschaft* 1 (May 15, 1924): 32–36.

Vertovec, Steven, and Robin Cohen, eds. *Conceiving Cosmopolitanism: Theory, Context, and Practice*. Oxford: Oxford University Press, 2002.

Vidler, Anthony. "The Third Typology." 1977. In *Architecture Theory since 1968*, edited by Michael Hays, 284–94. Cambridge: MIT Press, 1998.

Vieira, Else Ribeiro Pires. "Liberating Calibans: Readings of *Antropofagia* and Haroldo de Campos' Poetics of Transcreation." In *Post-Colonial Translation: Theory and Practice*, edited by Susan Bassnett and Harish Trivedi, 95–113. London: Routledge, 1999.

Vogt, Adolf Max. *Le Corbusier, the Noble Savage: Toward an Archeology of Modernism*. Translated by Radla Donnell. Cambridge: MIT Press, 1998.

Von Bischoff, Norbert. *Ankara: Eine Deutung des Neuen Werdens in der Türkei*. Vienna: A. Holzhausens, 1935.

"Von Flandern bis Liegnitz." *Wohnungswirtschaft* (January 1, 1925): 1–3.

Von Huber, Theodor. *Das deutsche Haus zur Zeit der Renaissance*. Berlin: Karl Habel, 1882.

Wagner, Martin. "Büyük Şehirler Nasıl Tadil Edilir?" parts 1–2. *Arkitekt*, no. 2 (1937): 57–58; no. 3 (1937): 71–74.

———. "Englische Gartenstädte," parts 1–2. *Wohnungswirtschaft* 2 (September 1, 1925): 136–39; (September 15, 1925): 145–47.

———. "Gross-Siedlungen. Der Weg zur Rationalisierung des Wohnungsbaues." *Wohnungswirtschaft* 3 (June 1, 1926): 81–114.

———. "Her mit den Wohnungsbauprogrammen." *Wohnungswirtschaft* 4 (January 15, 1927): 4–7.

———. "Industrie, Wohnungsbau und Baumarkt." *Wohnungswirtschaft* 2 (June 1, 1925): 85–86.

———. "İstanbul Havalisinin Planı," parts 1–2. *Arkitekt*, no. 10–11 (1936): 301–6; no. 12 (1936): 333–37.

———. "İstanbul Nufusunun Yayılışı ve Münakele." *Arkitekt*, no. 4 (1937): 112–14.

———. "İstanbul Şehrinin Düzeltilmesi Meseleleri." *Arkitekt*, no. 8 (1936): 217–18.

———. "İstanbul'un Münakele Tarihi." *Arkitekt*, no. 5–6 (1937): 143–46.

———. "İstanbul'un Seyrisefer Meselesi." *Arkitekt*, no. 9 (1936): 252–56.

———. "Jedem Deutschen eine gesunde Wohnung." *Wohnungswirtschaft* 2 (November 1, 1925): 169–71.

———. "Minimalwohnungen." *Wohnungswirtschaft* 7 (July 1, 1930): 247–50.

———. "Neue Wege." *Wohnungswirtschaft* 1 (July 15, 1924): 73–79.

———. "Neusiedlungen –Ein Wirtschaftlicher Wahnsinn." *Wohnungswirtschaft* 1 (June 1, 1924): 41–46.

———. "Die Organisation des Städtebau." *Wohnungswirtschaft* 3 (February 15, 1926): 21–27.

———. "Das Problem der reinen Gartenstadt." *Wohnungswirtschaft* 3 (October 1, 1926): 15–159.

———. "Şehir İnşasında Sermayenin Rolü." *Arkitekt*, no. 5–6 (1936): 139–41.

———. "Şehircilikte Sermayenin Yanlış İdaresi." *Arkitekt*, no. 7 (1936): 187–88.

———. "Städtebau als Wirtschaftsbau und Lebensbau." *Das Neue Frankfurt* (November 1932): 162–78.

———. "Türk Şehirleri ve Mevcut Sahalardan İstifade Ekonomisi." *Arkitekt*, no. 3 (1938): 82–86.

———. "Typ und Norm in Wohnungsbau." *Wohnungswirtschaft* 6 (February 1, 1929): 23–24.

———. "Zivilization, Kultur, Kunst." *Wohnungswirtschaft* 3 (October 20, 1926): 165–68.

Walter, Friedrich. *Das westfälische Bauernhaus*. Dortmund, Germany: Wilh. Ruhfus, 1936.

Ward, Stephen V., ed. *The Garden City: Past, Present, and Future*. London: E. and F. N. Spon, 1992.

———. "Garden City Introduced." In *The Garden City: Past, Present, and Future*, edited by Stephen Ward, 1–27. London: E. and F. N. Spon, 1992.

Watanabe, Shun-ichi. "The Japanese Garden City." In *The Garden City: Past, Present, and Future*, edited by Stephen Ward, 69–87. London: E. and F. N. Spon, 1992.

Weidle, Wladimir. "Tercüme Sanatı." Translated by B. Tuncel, *Tercüme* 1, no. 4 (1941): 25.

Weiß, Albert. "Die Garten-Wohnstadt Margaretenhöhe bei Essen." *Gartenstadt* 7, no. 10 (1913): 204–8.

"Werkbund *Siedlung*." *InnenDekoration* 43 (August 1932): 273–312.

Werner, Frank. "The Myth of the Atemporal: History of the Stuttgart Station." *Lotus* 59, no. 3 (1988): 114–32.

"Wettbewerb Gross-Berlin 1. Prize: Hermann Jansen." *Bauwelt* (May 11, 1910).

"Wettbewerbsentwürfe zur Ausgestaltung der Frankfurter Wiesen in Leipzig." *Städtebau* 9, no. 8 (1912): Pl. 45.

Whyte, Ian Boyd. *Bruno Taut and the Architecture of Activism*. Cambridge: Cambridge University Press, 1982.

Widmann, Horst. *Exil und Bildungshilfe: Die deutschsprachige akademische Emigration in die Türkei nach 1933*. Frankfurt: Peter Lang, 1973.

Wiedenhoeft, Ronald. *Berlin's Housing Revolution: German Reform in the 1920's*. Michigan: UMI Research Press, 1985.

"Wien-Berlin." *Wohnungswirtschaft* 1 (May 1, 1925): 69–71.
Wigley, Mark. *The Architecture of Deconstruction: Derrida's Haunt*. Cambridge: MIT Press, 1993.
Wilde, Hans. *Brussa: Eine Entwicklungsstätte türkischer Architektur in Kleinasien unter den Ersten Osmanen*. Berlin: Ernst Wasmuth, 1909.
Willett, John. *The New Sobriety 1917–1933: Art and Politics in the Weimar Period*. London: Thames and Hudson, 1978.
Williams, Raymond. *The Country and the City*. New York: Oxford University Press, 1973.
Wittgenstein, Ludwig. *Tractatus-Logico Philosophicus*, 1921. Translated by D. F. Pears and B. F. McGuinness, 1961. London: Routledge, 2001.
"Wochenendhäuser." *Der Neubau*, no. 2 (1928): 29–33.
"Wochenendhäuser." *Wasmuths Monatshefte für Baukunst* 11 (1927): 289–93.
"Die Wohnungspolitik der Sowjetregierung." *Wohnungswirtschaft* (January 1, 1926): 1–4.
Wolf, Michaela, and Alexandra Fukari, eds. *Constructing a Sociology of Translation*. Amsterdam: John Benjamins, 2007.
Wolf-Dohrn. "Gartenstadt Hellerau." *Gartenstadt* 3, no. 1 (1909): 5–12.
Wolfrom, Erich. *Das Bauernhaus im Magdeburger Land*. Magdeburg, Germany: Magdeburger Kultur- und Wirtschaftsleben, 1937.
Wolin, Richard. *Walter Benjamin. An Aesthetic of Redemption*. New York: Columbia University Press, 1982.
Wood, Allen W. "Kant's Project for Perpetual Peace." In *Cosmopolitics: Thinking and Feeling beyond the Nation*, edited by Pheng Cheah and Bruce Robbins, 59–76. Minneapolis: University of Minnesota Press, 1998.
Worbs, Dietrich. "Paul Bonatz–ein Konservativer Reformer?" *Architekt* (December 1992): 605–11.
Yar, Incila. "Modern Ev İdaresi: Evimizde Taylorizm." In *İzmir Cumhuriyet Kız Enstitüsü Yıllığı*, 1935–1936. İzmir: Cumhuriyet Kız Enstitüsü, 1936.
Yavuz, Erdal. "19. Yüzyıl Ankarasında Ekonomik Hayatın Örgütlenmesi ve Kent-İçi Sosyal Yapı." In *Tarih İçinde Ankara*, edited by Ayşıl Tükel Yavuz. Ankara: ODTÜ Mimarlık Fakültesi, 2000.
Yavuz, Fehmi. *Ankara'nın İmarı ve Şehirciliğimiz*. Ankara: Ankara Üniversitesi Siyasal Bilgiler Fakültesi Yayınları, 1952.
———. *Prof. Ernst Reuter*. Ankara: Sevinç Matbaası, 1968.
Yavuz, Yıldırım. "Ankara Çankaya'daki Birinci Cumhurbaşkanlığı Köşkü." In *Tarih İçinde Ankara II*, edited by Yıldırım Yavuz, 341–412. Ankara: ODTÜ Mimarlık Fakültesi, 2001.
———. "İkinci Meşrutiyet Döneminde Ulusal Mimari Üzerindeki Batı Etkileri." *ODTÜ Mimarlık Fakültesi Dergisi* 2, no. 1 (1976): 9–34.
Yılmaz, Veli. *Birinci Dünya Harbi'nde Türk-Alman İttifakı ve Askeri Yardımlar*. İstanbul: Cem Ofset Matbaacılık, 1993.
Yücel, Hasan Ali. "Giriş." *Tercüme* 1, no. 1 (1940): 1–2.
Zantop, Susanne. *Colonial Fantasies: Conquest, Family and Nation in Precolonial Germany 1770–1870*. Durham: Duke University Press, 1997.
Zöller-Stock, Bettina. *Bruno Taut: Die Innenraumentwürfe des Berliner Architekten*. Stuttgart: Deutsche Verlags-Anstalt, 1993.

Zubaida, Sami. "Middle Eastern Experiences of Cosmopolitanism." In *Conceiving Cosmopolitanism: Theory, Context, and Practice*, edited by Steven Vertovec and Robin Cohen, 32–41. Oxford: Oxford University Press, 2002.

Zukowsky, John, ed. *The Many Faces of Modern Architecture: Building in Germany between the Wars*. New York: Prestel, 1994.

"Zum 70. Geburstag von Hermann Jansen." *Deutsche Bauzeitung* 73, no. 21 (1939): K165–72.

SOURCES OF ILLUSTRATIONS

1.1 "Ankara Construit" series in *La Turquie Kemaliste*, August 1938. *La Turquie Kemaliste* 25–26 (August 1938).
1.2 Carl Lörcher. Residential settlement, Ankara, 1925 (*Bauwelt* [1925]: 6). Collection Centre Canadien d'Architecture/Canadian Centre for Architecture, Montréal.
1.3 Ebenezer Howard. "The Three Magnets." Howard, *Garden Cities of Tomorrow*, 46.
1.4 Theodor Fritsch. Diagram of ideal city, 1896. Fritsch, *Die Stadt der Zukunft*.
1.5 Richard Riemerschmid, Heinrich Tessenow, Hermann Muthesius, and Karl Frick. *Gartenstadt* Hellerau. Information brochure (c. 2002).
1.6 Hermann Jansen. Greater Berlin Master Plan Competition, 1909 (Hermann Jansen, *Vorschlag zu einem Grundplan für Gross-Berlin*). Collection Centre Canadien d'Architecture/Canadian Centre for Architecture, Montréal.
1.7 Hermann Jansen. Comparison of existing and ideal building blocks in Berlin (Jansen, *Vorschlag zu einem Grundplan für Gross-Berlin*, 54, 57). Collection Centre Canadien d'Architecture/Canadian Centre for Architecture, Montréal.
1.8 Hermann Jansen. *Kleinwohnungssiedlung*, Berlin, 1910 (Jansen, *Vorschlag zu einem Grundplan für Gross-Berlin*, 55).

1.9 Hermann Jansen. Zoning in Master Plan of Ankara. AMTUB (Architecture Museum of Berlin Technical University), Nachlaß Hermann Jansen, 22600.1.
1.10 Hermann Jansen. Sections for residential streets, Ankara. AMTUB (Architecture Museum of Berlin Technical University), Nachlaß Hermann Jansen, 22981.
1.11 Hermann Jansen. Perspective of a street with a view of the Citadel. AMTUB (Architecture Museum of Berlin Technical University), Nachlaß Hermann Jansen, 22811.
1.12 Photograph of houses in the Citadel of Ankara.
1.13 Şevki Balmumcu's Exhibition Hall. *La Turquie Kemaliste*, December 1934.
1.14 Hermann Jansen. Workers' housing. Jansen, *Ankara Imar Planı*, 48.
1.15 Hermann Jansen. Sketch for houses organized around courtyards. AMTUB (Architecture Museum of Berlin Technical University), Nachlaß Hermann Jansen, 23091.
1.16 Clemens Holzmeister. Project for Governmental Complex. Holzmeister, *Clemens Holzmeister* (original drawing in Albertina Museum).
1.17 Clemens Holzmeister. *Volkswohnhaus* Urban apartments in Rottstrasse, Vienna, 1924–26 (*Neue Werkkunst Clemens Holzmeister*, 32). Collection Centre Canadien d'Architecture/Canadian Centre for Architecture, Montréal.
1.18 Vedat [Tek]'s renovation of Mustafa Kemal's house in Çankaya. Yıldırım Yavuz Personal Collection.
1.19 Lenz and Company. Proposal for Mustafa Kemal's Palace. Courtesy Ali Cengizkan, Middle East Technical University, Department of Architecture (also published in *Arredamento Mimarlık*, no. 12 [2002]: 41, 42).
1.20 Giulio Mongeri. Proposal for Atatürk's vacation house. Pierre de Gigord collection of photographs of the Ottoman Empire and the Republic of Turkey. Research Library, The Getty Research Institute, Los Angeles, California (96.R.14). Box 38: 33129011 201288.
1.21 Clemens Holzmeister. Presidential Palace, Ankara, 1930–1932. Photo. Probably J. Scherb (*InnenDekoration*, vol. 43 [1932]: 434). Collection Centre Canadien d'Architecture/Canadian Centre for Architecture, Montréal.
1.22 Clemens Holzmeister. Presidential Palace, interior, Ankara, 1930–1932. Photo. Probably J. Scherb (*InnenDekoration*, vol. 43 [1932]: 423). Collection Centre Canadien d'Architecture/Canadian Centre for Architecture, Montréal.
1.23 Clemens Holzmeister. Presidential Palace, floor plan, Ankara, 1930–1932 (*Wasmuths Monatshefte fur Baukunst* [Nov/Dec 1931]: 534). Collection Centre Canadien d'Architecture/Canadian Centre for Architecture, Montréal.
1.24 Clemens Holzmeister. Presidential Palace, gallery and courtyard. Ankara, 1930–1932 (*InnenDekoration*, vol. 43 [1932]: 419). Collection Centre Canadien d'Architecture/Canadian Centre for Architecture, Montréal.

1.25 Clemens Holzmeister. Presidential Palace, winter garden from the courtyard. Ankara, 1930–1932 (*InnenDekoration*, vol. 43 [1932]: 418). Collection Centre Canadien d'Architecture/Canadian Centre for Architecture, Montréal.
1.26 Clemens Holzmeister. Presidential Palace, dining room. Ankara, 1930–1932 (*InnenDekoration*, vol. 43 [1932]: 425). Collection Centre Canadien d'Architecture/Canadian Centre for Architecture, Montréal.
1.27 Bureaucrats concentrating on papers rather than their meals in the dining room of the Presidential Palace. Courtesy Şenol Cantek.
1.28 Ernst Egli. Fuat Bulca House. ETH Library, Zurich, Special Collections, Nachlaß Ernst Egli, 785-137(1).
1.29 Ernst Egli. Fuat Bulca House, interior perspectives. ETH Library, Zurich, Special Collections, Nachlaß Ernst Egli, 787a-110.
1.30 Seyfi Arkan. Waterfront House. Arkan, "Ev Projesi," 6.
1.31 Seyfi Arkan. Residence for the Foreign Minister. Arkan, "Hariciye Köşkü," 311.
1.32 Seyfi Arkan. Residence for Makbule Atadan. Arkan, "Çankaya'da bir villa," 186.
1.33 Portrayal of the new women. *La Turquie Kemaliste* 6 (April 1935): 9.
1.34 Seyfi Arkan. Residence for Makbule Atadan, early version. Arkan, "Villa Projesi [I]," 114.
1.35 Seyfi Arkan. Residence for Makbule Atadan, plan. Arkan, "Çankaya'da bir villa," 180.
1.36 Seyfi Arkan. Residence for Makbule Atadan, main hall. Arkan, "Çankaya'da bir villa," 183.
1.37 Seyfi Arkan. Residence for Makbule Atadan, women's room. Arkan, "Çankaya'da bir villa," 185.
1.38 Seyfi Arkan. Atatürk's house at Florya.
1.39 Atatürk in front of the house at Florya. Photograph publicly exhibited on the walls of the house.
1.40 İstanbul waterbaths of the Ottoman period.
1.41 Hermann Jansen. *Kleinsiedlung* Friesland, Emden, site plan and perspective from common green areas. De Fries, "Einige Siedlungspläne," *Wasmuths Monatshefte für Baukunst* (1919–20): 138, 139.
1.42 Student projects in Hermann Jansen's studio (publ. 1925) (*Der Städtebau* [1925]: 23). Collection Centre Canadien d'Architecture/Canadian Centre for Architecture, Montréal.
1.43 Hermann Jansen. Bahçelievler housing, aerial perspective. AMTUB (Architecture Museum of Berlin Technical University), Nachlaß Hermann Jansen, 23083.
1.44 Hermann Jansen. Site plan for Bahçelievler Housing Cooperative. AMTUB (Architecture Museum of Berlin Technical University), Nachlaß Hermann Jansen, 23063.
1.45 Hermann Jansen. Type A1 of Bahçelievler Housing Cooperative. AMTUB (Architecture Museum of Berlin Technical University), Nachlaß Hermann Jansen, 23108B, 23107A, 23114A.

1.46 Hermann Jansen. Perspective of a street with A-Type Houses. AMTUB (Architecture Museum of Berlin Technical University), Nachlaß Hermann Jansen, 23082.

1.47 Hermann Jansen. Type D1 of Bahçelievler Housing Cooperative. AMTUB (Architecture Museum of Berlin Technical University), Nachlaß Hermann Jansen, 23271.

1.48a Bahçelievler as constructed. *Belediyeler Dergisi* (1937).

1.48b Ernst Reuter's cooperative house in Bahçelievler. Permission granted by Edzard Reuter.

1.49 Hermann Jansen. Master plan of Mersin. AMTUB (Architecture Museum of Berlin Technical University), Nachlaß Hermann Jansen, 23454.

1.50 Bahçelievler c. 2000. Photo: G. Çizgen. Tuncer, *Tarihten Günümüze Anadolu'da Konut ve Yerleşme*, 356.

2.1 Guillaume Berggren. Wooden houses and Topkapı gate, circa 1885. Pierre de Gigord collection of photographs of the Ottoman Empire and the Republic of Turkey. Research Library, The Getty Research Institute, Los Angeles, California (96.R.14). Box 10, p. 12.

2.2 Guillaume Berggren. Wooden houses near the aqueduct, circa 1885. Pierre de Gigord collection of photographs of the Ottoman Empire and the Republic of Turkey. Research Library, The Getty Research Institute, Los Angeles, California (96.R.14). Box 35.

2.3 Photomontage by İstanbul Fire Department showing how to stop fire, circa 1890. Pierre de Gigord collection of photographs of the Ottoman Empire and the Republic of Turkey. Research Library, The Getty Research Institute, Los Angeles, California. Fire Department's Album (96.R.14). Box 29.

2.4 Guillaume Berggren. Galata apartments, circa 1885. Pierre de Gigord collection of photographs of the Ottoman Empire and the Republic of Turkey. Research Library, The Getty Research Institute, Los Angeles, California (96.R.14). Box 10, p. 18.

2.5 Guillaume Berggren. Pera apartments, circa 1885. Pierre de Gigord collection of photographs of the Ottoman Empire and the Republic of Turkey. Research Library, The Getty Research Institute, Los Angeles, California (96.R.14). Box 10, p. 48.

2.6 Antoine Ignace Melling. Engraving of İstanbul's waterfront houses. *Voyage pittoresque de Constantinople et des rives du Bosphore*, 1819. Research Library, The Getty Research Institute, Los Angeles, California.

2.7 Gülmez Frères. Panorama of Bosphorus, circa 1885. Pierre de Gigord collection of photographs of the Ottoman Empire and the Republic of Turkey. Research Library, The Getty Research Institute, Los Angeles, California (96.R.14). Box 121.

2.8 Abdullah Frères. Rumelihisar, Bosphorus, İstanbul, circa 1870. Pierre de Gigord collection of photographs of the Ottoman Empire and the Republic of Turkey. Research Library, The Getty Research Institute, Los Angeles, California (96.R.14). Box 12, 3a.

2.9 Abdullah Frères. Waterfront houses on the Bosphorus, İstanbul, circa 1885. *Cumhuriyet'in Devraldığı İstanbul'dan Bugüne*, 116.

2.10 Reşad Ekrem Koçu. *İstanbul Ansiklopedisi*. *İstanbul Ansiklopedisi*, vol. 2, no. 15.
2.11 C. Biseo. Drawing of wooden houses in a Jewish neighborhood. Reşad Ekrem Koçu, *İstanbul Ansiklopedisi*, 1st ed., 314.
2.12 Abdullah Tomruk. Drawing of the Köprülü Amcazade Hüseyin Paşa waterfront house. Reşad Ekrem Koçu, *İstanbul Ansiklopedisi*, 1st ed., 506.
2.13 Sedad Eldem. "Landhaus bei Angora." Sedad Eldem, sketchbooks, Book 3, Edhem Eldem Personal Collection.
2.14 Sedad Eldem. Watercolor of a Turkish house. Sedad Eldem, Office drawings and papers, Koç University, İstanbul.
2.15 Sedad Eldem. Sketch for individual houses. Sedad Eldem, sketchbooks, Book 5, Edhem Eldem Personal Collection.
2.16 Sedad Eldem. Sketches for urban apartments. Sedad Eldem, sketchbooks, Book 8, Edhem Eldem Personal Collection.
2.17 Sedad Eldem. Sketches inspired by Erich Mendelsohn. Sedad Eldem, sketchbooks, Book 2, Edhem Eldem Personal Collection.
2.18 Sedad Eldem. Sketch inspired by Paul Schultze-Naumburg. Sedad Eldem, sketchbooks, Book 2, Edhem Eldem Personal Collection.
2.19 Sedad Eldem. Sketches suggesting hybridization between the old Turkish houses and modernism. Sedad Eldem, sketchbooks, Books 2 and 3, Edhem Eldem Personal Collection.
2.20 Sedad Eldem. Sketch possibly inspired by Frank Lloyd Wright. Sedad Eldem, sketchbooks, Book 10, Edhem Eldem Personal Collection.
2.21 Sedad Eldem. Sketch that would probably inspire the Ağaoğlu House. Sedad Eldem, sketchbooks, Book 1, Edhem Eldem Personal Collection.
2.22 Sedad Eldem. The Ağaoğlu House. Sedad Eldem, "Maçkada Prof. A. A. Evi," *Arkitekt*, no. 10–11 (1938): 277.
2.23 Sedad Eldem. The Ağaoğlu House, plan with oval *sofa*. Sedad Eldem, "Maçkada Prof. A. A. Evi," *Arkitekt*, no. 10–11 (1938): 278.
2.24 Sedad Eldem. The Taşlık Coffeehouse. Sedad Eldem, "Taşlık Kahvesi," *Arkitekt*, no. 11–12 (1950): 209.
2.25 Sedad Eldem. Sketch of an interior showing a panoramic vision that would probably inspire the Taşlık Coffeehouse. Sedad Eldem, sketchbooks, Book 4, Edhem Eldem Personal Collection.
2.26 Abidin Mortaş. Single-family house. Abidin Mortaş, "Müstakil Evler," *Mimar*, no. 1 (1931): 42.
2.27 Arif Hikmet. Mansion in garden. Arif Hikmet [Holtay], "Köşk Projesi," *Mimar*, no. 4 (1933): 109.
2.28 Sedad Eldem. Indian Embassy. Sedad Eldem, "Hindistan Sefareti," *Arkitekt*, no. 2 (1965): 55.
3.1 Bruno Taut. *Gartenstadt* Falkenberg. Taut, *Die Stadtkrone*, 75.
3.2 Bruno Taut. *Dissolution of Cities*. Taut, *Dissolution of Cities* (n.p.).
3.3 Cover of *Wohnungswirtschaft*.
3.4 Th. Heine. Caricature of *Mietskasernen*. *Wohnungswirtschaft*, September 1, 1926, 141.
3.5 Arthur Köster. Bruno Taut. *Siedlung* Onkel Toms Hütte, Berlin, 1926–

1931 (c. 1931) PH1986:0099:060. Collection Centre Canadien d'Architecture/Canadian Centre for Architecture, Montréal.

3.6 Arthur Köster. Bruno Taut and Martin Wagner. *Siedlung* Britz, playground surrounded by row houses, Berlin, 1925–1931 (c. 1931) PH1986:0098:064. Collection Centre Canadien d'Architecture/Canadian Centre for Architecture, Montréal.

3.7 Arthur Köster. Bruno Taut and Martin Wagner. *Siedlung* Britz, horseshoe block, Berlin, 1925–1931 (c. 1931) PH1986:0098:067. Collection Centre Canadien d'Architecture/Canadian Centre for Architecture, Montréal.

3.8 Bruno Taut. *Siedlung* Freie Scholle. *Wohnungswirtschaft.*

3.9 Bruno Taut and Martin Wagner. *Siedlung* Britz, horseshoe block. Taut, *Mimari Bilgisi*, 195.

3.10 Arthur Köster. Bruno Taut. *Siedlung* Carl Legien, Berlin, 1928–1930 (c. 1930) PH1986:0095:019. Collection Centre Canadien d'Architecture/Canadian Centre for Architecture, Montréal.

3.11 Arthur Köster. Bruno Taut. *Siedlung* Carl Legien, Berlin, 1928–1930 (c. 1930) PH1986:0095:014. Collection Centre Canadien d'Architecture/Canadian Centre for Architecture, Montréal.

3.12 Bruno Taut. *Siedlung* Neukölln. Taut, *Mimari Bilgisi*, 193.

3.13 Arthur Köster. Bruno Taut. *Siedlung* Onkel Toms Hütte, Berlin, 1926–1931 (c. 1931) PH1986:0099:009. Collection Centre Canadien d'Architecture/Canadian Centre for Architecture, Montréal.

3.14 Arthur Köster. Bruno Taut and Martin Wagner. *Siedlung* Britz, street with row houses, Berlin, 1925–1931 (c. 1931) PH1986:0098:034. Collection Centre Canadien d'Architecture/Canadian Centre for Architecture, Montréal.

3.15 Kemal Ahmet Aru, 4th Levent housing. Aru, "4. Levent" *Arkitekt*, no. 285 (1956): 141.

3.16 Martin Wagner. Scheme for new city land. Wagner, "Städtebau als Wirtschaftsbau und Lebensbau," *Das Neue Frankfurt* (November 1932): 162.

3.17 Work by students at Ernst Egli's Studio at the Academy. Rehabilitation of İstanbul's historical peninsula. "İstanbul Planı Etüdü," *Mimar*, no. 8 (1932): 258, 259.

3.18 Wilhelm Schütte. From *Mietskasernen* to *Zeilenbau*. Schütte, "Bugünkü Kültür ve İkametgah," part 1, *Arkitekt*, no. 1–2 (1944): 28.

3.19 Bruno Taut. Own house at Dahlewitz. Taut, *Ein Wohnhaus*, 55.

3.20 Bruno Taut. Variations of "type." Taut, "Grundrißfrage," *Wohnungswirtschaft*, November 15, 1928, 316.

3.21 Jakobus Goettel. Variations for furnishing a housing unit. Goettel, "Beitrag zur Erhöhung des Wohnwertes der Kleinwohnungen," *Wohnungswirtschaft*, February 1, 1930, 34.

3.22 Arthur Köster. Bruno Taut. Interior of a unit in *Siedlung* Onkel Toms Hütte, Berlin, 1926–1931 (c. 1931) PH1986:0099:011. Collection Centre Canadien d'Architecture/Canadian Centre for Architecture, Montréal.

3.23 Arthur Köster. Bruno Taut. Kitchen of a unit in *Siedlung* Britz, Berlin, 1925–1931 (c. 1931) PH1986:0098:061. Collection Centre Canadien d'Architecture/Canadian Centre for Architecture, Montréal.

3.24 Student project for a *Siedlung* in Ankara. Taut, "Tip ve Sıra Evler," *Arkitekt*, no. 8 (1937): 212.

3.25 Abidin Mortaş. Typological study of small houses. Mortaş, "Tek katlı evler," *Mimar*, no. 9 (1931): 310.

3.26 Abdullah Ziya [Kozanoğlu]. Double house in Adana. Kozanoğlu, "Müşterek Evler," *Mimar*, no. 6 (1932): 179.

3.27 Ernst May et al. *Siedlung* Niederrad. May, "Fünf Jahre Wohnungsbautätigkeit in Frankfurt am Main," part 2, *Das Neue Frankfurt* (April–May 1930): 119.

3.28 Ernst May et al. *Siedlung* Westhausen. May, "Fünf Jahre Wohnungsbautätigkeit in Frankfurt am Main," part 1, *Das Neue Frankfurt* (March 1930): 56.

3.29 Margarete Schütte-Lihotzky. Frankfurt kitchen. Lihotzky, "Rationalisierung im Haushalt," *Das Neue Frankfurt*, no. 5 (1926–27): 120.

3.30 Margarete Schütte-Lihotzky. *Lehrküche*, Frankfurt, 1929 (*Das Neue Frankfurt*, 1 Jan. 1929, 21). Collection Centre Canadien d'Architecture/Canadian Centre for Architecture, Montréal.

3.31 Margarete Schütte-Lihotzky. House for Kemal Ozan, 1939, PRNR 137. Universität für angewandte Kunst Wien, Kunstsammlung und Archiv (University of Applied Arts Vienna, Collection and Archive). Nachlaß Margarete Schütte-Lihotzky, Nr. 137.

3.32 Cooking classes in Turkish Girl's Institutes. *La Turquie Kemaliste* 6 (April 1935): 8.

3.33 Seyfi Arkan. Türkiş workers' housing, site plan. Arkan, "Amele Evleri Ilkokul, Mutfak ve Çamaşırlık Binası," *Arkitekt*, no. 9 (1935): 253.

3.34 Seyfi Arkan. Türkiş workers' housing, blocks in the *Zeilenbau* model. Arkan, "Amele Evleri, Ilkokul, Mutfak ve Çamaşırlık Binası," *Arkitekt*, no. 9 (1935): 257.

3.35 Seyfi Arkan. Kömüriş workers' housing, director's and engineers' houses. Arkan, "Kömür-iş İşçi Uramı: Zonguldak Kozlu," *Arkitekt*, no. 1 (1936): 10.

3.36 The immigrant village in Thrace. "L'Immigration en Turquie," *La Turquie Kemaliste* 23–24 (April 1938): 15.

3.37 Margarete Schütte-Lihotzky. Site plan of a village school in Anatolia. "Yeni Köy Okulları Bina Tipleri Üzerine Bir Deneme" (government brochure).

4.1 Cover of *Arkitekt*.

4.2 Hans Wilde. Plans of the Turkish houses. Wilde, *Brussa*, 120, 121.

4.3 Celal Esad Arseven. Map showing the alleged immigration of Turkish tribes and influence of Turkish art. Arseven, *L'art Turc*.

4.4 Ernst Egli. Comparison of the evolution of Turkish, Saxon, Greek and Roman houses. Egli, "Türk Evi," *Ülkü* 9, no. 99 (May 1941): 196.

4.5 Waterfront house in Bebek that Ernst Egli used to illustrate his theory. Egli, "Türk Evi," *Ülkü* 9, no. 99 (May 1941): 203.

4.6 Rudolf Henning. "Saxon Farm-House." Henning, *Das deutsche Haus in seiner historischen Entwicklung*, 30.

4.7 Sedad Eldem. Sketch of urban house and country house. Sedad Eldem, "Anciennes Maisons d'Ankara," *La Turquie Kemaliste* 7 (June 1935): 10.

4.8 Sedad Eldem. Drawing of an outdoor *sofa*. Sedad Eldem, Office drawings and papers, Koç University, İstanbul.
4.9 Sedad Eldem. Turkish house with a central *sofa*. Eldem, *Türk Evi Plan Tipleri*, 146.
4.10 Propaganda against *Siedlung* Weissenhof as an Oriental village.
4.11 Paul Bonatz. Multifamily house. *Die 25 Einfamilienhäuser*, 50.
4.12 Caricature of Paul Bonatz leaving the office to show his projects to Hitler. "Kemali Söylemezoğlu," *Anılarda Mimarlık*, 126.
4.13 Ahmet Sabri Ozan. Student project for a mosque in İstanbul. Gerhard Graubner, *Paul Bonatz und seine Schüler*, 112.
4.14 Paul Bonatz. *Siedlung* Saraçoğlu, perspective of the common garden. Bonatz, drawings and papers, Peter Dübers's collection, Stuttgart.
4.15 Paul Bonatz. *Siedlung* Saraçoğlu. Bonatz, drawings and papers, Peter Dübers's collection, Stuttgart.
5.1 Bruno Taut. Illustration of a modern room. Taut, *Die Neue Wohnung*, 44.
5.2 Bruno Taut. Comparative body diagram. Taut, *Houses and People of Japan*, 41, and *Mimari Bilgisi*, 65.
5.3 Bruno Taut. Comparison of Japanese and European farmhouses in *Houses and People of Japan*, 112–13. Collection Centre Canadien d'Architecture/ Canadian Centre for Architecture, Montréal.
5.4 Bruno Taut. *Mimari Bilgisi*, cover.
5.5 Bruno Taut. Hiding the façade. Taut, *Mimari Bilgisi*, 45.
5.6 Bruno Taut. Zeppelin touring around the world. Taut, *Mimari Bilgisi*, 59.
5.7 Bruno Taut. Own house, İstanbul.
5.8 Bruno Taut. Own house, İstanbul, interior of the living room.
5.9 Bruno Taut. Own house, İstanbul, seen from different perspectives. Permission granted by Bülent Özer.
5.10 Bruno Taut. Exhibition opening at the İstanbul Academy of Fine Arts. Manfred Speidel Personal Collection.
E.1 *Gecekondu* settlements in Ankara.
E.2 Antenna for watching Turkish television. Der Bruno Taut Block, Berlin.

INDEX

Page numbers in italics refer to figures.

Abdülhamid II, Sultan, 112
Abdullah Frères, 112, *115*
Ağaoğlu House, 133, *134–35*, 140
Agency, 4, 5, 84, 98, 212
Akkaynak, Samih, 216, 313n88
Al'Kindi, 106
Allerweltstil, 90, 91
Alsaç, Orhan, 245
Altunç, Süheyla, 191–93
Alus, Sermet Muhtar, 137, 311n42
Anatolian romanticism, 208
Anatomy of Melancholy, The (Burton), 106
Ankara: Bahçelievler, 78–79, 83–93, *85, 87–89, 92*; Foreign Minister's Residence, 67, *68*; garden city model in, 30–34, 38, 41, 42–52, 76; *gecekondu* settlements in, 287, *287*; Jansen master plan, 33, 42–52, *45*; Lörcher plan, 32, *33*; Makbule Atadan House, 67–71, *68*, 71–73; Presidential Residence, 48, 54–58, *59–63*; *Siedlungen* in, 172–75; Turkish houses in, 111–12
Ankara (Karaosmanoğlu), 76–78
Appiah, Kwame Anthony, 24
Apter, Emily, 147
Arel, Süheyla, 191

Arendt, Hannah, 22
Arif, Burhan, 97, 164, 183, 286, 307n161
Aristotle, 106, 142, 143
Arkan, Seyfi, 27–28, 56, 64–76, *66*, *68*, *71*, *72*, *75*, 98, 140, 285, 304nn119–23, 304n131; workers' housing, 199, 201–5, *202–3*
Arkitekt (journal), 96, 137, 164, 175, 182, 216–18, *217*, 242, 245, 261, 264, 286, 304n122, 314n69, 329n104, 333n49. See also *Mimar* (journal)
Arkitekturüberlegungen. See *Mimari Bilgisi* (Taut)
Arseven, Celal Esad, 95, 221–23, *222*, 229, 230, 275, 285, 326n23, 326n31
Aru, Kemal Ahmet, 164, *165*, *184*, 185, 285
Asad, Talal, 20
Asım, B. E., 307n161
Ataç, Nurullah, 15–17
Atatürk, Mustafa Kemal: 2, 32, 64, 78, 222, 241, 261; marriage, 55; parties of, 63; Presidential Residence, 48, 54–58, *59–63*, 303n111; sister, 67, 73; vacation house, *58*, 73–76, *75*, 303n105, 303n108, 305n131
Atay, Falih Rıfkı, 81
Auerbach, Erich, 27, 145, 147
Auflösung der Städte, Die (Taut), 150, *151*
Aurelius, Marcus, 23

Bahçelievler Housing Cooperative, 78–79, 83–93, *85*, *87–89*, *92*, 95, 96–97, *97*, 98, 191, 202, 243, 244, 302n90, 306n155, 308n187
Baltacıoğlu, İsmail Hakkı, 95
Banguoğlu, Tahsin, 102, 141
Bassnett, Susan, 20
Baudelaire, Charles, 114, 116
Bauernhaus, 225, 226–27, *228*, 258. See also Farmhouses
Bauhaus, 66, 67, 128, 203, 298n28
Baumeister, Der (journal), 40
Beecher, Catherine, 191
Behne, Adolf, 164, 234, 327n67
Behrendt, Walter Curt, 176
Belediyeler Dergisi (journal), 173
Belling, Rudolf, 27

Benjamin, Walter, 12–14, 104, 143, 147, 163, 176, 293n26, 293n31, 293n33
Berlin, Charlottenburg Technical University, 64–67; garden city model, 38–42, *43–45*, 83. See also Siedlungen
Bischoff, Norbert von, 57–58
Blau, Eve, 53
Bletter, Rosemarie, 150, 249, 315n29
Block (group), 237
Boğaziçi Mehtapları (Hisar), 112, 114
Bohaeddin Molla waterfront house, 110–11
Bonatz, Paul, 27, 146, 184, 223, 235, 237–46, *238–40*, *244–45*, 260, 285, 328n90, 328n94
Borges, Jorge Luis, 6, 116
Bosphorus, 112–14, *112–13*, *115*, 116, 119, 133, 273–74
Bozdoğan, Sibel, 95, 219
Breuer, Marcel, 128
Breuhaus, Fritz August, 28
Brix, Joseph, 32, 41, 297n28
Bruno Taut Block, Der, *Siedlung*, 288, *289*
Burton, Robert, 106

Çambel, Halet, 147
Center for German-Speaking Residents, 29
Çetintaş, Sedad, 329n104
Chomsky, Noam, 11
City planning, emergence of, 30, 32, 34, 165, 172–73. See also specific planners
Class critique, 196–99
Climate and architecture, 22, 80, 139, 207, 224, 227, 234, 335–36n98; Taut on, 268–70, 272, 275, 278
Clonialism, 16
Collective housing: commitment to, 96; developments in, 152, 164, 288; garden city principles in, 34, 38, 148, 173; generic design for, 176–77; in master plans, 2, 48, 81, 207, 240; modernism in, 67, 175, 206, 286; National Socialism on, 237–38; private/public capital for, 167, 173, 306n146; theories of, 172, 307n172, 321n151. See also Cooperative housing; Siedlungen; specific projects

Colonialism: in architecture projects, 199; cultural criticism and, 5, 284; cultural politics and, 101; imperialist imagination, 21, 284; land possession and, 279; translation and, 18–19, 284

Cooperative housing, 37, 38, 42, 78–80, 85–86, 96–97, 151, 156, 175. *See also* Collective housing

Copyright and Translation Committee, 28

Cosmopolitan ethics: in architecture, 248–49, 258, 263, 272, 277–81; blocking of, 4–5, 17, 23; hybridity and, 22–23, 241, 247–48, 277; institutional, 24; intertwined histories and, 284; Kant and, 23–24, 269, 277–81; modernism and, 24–25; multiculturalism and, 25; nationalism/racism and, 236, 258, 259–60; normative, 24; practices of, 24–25; Taut and, 271–72, 277–81; translation and, 4–5, 17, 25–26; universality of, 23–24, 258

Cronin, Michael, 21

Cubic architecture: in Ankara, 57, 64, 65, 77–78, 223, 262; critique of, 133–35, 137, 230, 262, 270, 275; popularity of, 95; use of term, 183, 270; Viennese, 54

Dahlem, garden city model, 42
Dante Alighieri, 9
Derrida, Jacques, 11, 12, 13–14, 18, 25, 218, 279
Deutsche Gartenstadt-Gesellschaft e.v. *See* German Garden City Society
Deutsche Wohnungsfürsoge A.G. (DEWOG), 152, 156, 159, 179–80
DEWOG. *See* Deutsche Wohnungsfürsoge A.G.
DGG. *See* German Garden City Society
Dilaver Paşa Regulation (1867), 201
Dissolution of Cities. See Auflösung der Städte, Die (Taut)
Divan, 139, 140
Dresden, garden city model, 38
Dülge, Mithat, 308n178, 308n183, 308n187
Dursunoğlu, Cevat, 146

Ebert, Carl, 27
Eco, Umberto, 6–7
Education in Turkey, 145–47, 191
Egli, Ernst, 53–54, 98, 164, 170, 187, 285; background, 223–24, 303n105; cubic architecture and, 64, *65*, 223, 303n105; Girl's Institute, *69*; house comparisons, *226*; on preservation, 102, 167–70; on *Siedlung*, 164, *183*, *240*; on *sofa*, 228–29; Studio, *168*; on Turkish house, 218, 222, 223, 224–29, *227*, 232; in Zurich, 225–29

Ehn, Karl, 53
Eichholzer, Herbert, 147
Eidgenössische Technische Hochschule (ETH), 223, 225
Eldem, Sedad, *134–36*, *140*, 285; appropriating translations of, 140; background, 119–20; on colonization of Turkey, 17, 124; in England, 126–27; in France, 122–26, 312n62; in Germany, 127–33, 313n73; influences, 125, 128–33; nationalism of, 242–43; on preservation, 171; sketchbooks, 120–33, *121–22*, *126*, *129–32*, 312n53; on *sofas*, 122, 125–26, 129, 133, *135*, 137–40, 229, 231–32, *231–32*; studies, 27, 120; on Turkish house, 119, 133–43, 184–85, 218, 223, 229–33

Elsaesser, Martin, 169, 187, 191, 285, 297n18, 308n187, 318n84
Encyclopedia of İstanbul (Koçu). *See İstanbul Ansiklopedisi* (Koçu)
Eser, Lami, 195
ETH. *See* Eidgenössische Technische Hochschule
Ethnic groups of Ottoman Empire, 22, 219, 246
Eurocentrism: cosmopolitanism and, 249, 277–78, 280; ideologies of, 103, 256; Orientalism and, 107
Ex oriente lux (Taut), 250–52

Fanon, Fritz, 101, 142
Farmhouses, 225, 226–28, *228*, 253, 258–60, *259*, 271, 332n37
Fascism and architecture, 233–39, 242

Femininity, 69; women's place in the house and, 69–73
Feminism in architecture, 181, 188–91, 194
Ficino, Marcillo, 106
Fidelity, 6, 8, 10, 264
Finckh, Ludwig, 236
First National Style, 56
Fischer, Theodor, 164, 169, 239n18
Foreign Minister's Residence, 67, *68*
Foucault, Michel, 98, 116
Frank, Hartmut, 66, 237
Frank, Josef, 53, 234
Frankfurt kitchen, 169, 182, 187–91, *190*, 195, 286
Frederick, Christine, 182, 188
Freedom, 10, 188, 249, 275, 278
Freud, Sigmund, 101, 106–7, 142
Frick, Karl, 39
Fritsch, Theodor, 37–38, 48; ideal city, *39*, 300n58
Fuat Bulca house, 64, *65*

Garden city model, 1–2; in Ankara, 30–34, 38, 41, 42–52, 79; as antimetropolitan, 98; in Berlin, 38–42; city planning as discipline, 34; in collective housing, 34, 38, 148, 173; design principles, 148; in England, 34–36; German terminology in, 50–51; in Germany, 36–42, 50; modernization and, 95; objectives of, 36–37; spiritual regeneration and, 37; transformation and, 5, 19, 84, 148–49, 150–52, 157, 170, 248; translation of, 5, 98, 150–52, 164, 173, 283–86; unity and harmony in, 40–41; use of term, 34, 38; westernization and, 95
Gartenstadt (journal), 299n48
Gartenstadt Falkenberg, 38, 149
Gartenstadt Hellerau, 38, *39*, 149
Gartenstadt model, 36, 38, 48, 50–51. *See also* Garden city model
Gecekondu settlements, 287, *287*
Gemeinnützige Heimstätten A.G. (GEHAG), 151–53, 159, 233–34; Siedlungen, 152–53, 157, 163. *See also specific Siedlungen*

Gentile, G., 9
German Garden City Society (DGG), 36, 37, 38
"German house," 203, 219, 226, 227. *See also Bauernhaus*; Farmhouses
German-Ottoman Treaty of Commerce, 29
German-Turkish Friendship Association, 30
German-Turkish House of Friendship architectural competition, 30
German-Turkish Treaty of Friendship (1924), 30
German Women's Association of İstanbul, 29
Girl's Institutes, *69*, 191–94, *193*
Globalization, 4, 5, 14, 277, 287–88
Goethe, Johann Wolfgang von, 15
Goettel, Jakobus, 180, *181*
Gökalp, Ziya, 215–16, 217, 218, 224, 270
Gramsci, Antonio, 195
Gropius, Walter, 50, 66–67, 74, 162, 234, 260, 286, 297n18
Gülmez Frères, 112, 113
Güntekin, Reşat Nuri, 15, 16, 207–8
Gurlitt, Cornelius, 220

Habermas, Jürgen, 24
Hall, Peter, 36
Hamdi, Bedrettin, 216
Harem, 56, 69, 220, 221
Heimatstil, 203, 234, 260
Hellerau. *See Gartenstadt* Hellerau
Henning, Rudolf, 226–27, *228*
Hermann, Fritz, 55
Hikmet, Nazım, 206, 208–10
Hilberseimer, Ludwig, 177, 198
Hillinger, Franz, 145, 239, 261, 285
Hirsch, Ernst, 147
Hisar, Abdülhak Şinasi, 111–12, 114
Hoffmann, Ludwig, 41
Hol, 137, 138, 243
Holtay, Arif Hikmet, 28, 138, *139*, 223, 239, 285
Holzmeister, Clemens, 52–55, 57–64, 145, 223, 285; Ankara Governmental

Complex, 53; Presidential Residence, 54–58, 59–63
Houses and People of Japan (Taut), 253–60, 261, 271
Howard, Ebenezer, 34–36, 38, 96, 163; Three Magnets, 35
Huber, Victor, 37
Hüsnü, Nizamettin, 185
Hybridity: architectural, 22, 60, 131, 271, 283; cosmopolitan ethics and, 22–23, 241, 247–48, 277; defined, 22; exclusion and, 21; modernism and, 131; of populations, 7; richness of, 271; transculturation and, 5, 324–25n230; in translation, 8, 247

Ibn'Sina, 106
Ihsan, Bekir, 185
Imperialism: cosmopolitanism and, 23; cultural, 30; imperialist imagination, 21; missionaries and, 201; modernization and, 205–6; as racial, 22; urbanism and, 35
Inferiority, 32, 101–2, 141–42, 256, 263
İstanbul, 103–4, 105, 109–11; Bosphorus, 112–13, 112–13, 115; collective housing projects, 50; *gecekondu* settlements in, 287; German community in, 145–47; melancholy of, 107–19, 287; modernization in, 50; novel on, 107–9; as Ottoman symbol, 30; restructuring, 165–68; Turkish houses in, 102–3, 116; waterbaths, 74, 76; waterfront houses, 110–11, 111, 114, 115, 118
İstanbul (Tanpınar), 115–16
İstanbul Ansiklopedisi (Koçu), 116–19, 117–18, 286

Jansen, Hermann: on *Allerweltstil*, 90, 91; Ankara master plan, 33–34, 38, 42–52, 45–49, 96, 302–3n84; on artistic quality, 40; Bahçelievler, 78–79, 83–93, 85, 87–89, 92; in Berlin, 38–42, 83; Berlin master plan, 43–44, 83, 176; as city planner, 27; on collective housing, 81–82; on free-standing single housing, 33, 91–92; on garden city model, 33, 40–42, 95; on local architectural elements, 86–90; in master plan competition, 32, 41; on modernization in architecture, 1–2; on single-family housing, 40, 46, 48, 83; students' projects, 84; Turkish city master plans, 93–95
Japan, *Siedlungen*, 164
Jaussely, Léon, 32–33, 41
Jeanneret, Pierre. *See* Le Corbusier

Kampffmeyer, Bernhard, 299n51, 300n55
Kampffmeyer, Hans, 299n48, 299n54, 300n58, 300n61
Kant, Immanuel: on cosmopolitan ethics, 23, 24, 248–49, 269, 277–80; on hospitality, 279–80; on humanism, 248, 278; on knowing, 175–76; on peace, 23, 248–49; on universality, 250, 254
Karaosmanoğlu, Yakup Kadri, 76–78, 96–97, 107–9
Kasapoğlu Mansion, 303n107
Katsura Palace, 253
Kemalism: architectural program of, 11, 32, 102; on ethnic difference, 22; on master plans, 93; versus minorities, 22; modernization of, 51; on population exchange, 206; on translatability, 11, 14, 22; westernization project, 192; women's reforms, 68–73, 69, 192; on Zonguldak mines, 201
Kessler, Gerhard, 27, 79, 147
Khosla, Romi, 101
Kiralık Konak (Karaosmanoğlu), 107–9
Kitchens: Frankfurt kitchen, 169, 182, 187–91, 190, 195, 286; in German *Siedlung*, 182, 183, 187; in Turkey, 192–95; as women's realm, 189
Klein, Alexander, 236
Kleinsiedlung Friesland, 50, 82
Kleinsiedlung Johannisthal, 50
Koçu, Reşad Ekrem, 116–19, 286
Köni, Yunus Kazım, 15–17
Köster, Arthur, 152, 155, 158, 160, 161, 162, 182, 183, 276n38
Koyunoğlu, Arif Hikmet, 219

Kozanoğlu, Abdullah Ziya, 185, *186*, 216, 242, 286
Kracauer, Siegfried, 163
Kriegerheim-Mustersiedlung Bissingheim, 50
Küfu, 250
Kurasawa, Fuyuki, 24–25

Landhäuser, 40, 48, 54, 67
Leach, Edmund, 20
Le Corbusier, 49, 74, 122, 125, 128, 132–33, 140, 198, 199
Lenz and Company, 55, *57*
Letchworth, as garden city, 36
Lévi-Strauss, Claude, 20
Linneke, Richard, 152, 234
Loos, Adolf, 53, 64, 128, 140, 169, 187
Lörcher, Carl, 32–33, *33*, 145
Loti, Pierre, 209
Lurçat, Andre, 53, 234
Luxemburg, Rosa, 29

Makbule Atadan House (Ankara), 67–71, *68*, *71–73*
Mann, Thomas, 148
March, Otto, 176
Marx, Karl, 19, 196, 212
May, Ernst, 49, 148, 162, 169, 187–88, *189*, 191, 196–97, 208, 233, 260
Melancholy: causes of, 106; of East, 252–63, 271; Freud on, 106–7; of İstanbul, 107–17, 287; versus melancholia, 106; memory and, 114, 116; modernism and, 141, 143, 255; versus mourning, 106; versus nostalgia, 141; Orientalism and, 91, 101, 104–5, 107; transformation and, 116; translations and, 5; Turkish houses and, 116–19, 170; westernization and, 254, 263
Melling, Antoine Ignace, 112
Memory and melancholy, 114, 116
Mendelsohn, Erich, 122, 129, *130*, 297n18
Mercer, Kobena, 25
Mersin master plan, *94*
Meyer, Hannes, 128, 177
Mies van der Rohe, 74, 234–5, 328n73
Mietskasernen, 36, 41, 50, 81, 152, 154, *154*, 169, 170, *171*

Migge, Leberecht, 156, 157, 178
Milli Mimarlık Semineri, 222, 223, 224, 227, 229, 233, 275
Mimar (journal), 137, 182, 216, 304n122. See also *Arkitekt* (journal)
Mimari Bilgisi (Taut), 253, 260, 263–272, *264*
Modern Architecture (Taut), 268
Modernism: architectural expressions of, 6, 67, 95, 132, 133, 140–41, 261–62, 275, 298n38, 324–25n230; in collective housing, 67, 175, 206, 286; cosmopolitanism, 24–25; cubic as term for, 270; dialectic of, 163, 175–78; dissemination of, 272, 278; global, 14; health and, 210; hybridization and, *131*; melancholy and, 141, 143, 255; principles of, 74, 128; transformation and, 140; translation of, 1, 2, 11, 51, 170; as universal, 262, 268, 270; westernization and, 101–2, 124, 204–5
Modernization: chosen by Turkish Republic, 27, 51, 55, 191; garden city ideal and, 95; German, 2; Kemalist revolution and, 93, 192; myth of, 285; official program of, 2, 99; postcolonial, 205; residential culture and, 51; Turkish elite and, 95
Mongeri, Giulio, 56–57, *58*, 64, 303n111
Mortaş, Abidin, 95–96, 137–38, *138*, 184–85, *186*, 216, 286, 313n88
Muhit (journal), 216
Mustersiedlungen, 82, 83, 95. See also specific projects
Muthesius, Hermann, *39*, 40, 153

Naim, Ahmet, 200
National Architecture Seminar. See *Milli Mimarlık Semineri*
Nationalism: in architecture, 242, 245, 260, 270–71, 329n104; foreignness and, 4; housing and, 80, 238; old Turkish house and, 245; rationalism and, 217; rise of chauvinist, 21, 22–23; subaltern and, 205
National Socialism: exile of architects and, 2–3, 145, 251; fascism and archi-

tecture, 241–42; German community in Turkey and, 146, 148; on housing, 81, 198, 237–38; imperialism and, 22; nationalism and, 21
Navaro-Yaşın, Yael, 193
Nazi regime. *See* National Socialism
Neue Frankfurt, Das, 169, 187, 188, 191, 233, 298n38
Neue Frankfurt, Das (journal), 166, 187, 196, 234
Neues Bauen, 234, 237, 241
Neue Wohnung, Die (Taut), 180–81, 251, 275
Neumark, Fritz, 27
New Frankfurt Program. *See* Neue Frankfurt, Das
Nicolson, Harold, 163
Niranjana, Tejaswini, 19–20
Nissen, Rudolf, 27
Nussbaum, Martha, 24

O'Brien, Justin, 10
Oelsner, Gustav, 27, 145, 163–64, 170, 264, 285, 286
Oettermann, Stephan, 114
Onat, Emin, 28
Ongun, Burhan Arif. *See* Arif, Burhan
Orientalism: death of Orient, 102–3; as difference, 91, 250–51, 254; inferiority and, 101; melancholy and, 91, 101, 104–5, 107; as paranoia, 107; Western, 112, 269, 294n48
Osmanische Lloyd (newspaper), 30
Osmanische Post (newspaper), 30
Ottoman Empire: architect-builders of, 28; colonization by, 229; decline of, 74, 206; ethnic groups of, 22, 219, 246; German firms in, 29; İstanbul as symbol, 30; *Medrese* system, 146; modernization in, 50, 146; nation building and, 20; overthrow of, 28; semicolonialization during, 205
Ottoman-Prussian Pact of Friendship, 29
Ozan, Ahmet Sabri, 239, *240*

Pamuk, Orhan, 110
Panorama (Karaosmanoğlu), 96–97
Panoramic vision, 112–13, *112*–14, 133, *136*

Parker, Barry, 187
Paz, Octavio, 10
Perret, Auguste, 122, 123, 125, 132
Perriand, Charlotte, 128
Piano, Renzo, 148
Poelzig, Hans, 28, 52, 64–67, 235, 260, 297n18, 304nn121–23
Pollock, Sheldon, 24
Posener, Julius, 66
Postcolonialism: cosmopolitanism and, 24–25; modernization and, 205; translation theory, 18–21, 284
Prairie houses, 130–32
Preservation, 168–71
Presidential Residence (Ankara), 48, 54–63, *59*–*63*
Proportion in architecture, 265–66
Pure language, 13–14

Rational dwellings, 177–78, 182–85, 187, 246
Rationalization of household, 182, 187–91, 191–94
Red Vienna, 53
Reuter, Edzard, 148
Reuter, Ernst, 27, 145, 147, 148, 164, 199, 264, 286, 314n9; in Ankara, 172–75; Bahçelievler house, *92*; as city planner, 145, 172–73
Riemerschmid, Richard, *39*, 297n18
Rietveld, Gerrit, 53
Robbins, Bruce, 24
Rogers, Richard, 148
Roofs, flat, 2, 178, 187, 234–36, 239
Rüstow, Alexander, 27

Sabri, Behçet, 138
Safa, Peyami, 133
Said, Edward, 91, 107, 248, 251, 294n48
Sayar, Zeki, 97, 137, 138, 164, 175, 182, 216, 261, 286, 303n111, 313n88, 333n46, 333n49
Scharoun, Hans, 235, 260
Scheerbart, Paul, 249, 250, 315n29
Scheffler, Karl, 176
Schirren, Matthias, 66
Schlegel, August Wilhelm, 23
Schleiermacher, Friedrich, 6, 16

Schlesisches Heim (journal), 187
Schmitthenner, Paul, 223, 235, 236, 237
Scholer, Friedrich August, 237
Schultze-Naumburg, Paul, 129, *130*, 234, 237
Schütte, Wilhelm, 27, 102, 145, 147, 148, 164, 169–70, *171*, 174, 183, 191, 261, 264, 286, 314n12, 318n89
Schütte-Lihotzky, Margarete, 27, 53, 81, 145, 147, 148, 171, 191, *192*, 206, 208, 261, 286, 324n230; Frankfurt kitchen, 169, 182, 187–91, *190*, 195, 322n160; on subaltern, 210–13, *211*; Weimar housing, 81
Schwartz, Philipp, 27, 146, 147
Sebah, Pascal, 112
Selamlık, 221
Siedlung Britz, 152, *155*, 157, *158–59*, 162, *162*, 173, 176, 177, *183*, 288
Siedlung Carl Legien, 157, 159, *160*, 176, 288
Siedlung Dammerstock, 162
Siedlung Eden, 53
Siedlung Eichkamp, 153
Siedlungen: defined, 19; economics of, 156, 163, 175–76; garden city model, 5, 148, 149, 283; generic design of, 176–77; green areas and, 170; metropolis and, 148–75; national house and, 233–46; planning, 83; principles, 171; subaltern and, 195–213; translation of model, 163–71, 182–85, 199–206, 239–46; use of term, 315n23; values of, 246. *See also specific projects*
Siedlung Freie Scholle, 157, *158*, 288
Siedlung Ikomaberg, 164
Siedlung Lindenhorf, 153
Siedlung Neukölln, 159, *161*, 288
Siedlung Niederrad, 188, *189*
Siedlung Onkel Toms Hütte, 152, *155*, 157, *161*, 176, 182, 235–36
Siedlung Römerstadt, 188
Siedlung Saraçoğlu, 239–46, *244–45*
Siedlung Schillerpark, 288
Siedlung Siemensstadt, 173, 288
Siedlung Törten, 50

Siedlung Treptow, 82–83
Siedlung Weissenhof, 234–35, *235*, 237
Siedlung Westhausen, 159, 188, *189*
Single-family housing, *138*; Jansen on, 40, 46, 48, 83; nationalism and, 80, 239; National Socialism on, 81, 239; promotion of, 81
Sırrı, Nahit, 110
Sitte, Camillo, 40; Sitte-esque, 41, 83, 162n84
Small Housing Colony (Rüstringen), 153
Sofas: modernized, 126, 129, 137–40, 184–85; in Turkish houses, 86, 110, 122, 125–26, 133, *135*, 137, 140, 229, 231–32, *231–32*; use of term, 137, 228–29
Söylemezoğlu, Kemali, 239, 286, 328n90
Speer, Albert, 237, 241, 328n90
Spitzer, Leo, 27, 145, 147
Spivak, Gayatri, 18–19, 25, 195, 206, 218
Städtebau, Der (journal), 40, 83
Stadtkrone, Die (Taut), 149–50
Stapel, Wilhelm, 236
Streiffeld Worker's Colony (Aachen), 81
Stuttgart circle, 235, 236, 237
Subaltern: agency of, 212–13; Anatolia projects and, 206–13; architecture of equality and, 196–98; capitalist production and, 198; participation and, 149, 195; postcolonial studies and, 205; representability of, 19, 195, 206, 213; *Siedlung* projects and, 195–213; social housing failure and, 198–99; use of term, 195–96, 205; Zonguldak housing project and, 199–206

Tafuri, Manfredo, 19, 163, 176, 196–99
Tahsin Güner waterfront house, 133
Tan (newspaper), 137
Tanpınar, Ahmet Hamdi, 54, 102–3, 114–16, 215
Tanrıöver, Hamdullah Suphi, 219
Tanzimat reforms, 28, 308n180
Taşlık Coffeehouse, 133, *136*
Taut, Bruno, 23, 27, 67, 145, 146, 286; on climate, 268–70, 269–70, 272, 275, 278; cosmopolitan ethics of, 23,

24, 277–281; Dahlewitz house, 178, *179*; death, 261; on East, 249–52; escape from Germany, 236, 238; on farmhouses, 258–60, *259*; on garden city, 38, 156–58, *149*, 149–51; İstanbul house, 272–75, *273–74*, *276*; in Japan, 247, 248, 251, 252–63; on minimalist dwelling, 188, 198; on modern room, *252*; on national architecture, 270–71; on proportion, 265–66; on rational dwelling, 177–79, 182–85, 187; sketches and diagrams, *257*, *267*, *269*; theory of type, 177–81, *180*; in Turkey, generally, 164, 182, 187, 191, 240, 248, 260–63; on uniformity, 177; utopian books, 149–50; Weimar housing, generally, 49, 81, 148, 151–52, 157–63, 235. *See also specific works*

Taylorism, 182, 191, 194

Tek/Vedat. *See* Vedat/Tek

Tercüme (journal), 28

Tessenow, Heinrich, *39*, 40, 64–66, 83, 149, 236, 304n123

Thrace, *207*

Topçubaşı, Allaettin Cemil, 306n146

Tör, Vedat Nedim, 80

Trabantenprinzip, 187, 197

Transculturation, 5

Transformation: architect's role and, 197, 235; within communities, 24; defined, 291n2; of garden city ideal, 5, 19, 84, 148–49, 150–52, 157, 170, 248; melancholy and, 116; *Siedlung* and, 176, 187; subaltern and, 195; translation and, 3–4, 8–9, 12, 16–17, 50, 283; transportation and, 4; universality and, 12

Translatability: from above/below, 93–99; absolute, 11, 14, 17, 171; civilization and, 28, 215, 270, 281; difference and, 218, 281; essentialism and, 216, 293n26; hospitality and, 25; hybridity and, 247; notion of, 10, 12, 51; possibility/impossibility of, 2, 5, 9–14, 15, 17; postcolonial studies and, 20; pure language and, 13; smooth, 5, 11, 14, 93, 170, 171, 210; uniqueness and, 10. *See also* Subaltern

Translation Office, 28

Translation(s): appropriating, 5, 16–17, 37, 73, 88, 140, 263; colonialism and, 18–19, 284; cosmopolitan ethics and, 4–5, 17, 25–26, 280–81; cross-cultural exchange and, 10; defined, 7–8; ethical, 19; Eurocentrism and, 107; fidelity in, 6, 8, 10, 264; foreignizing, 5, 15–17, 50, 52, 70, 73, 140, 244, 265; of garden city model, 5, 98, 150–52, 164, 173, 283–86; German-Turkish exchange and, 19, 21; hybridization in, 8; meaning and, 20; melancholy and, 5; of modernism, 1, 2, 11, 51, 170; modification and, 2; neutrality and, 4; nonlinguistic, 6–9; postcolonial theory, 19–20; power and, 19; process of, 25–26; reciprocal, 5; of *Siedlung* model, 163–71; test of, 6; transformation and, 3–4, 8, 12, 16–17, 50, 283; unevenness of, 17–21; utopianism and, 14; visual, 6, 7–9, 22; zones of exchange and, 17

Translators: infidelity and, 6; on language differences, 124, 292n10, 293n31; on priority, 10; role of, 6, 16, 19–20; task of, 13–14; universality and, 12, 28

Türkische Post (newspaper), 30

Turkish houses, modern, 133–43, 244–46; *sofas* in, 133, *135*, 137–40

Turkish houses, old, 18, 88–90, *103–4*, *118*, *121–22*, *220*, *230*, *275*; construction of definition of, 218–33, 243; devaluation of, 77, 102–3, 107–9, 116, 166–67; Eldem and, 119–23, 125, 129–33, 229–33; hybridization in, 5; identity and, 219, 225; melancholy and, 110–19, 170; nationalism and, 245; *sofas* in, 86, 110, 122, 125–26, 133, *135*, 137–40, 185, 229, 231–32, *231–32*; taxonomy of, 229; validation of, 133

Turkish language, 15–17, 20–21, 44, 146–47, 164, 172, 263–71

Turkish Republic: discipline of, 172; founding of, 2, 27; governmental symbolism of, 52; on mines, 205; modernization of, 27; translation and, 28–29, 93, 215

Ülken, Hilmi Ziya, 28
Ülkü (journal), 225
Ulus (newspaper), 79, 244
Universality: abstract, 11; of cosmopolitan ethics, 23–24, 258; Eurocentrism and, 107; of modernism, 262, 268, 270; translatability and, 10; truth and, 250
Ünsal, Behçet, 135, 183, 185, 216, 242, 286, 325n7
Untranslatability. *See* Translatability
Unwin, Raymond, 187
Urbanism, 5–6, 34, 35, 132, 172
Uzgören, Nusret, 79
Uzman, Emin Necip, 28

Varlık (journal), 110
Vedat/Tek, 55–56, *56*, 64
Venuti, Lawrence, 15, 19, 293n34
Viennese cubic architecture. *See under* Cubic architecture
Visual translation, 6, 7–9, 22

Wagner, Martin, 27, 67, 145, 286; on city planning, 172; on Florya, 73, 74; on garden city theory, 153–56, 164–65; on old Turkish houses, 166–67; on restructuring İstanbul, 165–68, 317n71, 317n74; on smooth translatability, 170; Taut invitation to Turkey, 260; on Turks, 147; Weimar housing, 49, 81. *See also specific Siedlung*
Wagner, Otto, 176
Waqfs, 174
Ward, Colin, 36
Wasmuths Monatshefte für Baukunst (journal), 82, 129
Waterbaths, 74, 76, *76*
Waterfront houses, 110–11, *111*, 114, *115*, *118*, 227

Weekend house, 128
Weimar *Siedlungen*: Bauhaus and, 203; characteristics of, 81, 164; critical analysis of, 196, 198; criticism of, 236; failure of, 197; garden city model, 5, 148, 283; generic rational dwelling and, 175–182; influence in Turkey, 164, 170, 172, 174, 283, 288; kitchens in, 187; metropolis and, 148–75; *Zeilenbau* principle in, 159
Werkbund, 30, 53, 249, 297n18, 298n38
Westernization: chosen by Turkish Republic, 2, 5, 27, 31, 55, 99, 101–2, 191; city zones and, 93, 108; colonization and, 283; Egli on, 303n105; garden city ideal and, 86, 95; imperialism and, 204–5; Jansen and, 86; in Japan, 254, 255–56; Kemalist revolution and, 93, 192; melancholy and, 142–43, 254, 263; modernism and, 124, 204; myth of, 5, 285; residential culture and, 51; of Turkish elite, 18, 77–78, 95, 108
Wilde, Hans, 220
Williams, Raymond, 35
Wittgenstein, Ludwig, 9
Wohnhaus, Ein (Taut), 178
Wohnungswirtschaft (journal), 152, *153*, 177, 179, 196
Women: femininity, 69–73; feminism in architecture, 181, 189–91, 194; Kemalist reforms, 68–73; kitchen as realm of, 182, 187, 189, 192–95; unveiling of, 70
Wretched of the Earth, The (Fanon), 101
Wright, Frank Lloyd, 130–32, *132*, 141

Yedigün (magazine), 95
Yücel, Hasan Ali, 28

Zantop, Susanne, 21
Zeilenbau, 50, 81, 83, 159, 162, 170, *171*, 176, 177, 178, 187, 203, *203*, 243, 264, 316n56
Zonguldak, 199–206, *202*
Zubaida, Sami, 24

ESRA AKCAN is an assistant professor of art and architecture history at the University of Illinois, Chicago.

Library of Congress Cataloging-in-Publication Data

Akcan, Esra.
Architecture in translation : Germany, Turkey, and the modern house / Esra Akcan.
p. cm.
Includes bibliographical references and index.
ISBN 978-0-8223-5294-5 (cloth : alk. paper)
ISBN 978-0-8223-5308-9 (pbk. : alk. paper)
1. Architecture — Turkey — History — 20th century.
2. City planning — Turkey — History — 20th century.
3. Architecture and state — Turkey — History — 20th century.
4. Turkey — Relations — Germany.
5. Germany — Relations — Turkey.
I. Title.
NA1368.A33 2012
720.943′09561 — dc23   2011053090

www.ingramcontent.com/pod-product-compliance
Lightning Source LLC
Chambersburg PA
CBHW051534230426
43669CB00015B/2597